CRITICAL SURVEY
OF
SHORT FICTION

CRITICAL SURVEY
OF
SHORT FICTION

Current
Writers

Index

7

Edited by
FRANK N. MAGILL

Academic Director
WALTON BEACHAM

SALEM PRESS
Englewood Cliffs, N. J.

LIBRARY OF CONGRESS CATALOG CARD NUMBER: 81-51697

Complete Set: ISBN 0-89356-210-7
Volume 7:   ISBN 0-89356-217-3

PRINTED IN THE UNITED STATES OF AMERICA

LIST OF CURRENT WRITERS IN VOLUME 7

LIST OF CURRENT WRITERS IN VOLUME 7

LIST OF CURRENT WRITERS IN VOLUME 7

CRITICAL SURVEY
OF
SHORT FICTION

ROBERT H. ABEL

Born: Ohio, 1941

Principal short fiction
"Ajax in Richmond," 1974; "Flood #14," 1977; "The Making of the Chalices," 1978; *Skin and Bones*, 1979; "Black Bear at Lake Ecstasy," 1980; *Curses!*, 1980.

Analysis
The *Skin and Bones* stories are thematically centered on childhood and are as intent on conveying a childhood state of mind as evoking childhood memories or narrating a tale. This is a magic, but certainly not a sentimental world since there is considerable hardship, violence, death, and moral struggle in the life of these semi-outlaw rural boys, girls, and adults. The *Curses!* stories are more experimental generally in that the content is fantasy and nightmare, and an attempt is made to convey real states of mind in relation to real experiences (or realizations) on a more subconscious, perhaps mythical level. "What is the real mood and psychological character of our existence in a world of so much random violence and over-arching (nuclear) terror?" could be said to be the question these stories confront.

Major publications other than short fiction
NOVEL: *Freedom Dues, Or, A Gentleman's Progress in the New World*, 1980.

WALTER ABISH

Born: Austria, 1931

Principal short fiction

Minds Meet, 1975; *In the Future Perfect*, 1977; "Self-Portrait," 1977; "Inside Out," 1978; "Happiness," 1979; "Ninety-Nine: The New Meaning," 1979; "Self-Portrait," 1979; "The Alphabet of Revelations," 1980; "Auctioning Australia," 1980; "The Idea of Switzerland," 1980; "The Writer-to-be: An Impression of Living," 1980.

Analysis

The titles of Walter Abish's collections of stories, *Minds Meet* and *In the Future Perfect*, point to his abiding concerns. He gives us an obsessive, reflective world in which characters try to find the true meeting, the perfect end. The stories, however, insist that these characters—such as the heroine of "In So Many Words" or the narrator of "The English Garden"—can never rise above distorted, imperfect dreams of completion. They travel; they assume roles; they lie to themselves and others. Their adventures are finally unbalanced, "funny," impure. Abish insists on creating structures which not only describe the often circular quest of his characters but which apparently embody them. His fictions are disturbing because they "reflect" the arbitrary, inconclusive, and random encounters of minds and matter. The fictions are, in a profound sense, looking glasses; they strongly suggest that reality—the sincerity of the hero and the clichéd setting of Africa or Southern California— can never be "hemmed in," defined, and pinpointed.

Abish does not really write loose, unstructured stories, however; on the contrary, he describes the bizarre adventures of his characters in a painstaking, detailed, and cool manner. There is a breathtaking tension created by the tightness of the structure (including numbered paragraphs and alphabetical codes) and the dream-filled searching which is described. "Claustrophobia"; "agoraphobia"—such clinical words could elucidate mental states of the reader, the hero, and the writer; but they are ultimately insufficient. Abish is in fact "beyond psychology": he recognizes that it—or any dead language— can never render transcendental longings of the spirit locked in the imperfect cages of the body-language-sense.

Major publications other than short fiction

NOVELS: *Alphabetical Africa*, 1974; *How German It Is*, 1980.
POETRY: *Dual Site*, 1970.

Irving Malin

DUANE ACKERSON

Born: New York, 1942

Principal short fiction
Edson Benedikt Ackerson, 1972; *Assembly Room*, 1977; "From the Future Sportsman's Manual," 1977; *The Eggplant*, 1978.

Analysis
Short, even terse, Duane Ackerson's stories partake to various degrees of the fable, the parable, and the prose poem, with hints of science fiction and helpings of fantasy. Many suggest small, soap-bubble worlds operating by their own rules of logic (or illogic), often taking an absurd premise and pushing it to the point where the surface tension of the story seems ready to break and the words on the verge of flying off in all directions. Like the surfaces of soap bubbles, however, the world these stories reflect, although distorted, is our own. In a review of *The Eggplant*, Tim Barnes remarks that the author delights in a "mix of slapstick literalism and rapid wordplay" and that his works are "cousins to the pun, taking off on the connotations of stock phrases like 'Giving up the Ghost' or 'Mechanized Farming.'" In the latter story, delivered in the form of a short dramatic monologue, a future farmer complains of the effort of having to wind up the vegetables and animals on his farm in order for them to function properly; he even has to wind up the clouds, so they can rain on the garden, only to discover that the last salesman has sold him a defective cloud, which reverses its action and pulls all the garden up into the cloud, reversing itself again a moment later: "There's a real racket going on inside the cloud machine, and after a while, raindrops shaped like carrots, squash, and radishes begin to fall all over the farm, mangling the animals and scratching the paint on the fields." These stories are windup machines in which delight with words overrides the mechanical.

CAROL MADDEN ADORJAN

Born: Illinois, 1934

Principal short fiction
"Requiem for a Virgin," 1972; "Naked Lady," 1972; "The Year of the Baby," 1972; "Cicada Summer," 1974; "American Gothic," 1976; "The Magic Box," 1977; "Something Different," 1979.

Analysis
Carol Adorjan is concerned in her short fiction with middle-class, domestic life. Her characters inhabit the American suburbs of the late 1960's and the 1970's. She is interested in the family rather than in marriage. Her work focuses on the mother, specifically on the multiple demands made upon her in the family system, most typically by young children, but in some of her best stories by her own elderly mother. The Adorjan heroine is sometimes the bemused narrator of her own experience, sometimes the gently humorous subject of an omniscient narrator. Most typically this tolerant heroine faces the relentless, daily, mother-consuming problems of running a household and rearing children. The heroine solves the problems, and while resigning herself to the sacrifice of her time and energies to these problems, she triumphs by her own amusement at her plight and her deep enjoyment of her family. In some stories, however, the Adorjan heroine, also presented from both narrative perspectives, is a much darker figure. In one story, she watches an ostracized neighbor have a mental breakdown; in another, she methodically murders her three children; in a third, with fear, sympathy, and disgust, she watches her mother's disintegration and death. In these grim and powerful stories, Adorjan's prose becomes flat and plain. Horror is carried in the style which perfectly expresses the stunned apathy of the heroine. The full range of her stories, then, gives the reader an exploration both of the rewards of the life of the middle-class American mother and of its terrible costs.

Jeanne A. Flood

ILSE AICHINGER

Born: Austria, 1921

Principal short fiction
The Bound Man and Other Stories, 1955; "Where I Live," 1960; *Eliza, Eliza*, 1965; "The Young Lieutenant," 1967; *News of the Day*, 1970.

Analysis

A common theme in Ilse Aichinger's stories is lack of freedom. Many of her characters are imprisoned in their own ignorance, from which they cannot, or will not, break out. Aichinger juxtaposes a world of horror, war, and death against the calm of the human spirit. Throughout her works she is concerned with the value of the human spirit. In her stories she shows a warm understanding for human frailty and sympathizes with the suffering and loneliness of her characters. Her experiences during World War II form the background of several of her stories. Aichinger intertwines fantasy and reality. Dreams, parables, myths, and visions are interwoven with reality to such an extent that it is sometimes difficult to distinguish the fantasy world from the real. She depicts the anxieties and absurdities of modern life, fusing the normal and the grotesque in a manner reminiscent of Franz Kafka. The bound man in the story of the same name, for example, suddenly finds himself bound and accepts this strange situation unquestioningly in much the same way that Gregor Samsa in Kafka's "Metamorphosis" does not question why he has been transformed into a bug. Aichinger takes much of her imagery from the Bible or from folklore and folktales. Her style is simple and precise, often realistic and vivid; her vocabulary is that of everyday life. The tone of her stories is frequently dreamlike or lyrical.

Major publications other than short fiction
NOVEL: *Herod's Children*, 1964.

Jennifer Michaels

ROBERT AICKMAN

Born: London, 1914

Principal short fiction
We Are for the Dark, 1951; *Dark Entries*, 1964; *Powers of Darkness*, 1966; *Sub Rosa*, 1968; *Cold Hand in Mine*, 1975; *Tales of Love and Death*, 1977; *Painted Devils*, 1979.

Analysis
Like M. R. James, the predecessor he most resembles, Robert Aickman considers "ghost stories" and the like a serious avocaton rather than a profession. He is better known to the British public as the founder of the "Inland Waterways Association" and author of a popular nonfiction book, *Know Your Waterways* (1954). He is also active in opera and ballet operation and administration, as well as being a noted drama and film critic. Aickman began to write his supernatural fiction in the early 1950's and has gradually established a reputation as probably the finest exponent of the classic horror story, which emphasizes disciplined, stylish writing, indirection, implication, and in M. R. James's phrase, the "carefully managed crescendo," instead of the bloodletting and physical atrocity so popular in the genre today. In Aickman's best fiction he develops a sense of psychological horror within the characters; he creates terrifying atmospheres by suggestion rather than through sudden, overt supernatural intrusion. Perhaps his best-known story is "Pages from a Young Girl's Journal," which won the first World Fantasy Award for best short fiction in 1975. In this chilling tale a young girl chronicles her gradual metamorphosis from innocent tourist to committed, eager vampire. Almost alone among those of contemporary horror writers, Robert Aickman's tales justify Jack Sullivan's label for the British ghost story: they are, indeed, "elegant nightmares."

Major publications other than short fiction
NONFICTION: *Know Your Waterways*, 1954; *The Attempted Rescue*, 1966.

Keith Neilson

DAISY ALDAN

Born: New York, 1923

Principal short fiction
"To a Guanajuato Baby," *A Golden Story*, 1979; "Though We Sang As Angels," 1980.

Analysis

"One thinks of Daisy Aldan as a word artist," stated Charles Guenther in the St. Louis Post Dispatch, "who alternates between meticulous description of the outer world and minute self examination. . . . Her work at times seems outwardly calm with an inner turbulence, and at other times, tremulous on the surface but with an underlying composure. . . . The contemplative nature of this writer startles us with the 'artfully designed acorn spiral of Self' she reveals. Her background is broadly cosmopolitan. . . ."

"Aldan is a formalist," state the reviewers in *Booklist*, "using metaphor to describe moments of feeling. Her voice is mature, gauging and evaluating, sometimes continuing to the rational explanation of a feeling or situation, and sometimes staying with the fleeting images she employs. Her form is often a whirling vortex of resolution, and she manipulates line length . . . into an effect. . . ."

Daisy Aldan's work shows "a subtle understanding of human relationships," states Nona Balakian of the Sunday Times Book Review, ". . . ability to create characters so they seem real . . . , originality of style. . . . She never overworks the theme. The beautiful poetic descriptions and imagery reflect the psychic states of her characters. She is a wise and elegant writer."

Major publications other than short fiction
NOVEL: *A Golden Story*, 1979.
POETRY: *The Destruction of Cathedrals*, 1964; *Seven:Seven*, 1968; *The Masks Are Becoming Faces*, 1969; *Breakthrough*, 1971; *Or Learn to Walk on Water*, 1970; *Stones*, 1973; *Verses for the Zodiac*, 1975; *Love Poems of Daisy Aldan*, 1976; *Between High Tides*, 1978.
NONFICTION: *Poetry and Consciousness*, 1978; *Contemporary Poetry and the Evolution of Consciousness*, 1980; *Writers' Workshop*, 1980.

BRIAN ALDISS

Born: England, 1925

Principal short fiction

No Time Like Tomorrow, 1959; *Galaxies Like Grains of Sand*, 1959; *Starswarm*, 1963; *Who Can Replace a Man?*, 1965; *The Saliva Tree and Other Strange Growths*, 1966; *Neanderthal Planet*, 1969.

Analysis

Probably, along with J. G. Ballard, the most important British "New Wave" science-fiction writer in the 1960's and 1970's, Brian Aldiss has written a number of deft and provocative short fictions which mirror the themes and images of his novels. His short stories began to appear in the mid-1950's, when he wrote some of his most notable work, especially "All the World's Tears," "Poor Little Warrior," "Old Hundredth," "But Who Can Replace a Man?," and "A Kind of Artistry." The best of his later stories, "The Saliva Tree," won a Nebula Award in 1965. In addition, two of his major "novels," *The Long Afternoon of Earth* (1962) and *Barefoot in the Head* (1969), are actually "fix-ups"—that is, collections of short stories strung together into continuous narratives. Aldiss has always felt himself to be "just an author," rather than a "science-fiction writer," and the breadth of his work demonstrates this fact. Not only does it show the influences of the science-fiction masters, but also of such experimental novelists as James Joyce in *Finnegan's Wake* (1939) and the "French New Novel" writers. Aldiss' style, imagery, and literary excellence put him in the forefront of the shift in science fiction from the "hard" variety, with its emphasis on "gadgetry," scientific accuracy, and "ideas," usually at the expense of characterization and good writing, to a more literary approach that is closer to mainstream fiction in technique and sentiment.

Major publications other than short fiction

NOVELS: *Starship*, 1958; *The Long Afternoon of Earth*, 1962 (as *Hothouse*); *The Dark Light Years*, 1964; *Greybeard*, 1964; *Cryptozoic!*, 1967; *Report on Probability A*, 1968; *Barefoot in the Head*, 1969; *The Hand-Reared Boy*, 1970; *Soldier Erect*, 1971; *Frankenstein Unbound*, 1973; *The Malacia Tapestry*, 1976; *Brothers of the Head*, 1977.

NONFICTION: *The Billion-Year Spree*, 1973; *Science Fiction Art*, 1975.

Keith Neilson

SIDNEY ALEXANDER

Born: New York, 1912

Principal short fiction

"Part of the Act," 1948; "White Boat," 1948.

Analysis

Although he has been immersed for many years in longer and more complex narrative writing (a trilogy of historical novels, biography, history, a contemporary novel), Sidney Alexander is deeply attracted to the short story for its qualities of poetic concision and metaphorical evocation, its surprising burst and illuminating fall-out. Realistically grounded, the materials of his stories are carefully structured around a symbolic core that informs the most minute naturalistic elements of incident or dialogue into broader areas of significance. The stories are frequently set in Italy where the author has lived for twenty-five years.

Major publications other than short fiction

POETRY: *The Man on the Queue*, 1941; *Tightrope in the Dark*, 1949; *The Celluloid Asylum*, 1951.

NONFICTION: *The History of Italy*, 1969; *Lions and Foxes: Men and Ideas of the Italian Renaissance*, 1974; *Marc Chagall*, 1978.

HENRY ALLEY

Born: Washington, 1945

Principal short fiction

"The Festival," 1969; "Through Glass," 1975; "Getting Rid of Aristotle," 1976; "Tales," 1976; "Stains of Light," 1977; "Within the Dial," 1977; "The Museum," 1977; "The True and Only History of the Alexandria," 1978; "The Fish," 1978; "Elizabeth Tyson, Poet, Playwright," 1978; "The Baritone and the Tenor," 1979.

Analysis

Although plot and image are highly important in Henry Alley's stories, they do not form the crux. Over the eleven years that his stories have been appearing, the unifying factor has been found in the sense of disorientation which many of his characters feel. The reader is asked to identify with someone who is quite familiar, to adopt a very specific point of view and then subsequently witness an imaginative revision of the outer world. Thus, it is not the city, the town, or the country which forms the primary landscape but, rather, the distance between: the point where the protagonist discovers he does not know where he is.

Such a disorientation often comes about when one is shut off from the past—one's ancestral past or a more general tradition. This severance is frequently voluntary, willed, and done in the hope of greater freedom. The past, however, always does return, with varying and contradictory results. There could be the imaginative freedom that had been sought, or the imprisonment that had been feared. The difference resides in the form that the reentry into the past takes.

Characteristically, the settings of Alley's stories (Seattle, Central Washington, San Francisco, Western Oregon, Upstate New York, St. Louis, the Ozarks) have had little to do with their region of publication. The West Coast stories have been published in the Midwest and vice versa. With the recurring images and hieroglyphics which thread the whole of his work, the stories frequently seem to be set in the same imaginative realm—one which emerges sometimes in experimental form, other times in traditional, in accordance with how far the theme of dislocation is taken.

Major publications other than short fiction

NOVEL: *Through Glass*, 1979.

PLAY: *Haemon*, 1980.

NONFICTION: *The York Handbook for the Teaching of Creative Writing*, 1979.

RUDOLFO A. ANAYA

Born: New Mexico, 1937

Principal short fiction
"The Place of the Swallows," 1976; "The Closing of Mack-Ellens," 1978; "A Story," 1979; "The Apple Orchard," 1980; "The Road to Platero," 1980.

Analysis
The short story provides a change of pace from the novel, and Rudolfo Anaya finds that he usually writes short stories between novels. He aims at a story which totally engrosses the reader, so mood seems to play a dominant role in the stories. Character and the interactions of characters and the violent or subtle changes which happen to the characters are important to Anaya. The landscape he uses as background very often acquires a force which affects and shapes the characters. The short story is one of the most challenging literary forms he knows and practices. In spite of the rigidity of space, it does lend itself to his sense of a total impression which it should create in the reader, and thus mood and all the consequent emotions that create mood seem to fit the form for him. There are exciting, experimental possibilities in the form which Anaya enjoys discovering as he writes short stories and as he shapes and crafts them toward a complete and ultimate end.

Major publications other than short fiction
NOVELS: *Bless Me, Ultima*, 1972; *Heart of Aztlan*, 1976; *Tortuga*, 1979.
PLAYS: *The Season of la Llorona*, 1979; *Rosa Linda*, 1980.

ALFRED ANDERSCH

Born: Germany, 1914

Principal short fiction

My Disappearance in Providence and Other Stories, 1978.

Analysis

A central theme in Andersch's works is the theme of flight, flight from reality, from the self, and from dictatorship. His protagonists are often outsiders and introverts who are disappointed, bitter, and despairing. They cannot find a place in society, which they feel has banished them, yet they also do not want to accept society and long to lead isolated lives. Andersch believes in the freedom of the will, in individual responsibility, and in the ability of people to choose and decide. He believes in the decency of people's ethical instincts. In most of his works he raises ethical questions. His ideal person observes the world critically and does not get enmeshed in doctrines and ideologies. Andersch's notion of freedom implies the right and the ability of each person to formulate his own individual critique of society. Andersch's stories are realistic. In the autobiographical *The Cherries of Freedom*, he says that the task of the writer is description. Like Idris Parry, whom he quotes at the beginning of *My Disappearance in Providence and Other Stories*, he believes: "Art is not about abstractions or ultimate issues or infinity or eternity. Art is about buttons." In other words, art should show everyday things as they really are without any symbolic, parabolic, or allegorical intent. For Andersch, the task of the writer ultimately is to show people possibilities from which they can choose.

Major publications other than short fiction

NOVELS: *Zanzibar or the Last Reason*, 1957; *The Red*, 1960; *Efraim*, 1967. NONFICTION: *The Cherries of Freedom*, 1952.

Jennifer Michaels

MARIANNE ANDREA

Born: U. S. S. R., 1922

Principal short fiction
"Rysskaya Mysl," 1955; "Kings, Queens and Shirley," 1957; "Stepmother," 1960; "Dream for Antonia," 1972; "Week Out of Time," 1974; "Two Printing House Square," 1974; "A Special Christmas," 1975; "World of Their Own," 1975; "The Original," 1976; "The Concert," 1976.

Analysis
Marianne Andrea's stories are, in the main, psychologically and intra-psychically oriented. Aside from two or three—"Stepmother," "Two Printing House Square," and "A Special Christmas"—the rest of the stories deal mainly with introspective, exploratory landscape of psychosocial realism. They seem to question the "why" of a specific type of existence as seen through the conflict of self with self, and only occasionally of conflict of self with society as exemplified in "Dream for Antonia," and in particular in "Home," which attempts to bring out as forcibly as possible the struggle of a Polish-Jewish youth in German concentration camps and his struggle with evaluating reasons for the chosen of "The Terror." "Week Out of Time" poses more immediate questions of identity through the medium of fantasy. In the ultimate direction, most stories explore character and ask questions deeply rooted within, rather than emphasize plot.

Major publications other than short fiction
NONFICTION: "At the Click of a Door," 1976; "Edgar Allan Poe and Russian Symbolism," 1977; "How About Poetry," 1979; "Parents and Homework," 1979.

Alex Jackinson

RONALD ARIAS

Born: California, 1941

Principal short fiction
"El Mago," 1970; "Stoop Labor," 1974; "The Interview," 1974; "Helping the Poor," 1975; "The Story Machine," 1975; "A House on the Island," 1975; "Perros," 1976; "The Wetback," 1976; "The Castle," 1976; "Chinches," 1977; "Lupe," 1980.

Analysis
Interweaving fantasy and reality, Ronald Arias' stories are clearly inspired by and related to Latin American "magic realism." His characters and settings are often Southwestern Mexican-American without becoming sociological portraits. Arias' stories focus on human reactions to strange, often comic or bizarre situations. His stories reveal his basic optimism in human strength. The characters are treated with respect, warmth, sympathy, and humor. The human spirit always triumphs over the mechanical world; imagination enables the characters to escape, to endure, and to triumph over the absurdities of existence.

Major publications other than short fiction
NOVEL: *The Road to Tamazunchale*, 1975.
PLAY: *The Interview in Nuevos Pasos*, 1979.

Joan Arias

SHEILA ASCHER and DENNIS STRAUS

Born: New York

Principal short fiction
"City/Edge," 1973; "Facts in a Case," 1974; "Between Two Walls," 1975; "In Doubt," 1976; "Figures of Speech," 1976; "Winter/Winter," 1976; "An Ambiguous Condition," 1976; "Double/Profile," 1977; "The Diagram," 1977; "Dreams of a Bound Woman," 1977; "Even After a Machine Is Dismantled. . . ," 1977; "The Scar," 1978; "Snow," 1978; "How the Day Passes," 1979; *Letter to an Unknown Woman*, 1979.

Analysis
Complex structures and subtle internal codes which comment on the narrative and the phenomenology of the text and a visual, cinematic prose surface characterize Ascher/Straus stories. The physical existence of text as object and process; the ways in which the story mediates between author and reader as "an impossible conversation"; the implied context of reality surrounding writing and reading; and the ways in which language determines the limits of thought, feeling, and perception are typical Ascher/Straus concerns carried out in a world which resembles the violent, urban world of the Hollywood crime melodrama.

The stories abound with multiple possibilities, with "propositions," aphorisms, and poetic-philosophical discourse, which interrupt the detached, cool, and mysterious narration, lending it an urgent immediacy, spontaneity, and dynamism of freedom-within-rigor. The physical "look" of the contemporary world is often modeled in astonishing detail: in descriptive prose, in diagrams, maps, signs, catalogues, meticulously reproduced overheard conversations, and the like.

In the essay "On Literary Collectivity," Ascher/Straus wrote: "The seams in the text are the lines of consciousness: the lesson of cubism: exposure of process, so-called rationalization of the surface and so on, lend a new source of intellectual-poetic adventure to the surface." In later fictions the self-referential and participatory strategies are employed in combination with both first-person narration and essaylike discourse to place new ways of presenting problematic personal relationships in an "extra-narrative" moral and historical context.

Major publications other than short fiction
NOVEL: *Woman's Nightmare "A"/"Fiction If It's Anything. . . ."*, 1980.

INGEBORG BACHMANN

Born: Austria, 1926   **Died:** 1973

Principal short fiction

The Thirtieth Year, 1961; *Simultan*, 1973.

Analysis

In her Frankfurt lectures, given in 1959 to 1960, Ingeborg Bachmann said that art gives us the chance to experience where we are and where we should be. It extends our possibilities, even though the goals it shows may be ultimately unattainable. Most of Bachmann's protagonists strive for the absolute. They rebel against the old order with its conventions, rules, and laws and seek perfection in love, justice, and freedom. Yet these ideals are rarely achieved. Many of these idealistic rebels, who cannot come to terms with existence, eventually capitulate to a hostile society, giving up their ideals. They know that they want their world to be changed but are not clear about how this can be done. For most, their rebellion remains a daring dream. They are driven to rebel by uncontrollable feelings rather than by reflection. The constant travels and changes of location in Bachmann's stories are an image of the homelessness of modern man. Common themes in her works are fear, sadness, and despair. Many stories are set in Austrian towns of the 1950's. The stories are often surrealistic, lyrical, or elegiac. Her language is precise.

Major publications other than short fiction

NOVEL: *Malina*, 1971.

PLAY: *The Good God of Manhattan*, 1958.

POETRY: *Borrowed Time*, 1953; *Invocation of the Great Bear*, 1956; *Song Above the Dust*, 1977.

Jennifer Michaels

WILL BAKER

Born: Idaho, 1935

Principal short fiction
"Hidden Spring," 1960; "Bloat," 1973; "What I Know About Chemistry," 1974; "Left Over in Your Heart," 1977; "PG," 1978; "Shards," 1979; "The Other Side of a Fable," 1978; "Between Planes," 1979; "Of Thee I Sing," 1980; "The Job," 1980.

Analysis
Will Baker's work is eclectic and diverse in every way, in its subject, tone, style, and structure. There are three-page stories that are little more than quick, acid anecdotes and tiny novels of fifty pages that explore characters through major wrenches, rebirths, or dissolutions in their lives. The overall impression is that of an impersonator (or schizophrenic) who strives for perfect illusions, and in the longer pieces, transforms himself into the roles he has chosen. The early stories show a strong influence from the fabulists and metafictionists—Vladimir Nabokov, John Barth, Donald Barthelme—but the later, more extensive works temper this impulse and introduce a more direct, compact style, a more serious attention to character, without abandoning the edge of lunacy and deviance that are useful in portraying modern life.

Major publications other than short fiction
NOVELS: *Dawnstone*, 1975; *Chip*, 1979.
NONFICTION: *The Syntax of English Poetry*, 1967; *Jacques Prevert*, 1967.

HARRY BARBA

Born: Connecticut, 1922

Principal short fiction

3 By Harry Barba, 1967; *Love, in the Persian Way*, 1969; *One of a Kind: The Many Faces & Voices of America*, 1976; *The Day the World Sane*, 1979.

Analysis

Harry Barba's unique talent combines painstaking craftmanship; superbly suitable imagery, tropes, and insights; and steady and compassionate psychological and social probings toward possible resolutions or new beginnings. G. K. Smart writes about Harry Barba's works, "All of this is told in a spirit of bucolic good humor which might, in less skilled hands, become merely pleasant. Barba . . . has managed to give surface charm and psychological depth." A review in *The New York Times Sunday Book Review* states that the distinguishing quality of Barba's stories lies "in their descriptive power and their use of visual detail. Though a New Englander by birth and upbringing, Barba has the Southern writer's sense of the eccentric, the larger-than-life character who thrives on his individualism. His social criticism is subtly masked behind a gusty humor . . . he keeps his stories moving from episode to episode with an unfailing exuberance and aplomb."

Major publications other than short fiction

NOVEL: *For the Grape Season*, 1960.

NONFICTION: *How to Teach Writing*, 1969; *Teaching in Your Own Write*, 1970; *The Case for Socially Functional Education*, 1973; *Two Connecticut Yankees Teaching in Appalachia*, 1974.

HELEN BAROLINI

Born: New York, 1925

Principal short fiction
"Reclamation of a Tourist," 1964; "The Nuns' Shoes," 1968; "The Spinsters of Taos," 1968; "Up in Camonica Valley," 1970; "Love in the Middle Ages," 1970; "Live and Let Lib," 1972; "The Finer Things in Life," 1973; "Opera Libretti and a May Day Carol," 1976; "In Calabria," 1978; "Learning to Meditate," 1978; "Going to Sicily," 1980.

Analysis
From a wider view of life, Helen Barolini has narrowed her narrative focus onto the virtually untouched ground of the Italian-American experience, and her recent work has concerned itself with this thematic material. Always present in her work is what has been termed her strong story line. She is a traditionalist in using the short-story form to tell a story and to craft it into a meaningful evocation of character, situation, or place.

Barolini's interest is in human interaction, the workings of people with or against people, with or against their environment, their passions and frustrations. This interest is reflected as well in her literary essays, in which, as in her stories, personal behavior is examined and interpreted. Place has played an important part in Barolini's writing; her descriptive talent comes to the fore as she examines her characters in their various placements. She hears them, feels them, and makes understanding them the end of her writing.

Major publications other than short fiction
NOVEL: *Umbertina*, 1979.
POETRY: *Umbria*, 1953; *Duet*, 1966.

PAUL ALEXANDER BARTLETT

Born: Missouri, 1909

Principal short fiction
"Cue," 1944; "Grilled Windows," 1944; "Log," 1944; "The Little Box," 1945; "World's End," 1945; "Golden Gate," 1946; "Mary's Carpenter," 1946; "Stranger in the House," 1946; "Tale from an Old Port," 1946; "Barley Water," 1947; "Fireflies," 1948; "Woodcut," 1951; "Wait for the Day," 1952; "Mambu Land," 1953; "Fronds of Corn," 1955; "The Good Mother," 1955; "Raincoat," 1956; "Rocks and Stars," 1957-1958; "Maker of Dreams," 1958; "Mist," 1958; "The Old Explorer," 1962; "Beat of Time," 1963; "Ancient Seeds," 1965; "Diosbotic," 1969; "The Inner Ear," 1970; "Venom 1 and Venom 2," 1975; "Letter to Felipe," 1976; "Revenants," 1976; "Chickering," 1979.

Analysis
Paul Bartlett intends to "make you see," in the Conradian sense—details are important. He is stylistically experimental in some of his writing. James Purdy said of Bartlett, "I find great pleasure and interest in Bartlett's stories . . . most distinguished writing." His writing has been praised by many for "a humanity that is not too frequently encountered." Pearl S. Buck wrote, "His stories are excellent." Don M. Wolfe wrote, in the Introduction to Bartlett's collection, "Person, place and mood are revealed through an unerring arrangement of images . . . such images are instinct with a magic that comes only to a writer of long and dedicated apprenticeship. There is great stylistic skill in these stories, comparable to those of Cather, Lawrence, Lowry."

Major publications other than short fiction
NOVELS: *When the Owl Cries*, 1960; *Adios, Mi Mexico*, 1979.
POETRY: *Wherehill*, 1976; *Spokes for Memory*, 1979.

JONATHAN BAUMBACH

Born: New York, 1933

Principal short fiction
"Know Your Enemy," 1970; "Dream News and World Report," 1972; "The Fell of Knowledge," 1975; "Another Story," 1975; "The Last War," 1975; "The Frozen Yak Fields of Alaska," 1976; "The War Baby," 1976; "Tooth," 1977; "Passion?," 1978; *The Return of Service*, 1979; "Mother and Father," 1979; "The Conference," 1980; "A West Coast Story," 1980.

Analysis
Jonathan Baumbach's stories are illusions meant to deceive and surprise while appearing to offer insight into their own method. They are inventions, mirrors of imaginative possibility, whose subject may or may not be the workings of the imagination. These antistories are as compellingly readable as conventional narratives; they take apart the story in order to reimagine it in a way that permits the reader to discover the nature of fiction. As such, the stories analyze themselves; they become the agency of their own criticism. As Ivan Gold says about one of the longer fictions, they are "about that place—no small terrain—where cinema dream and memory meet and no other fiction has mapped it as well." The stories have the codifying obsession of films transformed into dreams.

Major publications other than short fiction
NOVELS: *A Man to Conjure With*, 1965; *What Comes Next*, 1968; *Reruns*, 1974; *Babble*, 1976; *Chez Charlotte and Emily*, 1979.

NONFICTION: *The Landscape of Nightmare: Studies in the Contemporary American Novel*, 1965.

William Frederick Greenfield

M. F. BEAL

Born: New York, 1937

Principal short fiction

"Gloria Mundi," 1959; "The Moment of Losing," 1960; "Joining Up," 1960; "Survival," 1968; "End of Days," 1969; "Gold," 1971; "Old Babes in Toyland," 1971; "Space Time," 1972; "Discontinuation," 1974; "The Money, The Pickup, The Mare . . . ," 1975; "The Letter," 1975; "Nail Soup," 1976.

Analysis

M. F. Beal became interested in writing short stories because of the challenge of the genre in the areas of craft and communication, in addition to the need for certain short stories to be written. There are events in man's experience, he feels, whose universality can be broadcast only through literature. He sums up his perception of the function of fiction with the following analysis:

> Fiction attempts to satisfy a human hunger to experience life's events as connections in a larger scheme. We learn things we would not otherwise be likely to know about even those people we live with and we identify ourselves as human based on the models literature provides. Individual acts and transits which seem trivial nonetheless touch us all and the story is a sounding board whereon reverberations arrive from our lives and the fictions we have experienced. To read is to be involved in a uniquely private and at the same time immemorially collective activity.

The form of the story—how it is framed, focused, and revealed—is of utmost importance to Beal. He desires to present the material in a straightforward manner so the reader does not become preoccupied with the method of exposition and his "art," and can move into the content freely with little thought concerning how the construct was deliberately devised.

Major publications other than short fiction

NOVELS: *Amazon One*, 1975; *Angel Dance*, 1977.

NONFICTION: "Cosmic Comix: Comic-strip Devices in the Work of Thomas Pynchon," 1974; *Safe House*, 1976.

JOE DAVID BELLAMY

Born: Ohio, 1941

Principal short fiction
"The Dropout," 1969; "Sand," 1970; "Adolescence," 1974; "Obits," 1974; "The Ladder," 1974; "Love and a Lion," 1976; "Irony," 1979; "Julie Christie Rescued in Guatemala," 1979; "Suzi Sinzinnati," 1980.

Analysis
Known primarily (during the decade of the 1970's) as an editor, reviewer, anthologist, and critic, Joe David Bellamy began to assemble a body of short fiction that reflected and paralleled, to some extent, his better known theoretical observations and formulations. The fiction ranges in form and technique from more-or-less straightforward traditional stories that attempt to "hold a mirror up to Nature," to experimental forays that reveal an interest in and awareness of the fashionable aesthetic controversies of the period and a knowledgeable perspective on the past literary/historical contexts of such issues. In the more conventional mode, Bellamy has written a series of amusing, mock-heroic initiation stories involving the character Moke Galenaille, a young man wrested from his social moorings by a callous girlfriend and (via Mayflower Vanlines) by his father's ridiculous version of the American dream. These pieces are characterized by a droll sense of character and situation, a sometimes elaborate attention to style (somewhat in the manner of John Updike), and a parodied but nevertheless apparent nostalgia for the American Midwest of the early 1960's. In his more innovative or unconventional fiction, Bellamy has experimented with the parable, with varieties of irony, and, most successfully (as in his story "Julie Christie Rescued in Guatemala") with a seriocomic (quasimythic, quasi-put-on) treatment of the mysteries of personality, celebrity, and women, and the effects of the media on our perceptions of character, time, and the imagination.

Major publications other than short fiction
POETRY: *Olympic Gold Medalist*, 1978.
NONFICTION: *The New Fiction*, 1974.

JOHN BENNETT

Born: New York, 1938

Principal short fiction

"The Angel of Death and Sonya Schmidt," 1972; "Anneke," 1972; "The Federal Government's Flower," 1975; "The Move," 1975; "Conway & Blume," 1975; *The Night of the Great Butcher*, 1976; *The Party to End All Parties*, 1976; "Sandy," 1976; "Harry the Indian," 1976; "The Wedding," 1978; "Überblick," 1980; "Janice," 1980.

Analysis

John Bennett's short stories are like piles of reality snow-shoveled together and left along the side of the road. He has a way of venturing startling and quite unique phrases that infuse his writing with vividness of scene and cut-break action. There is nothing ponderous or wordy, and little that is stock in his fiction. His recurring themes are the process of lost love, coping with the circumstances that flood the finely tuned carburetor of sanity, and overcoming the inertia brought about by the demands of whatever society his characters happen to be moving through. Bennett is at his best when he lets down his carefully guarded "tough," as seen in the sentiments expressed in "Throwing Frisbee with the Poet," or again in the outright intellectual challenges expressed in one of his most ambitious stories to date, "8-8-8-38." Bennett is a remarkable writer, ferocious in his intent and startlingly poetic in much of its execution.

Major publications other than short fiction

NOVEL: *The Adventures of Achilles Jones*, 1979.

POETRY: *Anarchistic Murmurs from a High Mountain Valley*, 1975; *Crazy Girl on the Bus*, 1979; *Whiplash on the Couch*, 1979 (prose and poetry).

CAROL BERGE

Born: New York, 1928

Principal short fiction

The Unfolding, 1969; *The Challenge*, 1973; *A Couple Called Moebius*, 1973; *In Motion*, 1973; "In Trouble, Winter," 1975; *Timepieces*, 1977; *Hanging Tough*, 1978; *The Doppler Effect*, 1979; *Secrets, Gossip and Slander*, 1981.

Analysis

In an oeuvre distinguished by subtle analysis of relationships, Carol Berge selects those catalytic societal events which transmute the characters' lives. Stories evolve as the interacting personae move to discoveries and then to conclusions evidencing change. Berge's knowledge of the precise anatomy of interior states is expressed in a concentrated diction serving clear narrative. Characters are defined by artifacts, speech-patterns, astrology, gestures, and choice of cityscape or countryside. This New Yorker uses as settings the coasts, deserts, and midlands she has moved through; however, her native city is described as by an extrinsic anthropologist. A major concern is with the apparent rigidity and actual mutability of roles. For a city nightclub singer, childbirth is the pivotal event for transformation; in a country story, a change of houses forces redefinition of a couple's reciprocities and quick assets. The novellas discuss intermarriage, generational sets, academia, ethnic attitudes, dyslexia. Moving between conventional forms and innovative fiction, Berge edits and writes for both traditional and experimental literary magazines. She makes use of classical themes, particularly myths and folktales; the "one-page novels" are *fabliaux* converted to "social science fiction," which are "written as if from the future—distance creates the power of these disturbing, compressed, sardonic yet compassionate" pieces. They define one or two characters' responses to contemporary structures and hungers: "food," "love," "religion," "parenting," "psychology." The more traditional longer works interweave the lives of up to seven people, who "represent the challenges of growth, closeness and difference in a society emphasizing a uniformity of response."

Major publications other than short fiction

NOVEL: *Acts of Love*, 1973.

PLAY: *Landscape with Figures*, 1966.

POETRY: *The Vulnerable Island*, 1964; *Lumina*, 1965; *Poems Made of Skin*, 1968; *The Chambers*, 1969; *Circles, as in the Eye*, 1969; *An American Romance*, 1969; *From a Soft Angle*, 1971; *The Unexpected*, 1976; *Rituals and Gargoyles*, 1976; *A Song, a Chant*, 1978; *Alba Genesis*, 1979; *Alba Nemesis*, 1979.

NONFICTION: *The Vancouver Report*, 1964; *A Chronograph: N. Y. Poets*, 1965.

Howard McCord

BRIGHAM BESMILR

Born: Mississippi, 1923

Principal short fiction
"The Death of Manual Garcia," 1971; "The Old Woman and the Garden," 1972; "The Cathedral," 1972; "Mariposo: The Man Who Saw the Black Butterfly," 1973; "Cassandro: The Elephants' Dance," 1974; "The Street Called Nightingale," 1978; "The Gaunt Wolves," 1978.

Analysis
Brigham Besmilr writes almost entirely of the natural world and does so with authority and with absolute, unswerving attention. She sees the natural world for itself, with a kind of primitive innocence. The inner life is revealed through the tone of her work, that of wonder, unflinching openness, and complete absorption in her central purpose, which is to describe what she senses outside herself: a radiant naïveté, a visionary quality. In "Mariposo," a man and a woman view sexuality quite differently. The woman observes it in the mating of two black butterflies and in the puberty of her son, who is mad. The man understands his own sexuality to be a dangerous mechanism, like a carnival fire-tower, and is more aware than she of the distorted way much of the world views sexuality, as something always verging on the evil or degenerate. The woman's innocence and ability to see what is natural as beautiful, whatever form it may take, is characteristic of the author herself. Pain can be comprehended and respected within the framework of the earth's patterns, and with suffering is placed within the context of a splendid but stern nature which exacts recognition from us. Now, when conditions on this planet demand that we understand our relationship to natural forces, most of us are urban, settled amid the constrictions of our possessions, and accustomed by heritage and habit to being enclosed within the perimeters of civilization. Perhaps her Choctaw ancestry has provided Besmilr with a special sensibility.

Major publications other than short fiction
POETRY: *Agony Dance: Death of the Dancing Dolls*, 1969; *Heaved from the Earth*, 1971.

Sandra Hutchins

ALFRED BESTER

Born: New York, 1913

Principal short fiction

Starburst, 1958; *The Dark Side of the Earth*, 1964; *The Light Fantastic*, 1976; *Star Light, Star Bright*, 1976; *Starlight: The Great Short Fiction of Alfred Bester*, 1977.

Analysis

Although his production has been modest, Alfred Bester has long been recognized as a major science-fiction writer, one of the very few able to bridge the gap between the "hardcore" science-fiction authors of the 1950's and the "New Wave" writers of the 1960's. His appeal to the usual reader is probably due to the fact that Bester's stories feature plot lines familiar in traditional science fiction, fully realized future worlds, replete with ingenious technologies and social arrangements, and the "power fantasies" so eagerly enjoyed by the young readers who have always made up the principal science-fiction audience. At the same time, "New Wave" partisans can appreciate the fact that Bester's stories really focus on the "inner space" of his characters, his exotic landscapes are actually projections of his characters' perceptions, needs, and desires, the "power fantasies" are demolished by his biting irony and ferocious wit, and the tales are replete with clever literary allusions. Both camps can appreciate the frenzied pace of the narratives and the colorful, adroit use of language. At the center of most of the stories is the driven, obsessed Bester hero (or "Besterman") who has the stature of the traditional science-fiction hero, but whose obsessions are strictly contemporary. Frequently, these figures have extraordinary talents which prove to be destructive, like the protagonist of "The Pi Man" whose ESP gives him a frantic obsession with "balance" at all costs, or the chemist in "The Four Hour Fugue" whose extra-sensitive smelling abilities excite him to benevolent homocide, or the "God figure" in "Oddy and Id" whose ability to project "good luck" brings disaster. Other "Bestermen" pursue their obsessions with exotic inventions which, like the talents, always backfire, such as the rocket ship that destroys the Earth in taking off in "Adam and No Eve" or the time machine that betrays its master in "The Men Who Murdered Mohammed." Still others manage to create fantasy worlds to live in, some successfully, as in "Disappearing Act," but more often disastrously, as in "Hell Is Forever" or "They Don't Make Life Like They Used To." Central to all of this is the ambiguous nature of reality itself, a theme that has pervaded not only science fiction, but mainstream literature as well. Few writers have dealt with it as imaginatively and forcefully as Alfred Bester.

Major publications other than short fiction

NOVELS: *The Demolished Man*, 1953; *The Stars My Destination*, 1956; *The Computer Connection*, 1974.

Keith Neilson

SALLIE BINGHAM

Born: Kentucky, 1937

Principal short fiction
The Touching Hand, 1967; *The Way It Is Now*, 1972; "Mending," 1978; "Lawing," 1979; "At Home in Harrodsburg," 1979.

Analysis
Sallie Bingham's stories tell about people who are stranded. The language is that of fine-tuned minds which speak in a vacuum. The South, as background and charm, is part of the stasis: the hot-weather river and the run-down state park hold the characters like dust baths. When women and men speak to each other, they are usually at cross-purposes; desperately, humorously, they talk of sharing when there is not enough for one. As the stories move into colder climates, the temperature of the irony drops. Choices must be made; it is no longer possible to get by on the past, on charm. Desolation and isolation light, by contrast, those odd emotional ties which still bind: the black chauffeur who loves his starving mistress, the under-rated nurse who loves the children who will never be hers. The search for compassion continues, in characters who do not matter in the eyes of the world; merely young, or older and lost, it is through their eyes that the minute daily lives of the world are seen.

Major publications other than short fiction
NOVEL: *After Such Knowledge*, 1959.

DAVID BLACK

Born: Massachusetts, 1945

Principal short fiction
"Laud," 1973; "Twilight Hero at Wally's Place," 1973; "Menu for the Vampire's Ball," 1973; "Discharge," 1973; "Relay Race," 1975; "Return," 1976; "Understanding," 1977; "Turning Thirty," 1977; "Past the Greenfield Exit," 1977; "Rummage and Loss," 1977; "Nostalgia," 1980.

Analysis
Apparently realistic fiction, David Black's stories live in their odd and oddly juxtaposed details. His flashes of figurative language illuminate motive and character like flares lighting up a dark landscape. "Black firmly controls the narrative pace, conveying scenes of intense and unexpected violence in tightly expressed sentences that explode on impact," *The Washington Post* said of his work; and violence of emotion seething beneath ordinary actions is a characteristic of his fiction. "I have never read anything quite like *Like Father* (Black's first novel)," said James Baldwin. "It is both painful and liberating." What makes his work both "painful and liberating" is fidelity to fact and lack of sentimentality. "The characters are described with such attentiveness, such respect, that they seem surprising," Larry McMurtry said. "Through diligence, honesty, and insight, the author has made it fresh." Experience rendered in all its vivid and resonant reality becomes so heightened in Black's work that it gives a hard-edged effect comparable to that seen in photorealistic paintings; and, as in photorealistic art, the apparent cold eye betrays a humor, humanity, even love for its subject at the same time the subject may be under the dissecting knife.

Major publications other than short fiction
NOVELS: *Like Father*, 1978; *Minds*, 1981.
NONFICTION: *Ekstasy*, 1975; *The King of Fifth Avenue*, 1981.

CLARK BLAISE

Born: North Dakota, 1940

Principal short fiction

"A Fish Like a Buzzard," 1962; "Giant Turtles, Gliding in the Dark," 1963; "Before Sundown," 1965; "A Scholar's Work Speaks for Itself," 1965; "Thibidault et Fils," 1965; "Burning Man," 1966; *New Canadian Writing, 1968,* 1968; "Is Oakland Drowning?," 1972; "The Voice of the Elephant," 1972; *A North American Education,* 1973; *Tribal Justice,* 1974; "Cut, Print," 1977; "Man and His World," 1980; "The Sense of an Ending," 1980.

Analysis

Clark Blaise has attempted to particularize, through the use of an autobiographical mode, a universal history of uprootedness, of cultural and class and racial/linguistic tension, and of sexual anxiety and fear of inadequacy in the world, as son, husband, lover, and father. For the most part, he has accepted the "facts" of his own upbringing as suitable for this kind of exploitation; therefore, his characters often find themselves with Canadian parents (French and English), living in the deep South, or with accomplished foreign-born wives whom they have in some way victimized. A persistent set of symbols, which have been remarked upon by critics, involve water, dance, and exhibitionism—a projection outward from fairly deep and obviously disturbing sexual signals. Typically, the Blaise "hero" is an inward, intellectual, physically awkward or even repulsive misfit, fully or acutely alive only in a private fantasy-life. At some point in the story, the self-sufficiency of that private life is challenged by "reality" in the form of social or natural violence, or by an urgent need from a loved one. He will struggle to remain in his dreamworld, or to return to it. There are, of course, strains in Blaise's fiction that are different from those described above—satiric, comedy-of-manners, surrealist—but when his stories are anthologized, these latter elements tend to be ignored.

Major publications other than short fiction

NOVEL: *Lunar Attractions,* 1979.

NONFICTION: *Days and Nights in Calcutta,* 1977 (with Bharati Mukherjee).

ROBERT BLOCH

Born: Chicago, 1917

Principal short fiction
The Opener of the Way, 1945; *Pleasant Dreams*, 1960; *Blood Runs Cold*, 1961; *Atoms and Evil*, 1962; *Yours Truly, Jack the Ripper*, 1962; *Bogey Man*, 1963; *Horror-7*, 1963; *Skull of the Marquis de Sade*, 1965; *Tales in a Jugular Vein*, 1965; *Chamber of Horrors*, 1966; *The Living Demons*, 1967; *Dragons and Nightmares*, 1969.

Analysis
Robert Bloch is perhaps best known for having authored the novel upon which Alfred Hitchcock based his classic film *Psycho*; but that is, in fact, only one detail in Bloch's long and very prolific career—many of his finest accomplishments are in the area of short fiction. As a boy and youth, Bloch was influenced by early horror films and the stories appearing in *Weird Tales*, especially those by H. P. Lovecraft that form the "Cthulhu Mythos." As a young man, Bloch corresponded with Lovecraft and was encouraged by him in his early efforts. During the 1940's, however, Bloch went beyond Lovecraftian imitations to develop his own style, and he became especially skillful in writing the short, grotesque tale which ends with the sharp, unexpected, usually horrific twist. Influenced by such other historical masters of the genre as Edgar Allan Poe and Joseph Sheridan Le Fanu, Bloch also explores the psychological as well as the overtly supernatural in his tales, exploiting that fragile, ambiguous distinction between the real and the imagined to reinforce the horror of his stories. Bloch has also been one of the first contemporary dark fantasists to appreciate the thin line that separates horror from humor; by combining the two in many of his best stories, he has produced memorable tales that are both funny and frightening at the same time. Although most of his writing has been in the suspense/horror genres, Bloch has also written mysteries and science fiction and has, paradoxically, won a science-fiction Hugo Award in 1958 for "That Hell-Bound Train," a story that is actually pure fantasy. Even though Bloch is an excellent novelist, as well as being a successful creator in other media, his short stories represent the finest crystallization of his remarkable talent.

Major publications other than short fiction
NOVELS: *The Scarf*, 1947; *The Kidnapper*, 1954; *Spiderweb*, 1954; *The Will to Kill*, 1954; *Psycho*, 1959; *Firebug*, 1961; *The Couch*, 1962; *Terror*, 1962; *Night Walker*, 1964; *The Dead Beat*, 1968; *American Gothic*, 1974.

Keith Neilson

S. DIANE BOGUS

Born: Illinois, 1946

Principal short fiction

"A Touch of Adultery," 1968; "Fallacy," 1973; "With Respect for Leonard," 1975; "The Bus Ride," 1977; "Goodwill and Foreign Shade," 1978; "A Measure by June," 1978; "The Second Apple," 1978; "The Fixed and Common Notion," 1978; "Patience and the Wages of Sin," 1979; "Dignity Be Thine," 1980.

Analysis

S. Diane Bogus' writing taps three wellsprings of human experience: those of the black, the lesbian, and the feminist. One of her finest stories, "A Touch of June," integrates all three of these levels of experience into a harmonious, well-knit whole. Her prose is sharp yet poetic; she is at her best when delineating character and the erratic, often frustrating flow of relationships. Indeed, the vagaries of human interaction under the stress of social disapproval is a major theme of Bogus' work. There is also an element of fantasy in some of her stories—not the dragons-and-elves type of fantasy, but a subtle, entirely plausible stretching of the limits of reality. There are some who say that the literary craft should not be used as a medium for social consciousness, that activism negates art. A reading of Bogus' stories would definitely contradict that view. Her work is eminently artistic—clean imagery and emotional verisimilitude are evident. Her social perspective shows with equal clarity. Thus, Bogus writes successfully on more than one level. To read her is a learning experience.

Major publications other than short fiction

POETRY: *I'm Off to See the Goddamn Wizard, Alright!*, 1971; *Woman in the Moon*, 1977.

Charles R. Saunders

THOMAS BONTLY

Born: Wisconsin, 1939

Principal short fiction
"Eurydice," 1967; "The Coward," 1971; "Eight Meetings," 1972; "Missing Persons," 1973; "How I Learned About Sex in the Boys' John of Good Old P. S. 39," 1973; "The Birth Day," 1975; "Papa," 1976; "The Blue Smile," 1976; "The Guardian," 1978; "One Year," 1979; "The Rescue," 1980.

Analysis
With a few not very notable exceptions, Thomas Bontly's short stories deal with domestic subjects and employ the traditional techniques of realistic fiction. The best are probably "Missing Persons," "The Birth Day," "The Blue Smile," "The Guardian," and "The Rescue," which all concern a character named Joe Kelsey and focus upon his experiences as husband and father. The theme of fatherhood is especially important. Bontly tries to capture both the pain and pleasure and the privilege and responsibility of fatherhood, and to understand the moral and psychological consequences of what James Joyce termed that "mystical estate." He comments on the various ironies of domesticity in the present age, putting these commonplace experiences into a cosmic perspective—although only as intuited from Kelsey's own finite perspective. Technically, these stories use a single episode in Kelsey's life and attempt to monitor its spiritual meaning through a careful interweaving of image and symbol, action and reflection. Bontly's other published stories, while less important, are more experimental and usually involve an ironic commentary on some aspect of the literary or academic scene.

Major publications other than short fiction
NOVELS: *The Competitor*, 1966; *The Adventures of a Young Outlaw*, 1974; *Celestial Chess*, 1979.

WOLFGANG BORCHERT

Born: Germany, 1921   **Died:** 1947

Principal short fiction
The Sad Geraniums, 1962.

Analysis

In "That Is Our Manifesto," Wolfgang Borchert explains his concept of the writer's role. He says that his age does not need poets with good grammar but rather those with "hoarse emotion" who call "a tree a tree, and a woman a woman, and who say 'yes' and 'no' loudly and clearly." This belief is evident in Borchert's writing. His style is laconic and direct, his language clear and concise. He uses repetition to emphasize important points. The tone of the stories is often shrill and aggressive, often bitterly ironical. In his stories, Borchert portrays a harsh world: youth senselessly slaughtered in a brutal war (he draws from his own experiences on the Eastern Front in World War II where he was sent as punishment for having written anti-Nazi comments in private letters), people who are desperately lonely, and people who suffer mental and physical anguish. Many of his protagonists are likened to puppets who are not in control of their own fate. Borchert depicts a world in ruins which contains shattered people. Despite the bleakness of these stories, there is a ray of hope for a better world in the future. Nevertheless, he called himself a nihilist, but claimed that this was not out of despair but rather out of protest: he wanted to bring some meaning into the void that surrounded him. Borchert's stories exerted a strong influence on the stories of Heinrich Böll.

Major publications other than short fiction
PLAY: *Man Outside*, 1947.

Jennifer Michaels

AUDREY F. BORENSTEIN

Born: Illinois, 1930

Principal short fiction
"The Roses Are Dying," 1961; "The Birth of Abraham Dooley," 1961; "An Heir for Horowitz," 1965; "Regards to Miss Sedonia," 1965; "Parting Gift," 1966; "At Lady Michelangelo's Exhibit," 1966; "Rachel in Search of Her Breasts," 1966; "The Natural History of a Friendship," 1966; "A Fragment of Glass," 1967; "Gloria in Excelsis," 1968; "The Magic Brooch," 1969; "Who's Dreaming Now?," 1971; "The Visions," 1973; "Wake Up, Maggie, Were You Dreaming?," 1973; "A Time for Good-bye Forevers," 1975; "Increase and Multiply," 1975; "Sacrilege, Sophie-style," 1976; "Tide of the Unborn," 1978; "Blue Sunday," 1979; "Sowing in the Shadows," 1980.

Analysis
These lyrical short fictions of magic realism, social realism, and satiric vision are told in Irish voices, Jewish voices, Southern voices—one, the grieving of a black woman, is the prayer of Pietà. In irruptions of inner life, in narratives following a sequential pattern, and in the transformative wonder-working of compositions moving through dreams, imaginative fecundity and emotive power interfuse in the achievement of the miraculous. Glass is the *materia magica*. The image of a dying friend imprints itself on glass. For one dreamer, the entire world becomes a piece of glass. In a fragment of glass embedded in his navel, a man beholds his Other. In the glass jugs of the Futura Sperm Bank, boys and girls dance on the ashes of our ashes. Loss and longing and orphanhood are the themes of these stories set in the South and the Midwest, stories of the 1950's, the 1960's, and the 1970's, stories of public events—wars, assassinations—and private happenings—an abortion, a fatal illness, a vasectomy. Characters are in search—an Irish father for his lostling daughter, a Jewish father for his lostling son, an aging woman for her breasts, a rabbi for another flock. Friends and lovers seek confessors in each other—healers. Each protagonist is a soul dismembered, seeking another of its many selves. Humor and mysticism are gates opening to recognition of selves to be realized, lives to be lived, chances to be taken to redeem Time past and Time passing.

Major publications other than short fiction
NONFICTION: *Redeeming the Sin: Social Science and Literature*, 1978.

BRUCE BOSTON

Born: Illinois, 1943

Principal short fiction

"Carmichal and the City," 1968; "Julia and Richard," 1970; "Burning Man," 1973; "The Monster and the Moon," 1973; "Headed for the Big Time," 1973; "She Comes When You're Leaving," 1975; *Jackbird*, 1976; "Limb Still Kicking from a Stillborn Novel," 1976; "Interview with a Gentleman Farmer," 1976; "Broken Portraiture," 1976; "Sunday Review," 1976; "All the Clocks Are Melting," 1977; "The Poets' War," 1977; "The Chosen," 1978 (with Carl Wittnebert); "Short Circuits," 1978; "South Coast," 1980; "The Opening," 1980.

Analysis

Bruce Boston's stories range from science fiction/fantasy to contemporary realism, though in most cases the thematic concerns center on illusion, reality and the search for an individual identity. The language tends to be dense and descriptive, employing many of the techniques of poetry; a number of the later stories read like extended prose poems. Reviewing the collection *Jackbird* in *Library Journal*, Bill Katz wrote: "The twilight between science fiction and the subconscious nightmare is handled generally well, and sometimes with breathtaking skill."

JAMES BOWDEN

Born: Kentucky, 1934

Principal short fiction
"Go, Purple," 1977; "The Grief of Terry Magoo," 1977; "Why We Like Snow at Christmas," 1979; "Don't Lose This, It's My Only Copy," 1979.

Analysis
These are carefully crafted pieces that for the most part depict people behaving existentially (the author accepts Sidney Hook's definition of existentialism as "cosmic hypochondria") in a basically nonexistential world. They are mostly modern unbelievers who fancy themselves situated on the slanting deck of a sinking ship that happens not to slant very much and apparently is not sinking at all; thus the stories go against contemporary sensibility and sentiments. Perhaps because of this there is a tendency toward parody in James Bowden's work. Limited third-person point of view is usual, although more than one character may use it. Punctuation, to include quotation marks, is eschewed, except for the colon and the period. A slight sense of unreality sometimes results. John Gardner has called his work "glorious."

Major publications other than short fiction
NONFICTION: *Peter De Vries: A Critical Study*, 1981.

JOHN BRANDI

Born: California, 1943

Principal short fiction
Desde Alla, 1971; *Y Aun Hay Mas*, 1972; *Narrowgauge to Riobamba*, 1975; *Diary from a Journey to the Middle of the World*, 1979.

Analysis
"We are children of our landscape; it dictates behaviour and even thought in the measure to which we are responsive to it," exclaimed Lawrence Durrell in "Justine." John Brandi (whose writing has been compared to Durrell's) submerges himself in the peasant landscape—daily rituals and religious festivals of Andean mountain people—stringing together a series of prismatic tableaus in four books spanning ten years of travels. He is the observer (the itinerant painter, poet, sometimes social worker) closely linked to the farmer, shaman, milkmaid, and common laborer; yet stranded with the realization that he is "a foreigner everywhere." Thus, Brandi's collected stories are like miniature cyclones swirling with conversations, situations, emotional vortex, color, and phantasma of a world not completely understood, but appreciated for its symbols and archetypal reminders. "The world is one big confusing ideogram and I am the masked effigy wondering who's in control of the pulley and where exactly I'll come down. Dreams. Fantasy. Reality. All is blank. And I have amazingly landed."

Major publications other than short fiction
POETRY: *Firebook*, 1974; *Looking for Minerals*, 1975; *Poems from Four Corners*, 1978; *Andean Town Circa 1980*, 1979; *Skyhourse*, 1980; *Hiding Behind Open Doors*, 1981.

NONFICTION: *Chimborazo: Life on the Haciendas of Highland Ecuador*, 1976.

CHARLES BRASHERS

Born: Texas, 1930

Principal short fiction

The Other Side of Love, 1963; "Crack, Crash Orange Flare," 1967; "Growing Pains," 1968; *Eight Stories*, 1975 (with three other authors); "A Cup of Fresh Rainwater," 1977; "Betjegen," 1978; "Eggs in Cow Country," 1979; "Rough Creek, Texas—1888," 1979; "The Battle of Wounded Thigh," 1980.

Analysis

Charles (Howard C. or H. C.) Brashers' short fiction is in the "well-made" tradition of Henrik Ibsen, Anton Chekhov, and Katherine Anne Porter. Usually there is a strong sense of a central controlling idea, moving toward a revealing climax and close. Brashers' characters often move through cycles of experience, often generating or echoing mythic patterns. His forte in style is his use of vivid detail to evoke a physical scene which acts as the "objective correlative" of the psychological states of his characters. His subjects are taken from his boyhood in Texas, grandmothers and little sisters, and the interface of American/Indian cultures in contemporary and historical situations. The historical situations tend to be "documentary," that is, built around real characters in real places, performing historically docu-actions.

Major publications other than short fiction

NOVEL: *A Snug Little Purchase, How Richard Henderson Bought Kaintuckee from the Cherokees in 1775*, 1979.

POETRY: *Whatta Ya Mean, 'Get out o' That Dirty Hole'?—I LIVE Here*, 1974.

NONFICTION: *Introduction to American Literature*, 1965; *Creative Writing, Fiction, Drama, Poetry, The Essay*, 1968; *Developing Creativity, an Introduction*, 1974.

JOSEPH PAYNE BRENNAN

Born: Connecticut, 1918

Principal short fiction

Nine Horrors and a Dream, 1958; *The Dark Returners*, 1959; *Scream at Midnight*, 1963; *The Casebook of Lucius Leffing*, 1973; *Stories of Darkness and Dread*, 1973; *The Chronicles of Lucius Leffing*, 1977; *Act of Providence*, 1979 (with Donald M. Grant); *The Shapes of Midnight*, 1980.

Analysis

The best of Joseph Brennan's short stories lie in the field of imaginative or fantasy fiction. Compressed and carefully written, they possess sustained power and impact. Brennan relies more heavily on compelling atmospheric touches and disturbing aspects of milieu than on mere plot gimmickry. Stylistically, he eschews the flowery and the ornate. "He writes," says Stephen King, "in what E. B. White called 'the plain style' . . . a sturdy style, capable of wielding enormous power. . . . The only stories which come to mind as equals of Brennan's *"Canavan's Back Yard"* in terms of cumulative effect and quiet overall success are Charlotte Perkins Gilman's *The Yellow Wallpaper* and William Faulkner's "A Rose for Emily." The late August Derleth mentioned Brennan's "Sure sense of scene and dramatic effect." Even though much of the author's work is classified as fantasy fiction, he invariably strives for an aura of verisimilitude—Edgar Allan Poe's "momentary suspension of disbelief." With few exceptions, he succeeds. Brennan's best stories go beyond simple entertainment; thematically they touch on some of the most important problems and dilemmas confronting the human psyche and mankind itself. If Brennan's work has been called "too terrifying and macabre," it can be said that world crises today are little less than "terrifying and macabre." Brennan's straight detective stories, featuring Lucius Leffing, a private investigator, have been favorably compared to Arthur Conan Doyle's Sherlock Holmes narratives, even though their setting is the United States and their time the twentieth century.

Major publications other than short fiction

POETRY: *Heart of Earth*, 1950; *The Humming Stair*, 1953; *The Wind of Time*, 1962; *Nightmare Need*, 1964; *A Sheaf of Snow Poems*, 1973; *Edges of Night*, 1974; *As Evening Advances*, 1978; *Webs of Time*, 1980.

CHRISTOPHER BROOKHOUSE

Born: Ohio, 1938

Principal short fiction
"If Lost, Return," 1969; *If Lost, Return*, 1973; "A Short History of North Carolina with Some Names Changed to Protect the Innocent, the Guilty, and the Dead," 1976.

Analysis
Clearly within Christopher Brookhouse's short stories, as well as his longer fiction and poetry, there is a strongly developed sense of place, and the idea, or metaphor, of a journey is continually present. His characters seem constantly on the move, whether their journeys be outward, physical ones, or inner, spiritual ones. His characters are not neccessarily products of actual geographies; place does not form character; the characters do, however, seem to function in relation to place. For example, in much of Brookhouse's work there is a division of north and south. People, such as the woman in the story "The Woman Who Read Wallace Stevens," have left the North for the South and have abandoned, in the process, a world where their lives were distinct and whole for a new landscape that signifies a spiritual confusion which often results in violence. To some degree Brookhouse's short fiction has links to his poetry, particularly the omission of exposition in favor of implications and resonances. His stories, among them "The Afternoon Gordon Dies," are fragmentary, or developed in sections which resemble stanzas in poetry. One influence on such work is Anaïs Nin.

Major publications other than short fiction
NOVELS: *Running Out*, 1970; *Wintermute*, 1978.
POETRY: *Scattered Light*, 1969.

C. B. Clark

BEN BROOKS

Born: Washington, D.C., 1948

Principal short fiction

"Rage," 1976; "Julia," 1977; "Feldman's Mother," 1977; "The Babysitter," 1978; "Blue," 1979; "Cheese," 1979; "No More Bettys," 1980; "Tools," 1980; "Dharna," 1980; "A Postal Creed," 1980; "Turtles Move Slowly," 1980.

Analysis

Ben Brooks's first-person narratives remind one of Franz Kafka and of certain other European writers of the tales that survivors tell. His characters are pinned to chance, seeming to have no control over their lives—or have they simply given themselves over to willed loss, to the play of unconscious drives? These tales are almost primal in their intensity. There is rage in these stories, but Brooks moves through it with muffled oars. Mutilations, indignities: they are met with impotence or indifference. Characters are swamped by their own physical sensations. Thus, situations and even space itself becomes claustrophobic. Images of disgust pervade: food viewed more as endproduct than as by-product, sexual transgressions and aberrations, the intimate life of the body and its decay. The body is viewed as a conglomerate of parts, perhaps no more the Self than the "world of externals" ("Blue") which we inhabit. What gives life its meaning is the personal quest, a life governed by passion and intuition. This alone is pure, and any pretention to the communal life is a lie. Personal quest tempts exposure and humiliation—there is no solidarity anywhere, except for that tenuous connection which arises at the moment of common need. This connection, once systematized or instituted, brings about its own demoralization. The perfect life, in order to be lived, requires its scapegoat somewhere. Brooks's characters, having been the scapegoats, wait for it to happen again.

Major publications other than short fiction

NONFICTION: "Artists at Work: One Place," 1978; "The Permanent Collection." 1978.

Vanessa Ryder

FREDRIC BROWN

Born: Ohio, 1906   **Died:** Arizona, 1972

Principal short fiction

Space on My Hands, 1951; *Angels and Spaceships*, 1954; *Honeymoon in Hell*, 1958; *Nightmares and Geezenstacks*, 1961; *Daymares*, 1968; *Paradox Lost*, 1973; *The Best of Fredric Brown*, 1976.

Analysis

Although perhaps best known to the general public as a mystery-story writer for such works as the Edgar Award-winning *The Fabulous Clipjoint* (1947), Fredric Brown has done his finest writing in the short-short-story genre. Most of his science fiction is characterized by a sharp wit, acute observation, and provocative sense of irony. Usually his works, even the novels, turn on a marvelously clever central idea—even a joke—and, for that reason, the shorter the piece, the greater the impact of the "punch line." Sometimes, the ideas are clever enough to sustain an entire novel: for example, in *Martians, Go Home* (1955) the Martian invaders are actually "little green men" who do nothing, but who appear everywhere, know everything, and disrupt every human activity from gambling to sex by a constant barrage of sarcastic one-liners. The central ideas of his stories demand a succinct presentation, and Brown is a master at setting his reader up and then deftly turning him upside down. The crucial ingredient, of course, is humor, a quality generally missing from pre-1960's science fiction. For sheer wit and ingenuity, in the short forms at least, no science-fiction writer has yet matched Brown. Perhaps this fact can be best conveyed by reprinting, in toto, one of his most famous short-shorts, the story that Swedish critic Sam J. Lundwall uses in his book *Science Fiction: What It Is All About* (1971) to illustrate the capacity of science fiction to stimulate awe in a reader:

> After the last atomic war, Earth was dead; nothing grew, nothing lived. The last man sat alone in a room. There was a knock at the door. . . .

Major publications other than short fiction

NOVELS: *The Fabulous Clipjoint*, 1947; *What Mad Universe?*, 1949; *The Lights in the Sky Are Stars*, 1953; *Martians, Go Home*, 1955; *Rogue in Space*, 1957; *The Office*, 1958; *The Mind Thing*, 1961.

Keith Neilson

ROSELLEN BROWN

Born: Pennsylvania, 1939

Principal short fiction
"Good Housekeeping," 1970; "What Does the Falcon Owe?," 1970; "Fingerprints," 1971; "Mainlanders," 1971; "Re:Femme," 1971-1972; "A Letter to Ismael in the Grave," 1972; *Street Games*, 1974; "How to Win," 1975; "Why I Quit the Gowanus Liberation Front," 1976; "How Mrs. Fox Married Again," 1978; "The Wedding Week," 1979.

Analysis
Fourteen of Rosellen Brown's stories are gathered in *Street Games*, a series of interrelated glimpses of life on a (hypothetical) block in Brooklyn in the 1970's. "Slocum Hill" is a neighborhood under renovation, which accounts for the wide range of characters who coexist on a single block of "George Street," whose lives are in dissimilar state of de- and reconstruction. There is the owner of a failing bodega who tries, in "I Am Not Luis Beech-nut," to defend his modest hopes but sees himself finally overtaken, mugged by the advancing spectre of the A & P. There is Cecil, a Jamaican with an inclination to straightforward satisfactions whose view of the world is complicated by a visit from his mysteriously unhappy sister; and there is a woman who, beyond loss, sits down to reason with the burglar who has her jewelry in his pocket. The reader meets upwardly mobile Puerto Ricans trying to put distance between themselves and their childhoods and white middle-class parents struggling with their children and their comprehension that this "integrated" neighborhood is less of a triumph of democracy than it seems. The voices in *Street Games* are varied, some a realistic first person, others a more heightened, poetic first or third-person prose. Half the stories were published separately in magazines, and the others were written expressly for the book. Of the uncollected stories, the first published, "What Does the Falcon Owe?," is a melange of "leavings, clues" gathered to provide a cryptic explanation of a wife's departure from her marriage. "Re:Femme" is a series of letters, bitter and humorous but striving for hopefulness, between a senator's wife and two women who are magazine editors of different generations. "Good Housekeeping," originally written as part of Brown's first novel, *The Autobiography of My Mother* (1976), is a very short glimpse of a mother-as-artist, desperate for some concentration unbroken by her baby. "The Wedding Week" is a portrait of his old-world father by a son who is afraid he is doomed to repeat his father's personality in the "new world."

Brown also published in the late 1960's and early 1970's a series of "collage" fragments—prose, poetry, quotations—with a thematic order. These might be seen as a bridge between her poetry and the more conventionally formed stories in *Street Games*. She continues to represent many kinds of voices of both sexes and many classes and races, most of them made articulate by her belief that people feel more complexly than they talk in so-called "real life," and that, consequently, the sympathetic writer must imagine those thoughts and give them dignity and shape on the page.

Major publications other than short fiction
NOVELS: *The Autobiography of My Mother*, 1976; *Tender Mercies*, 1978.
POETRY: *Some Deaths in the Delta and Other Poems*, 1970; *Cora Fry*, 1977.

FREDERICK BUSCH

Born: New York, 1941

Principal short fiction
Breathing Trouble, 1973; *Domestic Particulars*, 1976; *Hardwater Country*, 1979.

Analysis
Frederick Busch's short fiction flowed from his early attempts to be a poet. The first works are obsessed with rhythm, even rhymes within lines, a refusal to disclose data that cannot be inferred from dialogue and minimal description. The stories in *Breathing Trouble* substantiate those dogmas. They slackened, or grew flexible, as Busch grew up, and as he became more conscious of his self-consciousness and less comfortable with it. From the start, the family as central tragic unit has been crucial to Busch's writing, and remains so; but the stories were influenced by his working at novels and his growing love of the works of Dickens. *Story*, in the stories, grew terribly important to him. His love of, and insistence upon, disclosure through dramatic dialogue grew even stronger, and so did affection for the world outside the sensibility of the writer and his personae. Busch's stories are about self-enclosed people and the startling, wonderful natural world they crawl upon—and about their efforts to pierce the membrane of self in which they are locked, and finally touch one another.

Major publications other than short fiction
NOVELS: *I Wanted a Year Without Fall*, 1971; *Manual Labor*, 1974; *The Mutual Friend*, 1978; *Rounds*, 1980.
NONFICTION: *Hawkes: A Guide to His Fictions*, 1973.

DEAN CADLE

Born: Kentucky, 1920

Principal short fiction
"We Have Returned," 1947; "Anthem of the Locusts," 1949; "The Wedding Warriors," 1949; "The Bootleggers," 1952; "Deep Furrow," 1952; "Proposal of the Republic," 1955; "Cry in the Wilderness," 1956; "Dance by the Sea," 1958.

Analysis
Traditional in their balance of plot and characterization. Dean Cadle's stories thematically reflect man's continuing struggle to prevail over an often inimical atmosphere. The isolated coal-mining camps of eastern Kentucky and the towns and barrios of the Philippines provide settings for his portrayals of simple people who search for freedom, permanence, and love in a world governed by uncertainty, authority, and fear. The dominant character in Cadle's stories is the child or child-like adult who, unencumbered by urban values, is most in touch with those needs. The tone of the stories varies from playful to ironic to solemn. While the Filipino stories are more tightly constructed and more thematically oriented, those set in Appalachia are more relaxed, "natural," and humorous, perhaps illustrating Cadle's statement that "a writer must live a long time with a people before he can write humorously about them." Cadle's style ranges from the mountain-inflected dialogue of two young boys theorizing that "Fire on the tail'll make anything move" to the fantasy-like description of an island prison rising out of the ". . . fragments of mist that hovered like gray head-veils of invisible women strolling the water." There are similarities in character and theme, but what most obviously ties together these stories from two sides of the world is a pervading tenderness on the part of the author toward his people. The evil in the stories is not an inherent or developed trait of the people but an outside force imposed on them.

Lynne Baber

JACK CADY

Born: Ohio, 1932

Principal short fiction
The Burning; *Tattoo*.

Analysis
The short story lives best in the realm between poetry and fiction. Like poetry, there is no room in a short story for an extra word. Cady's stories represent both intellectual and emotional development, for they begin in an existential mode and gradually move toward a critical compassion. The stories are tinged with a hint of Americanism, since the writer is deeply concerned with American history and literature. There is an unlevel quality about the stories. The ones listed are excellent, and some of the others are rather hasty. The best is prose-poetry, and it is titled "The Priest."

Major publications other than short fiction
NOVEL: *The Well*, 1980.

JOHN W. CAMPBELL, JR.

Born: New Jersey, 1910   **Died:** 1971

Principal short fiction

Who Goes There?, 1948; *The Cloak of Aesir*, 1952; *Who Goes There? and Other Stories*, 1955; *The Planeteers*, 1966; *The Best of John W. Campbell*, 1973.

Analysis

John W. Campbell, Jr., is generally regarded as the most influential figure in the shaping of modern science fiction between Hugo Gernsback and the "New Wave" of the 1960's. Campbell's major impact was made as the editor of *Astounding Stories* (later *Analog Science Fiction/Science Fact*) from 1937 until his death in 1971. In that capacity he discovered, stimulated, and guided a group of writers, including Isaac Asimov, Robert A. Heinlein, Theodore Sturgeon, and A. E. van Vogt, that came to dominate the field for more than two decades. If Campbell had never edited at all, his influence on the genre would have been considerable, especially in the short story. In the early 1930's, he built a solid reputation writing "space operas," mostly for *Amazing Stories*, in the style of the times. Ironically, he also began to write a different kind of story under the pen name of "Don A. Stuart," the first being "Twilight" (1934), a lyrical, philosophical "mood" tale about a visitor from the distant future. It was under the Stuart pseudonym that Campbell wrote his most memorable stories, which, in turn, crystallized his ideas about the nature, purpose, and standards of science-fiction writing—criteria that he then imposed on his growing "stable" of writers. Campbell probably reached his peak as a story writer with the classic "Who Goes There?" (1938), a chilling story of an Arctic encounter with a shape-changing alien, later adapted to film as *The Thing* (1951), without most of Campbell's imaginative touches. He wrote little fiction after "Who Goes There?," preferring to concentrate on editing and nonfiction (primarily editorials in *Astounding Stories*).

Major publications other than short fiction

NOVELS: *The Mightiest Machine* 1947; *The Black Star Passes*, 1953; *The Moon Is Hell*, 1950; *Islands of Space*, 1957; *Invaders from the Infinite*, 1961; *The Ultimate Weapon*, 1966.

NONFICTION: *The Atomic Story*, 1947.

Keith Neilson

ELI CANTOR
Gregory A. Douglas

Born: New York, 1913

Principal short fiction

"Day of Days," 1940; "Adventure in the Morning," 1941; "Take Me, Missus, Take Me!" 1941.

Analysis

As the book jackets on the novels *Enemy in the Mirror* (1977) and *Love Letters* (1980) point out, Eli Cantor has had several successful careers, but he started as a writer—honored by E. J. O'Brien along with William Faulkner, D. H. Lawrence, Sean O'Casey, Katherine Anne Porter. That was in 1940; his first novel was published in 1977. The years between were devoted to journalism as editor of *Esquire*, then as editor-in-chief of "The Research Institute Report," and to printing (as board chairman of Printing Industries of America)—a somewhat unusual combination for a novelist. At the time of Cantor's short stories, a grimness of "social consciousness" prevailed. Looking back, he finds the stories nevertheless resonant with the humor and courage of individuals who, although caught in an economic vise, never forfeit their inner spirit. His novels currently echo the same basic theme: individuals struggle always, against themselves as well as others, but always with a grace of humor and, ultimately, compassion. Unlike some contemporary writers, Cantor believes in Aristotle's views of structure and teaches them in his fiction workshop at P. E. N. Centro Internacional in San Miguel de Allende, Mexico. It seems to him that without the conflict, the rising of climaxes, and the catharsis of resolution, a story—whatever its other strengths and illuminations—simply does not get off the page to the reader.

Major publications other than short fiction

NOVELS: *Enemy in the Mirror*, 1977; *The Rite*, 1979; *Love Letters*, 1980; *The Nest*, 1980.

PLAYS: *Old Lady*, 1938; *Candy Store*, 1948; *Armstrong TV Theatre*, 1951; *The Golden Goblet*, 1960; *Screenplay, Love Letters*, 1980.

ROBERT CANZONERI

Born: Mississippi, 1925

Principal short fiction
Barbed Wire and Other Stories, 1970; "The Hill," 1973; "The Boot," 1973; "And I Made a Lovely Salad," 1974; "Blue Leaf in August," 1977; "Human Voices," 1979.

Analysis
Much of the clarity, vivid reality and warmth of Robert Canzoneri's short fiction stems from his easy familiarity with the small Southern towns and the academic communities in which most of the stories are set. He often depicts the world of children as they struggle to understand the strange terms of their existence in an adult world. In "Freddy-Bear" the encounter embodies a terror reminiscent of another Southern writer, Flannery O'Connor, but more often such stories are characterized by a gently ironic humor, as in "The Prodigal Uncle." The short stories integrated into the memoir, *A Highly Ramified Tree* (1976), evoke the author's real and imagined childhood affectingly but without bathos; the child's world here is less frightening than in the *Barbed Wire* stories, because less dependent on the adult world and populated by more reassuring adults. Another important theme in the stories is the search for the past; a teenager tries to find the truth about his long-dead father in "Barbed Wire," discovering enough to make him realize that he cannot build his own life on a romanticized image of the dead parent; a young man in "Blue Leaf in August" returns to the town his parents had fled years before to find out why they had left, but he is unable to decide how to deal with what he finds. Harsher but sometimes funnier ironies characterize the academic stories: an encounter between a genteel poetess and a macho poet, the odd relationship between a stupid but beautiful student and a fat old professor, and the self-pity of a hypochondriac who is driven to make others' diseases his own. In all of the stories the prose is lucid, easy and evocative, the settings are sharp, and the sense of life is immediate.

Major publications other than short fiction
NOVEL: *Men with Little Hammers*, 1969.
PLAYS: *The Peace Gimmick*, 1962; *Siege! The Battle of Vicksburg*, 1975.
POETRY: *Watch Us Pass*, 1968.
NONFICTION: *I Do So Politely*, 1965; *A Highly Ramified Tree*, 1976.

John M. Muste

RON CARLSON

Born: Utah, 1947

Principal short fiction

"Be not marooned," 1971; "How to analyze a short story," 1972; "Martha's Vineyard: Three days from the end . . . ," 1974; "A story: Things fall locally," 1976; "Solo," 1977; "The uses of videotape," 1979.

Analysis

Frequently humorous, with moments of poignance drawn from observations of everyday experience, Ron Carlson's stories each have the quality of a vignette with a single episode told from the narrator's point of view. Most are boyhood stories related in the "smart-alecky" voices of adolescence. Primarily a novelist, Carlson, in his stories, brings his vivid imagination to a traditional form. In these stories he employs puns and other wordplay and he frequently weaves references to old movies with the experiences of growing up in a neighborhood with backyards for camping overnight, trees and fences to climb, and pick-up ballgames. The plot lines are clear and direct, with imagination, wry observation, and narrative voice bringing the special character to the stories.

Major publications other than short fiction

NOVELS: *Betrayed by F. Scott Fitzgerald*, 1977; *Truants*, 1980.

Walter DeMelle, Jr.

PAT CARR

Born: Wyoming, 1932

Principal short fiction
"El Santa," 1966; "Desire Is a Bus," 1967; "Life and Death of a Roustabout," 1969; *From Beneath the Hill of the Three Crosses*, 1970; *The Grass Creek Chronicle*, 1976; *The Women in the Mirror*, 1977; "Buffalo Man," 1978; "Penelope at the Loom," 1979; "The Emergence," 1979; "Atocle Woman," 1980.

Analysis
Strongly influenced by Anton Chekhov, Pat Carr strives for exactness, compression, and intensity, for a precise "objective correlative" of setting and atmosphere that will expose the emotion of each story's core incident. All of her fiction is anchored in actuality and is based on psychological reality, and she readily admits that she has no patience with Modernist antiheroes or motiveless, absurd behavior. She feels that twentieth century literature has too often featured the weak who are mired in self-indulgent ennui, loneliness, and contempt, and she believes that it is time once more for fiction to deal with the strong who are capable of sympathy, acts of kindness, and genuine passion. She has a deep commitment to express as clearly and as truthfully as possible what one actually experiences in "boundary situations"; and she is more concerned with telling a dramatic, nonconfessional story than with exhibiting stylistic virtuosity. As Leonard Michaels says,

> Pat Carr's stories have solid, traditional virtues—excellent prose, skillful dramatic struc-
> ture—and they are especially impressive for the variety and depth of their subjects. A
> clear moral vision prevails throughout; and the most delicate and exquisite psychological
> situations are rendered with subtlety and good effect. She is the kind of writer who, with
> remarkable consistency, produces stories that are at once finely controlled and significantly
> moving.

Major publications other than short fiction
NONFICTION: *Bernard Shaw*, 1976; *Mimbres Mythology*, 1979.

LILLIE D. CHAFFIN

Born: Kentucky, 1925

Principal short fiction
"Beyond the Curve," 1968; "A Patch of Spring," 1970; "Third Hand," 1970; "Whistler's Mother," 1978; "Public Assistance," 1972; "Whole Sky," 1978; "Out of Chaos," 1970; "Bread for a Journey," 1980.

Analysis
Deceptively simple, Lillie D. Chaffin's stories center on tender characters who are basically unsophisticated and who deal with the essential elements in their lives: food, clothing, love, dreams, death. Many of the stories are set in central Appalachia, an environment restricted by religion and poverty. Her best works involve children, the true people, learning from adults by observation and imitation.

Major publications other than short fiction
NOVELS: *John Henry McCoy*, 1971; *Freeman*, 1972.

THALIA CHERONIS-SELZ

Born: Illinois

Principal short fiction
"The Death of Anna," 1957; "The Education of a Queen," 1961; "The Elbow," 1966; "Three-Thirty A.M.," 1972; "The Algerian Hook," 1976; "Peace," 1977; "It Is Well That You Came.—It Is Well That We Found You.," 1977; "Relationships," 1978; "A View from the Tumulus," 1980; "The Greek Garden," 1980.

Analysis
Thalia Cheronis-Selz has been called a traditionalist because of her preoccupation with plot, character, theme, and setting, and she agrees that what interests her is the influence of the social scene—at a given historical moment—upon character. Richard Poirier comments on her novella-length story which won an O. Henry Award that while it is comic, it "offers an implicit criticism of people who live by dependence on the manners and roles of some particular in-group, even while the author takes pleasure from the mannered self-assurance with which they express themselves." She is, however, equally intrigued by the impact of formidable individuals upon society, and her short fiction seems crowded with lives and events which extend themselves far beyond the story framework. Fittingly, her most recent stories are self-contained excerpts from a long novel-in-progress, *The Greek Garden*. Her subject matter ranges from the Chicago Greek-American background of her childhood through the contemporary urban singles scene to the most gifted and privileged circles of the New York art world. Her scenes are full of "a magic sense of surprise, rich invention, and lush detail," but her tone is humorous—even her tragedies tend to be funny—and she has an ear for the absurdly characteristic turn of phrase. Cheronis-Selz is a self-conscious, precise stylist whose narrative passages are as compelling as her dramatic scenes. She has won two major short-story awards and has been anthologized in three collections.

KELLY CHERRY

Born: Louisiana, 1940

Principal short fiction

"An American Arcady," 1967; "Tycho Brahe's Gold and Silver Nose," 1967; "Covenant," 1971; "Braumiller and His Daughter Discuss Feminism at Dinner," 1974; "Portraits; or, Four Tests of Authenticity," 1975; "The Woman Who Was Not Pretty Enough," 1975; "Where the Winged Horses Take Off into the Wild Blue Yonder From," 1976; "Soundings," 1976; "Of Silence and Slow Time," 1976; "Conversion," 1976; "Creation," 1977; "The Day That Waldo Did It," 1978.

Analysis

The text referred to in the subtitle of Cherry's collection in manuscript, *The Lost Traveler's Dream: Commentary on a Text*, is a poem by William Blake. Each of the stories in the collection is a comment on this poem, and the three parts of the collection were suggested by a line in the poem. The book is concerned with the act of creation in its theological, aesthetic, and sexual dimensions. The major motifs of the three sections of the book are correspondingly religion, art, and science. In anything Cherry writes, prose or poetry, fiction or nonfiction, she is most compelled by the developmental passages. It is structure in time, the logic of change, that most interests her. Most of her stories are relatively long, and it is their coherence on a still larger scale that was her reason for doing a collection.

Major publications other than short fiction

NOVELS: *Sick and Full of Burning*, 1974; *Augusta Played*, 1979.

POETRY: *Lovers and Agnostics*, 1975; *Relativity*, 1977; *Songs for a Soviet Composer*, 1980.

ALAN CHEUSE

Born: New Jersey, 1940

Principal short fiction
Candace & Other Stories, 1980.

Analysis
Alan Cheuse has published one collection of short stories which indicates his wide range and variety. "Candace," the title piece, has been conceived as an extended interpolation to Faulkner's *The Sound and the Fury*, as Cheuse brilliantly provides for Caddy a history between the lines. He takes the original text and fills in the blank time between her disappearance and reappearance in the photograph beside a Nazi officer. It is a virtuoso performance, deeply literate yet supple on the surface. "Incidents of Travel in the Yucatan" employs John Stephens' original text as counterpoint to a contemporary travel-tale; "The Quest for Ambrose Bierce" does much the same. Two stories in the collection, "The Call" and "Fishing for Coyotes," illustrate further Cheuse's keen ear for dialogue and the sense of menace that hovers, always, just out of easy eye-range. An uncollected story titled "Accident" perhaps best indicates the Cheuse protagonist: a decent, troubled witness whose daily round gets shattered by a shot. Love and responsibility are often at odds in the stories. The resolution fuses them. A Northerner, Cheuse has elected the South. At home in the slums or suburbs, he works within several traditions and is perceptibly forging his own.

Nicholas Delbanco

B. J. CHUTE

Born: Minnesota, 1913

Principal short fiction

The Blue Cup, 1957; *One Touch of Nature*, 1965; "The Temptation of Mrs. Logan," 1966; "Turn of the Tide" 1973; "The Meadow," 1975.

Analysis

In her short stories, as in her novels, B. J. Chute has always gone her own way, neither in fashion nor out of it but obedient to her own sense of truth. She began her career with sports stories for young people, stories which have been extremely popular because of their lively characterizations, vivid action, and impeccable accuracy. When she moved into the adult field to write about men—prizefighters, tycoons, policemen, other representatives of a male world—this quality persisted. Her empathy has served her equally well in the female world—from a nine-year-old tomboy to an aging actress, from a pregnant slum girl to a happy suburban housewife. Chute's work demonstrates a wide familiarity with all kinds of people and backgrounds. Two of her best-known stories, "The Outcasts" and "Birthday Gift," deal head-on with racial prejudice and were published in leading popular magazines at a time when the subject was virtually taboo. Her range extends to her use of language. Sometimes poetic as in "The Meadow," sometimes folkloric as in "The Jukebox and the Kallikaks," sometimes matter-of-fact and tough as in "Rookie Cop," the function of her style is always to mirror a particular world. A critic has called her "one of the few masters of short-story writing alive who can still weave the patterns of a story into a distinguishable whole." She looks upon herself as a storyteller, and she rejoices in the infinite variety of human beings—their happiness, sorrow, failure, triumph, and, perhaps most of all, their capacity for love.

Major publications other than short fiction

NOVELS: *The Fields Are White*, 1950; *The End of Loving*, 1953; *Greenwillow*, 1956; *The Moon and the Thorn*, 1961; *The Story of a Small Life*, 1971; *Katie: An Impertinent Fairy Tale*, 1978.

JANE CIABATTARI

Born: Kansas, 1946

Principal short fiction
"Hiding Out," 1974; "Totems," 1975; "Pulling Pieces Together," 1976; *Deadlines*, 1980.

Analysis
Jane Ciabattari writes stories about people who are caught up in the pressures of the everyday, or who are "on the edge"—in peril psychically or intensely aware of being in a state of transition. There is a strong sense of immediacy in her work. The stories are presented from a strong central point of view, often in first person. They proceed by accumulation of scene and rely more on the power operating within language and image than on linear plot development. Often the stories contrast the interior contemplative world of the individual with a busy and demanding exterior world.

A sense of place and the natural setting are important in Ciabattari's work, often mirroring subjective events. "Hiding Out" is set in a frozen New England village. There is a mood of madness and withdrawal in this story that borders on the surreal. In "Totems," which takes place in Vancouver, the protagonist is searching for magical connective words, places, and rituals to comfort her in a time of grief. "Pulling Pieces Together" is set in San Francisco; it details one day in the life of a woman who is searching for a sense of self in her roles as newspaper reporter, wife, and mother. The shifts in consciousness required by the changing demands of her day create the structure of the story.

The fragmentation and stressfulness of contemporary life and the ever-present potential for obliteration of the individual are givens in these stories. The characters search for balance, for connection with others, for compassion, for a fleeting sense of peace. In exploring the texture of common experience, Ciabattari offers the readers moments of individual choice and courage and illumination.

SYBIL CLAIBORNE

Born: England, 1923

Principal short fiction
"Great Western Civilization Caper," 1970; "The Object of My Affections," 1974; "Okinawa's Wife," 1977.

Analysis
Sybil Claiborne's stories are of ordinary people in extraordinary situations, funny, absurd, and satirical. Like insects trapped inside a room, the people in these stories struggle to free themselves. Some are trying to escape an impossible situation. A young man living in an old people's home secretes India ink. He tries to invent a device that will catch the flow so that he can leave and resume his life. An elderly woman with nothing to do because her retired army husband has taken over all the housework tries to start a new career. A man whose mistress and wife become best friends fears they are planning a vacation without him. These are some of the problems the people try to overcome, and the intensity of their struggle and their determination to survive are recurrent themes throughout these short fictions.

JEAN C. CLARK

Born: Connecticut, 1920

Principal short fiction
"This Was Madness," 1955; "Something to Give," 1956; "Watch the Sunset," 1956; "Fifty-Cent Guess," 1956; "The Fabulous Success of Riley MacNeal," 1956; "Sorry—Right Number," 1956; "Little 'It'," 1957; "Treasure Each Day," 1958; "Valedictory," 1959; "A Kind of Make-Believe," 1959; "Only for Now," 1959; "Lest Old Acquaintance," 1960; "More Than a Prayer," 1960; "Little Boy Bluebird," 1962.

Analysis
Jean Clark writes an essentially structured story that has a beginning, a middle, and an end. The emphasis, however, is on the characters involved. Although not conceived in terms of plot, each story has a pattern that grows naturally out of the main character's responses to the situations that confront her or him. In most of the stories the reader meets the characters at a time of crisis or at a time when a new element has been introduced into the protagonist's life, an element that will cause her or him to speak or act, and, in so doing, to reveal individual characteristics as well as to move the story forward to a climax and denouement. The resolution finds the protagonist in some way changed. Clark's stories are concerned with moments of truth, moments of awareness, or moments of crisis as experienced by people facing the exigencies of modern life. Consisting of three to five scenes and a small cast of characters, they largely involve marital or family situations. In most cases the stories take place within the time span of one day or even one hour.

Major publications other than short fiction
NOVEL: *Untie the Winds*, 1976.

LAVERNE HARRELL CLARK

Born: Texas, 1929

Principal short fiction
"Big Damon's Quilt," 1977; "Three to a Window," 1980; "Craig Rock," 1980; "Reflections at the Door," 1980; "The Sign from Luke XVIII," 1981.

Analysis
The cadence that marks LaVerne Clark's oral presentations of her published stories is heavily influenced by her lifelong work as a folklorist and collector of tales from oral traditions, as well as her personal associations for over twenty years with poets of the 1960's and 1970's. Besides being the foundling director of the University of Arizona Poetry Center, Tucson, she has also edited and photographed two anthologies and reference works upon contemporary poets. Singling Clark as one of the significant contributors of the "more than 150" presented in *Southwest: A Contemporary Anthology*, a reviewer noted that "the focus of [her] . . . prose . . . is 'place,' [a focus, which] assur[es] us that [she is] rooted in Southwestern soil. [She] understand[s] where they are; they are deeply involved in and comfortable with their home." Elsewhere other Clark stories have been described as "having a tone which is Texas-southern, lonely, and somehow elegiac." At readings of her "Big Damon's Quilt," Clark explains that "this story follows a contrapuntal structure, an inter-weaving of themes through a free association of images. Basically set in first person, I have also devised a third person dimension to move along various layers of action occurring in the story's present action, but contrasted consecutively by its living past." Of "Three to a Window," Clark says:

> It's the only humorous, or satirical story I've ever published. I put it in first person using one of three old maids as the narrator so as to bring the characterization of these women, their humdrum existences and provincial viewpoints, as well as their manner of speech into what I feel is a sharper focus than a use of third person would have provided. Hopefully, by employing this medium, I have achieved my goal for this, or any story: that, of writing convincingly about my characters, and therein of the *universality* we share *wherever in being*.

Major publications other than short fiction
NONFICTION: *They Sang for Horses*, 1966, 1971; *Revisiting the Plains Indian Country of Mari Sandoz*, 1977; *Focus 101: Biographies of 101 Poets of the '60's & 70's*, 1979.

STANTON A. COBLENTZ

Born: California, 1896

Principal short fiction
"Older than Methuselah," 1935; "Triple-Geared," 1935; "The Midgets of Monoton," 1939; "Missionaries of Mars," 1940; "The Crystal Planetoids," 1942; "The Treasure of Red Ash Desert," 1942; "The Cosmic Deflector," 1943; "The Glass Labyrinth," 1943; "The Enchantress of Lemuria," 1951; "Microcosm," 1958.

Analysis
Stanton Coblentz has written on the theory that it is possible to fuse entertainment and meaning. With one or two exceptions, such as a dog story contributed years ago to *Household Magazine*, all Coblentz's short tales have entered the field of science fiction or fantasy. They are characterized by soaring imagination and vivid descriptive powers, which take the reader from the depths of far galaxies to the heart of the atom, with suggestions of a Poe-like weirdness and the satire of Jonathan Swift or Voltaire. The stories combine arresting storytelling with analyses of the perils and possibilities of science, and cover such diverse subject-matter as the reincarnation of an abused and remembering dog, the love between a man and a phantom, the unwitting transportation of a scourge from space to earth, and the attempt of "missionaries from space" to convert our planet. Despite the novel background, however, the reader encounters men and women who aspire, struggle and suffer, love and hate, hope and despair, and triumph like members of the human family in all ages and lands.

Major publications other than short fiction
NOVELS: *The Wonder Stock*, 1929; *When the Birds Fly South*, 1945; *The Sunken World*, 1948; *After 12,000 Years*, 1950; *Into Plutonian Depths*, 1950; *The Planet of Youth*, 1952; *Under the Triple Suns*, 1955; *Hidden World*, 1957; *The Blue Barbarians*, 1958; *Next Door to the Sun*, 1960; *The Runaway World*, 1961; *The Lizard Lords*, 1964; *The Moon People*, 1964; *The Lord of Tranerica*, 1966; *The Crimson Capsule*, 1967 (reprinted as *The Animal People*, 1970); *The Day the World Stopped*, 1970; *The Island People*, 1970.

SHIRLEY GRAVES COCHRANE

Principal short fiction

"Remember Charlie Mock?," 1966; "A Change of Heart," 1971; "Sully," 1972; "Noon Special," 1973; "Leaving," 1973; "The Lambs of Summertime," 1974; "Middle Distance," 1976; "The Other Table," 1976; "Journey There, Journey Back," 1976; "Homecoming," 1977; "Volts," 1978; "Family Reunion," 1978; "The Camper," 1978; "Red Carpet," 1979.

Analysis

"Tell it all," Emily Dickinson said, "but tell it slant." Shirley Cochrane tells it slant. Large direct confrontations are few in her haunting, dreamlike commentaries. Even the grand passion, the breathless crisis, is refracted through the inescapable trivia of everyday existence: the bed that has to be made before the lovers use it, the meal that must be cooked even as it becomes apparent that the husband of a lifetime has taken off. Often the high moment toward which the action moves is never put into words, merely foreshadowed—deftly and satisfactorily—as the story ends or, rather, fades away. An example of this is the story called "Volts," even as the one called "Waltzing" is an example of the frequency with which Cochrane makes memory the major, the overwhelming, time element of the episode. For by and large Cochrane eschews beginning, middle and end, preferring to fuse past with present and history with immediate event, and to let recollection act as surrogate for chronology. She has a genius for bringing her characters quickly into focus with a few brief strokes. Always they are recognizable, coming all the nearer to us because they are also a trifle distorted, like the figures in a Picasso painting. Distance is another noticeable element of her work. She does not let us see many things close up, requiring her readers to squint a bit to take in the scenes. In "The Eyes of Carlo Cresca," one of the most fulfilling of her narratives, she somehow manages to give us the whole of a remarkable affair between an old man whose sight and powers are failing and a middle-aged woman married to an alcoholic, achieving her effects with subtle shiftings of the point of view, handled with uncanny skill. If one or more persons coping with a problem is an acceptable definition of a short story, then Cochrane's offerings must be regarded as occupying another plane. She goes her own way, committed to no known formula. Properly to categorize her tales we must preempt a term from a nonliterary art form: "nonobjective" would seem to be the appropriate designation.

Milton Lomask

ANDREI CODRESCU

Born: Romania, 1946

Principal short fiction
Why I Can't Talk on the Telephone, 1971.

Analysis
Small masterpieces of "apocalyptic realism," these tales eradicate the few remaining (in American critical terms, at least) distinctions between prose and poetry. "Language under the gun," "sentence-theatre," "liberation euphoria vampires," these pieces have been perceived variously to do to language what light does to things: to reveal, develop (as in photography), and at times devastate. Disguised as small, unperformable plays, speeches proceeding from the hitherto mute organs (the hand, the hair), wills (last), legal writs, memos, and so forth, these pieces consistently deny their connections to the genre. Codrescu will be known definitively as the creator of at least two new fictional forms: *the contributor's note* (he has never repeated his biography) and *the memo* (often written to "no one"). He has also rewritten "Monsieur Teste" in "Monsieur Teste in America," "A Simple Heart" in "Three Simple Hearts," and "The Turn of the Screw" in "The Screw Keeps Turning." He has done many reviews of imaginary books, set up elaborate "movements" such as "Akt-up," "The Bowel Movement," "The Euphoria Liberation Vampires," and "The Dada Council of World Revolution" through the short-story medium of the *communique*. Words in Codrescu's sentences exist in a tensionless relation to one another in that they exist only to set up largely imaginary referential revolutions. His literary family would include Max Jacob, Malcolm de Chazal, Raymond Roussell, and the family and comix pages of the yellow press.

Major publications other than short fiction
NOVELS: *How I Became Howard Johnson*, 1970; *Meat from the Goldrush*, 1971; *The Life and Times of an Involuntary Genius*, 1975; *Monsieur Teste in America*, 1975; *The Repentance of Lorraine*, 1976; *The Organic Princess*, 1980.
POETRY: *License to Carry a Gun*, 1970; *The History of the Growth of Heaven*, 1973; *Necrocorrida*, 1980; *Selected Poems*, 1981.

Faye Dargenti

ARTHUR A. COHEN

Born: New York, 1928

Principal short fiction
"Hans Cassebeer and the Virgin's Rose," 1975; "The Monumental Sculptor," 1978.

Analysis
Densely written, intellectually demanding, Arthur Cohen's novellas and uncollected stories are marked by the same qualities as his longer fictions: picaresques of the mind in which what is thought possible is set forth as having occurred. Cohen is obviously not bothered by writing about cultures and societies of which he has no first-hand knowledge. The undertaking is constructed as a demand upon himself which can be mastered if the imagination (supported by intense reading) succeeds in conjuring the psychological complexities of character and sustaining his preoccupation with the mythic and sacral foundations of human life. His practice is traditional—caring for precisely those elements in fiction eschewed by modernist practitioners. Cohen infiltrates his characters and situations with a language and metahistorical preoccupation that all but annihilates conventional notions of causality, time, and plot.

Major publications other than short fiction
NOVELS: *The Carpenter Years*, 1967; *In the Days of Simon Stern*, 1972; *A Hero in His Time*, 1976; *Acts of Theft*, 1980; *An Admirable Woman*, 1981.

KEITH COHEN

Born: Virginia, 1945

Principal short fiction
"Vizcaya," 1965; "Strands Growing Downward," 1965; "Water," 1966; "You Froze the Light and Flew," 1966; "The Balustrade," 1967; "At the Inlet," 1968; "Grecian Dreams," 1968; "Phenomenal Feelings," 1971 (prose-poem); "Natural Settings," 1973; "Quiché," 1974; "Feast," 1977 (prose-poem).

Analysis
Keith Cohen's writing is highly descriptive and compact, tending toward complex structure. There is little or no plot and virtually no character "development" in most of his short stories. His voice tends toward the lyrical, at times highly abstract. Perhaps Cohen's greatest accomplishment is to have forged a flexible lyric voice in prose. Some of his finest pieces are prose-poems, published in part in *The Paris Review*. Cohen's current work, *Domestic Tranquillity*, is a meditation on family life, especially father-son relations, in a characteristically no-action, lyrical, collage format. Readers of Cohen's fiction tend to be fascinated but lost for words; there is no attempt to make them "identify." Critics have identified in his work the influence of Marcel Proust and Alain Robbe-Grillet and compared his "meticulousness" to that of Mozart. They point consistently to the obsessive imagery of photography and cinema, pictures-within-pictures, stories-within-stories—but not really stories, so much, as "highly wrought technical sketches of great economy."

Major publications other than short fiction
NOVEL: *Natural Settings*, 1980.
NONFICTION: *Film and Fiction: the Dynamics of Exchange*, 1979.

ANN COPELAND

Born: Connecticut, 1932

Principal short fiction
At Peace, 1978; "Meeting," 1978; *The Back Room*, 1979; "The Garage Sale," 1979.

Analysis
Ann Copeland has produced two very different volumes of short fiction. The first, *At Peace*, is a collection of stories about convent life. Although the stories describe nuns in a variety of settings, their situations trace a very coherent pattern, from a young teacher's encounter with brutal violence, to a rededication by a very old woman, to the death of an odd sister and her recollection by a woman who has left religious life. The second collection, *The Back Room*, contains very disparate stories, often concentrated on shifts of perception by men and women of various ages and circumstances in secular life. Most of Copeland's stories are traditional, third-person narratives, and their effects sometimes arise from the affirmation of commonplace human feelings in the midst of cloistered, dedicated silences, and from the disclosure of transcendence in seemingly shabby situations. The narrator's sympathies usually reach deep beneath a surface, and as a result the author has been criticized for sentimentality and thinness of plotting. At her best she penetrates to the hearts of characters who are struggling to comprehend the ideals by which they live.

A. J. Furtwangler

PAUL COREY

Born: Iowa, 1903

Principal short fiction

"Onlookers," 1930; "Washington Slept Here," 1930; "Barn Dance," 1930; "A Few Goats," 1933; "Mid-American Sketches," 1933; "A Good Recommendation," 1933; "Run Rabbit," 1934; "A Bridge Is Built," 1934; "Nine Pennies," 1934; "They Could Do Something Big," 1934; "Their Forefathers Were Presidents," 1934; "Soft Pine," 1934; "Tombstone of Straw," 1935; "A Son of My Bones," 1935; "The Farmer and the Gold Stone," 1935; "Death in the Valley," 1935; "When Farmers Sang," 1935; "Aunt Birdie's Cookies," 1936; "There's Always an Accident," 1936; "The Green Jackrabbit," 1938; "Water in the Hills," 1942; "Sudden Autumn," 1947; "The Bridge Over the Grand Vallat," 1951; "Barn Crazy," 1952; "Meatballs on the House," 1960; "Operation Survival," 1962; "If You're So Smart," 1969; "Napoleon of Motu Tari," 1973; "Conversation with a Mountain Lion," 1973; "Name Your Handicap," 1975; "Red Carpet Treatment," 1977.

Analysis

It is as if Paul Corey lived three lives as a writer. His first group of writings dealt with his Midwestern background. Lewis Mumford described his work as "The best novels of agricultural America that anyone has produced in our generation." Louis Bromfield said of his work, "Beautiful and important books of our time . . . full of truth and understanding and beautifully done." *The New York Times* judged his writing as "The best farm fiction that has come along in many a day. His second incarnation, so to speak, covered his years of do-it-yourself house-building and books about how to build furniture and repair and improve things around the home. *Mechanix Illustrated* said of *Holiday Homes*, "An excellent book . . . covers a myriad of subjects from design to construction." Virginia Kirkus characterized it as "All you need to know to get a place for yourself and your family among the second home set." Corey's expertise in how-to and do-it-yourself building is one of the characteristics in almost all his stories, including how to blow up a munitions train in "The Bridge Over the Grand Vallat."

In Corey's third period, his interests fix on science fiction and animal behavior. E. J. Carnell, the British commentator, says of his story "If You're So Smart," "Empathy between human beings and other species is often strong but indefinable. We may well need a different kind of link to find out." To all of the subjects Corey brings his wide spectrum of knowledge and understanding.

Major publications other than short fiction

NOVELS: *Bushel of Wheat, Bushel of Barley*, 1936; *Three Miles Square*, 1939; *The Road Returns*, 1940; *County Seat*, 1941; *Acres of Antaeus*, 1946; *The Planet of the Blind*, 1968.

NONFICTION: *Buy an Acre*, 1944; *Build a Home*, 1946; *Homemade Homes*, 1950; *Holiday Homes*, 1967; *Home Workshop Furniture Projects*, 1968; *How to Build Country Homes on a Budget*, 1975; *Bachelor Bess, My Sister*, 1975; *Do Cats Think?*, 1977; *Are Cats People?*, 1979.

R. L. C.

JOHN WILLIAM CORRINGTON

Born: Tennessee, 1932

Principal short fiction
The Lonesome Traveller, 1968; *The Actes and Monuments*, 1978; "Nothing Succeeds," 1979.

Analysis
The purpose of John Corrington's short fiction is to deal with human beings at the edge, faced with realities they had never supposed they would have to meet. Whatever the concrete particulars may be in a given story, the question at issue is how men and women will manage to reestablish order in their lives and in their sensibilities. Suddenly, people find themselves involved in history, in circumstances flowing out of the past, and forced to come to terms with a past which, in Faulkner's phrase, "Isn't dead. It isn't even past." Thus, in many of the stories, the Southern past is part of the present, a living element in the choices and decisions of the people whose lives might be easier if they were from New Jersey or New Hampshire and had no past of any importance to weigh in the scale of their actions. In all the stories, there is a fundamental tension between the present world and what it demands or seems to demand, and another world perceived by those who must act not according to fashion or trend, but in some ultimate way—according to a *Logos* which possesses them—outside of and beyond mere time and space.

Major publications other than short fiction
NOVELS: *And Wait for the Night, 1964; The Upper Hand*, 1967; *The Bombardier*, 1970.
POETRY: *Where We Are*, 1962; *Mr. Clean & Other Poems*, 1963; *The Anatomy of Love*, 1964; *Lines to the South*, 1965.

MARY ELIZABETH COUNSELMAN

Born: Alabama, 1911

Principal short fiction
African Yesterdays, 1977; *Half in Shadow*, 1978; *New Lamps for Old*, 1979; *The Fifth Door*, 1980.

Analysis
Mary Elizabeth Counselman's favorite genre is symbol-writing of universal appeal that reveals many phases of human struggle, with human error in the guise of mythical "bogies." Her understanding of the human mind is penetrating but tender. Intricately plotted, her action and character delineation work always toward some definite premise, sometimes ironic but always with a common-sense moral conclusion. Dorothy McIlwraith, the editor of *Weird Tales*, described the author's prolific work for that magazine as "always adequate, often superb." Not with a strict feminist viewpoint, and quite often with a male protagonist, Counselman strikes a happy balance between male and female attitudes, with an especially astute knowledge of the child-mind in its confused efforts to grow up. Counselman is widely reprinted in fifteen languages, with large print, tapes, and Braille for the handicapped. It is apparent that her most ferocious horror tales, however, are designed to counsel rather than frighten the reader, young or old. Foremost is her gentle effort to help one "make friends with Death," as a mere transition state, with honor, in life, for old beliefs that are a part of one's local heritage anywhere in the world. Primarily a magazine writer, her work reflects our changing times.

Major publications other than short fiction
POETRY: *The Eye and the Hand*, 1976.
NONFICTION: *Move Over—It's Only Me*, 1975; *Krazy Kustoms Kookbook*, 1978.

Steve Eng

GEORGE CUOMO

Born: New York, 1929

Principal short fiction
"The Lake," 1956; *Sing, Choirs of Angels*, 1970.

Analysis
In "The Unholy Trio," George Cuomo has a potter tell a beginning student, "You want to learn to like the clay. That's what counts, that's what you have to learn to respect—the clay, the material in your hands." That is what counts for Cuomo, too. He *likes* the characters in his short stories. He even likes the world they live in, and in this he is an anomaly among serious contemporary storytellers. He writes tales in the old sense of the word, tales in which causes and effects are clearly linked, events are intelligibly related, and characters one cares about undergo changes in response to their experiences. Faintly satirical and sardonic, but humorous and warmly tolerant, Cuomo tells about the world's absurdities and ironies, its surprises, its evil, its good. His themes are marital infidelity, the generation gap, the liberated woman, the collapse of the work ethic, and the preoccupation with one's self-image. Without banality or maudlin tearfulness, he writes his characters into moral difficulties to see where they get the strength to survive. It comes from the bonds between people and from the best of America's national past: duty, self-sacrifice, ideals, compassion, a belief in the continuity of the American tradition. No less probing of modern experience than more experimental writers, Cuomo believes that the lives of the little people he writes about are coherent and value-based and that the traditional short story is an appropriate form for talking about them.

Major publications other than short fiction
NOVELS: *Jack Be Nimble*, 1963; *Bright Day, Dark Runner*, 1964; *Among Thieves*, 1968; *The Hero's Great Great Great Great Great Grandson*, 1971; *Pieces from a Small Bomb*, 1976.
POETRY: *Geronimo and the Girl Next Door*, 1974.
NONFICTION: *Becoming a Better Reader*, 1960; *Becoming a Better Reader and Writer*, 1977.

Jerry H. Bryant

PEGGY SIMSON CURRY

Born: Scotland, 1911

Principal short fiction

"In the Silence," 1973; "Gypsy Trainer," 1978; "In the Silence," 1979; "All Shaded Up," 1981.

Analysis

These short stories, slanted for a wide reading audience, draw their distinction from realistic background detail that supports and contributes to characterization, plot, and emotional impact. The majority of the stories are based in the American West in an attempt to make that West, past and present, more real than portrayed in the usual "Wild West" fiction. Whether dealing with cowboys, sheepherders, haymakers, or fishermen, the author draws her material from personal experience and careful research. The impact of land itself is a dominant influence in most of Curry's short stories. Apart from the Western background, the same attention to realistic detail is used in portraying harness racing in Central Illinois. "I consider realistic detail significant in creating a believable story. In this approach plot and characterization become informative as well as entertaining, not only about the inner world of mankind but also about the outer world around us. One won't survive without the other." Curry won the Golden Spur Award of Western Writers of America for "distinguished short fiction of the American West" in 1957 and 1970.

Major publications other than short fiction

NOVELS: *Fire in the Water*, 1951; *So Far from Spring*, 1956; *The Oil Patch*, 1959; *A Shield of Clover*, 1969 (Juvenile).

POETRY: *Red Wind of Wyoming*, 1955.

NONFICTION: *Creating Fiction from Experience*, 1964.

DANIEL CURZON

Born: Illinois

Principal short fiction

"A Christmas Miracle at the B.O.O.M.," 1974; "Man and Wife," 1978; *The Revolt of the Perverts*, 1978; *Human Warmth*, 1981.

Analysis

Daniel Curzon's stories are noted for the variety with which they portray the lives of gay people. He shows that it is difficult to generalize about a "homosexual lifestyle," because he shows how many lifestyles there can be. The stories usually deal with gay characters as they come into contact or conflict with the larger society. At times the events may be about specifically gay realities, such as "coming out" to a relative; but often they are about problems that any person may experience, such as sexual rejection or unwanted desire. Curzon believes that the novelty of his subject matter makes "experimental" narrative devices unnecessary. He wishes to be clear and direct. He tries to tell a story first and sees himself as putting the homosexual into the mainstream of Western literature. He agrees with the *San Francisco Review of Books* that it would "be unfair to categorize Curzon as a 'gay writer' when he reveals a talent for story-telling that is characterized by wit, compassion, objectivity, and a certain toughness of mind that can come only through years of experience and introspection." Above all, Curzon's stories are as universal as those of any writer who selects a wide, if taboo, canvas, and feels that in time his work will be of interest to the general reader, just as the general reader does not read William Faulkner only because he is a "Southern writer" or Anton Chekhov only because he is a "Russian writer."

Major publications other than short fiction

NOVELS: *Something You Do in the Dark*, 1971; *The Misadventures of Tim McPick*, 1975; *Among the Carnivores*, 1979.

NONFICTION: *The Joyful Blue Book of Gracious Gay Etiquette*.

CECIL DAWKINS

Born: Alabama, 1927

Principal short fiction
The Quiet Enemy, 1963.

Analysis

Cecil Dawkins' stories are exercises in the storytelling art of action-as-metaphor. In these deceptively traditional tales, the energy is everywhere evident but held in check, and the voice is true and sure but underspoken. These restraints balance an audacity of conception to account for the vibrance of these balancing acts of hope and despair. Time and again the characters confront the possibility of love with its demand for growth, which they inevitably betray, retreating in fear to safeguard an empty status quo. There is integrity in the despair, however, for the characters are the authors of their own fate, not pawns in a larger game. Relief from this relentless process as each story discovers what it is about comes from the language, the humor, the accuracy of observation, and a certain magnanimity with which they surprise and delight. Man is here the center and value in a universe which is not, therefore, relative. The virtue of the stories lies in their willingness to confront the human condition with an unpretentious courage.

Major publications other than short fiction
NOVEL: *The Live Goat*, 1971.
PLAY: *The Displaced Person*, 1966.

ANN DEAGON

Born: Alabama, 1925

Principal short fiction
"Man Woman and Child," 1977; "The Same River," 1978; "A Natural History," 1978; "The First Youth of Faust," 1978; "The Silver Apples," 1979; "The Second and Final Vision of Mrs. Fuquay," 1979.

Analysis
The correspondences and tensions between mythology and psychology provide the backdrop for Deagon's stories, which are more discursive than dramatic. The significant dialogues are less frequently between characters than between a character and her past. Although violence underlies most of the stories, the apparent violence is usually played in a minor key, implying or anticipating more dramatic violence, which usually comes—if at all—in metaphorical terms. Many of Deagon's characters attempt to bridge the distance between age and youth, and most are actively engaged in the "war between the sexes." Deagon's stories are more often structured around motif and image than around narrative sequence, although the events of the stories are neither indecipherable nor lacking in suspense. Frequently the narrator takes an active role in the story, occasionally intruding to usurp the autonomy of a character. Dreams affect the motives of the characters, and underlying the dreams is an acute sense of myth, either the traditional Greco-Roman mythology or myth in the sense of pattern, repetition, and ritual. The characters seldom know how to fulfill these molds from which they emerge and attempt to take control of their lives in the face of adversity. While many of Deagon's protagonists succeed in finding a subtle, inward satisfaction, imperceptible to the other characters around them, the "solutions" are seldom conventional and never easy or sentimental.

Major publications other than short fiction
POETRY: *Poetics South*, 1974; *Carbon 14*, 1974; *Indian Summer*, 1975; *Women and Children*, 1976; *There Is No Balm in Birmingham*, 1978.

R. T. Smith

EMILIO DEGRAZIA

Born: Michigan, 1941

Principal short fiction

"The Enemy," 1973; "The Trip Back Home," 1975; "Inflation," 1975; "Gooks," 1976; "The New House," 1977; "The Girl and Two Old Men," 1977; "The Death of Sin," 1977; "The Mask," 1977; "A Minnesota Story," 1979; "The Sniper," 1979; "Lanternlight," 1980; "Grandmother's Secret Places," 1980; "The Man Who Murdered the Family Car," 1980; "Marking Time," 1980.

Analysis

Fidelity to others, faith, the search for self-knowledge, and the clash between generations intensified by immigration all recur in Emilio DeGrazia's fiction. He has explored the problems of youth, middle years, and old age, but he offers no easy solutions. The stalwart farmer of "A Minnesota Story," seen battling the apathy of his neighbors over a number of decades, is a very different old man from the narrator of "Lanternlight," who has never succeeded in knowing himself. In DeGrazia's insistence on the importance of the examined life, and with his stress on the centrality of ethical concerns, his fiction does, at times, become too didactic, temporarily losing its effectiveness as fiction, but these concerns are generally a strength in his work. Most of his stories are told in traditional styles, and in his devotion to his craft, he has developed a mastery of his material so that his style is usually at one with his subject. He has used a number of settings, including Vietnam; his more recent work focuses on the Minnesota scene.

Jean Ervin

NICHOLAS DELBANCO

Born: England, 1942

Principal short fiction
"The Executor," 1978; "Ostinato," 1979; "Composition," 1979; "Traction," 1979; "Marching Through Georgia," 1980.

Analysis
Nicholas Delbanco's short fiction is of recent vintage; he published his first short story after his ninth novel. The uncollected pieces that have appeared thus far, however, are thematically linked. Each protagonist—a lawyer, a concert pianist, a curator, a history professor and so forth—is a family-man approaching middle age. He is committed to his professional life but at odds with its restrictions; he is, often, on the road. In "Traction" the distance is geographic and the obstacle a snowstorm; a father tries to rejoin his hospitalized daughter and reaches her in his imagination if not in actuality. In "Ostinato," the distance is psychological; a husband and wife find their intimacy shamed by the letters of a foreigner who wishes them both well. The language is spare, the circumstance domestic, the resolution seemingly almost irresolute. Always, however, the man attempts to make a present whole out of the shards and scattered fragments of his past. It is, as one of Delbanco's characters observes, "What you carry." In the root sense of the word, therefore, the stories deal with integrity—how to make a unity of what appears disorganized, disjunct.

Major publications other than short fiction
NOVELS: *The Martlet's Tale*, 1966; *Grasse 3/23/66*, 1968; *Consider Sappho Burning*, 1969; *News*, 1970; *In the Middle Distance*, 1971; *Fathering*, 1973; *Small Rain*, 1975; *Possession*, 1977; *Sherbrookes*, 1978; *Stillness*, 1980.

NEPHTALÍ DE LEÓN

Born: Texas, 1945

Principal short fiction

Aztlan Fairy Tales/Fábulas de Aztlán, 1980.

Analysis

The short stories of Nephtalí De León represent an amusing, highly individualized style which uses cultural reflections to create unexpected but delicious comedy—such as, ". . . Tamales the Elder having been a kernel in Montezuma's army. . . ." Her recurring themes are foods, customs, traditions, and other reflections that poke fun at the Chicano way of life but which are unequivocally uplifting with every turn of event. Parodies of other traditional stories are "Los Tres Little Pigs," who are not the happy-go-lucky piglets afraid of the big bad wolf but rather the hunted and disenfranchized but rebellious little pigs pitted against the industrial technical computer age; and, another such story, "Pedro Gets a Donkey"—given to him by a Yankee from Connecticut. Pedro has always wanted a donkey and when he gets it, the whole village has a feast. Pedro did not want to ride the donkey but rather to provide food for his people. De León's fairy tale fables feature mythological beings, wizards, magic mountains, and even fire-breathing dragons who use their fire to warm tortillas. Unexpected characters abound such as a hopping kangaroo who carries hot sauce in his pouch and giant dogs who carry bushels of bones in a ferry. The style is fast paced with puns in two languages (English and Spanish), and the unlikely but credible action takes place in immediately believable but far-fetched settings. In the somewhat depressing and haunting situations, the author also manages to leave us with a high note of hope, understanding, and even huge doses of human compassion. As it was once stated by Dr. Larry Tjarks in *Children's Literature*, Nephtalí De León "Celebrates the human spirit that permeates all ages and all ethnic traditions."

Major publications other than short fiction

PLAYS: *Five Plays*, 1972; *Tequila Mockingbird*, 1979.

POETRY: *Poems by Nephtalí*, 1971; *Chicano Poet*, 1973; *Coca Cola Dream*, 1973; *Hey Mr. President Man!*, 1975.

RICHARD DE MILLE

Born: California, 1922

Principal short fiction
"Safety Valve," 1953; "The Phoenix Nest," 1954; "Family Secret," 1954; "The Other Door," 1955; "The Last Chance," 1955; *Two Qualms & A Quirk*, 1973;

Analysis
Richard de Mille's early, uncollected stories retain interest mainly for connoisseurs of science fiction. His later collected stories are satirical fantasies. "The Royal Banquet" is a subtly erotic dream of public embarrassment. "The Ultimate Prosthesis" is an inexorable nightmare of bodily and mental annihilation. The two narratives are simple, direct, somewhat old-fashioned, offering no difficulty. After these two "Qualms" comes the "Quirk" of the title. "The Transuxors, Duet for Whangbox and Quimbone," is a paronomastical *tour de force* combining intricate, erudite, bawdy punning with profuse, sarcastic anagramming of two familiar names: Gore Vidal and Myra Breckenridge (sic). Literary diversions rather than serious short stories, the three pieces merit attention because of their economy, precision, humor, metaphor, and imagery.

Major publications other than short fiction
NONFICTION: *Castaneda's Journey: The Power and the Allegory*, 1976; *The Don Juan Papers: Further Castaneda Controversies*, 1980.

DAVID DIEFENDORF

Born: Ohio, 1944

Principal short fiction
"Fables," 1975; "Woman Followed by Blue Lines," 1975-1976; "The Test," 1978; "Disjecta Membra," 1980.

Analysis
David Diefendorf views traditional narrative structures as enlarged and invisible clichés. His short fiction draws attention to the medium of language itself and attaches great value to the proliferation of ambiguities. Diefendorf has stated that a primary aim of his work is to "undermine the sanctity of 'tone' "—enigmatic, eerie, droll, understated, or flat.

MILLICENT DILLON

Born: New York, 1925

Principal short fiction
Baby Perpetua and Other Stories, 1971; "All the Pelageyas," 1979; "Walter Walter Wildflower," 1980.

Analysis
The men and women of Millicent Dillon's stories are prey to dilemmas that cannot be overcome by willful, explosive action. Their lives are driven by a perpetual effort to hold their problems down to habitable size, aware as they are that irresolution has come to be the condition of their daily routine. Psychological entrapment comes in many guises in these stories, from the delusions of an artistic mind to those of a criminal one. Yet in their entrapment, the characters offer a resistance to destiny that makes for comic elation. The bravest of them play out their dramas on the most restricted stages.

Major publications other than short fiction
NOVEL: *The One in the Back Is Medea*, 1973.
NONFICTION: *A Little Original Sin*, 1981 (biography of Jane Bowles).

ALBERT DEE DRAKE

Born: Oregon, 1935

Principal short fiction
"Father to Son," 1969; "The Hem of Harvest," 1969; "The Chicken Which Became a Rat," 1970; "I Remember the Day James Dean Died Like It Was Yesterday," 1973; "Won't You Please Sit Down?," 1975; *The Postcard Mysteries*, 1976; *In the Time of Surveys*, 1978.

Analysis
Albert Drake's earlier published stories alternated between "traditional" modes of narration (*In the Time of Surveys*) and "experimental" modes (*The Postcard Mysteries*). Stories in both categories share a concern for craft, for a language which is visual and active, for economy, and for the exploitation of narrative techniques. Those earlier concerns continue, but the subject matter has become more limited. For the past dozen years, Drake has focused on a central character, Chris, and on a place, Oregon; these uncollected stories form a *Bildungsroman* sequence. In *One Summer* Drake develops the character (Chris), the time (1948), and the place (Portland), and promises that this is the first in a projected quartet of novels related by character and place—the latter taking on increasing importance for Drake, who considers himself a Northwest writer.

Major publications other than short fiction
NOVEL: *One Summer*, 1979.
POETRY: *Three Northwest Poets*, 1970; *Poems*, 1972; *Riding Bike*, 1973; *By Breathing In & Out*, 1974; *Returning to Oregon*, 1975; *Cheap Thrills*, 1975; *Tillamook Burn*, 1977 (poetry, art, photos, three stories); *Reaching for the Sun*, 1979; *Garage*, 1980.

JAMES W. DROUGHT

Born: Illinois, 1931

Principal short fiction
Green Brown & Red, 1964.

Analysis

James Drought's thirty-year career in fiction, 1950-1980, falls into three categories. The works written between 1950 and 1958 are marked by classical structure, superb technique, and powerful characterization which blend into memorable, meaningful myths for his country at that time. *The Gypsy Moths* (1955), when published in Europe in 1966, was called by the contemporary critic Karl Krolow in *Die Welt* "the best depiction of the death-defying performer's art since Hemingway's *Death in the Afternoon*." British critic Colin Wilson described Drought's *Memories of a Humble Man* (1957) when he read it in England in 1966 as "a mysterious, absorbing study of apathy that actually draws considerable blood." Between 1959 and 1969, Drought took on American political problems and incorporated them into his fiction. *Mover* (1959) accurately assays the coming experience of racial desegregation; *The Secret* (1962) assails the society with a youthful voice determined to overcome the repressive loss of civil rights in the early 1960's; and *Drugoth* (1965) describes the desire which later swept the country for the right of dissent and the ultimate control of one's life and work. *The Enemy* (1964) has been noted by Max Peters, editor of the environmental magazine *Survival Rights*, as being the "first 'ecological' novel to appear and perhaps the best." From 1970 to 1980, Drought confidently exhibited a new view from "above the battle," in works such as *The Master* (1970), which portrays a new American version of the "savior-Christ," and *Blessed Bob Bunyon* (1974), which portrays in a journey of searching the inevitable passing of responsibility from one generation to the next. Drought was nominated for the Nobel Prize in Literature in 1973 by European critics.

Major publications other than short fiction

NOVELS: *Boxed in by the Rich*, 1950; *The Gypsy Moths*, 1955; *Memories of a Humble Man*, 1957; *Mover*, 1959; *Way of the Fifties*, 1962; *Dead Body in Burtonville*, 1962; *The Secretl*, 1962; *The Enemy*, 1964; *Drugoth*, 1965; *The Master*, 1970; *Blessed Bob Bunyon*, 1974; *Book of Names*, 1976; *Superstar for President*, 1978; *Learning to Laugh*, 1980.

PLAYS: *The Wedding*, 1953; *Alivemovie Book*, 1967.

NONFICTION: *A Treatise on "Nuclear Communication"*, 1976.

Lorna Carlson

ROCHELLE H. DUBOIS

Born: Illinois, 1949

Principal short fiction
Bushels of Broken Glass, 1970; "Some Time When You've Some Time," 1972; "Like a Prism," 1973; "Faith in Xanadu," 1974; "A Divine Prospect," 1977; "The Stones of Spring," 1977; "The Mask," 1978; *A Legend in His Time*, 1979; "Welcome to Love in Mississippi," 1979; *Pangs*, 1980; "Love Is a Square Knot," 1980.

Analysis
The short stories of Rochelle H. Dubois are well structured, evocative, sensuous, and compelling. Her imagination and lyrical sense drive the subject of her stories, who is generally the young woman as creator. Sharon Spencer describes Dubois' art in her essay "A Creative Dreamer":

> Almost without exception, [Dubois'] writings focus on the woman as aspiring creator. . . . The focus is almost always on the heroine's attempt to transcend disappointment and despair through the visionary power of the beautiful—through the splendid work of art or of imaginative fantasy. . . . [Dubois] shows how imagination provides the key to the prisons in which her protagonists seem to languish. . . . [She] is very much an individual whose writing explores a virtually new subject at the same time that it proposes a universe of new structures and new language.

Major publications other than short fiction
POETRY: *To Make a Bear Dance*, 1970; *From One Bird*, 1978; *Ecstasy*, 1979; *The Train in the Rain*, 1981.

HÉLÈNE DWORZAN

Born: France, 1925

Principal short fiction
"La Légende de Gaspard Ravion," 1948; "A Husband for Bluma," 1953; "The Almighty Power," 1955; "The Healer," 1978.

Analysis
Hélène Dworzan's published short fiction grows out of her youth in the Jewish *Pletzel* in Paris. Her writing is distinguished by careful observation and precise delineation of—as well as deep compassion for—characters trapped by their environments. Her themes involve the compromises that human beings must make between their ideals and the harsh realities they face—the Gestapo, poverty, or blind tradition. A warm, compassionate humor lightens the mood of "The Healer," which was awarded the *Prairie Schooner*'s 1978 prize for fiction.

Major publications other than short fiction
NOVEL: Le temps de la chrysalide, 1957.

Donald H. Reiman

STUART DYBEK

Born: Illinois, 1942

Principal short fiction

"Blanche: A Baker's Dozen," 1973; "The Maze," 1975; "Divorce & Suicide/ True Confessions," 1975; "The Conductor, the Nun, and the Streetcar," 1976; "Gum," 1976; "Midwest," 1976; "Prayer," 1976; "Old Grandma Rockingchair," 1978; "Tarantella," 1978; "Transients Only," 1978; "Death of the Right Fielder," 1980; *Childhood and Other Neighborhoods*, 1980.

Analysis

The range of these stories is broad—from naturalistic pieces with linear narratives to fragmented, lyric stories such as "Tarantella" which are developed through an associative flow of images. In these lyric fictions Stuart Dybek's interest in the prose poem, a form which appears frequently in his collection of poetry, *Brass Knuckles*, is evident. The lyric stories explore several levels of speculative fiction: the grotesque, the fantastic, myths, fables, fairy tales, surrealism, and science fiction.

Many of the stories, in particular those collected in *Childhood and Other Neighborhoods*, are urban, set in the ethnic working-class neighborhoods of Chicago. For this reason the book has invited comparison with the work of other Chicago writers such as Nelson Algren, Saul Bellow, and James T. Farrell. As reviewers such as Bruce Cook have pointed out, however, "Dybek has his own voice. . . . There is a kind of transcendental, magical quality to certain of the stories that is quite new to Chicago writing." When the book of stories and collection of poems are taken together, it becomes clearer that what is being evoked is a single vision of an urban world in which realism collides and merges with the fantastic.

Major publications other than short fiction

POETRY: *Brass Knuckles*, 1979.

CHARLES EAST

Born: Mississippi, 1924

Principal short fiction
Where the Music Was, 1965; "The Summer of the White Collie," 1965; "The Last Person," 1976.

Analysis
In the *Harvard Guide to Contemporary American Writing* (1979), scholar and editor Lewis P. Simpson writes that East, "like [Peter] Taylor, has a gift for conveying, within the miniature scope of the short story, the unobtrusive but resistless destruction of accepted reality by historical actualities." The small-town Deep South is the setting for most of East's stories, which are characterized by a quiet, reflective tone, an economy of words, and a deceptively simple style that is sometimes almost lyric. The care with which he constructs his stories has been commented upon by John William Corrington, among others: "Rather than participate in his fiction, he chooses to control it, to refine and to telescope his material until, to an uncanny degree, the audience is forced to respond outside the area of literary-conditioned responses, and to reenact in reading the kind of precise understanding East has exercised in writing." East has stated his preference for the short story over the novel emphatically and has described his technique in part as "looking for the right moment" ("in every good story there is one moment when everything seems to hang in the balance"). What is especially notable about East's work is his instinct for character.

Major publications other than short fiction
NONFICTION: *The Face of Louisiana*, 1969.

WILLIAM EASTLAKE

Born: New York, 1917

Principal short fiction

"Ishimoto's Land," 1952; "Little Joe," 1954; "Two Gentlemen from America," 1954; "Homecoming," 1954; "The Medicine Men," 1955; "The Quiet Chimneys," 1955; "The Chrome Covered Wagon," 1955; "Where the Warriors Crossed," 1956; "The Unhappy Hunting Grounds," 1956; "The Bandits," 1956; "Flight of the Circle Heart," 1957; "Man Trap," 1958; "Portrait of an Artist with Twenty-Six Horses," 1958; "The Barfly and the Navajo," 1959; "Three Heroes and a Clown," 1959; "What Nice Hands Held," 1960; "A Bird on the Mesa," 1961; "Something Big Is Happening to Me," 1962; "In a While Crocodile," 1963; "A Long Day Dying," 1963; "Jack Armstrong in Tangiers," 1965; "There's a Camel in My Cocktail," 1966; "The Last Frenchman in Fez," 1967; "The Biggest Thing Since Custer," 1968; "Now Lucifer Is Not Dead," 1968; "The Hanging at Prettyfields," 1969; "The Bamboo Bed," 1969; "A Dead Man's Guide to Mallorca," 1969; "The Secret of the War," 1969; "The Dancing Boy," 1970; "The Death of Sun," 1972; "Sings in Pretty Places," 1973; "Smoke," 1973; "Dancers in the Scalp House," 1973; "Coyotes Love Me," 1974; "Music on the Painted Bird," 1974; "The Naked Bike," 1975; "The Gentleman from Japan," 1975; "Mrs. Gage in Her Bed of Pain with a Nice Cup of Gin," 1977.

Analysis

William Eastlake learned early that one cannot master the novel without first mastering the short story. His first published novel was actually a result of a raid on his short stories that appeared in *Harper's Magazine*. Eastlake believes that the problem in writing the short story at this time, or the time of a hundred years ago when Herman Melville was around, is the same—to write well. One can be—and most writers are—professional without being an artist; but one cannot be an artist without being a professional. In his view, the only quality that genius everywhere has in common, whether it be music, painting, or science, is the professionalism, the discipline, of turning out a body of work. The importance about a piece is to write it, then write another and another. One should not be discouraged because junk writing is popular. Survival value is what counts. A writer should be encouraged that the competition is less at the top; very few people write well or seem to try. Eastlake had an advantage in his youth over the young writers of today, for then the great masters were alive, men such as Ernest Hemingway, Eugene O'Neill, Thomas Wolfe, and William Faulkner, whom he had the good fortune to know. "They don't make them like that any more, and that loss has denied the young of this time. No good writer stands alone; we are all in debt to one another," admits Eastlake. "I never would have appeared in thirty-five anthologies and textbooks without the aid and comfort of the masters, and for this luck I shall always be in fantastic debt—and gratitude."

Major publications other than short fiction
NOVELS: *Go in Beauty*, 1956; *The Bronc People*, 1958; *Portrait of an Artist with Twenty-Six Horses*, 1963; *Castle Keep*, 1964; *The Bamboo Bed*, 1970; *Dancers in the Scalp House*, 1975; *The Long Naked Descent into Boston*, 1977.
POETRY: *A Child's Garden of Verses for the Revolution*, 1970.

CHARLES EDWARD EATON

Born: North Carolina, 1916

Principal short fiction

Write Me from Rio, 1959; "The Motion of Forgetfulness Is Slow," 1966; *The Girl from Ipanema*, 1972; *The Case of the Missing Photographs*, 1978.

Analysis

"Why do human beings keep toying with each other past the point of reason and civilized endurance?" the narrator asks in "The Case of the Missing Photographs." This could be taken as an epigraph for a primary aspect of Charles Eaton's work. Balancing this analytical approach, which incorporates Gustave Flaubert's notion that *ideas* are action, is a steadfast belief in coherence, consummation, ecstasy—strong thematic concerns in the Brazilian stories. About these results of Eaton's experience as Vice Consul in Rio de Janeiro, Alceu Amoroso Lima has written: "It is the first time a North American author has really been deeply affected by the mystery of our nature and of our people. Eaton has with much skill shown the continuity between men, cities, and forests in our country." Both the North and South American stories embrace the claims of style and content—one cannot "tell the dancer from the dance." Eaton's work has obviously been influenced by the study of philosophy just as his interest in painting gives a strong visual dimension. Dave Smith perhaps best summarizes the work as a whole:

> For more than two decades, Eaton has slowly crafted a literature of the psyche in which he has made a consistent attempt to envision a balanced, rational, and passionate man. His fictions speak to all men of sense and sensibility with what is the only convincing argument, the argument of art and the imagination which says that there is a condition of joy to which we must not only aspire but also actively and at any cost struggle.

Major publications other than short fiction

POETRY: *The Bright Plain*, 1942; *The Shadow of the Swimmer*, 1951; *The Greenhouse in the Garden*, 1955; *Countermoves*, 1962; *On the Edge of the Knife*, 1970; *The Man in the Green Chair*, 1977; *Colophon of the Rover*, 1980. NONFICTION: *Karl Knaths: Five Decades of Painting*, 1973.

PAGE EDWARDS

Born: Idaho, 1941

Principal short fiction
"The Thaw," 1972; *Staking Claims*, 1980.

Analysis

Page Edwards is primarily interested in the revelation of character, in writing stories which unveil the essential identity of an individual, that particular quality which makes him unique, and the way he sees himself as compared with the way he is seen by others. The change which occurs in a person who stops looking at himself with his own eyes and considers himself as others see him, frozen in a role, is a tragic death to an individual. Still, the man who lives only by his own light is doomed to solitude, which man cannot bear. Edwards' stories concern themselves with this dual between the self and society as forces which mold the individual's identity.

Major publications other than short fiction

NOVELS: *The Mules That Angels Ride*, 1972; *Touring*, 1974.

GARY ELDER

Born: Oregon, 1939

Principal short fiction
"Dorian Woman," 1960; "Lady Fogelsang's Passage," 1961; "In Beautiful Devonian Slime," 1965; "Jazzwitch," 1965; "Adam & Eve & Vipe," 1966; "Rabbit Dance," 1967; "One Fast Life," 1969; "High Sam Sees Through," 1974; "King of the Lear Wind," 1977.

Analysis
Except for three satiric fables, the published short fiction of Gary Elder has been concerned with the experience of the American West, both historical and contemporary. The most successful of these, in Elder's own estimation, are those he calls "located," which take their vision directly from his roots in the Pacific Northwest, operating characteristically through an emotionally charged poetic language that tends, at its best, to elevate "the vital circumstantial instant" beyond plot and event. These elements combine most effectively in the story, "Rabbit Dance," which critic Ripley Schemm, writing in *Small Press Review*, notes as working "with such sureness of mind, mood, and the insult of 200 years of history that grief seems a word your mind never uttered before this story."

Major publications other than short fiction
POETRY: *Arnulfsaga*, 1970 (second edition, with commentaries, 1979); *Making Touch*, 1971; *A Vulgar Elegance*, 1974; *Eyes on the Land*, 1980; *Hold Fire*, 1980.

WILLIAM D. ELLIOTT

Born: Minnesota, 1938

Principal short fiction
"Stopping Off in Switzerland," 1968; "People Are Too Sentimental," 1969; "Isabella," 1969; "Flight," 1969; "In Flight," 1969; "Getting It All Out," 1970; "So Much Secret Timing," 1971; "The Road to Monterrey," 1971; "To All Parent of Our Youth," 1972; "Moving Out," 1972; "Elk War," 1972; "Interface," 1974; "Blue River," 1979; "Ahna Andersen," 1980.

Analysis
Lean, spare, ironic in tone, and often satiric, William Elliott's most characteristic scene is confrontation with past events or people on the major character's side and the psychological implications of the action. The basic unit is an expository spring that returns the protagonist to a past faced only with difficulty and the complication of how he will work his way through to a resolution. Influenced by both the realists and the naturalists, particularly the English writer Alan Sillitoe, the Australian writer Henry Handel Richardson, and the American writer James T. Farrell, Elliott's work relies on the gesture of individual characters within a scene, modified stream-of-consciousness sequences which work to clarify and deepen the often painful journey and return motif possessing the characters' consciousness, and satire to highlight the minor characters who see time as easily dealt with and simply linear.

Major publications other than short fiction
NOVELS: *Stopping Off in Switzerland*, 1968; *Blue River*, 1979.
POETRY: *Pine and Jack Pine*, 1973; *Winter in the Rex*, 1974; *Timber Drive*, 1977; *The Paul Bunyan Poems*, 1979.
NONFICTION: *Henry Handel Richardson*, 1977.

DAVID ELY

Born: Chicago, 1927

Principal short fiction

"Court of Judgment," 1961; "The Last Friday in August," 1961; "The Wizard of Light," 1962; "The Alumni March," 1962; "McDaniel's Flood," 1963; "The Captain's Boarhunt," 1964; "The Assault on Mount Rushmore," 1966; *Time Out*, 1968; "The Language Game," 1970; "The Carnival," 1971; "No Time to Lose," 1972; "The Gourmet Hunt," 1972; "The Many Faces of John Dobbler," 1973; "The Prince," 1974; "A Middle-aged Nude," 1974; "A Place to Avoid," 1974; "The Light in the Cottage," 1974; "Always Home," 1975; "Rockefeller's Daughter," 1975; "Starling's Circle," 1976; "Last One Out," 1976; "The Squirrel," 1976; "The Running Man," 1976; "The Partisan," 1977; "The Weed Killer," 1977; "The Looting of the Tomb," 1977; "Counting Steps," 1978; "The Temporary Daughter," 1978; "The Rich Girl," 1978; "The Man in the Park," 1978; "Going Backward," 1978; "Grandfathers," 1979; "Methuselah," 1980.

Analysis

David Ely's stories in general have been traditional in form and use of language, varied in style and subject. Ely has written many satiric stories with elements of fantasy or farce, many straight narratives with touches of the grotesque, and some experimental stories. Thematically, he has dealt less with psychological studies of character and family or other personal inter-relationships than with man in society—that is, he has written criticism of social institutions, satires on modern life. He believes these themes are important for writers, particularly writers in a society so many of whose dreams have become nightmares inflicted on the rest of the world. He tries to keep his writing clear and succinct and to avoid what he feels are the worst American writing characteristics: self-indulgence, sloppiness, faddism, and parochial disregard for other peoples.

Major publications other than short fiction

NOVELS: *Trot*, 1963; *Seconds*, 1963; *The Tour*, 1967; *Poor Devils*, 1970; *Walking Davis*, 1972; *Mr. Nicholas*, 1974.

CHARLES ENTREKIN

Born: Alabama, 1941

Principal short fiction
All Pieces of a Legacy, 1975; "Lot's Wife," 1980; "To Talk with the Dead," 1980; "Hidden Plants," 1980.

Analysis
With their moments, places, and voices, Charles Entrekin's stories are set somewhere between the insides and outsides of our inherited expectations and our capricious realities. Entrekin uses the short story—plot, character, setting—as a compact unit of understanding; he attempts the transformation from point of·view into tactile experience, always moving inward at crucial moments of conscious or unconscious realization toward universal human experiences. The end result brings us a fiction and a poetry, as Jon Ford put it in his review *Poetry Flash* in 1976, that "treats the epiphany, the shining moment when things suddenly crystalize, for better or worse, and our lives assume the full contour of their unique sort of fullness."

Major publications other than short fiction
POETRY: *Casting for the Cutthroat*, 1977; *Casting for the Cutthroat & Other Poems*, 1980.

IRVIN FAUST

Born: New York, 1924

Principal short fiction

"The Dalai Lama of Harlem," 1964; "Operation Buena Vista," 1965; "The Double Snapper," 1965; *Roar Lion Roar and Other Stories*, 1965, "Simon Girty Go Ape," 1966; "Gary Dis-Donc," 1967; "Into the Green Night," 1969; "Philco Baby," 1970; "The World's Fastest Human," 1970; "Jake Bluffstein and Adolph Hitler," 1973.

Analysis

The portrayal of a charcter from his own point of view without filtering his feelings or behavior through the writer's sensibilities; depicting his desires, dreams, responses (some of which society may perceive as "problems" or "defects") without judging, condescending, or moralizing (sometimes demonstrating that a life perceived as "deprived" might be rich, diverse, and rewarding to the protagonist)—these are the aims and remarkable achievements of the Irvin Faust story. His ability to explore emotions, tensions, fears, and anxieties plugs the reader into an experience of the character's mind, body, and soul that can be exhilarating, fascinating, hilarious, or shocking. Intensely aware of the influence of pop culture—especially sports, radio, and films—Faust uses brand names, song titles and lyrics, advertising slogans and jingles, celebrity names and deeds as trail markings of time and place as well as landmarks to the interior of the character. A post-motion picture era writer, he limits descriptions of place, scenery, and physical appearance, allowing the reader to fill in details. His skill with language—street dialects, hip talk, ethnic speech—links the reader to the consciousness of the character, encourages him to "be" the character. No slave to convention, Faust occasionally surprises and delights by stretching usage—changing nouns into verbs, inventing speech patterns that shatter syntax—simultaneously revealing the character-defining possibilities of language. By the end of a Faust story, the reader has connected with another person revealed direct, as if there had been no writer intervening.

Major publications other than short fiction

NOVELS: *The Steagle*, 1966; *The File on Stanley Patton Buchta*, 1970; *Willy Remembers*, 1971; *Foreign Devils*, 1973; *A Star in the Family*, 1975; *Newsreel*, 1980.

NONFICTION: *Entering Angel's World*, 1963.

RAYMOND FEDERMAN

Born: France, 1928

Principal short fiction
Double or Nothing, 1971; "The Toothbrush," 1973; "Inside the Thing," 1974; *Take It or Leave It*, 1976; "Playgarism," 1977; "Premembrance," 1978; *The Voice in the Closet*, 1979; "Parsifal in Hamburg," 1980.

Analysis
Attempting to divide Federman's fiction into "stories" and "novels" is a fruitless and irrelevant task, for all of his published fiction to date forms a single project—essentially the story of Federman's life, especially the fiction-alized re-creation of the traumatic but stimulating period of his life from 1942 until 1958. The central event of Federman's life, which his fiction constantly circles, storifies, and evades, concerns the morning in 1942 when the Nazis knocked on the door of his family's apartment. Federman was hidden in a closet while his parents were shuffled off to extinction in the concentration camps. This unspeakable event—always designated by Federman by the ty-pographical symbols X-X-X-X—thrust Federman into a new world: he was forced to abandon his home, his family, his native country, and his language. His highly self-conscious, often humorous, and typographically playful fiction usually deals with this event and with his subsequent arrival in America by inventing numerous variations of his past with which his narrators freely play.

Samuel Beckett and Louis-Ferdinand Céline are the two most obvious influences on Federman's prose style, which is a unique blend of delirious, energetic, and poetic language. Although his two "novels," *Double or Nothing* and *Take It or Leave It*, are loosely based on the journey motif, both rely on highly digressive structures composed of anecdotes, tall tales, and metafic-tional self-commentaries, many of which originally appeared separately. *The Voice in the Closet* would appear to be Federman's one true "short story," since it is a twenty-page narrative with a French translation included in the text. In fact, however, this piece is accurately described by one of Federman's own characters as being "a twenty page novel." Closest in tone and language to Beckett's recent fragmented, densely layered narratives, this work is a condensation of all of Federman's earlier symbolic and thematic obsessions. Here the voice of all his earlier works confronts the typewriter producing it (the "selectricstud"), assaulting its creator for its previous failures to do justice to its "real story." All of Federman's fiction insists on its fictional, linguistic basis and defies all distinctions between reality and fiction. Above all, Fed-erman insists on the power of language which underlines our imaginative activities and allows us to generate fictional forms that vitalize and sustain us. As in Beckett, there is always the suggestion that no matter how bleak our condition may be, man possesses the ability to prevail so long as his words continue.

Major publications other than short fiction

NONFICTION: *Journey to Chaos: Samuel Beckett's Early Fiction*, 1965; *Samuel Beckett: His Works and His Critics*, 1970; *Surfiction: Fiction Now and Tomorrow*, 1975.

Larry McCaffery

ERIC FELDERMAN

Born: New York, 1944

Principal short fiction
"The Old Story," 1980; "The System," 1980.

Analysis
Eric Felderman's *Garden Street* (1977) concerns childhood and the memories of childhood; *Small Press Review* termed it "a minor masterpiece." In *Animal Book* (1978), Felderman presents a religious view of the world in conflict with the everyday horrors of reality. *The Book of Lies* (1975) presents a cycle of anecdotes about hell. *My Adventures on the Earth* (1980) presents a collection of short prose, poetry, and visionary jokes. *Elegy of Dreams* (1981) developed from a twelve-hundred-page record of dreams.

GARY FINCKE

Born: Pennsylvania, 1945

Principal short fiction

"Game of Games," 1973; "Caps," 1974; "Sleeping," 1974; "Beneath the Underbrush," 1975; "Cold Front," 1975; "Flip Side," 1975; "Night Watch," 1975; "A Mumbling Has Reached Me," 1976; "Autistic," 1978; "Calculating Very Carefully," 1978; "Cave Drawings," 1978; "The Deposit Box Scandal," 1978; "The Frigid Air Unchanging," 1978; "The Last Supper," 1978; "Three Short Fictions," 1978; "Afterbirth," 1979; "Corrective Lenses," 1979; "Swimming," 1980.

Analysis

Often fragmented, the stories of Gary Fincke are disjointed to reflect the coming apart of contemporary life. Structure as much as plot is used to show the de-evolving of the protagonists as they discover their lives retrogressing toward a kind of primitive, psychological survival of the fittest. There is a sense in these stories that the characters are not in control and are well aware of it. Through series of telling incidents, Fincke seeks to draw the reader into the breakdown of illusion and stability in what appear to be ordinary lives. His characters, like a "dwarf beneath the bed," are afraid of light, contact, and space, each of which makes them feel smaller in an expanding world. Although his more recent work has become more tempered with redeeming relationships and occasional humor, Fincke's stories are generally supplied with characters who suffer from a quiet panic.

Major publications other than short fiction

POETRY: *Emptied*, 1974; *Victims*, 1974; *Permanent Season*, 1975; *The Pattern of Destruction Was Obvious from the Air*, 1980.

ROBERT L. FISH

Born: Ohio, 1912

Principal short fiction

"Personal Appearance," 1960; "Clancy and the Subway Jumper," 1961; "Clancy and the Paper Clue," 1962; "Clancy and the Shoeshine Boy," 1962; "Clancy and the Cat's Eye," 1963; "Not Counting Bridges," 1963; "Lady in the Soup," 1964; "Bedtime Story," 1965; "Sonny," 1966; *The Incredible Schlock Homes*, 1967; "Spy Story," 1967; "To Hell with the Odds," 1968; "Double Entry," 1969; "In a Country Churchyard," 1970; "Instead of the Wall," 1971; "Moonlight Gardner," 1971; "Don't Worry, Johnny," 1972; "Hijack," 1972; "In the Bag," 1973; "Muldoon and the Numbers Game," 1973; "No Rough Stuff," 1973; *The Memoirs of Schlock Homes*, 1974; *"Kek Huuygens, Smuggler*, 1976; "The Patsy," 1976; "One of the Oldest Con Games," 1977; "The Adventure of the Elite Type," 1977; "The Adventure of the Common Code," 1979; "The Adventure of the Animal Fare," 1977; "The Art of Deduction," 1979; "The Adventure of the Patient Resident," 1980; "Punishment to Fit the Crime," 1980; "The Adventure of the Short Fuse," 1980.

Analysis

Robert Fish's short fiction nearly defies categorization, for while he eschews the shock qualities of a Robert Bloch or the grisly trickeries of a Roald Dahl, he also belongs to that pantheon with full honors. O. Henry is solidly at work in Fish, but somehow the quality he purveys in the short story is uniquely his own. There are no more beguiling stories in the genre than the Schlock Homes pastiches of the immortal sleuth from Baker Street; the remarkable plot-juggling and gaslight fun in these tales have to be read to be believed. There is more to Fish in the short story, however, than mere fun and games. Solidly structural and noncynical, utterly straightforward in the telling, a Fish short story is more likely to be a great piece of reading entertainment than a polemic on his fellowman. Fish has no time for condemnation, cruelty, or judgment. He simply is a masterful storyteller, the basic tools of the craft completely under control. He is an original, whether one is reading tales of Kek Huuygens, smuggler extraordinary, or Schlock Homes, or yet one of those dazzling exercises in suspense and trickery that have won him two Edgars from the Mystery Writers of America for his short work.

Major publications other than short fiction

NOVELS: *Isle of the Snakes*, 1963; *The Shrunken Head*, 1963; *Mute Witness*, 1963; *The Assassination Bureau*, 1963 (completion of an unfinished work by Jack London); *The Quarry*, 1964; *The Diamond Bubble*, 1965; *Brazilian Sleigh*

Ride, 1965; *The Police Blotter*, 1965; *The Hochmann Miniatures*, 1967; *Always Kill a Stranger*, 1967; *The Bridge That Went Nowhere*, 1968; *The Murder League*, 1968; *The Xavier Affair*, 1969; *Reardon*, 1970; *Whirligig*, 1970; *Rub-A-Dub-Dub*, 1971; *The Green Hill Treasure*, 1971; *The Gremlin's Grampa*, 1972; *Tricks of the Trade*, 1972; *A Handy Death*, 1973 (with Henry Rothblatt); *Trouble in Paradise*, 1974; *Bank Job*, 1974; *The Wager*, 1974; *Pursuit*, 1978; *A Gross Carriage of Justice*, 1979; *The Gold of Troy*, 1980.

Michel Avallone

ROBERT R. FOX

Born: New York, 1943

Principal short fiction
"A Fable," 1970; "Love Stories, Fables, and Other Tales," 1974; *Destiny News*, 1977.

Analysis
After his first reading of Robert R. Fox's collection *Destiny News*, critic Martin Kich began to identify with "certain moments and feelings" in the stories. His second reading brought the revelation that Fox's stories "are thrilling because they embody common emotions in a hauntingly real artistic framework." The impact of the stories is delayed because of Fox's subtle style: "The emotional force of Bob Fox's stories is almost sinisterly surreptitious. The author's style is almost somnolently poetic." Gabriel Taliaferro credits Fox's stories with traditional as well as surrealistic influences. In *Newsart* he states that the Frito stories "are reminiscent of F. Scott Fitzgerald's Pat Hobby Stories, neat, clear, reportorial, well-turned." The traditional heritage of the stories is well balanced by Fox's sensitivity to change, displayed through his rhetoric and his exploration of fantasy.

Major publications other than short fiction
NOVEL: *Tuscarora Tunnel's Touchdown*, 1981.

H. E. FRANCIS

Born: Rhode Island, 1924

Principal short fiction

"The Broken Bottle," 1951; "Journey to Emily," 1952; "The Darkness Is So Big," 1953; "The Rock Garden," 1953; "An Anchor in the Land," 1953; "The Journey of Annie Bliss," 1954; "The Kettle," 1955; "The Choice," 1956; "The Mandrake Heart," 1957; "Tom and Letty's World," 1958; "The Indifferent Wind," 1957; "The Keepers," 1958; "Vigil," 1958; "The Singer and the Song," 1959; "Let the Weariness Go," 1959; "You'll Hear from Me Saturday," 1959; "Something for a Rainy Day," 1959; "The White Duck," 1960; "Through a Certain Window," 1960; "Five Miles to December," 1960; "The Dark Woman," 1960; "The Visitor," 1961; "The Inheritance," 1961; "As fish, as birds, as grass," 1962; "The Fallen," 1962; "Sailor in Malaga," 1963; "Don't Ask for Beauty Twice," 1964; "Does He Treat You All Right?" 1965; "The Moment," 1966; "Summer Is the Suffering Time Here," 1967; "In Transit," 1968; "Moments in the Definition of Space," 1968; "The Listener," 1968; "Her," 1969; "Something Just Over the Edge of Everything," 1969; "The Shaping Sky," 1971; "Sully," 1971; "Tomorrow," 1973; "Parts," 1973; *The Itinerary of Beggars*, 1973; "The Finer Cadence," 1974; "The Electrician," 1974; "The Long Way to Go," 1974; "The Emptiest Corner," 1974; "The Lessons of Particular Love," 1974; "The Interior Landscape," 1974; "This," 1974; "Distances," 1974; "I am trying to reach you, a long way off, from this my body lying beside you, so please listen—," 1975; "Begin, Begin," 1975; "Bones," 1976; "Tracks," 1976; "The Impossible," 1976; "Answers," 1976; "The Fever," 1976; "Thief," 1976; "A Circle of Light," 1976; "Hurricane," 1976; "Out There," 1977; "Down," 1977; "A Thing of Beauty," 1977; "Under," 1977; "What Is the Color of Eternity?" 1978; "The Alien Concept," 1978; "The Advancement of Learning," 1978; "Subject, Object, and the Nature of Love," 1978; "The Long Haul," 1978; "The History of a Man in Despair," 1978; "The Visitation," 1979; "Walls," 1979; "The Ballad of the Engineer Carl Feldmann," 1979; "The Killing Station," 1979; *Naming Things*, 1980.

Analysis

H. E. Francis' stories frequently attempt to capture the drive which pulses through all nature and to probe the dark mysteries of the soul as he focuses on moments in his characters' struggles toward wholeness. He writes of a broad range of characters in diverse structures, traditional or experimental. A key recurrence is the quest for ultimate values in a world of confused or vanished absolutes. Often isolates or failures, his characters attempt to break through aloneness, to affect another being deeply. The pursuit carries them, sometimes with uncompromising gallantry, to the edge of intuitions, the ironic cost of which may be violence, madness, or death. Francis uses an elliptical method, deceptively casual, which creates taut, intricate—sometimes difficult—structures reflective of the multiple aspects of his vision. His is a strong personal voice, essentially lyrical, in a language ordinary and familiar, yet dense and multileveled in texture. A mood at times brooding and monstrous is balanced in tension with an overriding compassionate tone. As John Hawkes stated, in his concentration on "the oneness of all things, the terrifying completion of the individual who contains within himself the entirety of life," Francis insists on a subtle nature and space imagery to suggest man's relationship to the cosmos.

MARJORIE FRANCO

Born: Illinois, 1926

Principal short fiction

"I Am a Gentle, Peaceful Man," 1967; "The Rite of Spring," 1970; "An Uncompromising Girl," 1972; "The Boy Who Cooked," 1974; "A Day In Bed with Anthony Adverse," 1975; "The Girls," 1975; "Two of a Kind," 1976; "The Day We Had Lunch at the Palmer House," 1979; "Alexander's Life and Death Struggle," 1980.

Analysis

The stories of Marjorie Franco are about gentle, peaceful people. No murderers, no rapists, not even a neurotic housewife. Yet the characters are not ordinary people; ordinary suggests dullness and these people are described with a gentle humor that is never dull. Their problems are common ones— whether to adopt a child or a father's worries about his daughter's first date. Franco understands that most people never cope with marrying one's mother or risking an atomic war. Her characters are not omniscient persons who influence the destiny of millions. Instead, they must cope with their own destinies. Through all her prose there is a chain of optimism, a feeling that the unimportant individual will survive and the world will survive with him. That optimism, perhaps, makes them more important than the assassins and power brokers of other people's fiction. Franco describes her scenes with deft, fluid prose that seems effortless but is the result of much polishing and rewriting. Franco creates a mood with many sensory details: a red umbrella, breeze-puffed yellow curtains (red, pink, and yellow recur frequently), the sounds and smells of a city. We see what her characters see and feel what they feel. When the story is over, we are contented that we have shared in the solution of their problems.

Major publications other than short fiction

NOVEL: *So Who Hasn't Got Problems?*, 1979 (juvenile).

Marion M. Markham

LEONHARD FRANK

Born: Germany, 1882   **Died:** 1961

Principal short fiction
Der Streber: Drei Erzählungen, 1928; *In the Last Coach and Other Stories*, 1935; *Desire Me and Other Stories*, 1948; *Sieben Kurzgeschichten*, 1961.

Analysis
More than most writers, Leonhard Frank took his material from events in his own life as well as from political events of his time. A common theme is the conflict of the individual with society, leading to neurosis in the individual. Frank's protagonists frequently are alienated from themselves as well as from society. They feel lost, they suffer, and often they long for death as an escape. Frank portrays people forced to adapt to society, losing their identity and spontaneity in the process. By nature, Frank believed, people are good, but a ruthless society does not allow people to retain their essential goodness. Frank demanded radical changes in society, especially in the family and the school, which, for him, are microcosms of society as a whole. Only then can a better world come into being in which people can live in harmony with themselves and with nature. Frank's analysis of social problems owes much to Marxism, and his description of neuroses is based on Sigmund Freud and other members of the Vienna psychoanalytic movement. Frank's later stories are more resigned in tone; here he has less hope of changing society. Instead, he focuses on the private sphere of human relationships and on erotic problems, believing that suffering and loneliness can be healed only by love.

Major publications other than short fiction
NOVELS: *The Robberband*, 1928; *The Cause of the Crime*, 1928; *Carl and Anna*, 1929; *A Middle-Class Man*, 1930; *Brother and Sister*, 1930; *The Singers*, 1932; *Three of Three Million*, 1936; *Dream Mates*, 1946; *Mathilde*, 1948; *The Baroness*, 1950.
NONFICTION: *Heart on the Left*, 1954.

Jennifer Michaels

EDITH FREUND

Born: Illinois, 1932

Principal short fiction

"The Red Glove Kid Rides the Full Fare Ride," 1974; "Parts of the Machine," 1977; "We Were Not Poor in Lupco," 1978; "Return of the Marmalade," 1978; "The Girl Who Lived in Graceland in the Spring," 1978; "The Devil's Disciples," 1980.

Analysis

Writing short fiction and poetry with equal ease, Edith Freund often uses the disciplines of one to enhance the other. Thus, many of her poems are plotted; they tell a story as clearly as any prose. In her fiction, the entire storyline is not always clearly defined. At times the story starts in the middle and we only sense the beginning, or there may be a beginning and a middle, but the end is unwritten. We know, however, what it will be. We even know the end beyond the end until the moment of death, because we know the people about whom she has written. She uses a poet's eye to see beneath the surface of her characters—they are surely people she has met. We have met them too, but never understood them until Freund dissected them for us. The dissection is skillfully done and it is important to know none of the stories appear to be autobiographical. She has the poet's ear for the sounds as well as for the meanings of words. Her sentences are rhythmical, yet never cadenced. Her choice of words is often unexpected, yet the words seem exactly right. Her vision is clear; yet, sometimes it does not become clear for her reader's until a second or third reading. Perhaps the final test is that her stories are worth reading again.

Marion M. Markham

THOMAS FRIEDMANN

Born: Hungary, 1947

Principal short fiction
"Weekend Fruit," 1971; "Magic Mirror," 1974; "Handgames," 1975-1976; *Hero Azriel*, 1979; *Fathering and Other Sins*, 1980.

Analysis
The "magical realism" apparent in two of the pieces in *Hero Azriel* dominates *Fathering and Other Sins*. The earlier collection is unabashedly Jewish, the author deliberately refashioning Hebrew myths and legends in the six stories. Although Thomas Friedmann seems to be at home writing about New York, determined jogging, and chance sex, he is equally comfortable writing about the High Priest's court. The language is formal and precise, owing more to the Bible and Commentaries than to the informality and wisecracking of Yiddish. The humor and irony are gentle. Within the formal restrictions of the folktale, Friedmann does manage to address a striking variety of modern themes. Two of the stories, "Azazel" and "Azriel: A Legend," point very clearly toward new interests in *Fathering and Other Sins*. Both pose "what if" situations: what if the Temple and the office of the High Priest existed in modern days; what if a superhero who combined Superman and the Angel Gabriel kept watch over Jews in America? The stories in the second collection are similarly magical although totally modern. Beyond the initial situations— a father appears after a ten-year absence for a Sunday in the zoo with his grown son, a Jewish mother coaches her son in the pros, a mistress moves in with a wife who seems unaware of her presence—the stories observe the strict demands of verisimilitude. The material is imaginative yet autobiographical, the first-person voice authentic even while rendering surrealistic or dreamlike events. The situations are ordinary, even domestic, but slightly skewed so that familiar moments between parents and children or husbands and wives are revivified. The cycle of stories does concentrate on the responsibilities and repercussions of being a father, the narrator moving from childhood to adulthood to fatherhood in the course of the book. The Jewishness, while apparent, is in the background, making this an accessible group of stories. The language is handled with a poet's craft, while the humor utilizes the ear of a foreigner finely tuned to the peculiarities of English.

Major publications other than short fiction
NONFICTION: *The Copy Book*, 1980 (with J. MacKillop).

James MacKillop

DANIEL FUCHS

Born: New York, 1909

Principal short fiction
The Apathetic Bookie Joint, 1979.

Analysis
Daniel Fuchs tries for an artistic effect and is interested in continuity, form, or shape; in hitting off characters for the artistic worth in them; and in capturing the good of moments, of scene, and of events. He depends on humor and mimicry. The idea is to advertise the allurements of life, reality, and experience.

Major publications other than short fiction
NOVELS: *Summer in Williamsburg*, 1934; *Homage to Blenholt*, 1936; *Low Company*, 1937; *West of the Rockies*, 1971.

ROCCO FUMENTO

Born: Massachusetts, 1923

Principal short fiction
"It Had to Be You," 1948; "Alfredo's Sweetheart," 1949; "The Fig Tree," 1950; "Nonna's Pet," 1955; "Season of Atonement," 1961; "Neighbors and Crosses," 1962; "A Decent Girl Always Goes to Mass on Sunday," 1975.

Analysis
Rocco Fumento's Roman Catholic upbringing is strongly reflected in his stories through his characters' eternal struggles between the spirit and the flesh. His characters race headlong toward salvation or damnation, they are guilt-ridden, and sometimes they are possessed or think they are possessed. They are usually either Italian or Italian-Americans, and often there is a love-hate relationship between them and their Italian-Catholic heritage. Fumento deals with complex ideas in prose that are intense yet simple. To quote Dr. Frank Rosengarten in *The Italian American Novel*:

> One of the most powerful and complex novels to appear on the American scene . . . is Fumento's *Tree of Dark Reflection*. . . . In its exhaustive probing of the psychic and social causes of an American family's descent into the pit of self-destruction, this novel rivals William Styron's *Lie Down in Darkness*, and is one of the few American works of fiction . . . to approach the intensity of conflict achieved in another literary sphere, that of the drama, by such playwrights as Eugene O'Neill and Tennessee Williams. . . . *Tree of Dark Reflection* is also a novel about a human being's attempt to reconcile the two main elements in his cultural heritage, the Italian and the American experiences.

What Rosengarten says of Fumento's novel can also be said of his short fiction.

Major publications other than short fiction
NOVELS: *Devil by the Tail*, 1954; *Tree of Dark Reflection*, 1962.
NONFICTION: *Introduction to the Short Story*, 1962.

EUGENE K. GARBER

Born: Alabama, 1932

Principal short fiction

"The Black Prince," 1974; "The Lover," 1976; "The Host: Homage a Teilhard de Chardin," 1976; "Three Metaphysical Tales," 1977; "The Poets," 1978; "The President," 1978; "The Women," 1979.

Analysis

Perhaps the best introduction to Eugene Garber's techniques and themes is an essay he wrote for a set of three metaphysical tales published in the *Iowa Review*, Winter, 1977. In that essay, sometimes critical and sometimes speculative and metaphorical, Garber acknowledges his chief mentors (Edgar Allan Poe, Franz Kafka, Isak Dinesen, Jorge Luis Borges). He also tries to characterize the two key interrelated aspects of his fiction. First, his works are *tales*, as distinguished from short stories—nonrealistic, densely atmospheric, archetypal, and occasionally open to the preternatural. Second, his works are *metaphysical*—he attempts quite literally to go beyond the physical world in the direction of the substructure of reality, which, assuming it is there at all, we can know only metaphorically, mythically. The other quality of Garber's fiction is the density of the style. This characteristic derives from his belief (biblical, Joycean) that language, both lexicon and syntax, is talismanic. The chief nonliterary sources of his work are myth and religion: the Bible, Eliade, Levi-Strauss, Teilhard, among others. Garber is indebted to many contemporary writers, especially Robert Coover, whose *Pricksongs & Descants* has served him as a treasure trove of post-modernist techniques, and to Norman Lavers, whose careful reading of Garber's work in draft, as well as the model of his own writing, has been of enormous help.

RICHARD GARDNER

Born: Washington, 1932

Principal short fiction
Brass Necks and Basket Cases, 1961; "A Step Backwards," 1963; "The Perfect Woman," 1964; "The Devil's Sister," 1974; "O'Conner's Last Stand," 1975; *Hillbilly Heaven*, 1979.

Analysis
Between his first collection of stories and the most recent collection, Richard Gardner has written and published several dozen stories of such a variety as to defy critical classification. Some were genre pieces—science fiction, mystery, pornography—many were sprung pure and whole from events and emotion but found no publisher and fit no category. The stories of the two collections, however, do have much in common. Both collections bind the stories together in a common time and place. All are told chronologically in straightforward prose, with never a flashback in block, only in passing insertion. They concern themselves with no more than four people, often with only one. The first collection concerns itself with human loneliness, the second more specifically with fear of death. Plots are not of the sort that demand climax; the only resolutions are modest emotional-spiritual events. The characters are of humble origins and small distinction, but they all evidence humor and courage.

Major publications other than short fiction
NOVELS: *Scandalous John*, 1963; *The Bridge*, 1963; *The Adventures of Don Juan*, 1974; *The Dragon Breath Papers*, 1976; *Mandrill*, 1977.

RUTH GELLER

Born: New York, 1945

Principal short fiction
Pictures from the Past, 1980.

Analysis
The witty working-class perspective evident in Ruth Geller's stories takes as its starting point a deceptively simple incident that reveals various characteristics of contemporary American life. These everyday circumstances— driving to work, meeting a stranger at a bar—illustrate the basic questions about which Geller is concerned: how do race, sex, class, and sexual preference divide people; what is the individual's responsibility for suffering and social injustice; how does the average person face something so shattering as ecological catastrophe? Displaying traditional structure and basic language, the stories are evocative and understated, often hinting at an imminent violence. Cited for her realistic dialogue, Geller lets the characters speak for themselves; and many of the stories are in the first person, as in "Dreckula," about the trials and tribulations of a Jewish vampire. Even in the most humorous stories that approach parody, political concerns are evident. In the stories as a whole, one sees the individual in relationship to society and nature, struggling to understand and overcome the alienation with which we all live.

Major publications other than short fiction
NOVEL: *Seed of a Woman,* 1979.

MERRILL JOAN GERBER

Born: New York, 1938

Principal short fiction
Stop Here, My Friend, 1965; "Chipping," 1965; "Baby Blues," 1965; "Ten Cents' Worth of Love," 1966; "Invitation to the Dance," 1966; "The Stork Is a Wonderful Bird," 1967; "The Bargain," 1968; "Explain That to a Baby Sitter," 1968; "What Do I Want to Do Today?," 1969; "The Ultimate Friend," 1970; "Things in Their Proper Order," 1970; "Daydreams," 1970; "Can a Girl Find Happiness," 1971; "May I Ask Who's Calling?," 1971; "Inside the Castle," 1972; "Poor Katie," 1972; "Moon Life," 1972; "The Diary," 1972; "The Bottle of Shrieks," 1972; "A Woman of the Night," 1972; "Must You Go?," 1973; "Candy Corn," 1973; "To Life," 1973; "The Sunday Visit," 1973; "Sadzia, The Sultan's Sweetmeat," 1975; "I Am . . . the Queen . . . of England," 1975; "How We Spent Our Family Vacation," 1976; "The Three Princesses," 1976; "A Gambling Woman," 1977; "The Key Word," 1977; "Lover's Knot," 1977; "I'm Fine, Where Are You?," 1978; "A Personal Decision," 1978; "Rest, You'll Live Longer," 1978; "Taking the Chance," 1979; "The Peaceable Kingdom," 1979; "The Mistress of Goldman's Antiques," 1979.

Analysis
The most distinctive feature of Merrill Gerber's stories is the everyday, commonplace situations which she relates with credibility. Her craftsmanship involves the point of view of a sympathetic, often amused observer who records real life effortlessly but with practiced control.

Major publications other than short fiction
NOVELS: *An Antique Man, 1967; Now Molly Knows*, 1974; *The Lady with the Moving Parts*, 1978; *Please Don't Kiss Me Now*, 1981.

MORGAN GIBSON

Born: Ohio, 1929

Principal short fiction
"Madonna," 1950; "Through a Glass Darkly," 1950; "Nice Work If," 1961; "Palely Loitering," 1964; "Patiently," 1978; "Wormy Toes," 1978; *The Great Brook Book*, 1980; "The First Woman of Japan," 1980.

Analysis
Morgan Gibson's fiction expands the vision of his poetry. Like poetry, his fiction is melodic in style, passionately imagistic, and suited for oral performance. The narrator, often hovering between dreaming and waking, explores the origins of consciousness—the onset of feeling, sensing, thinking, imagining—and tells tales out of time, in which events occur in the eternal present, sequential time turns out to be illusory, and characters are focuses of self-awareness. Gibson's stories are lyrical awakenings of heart-mind, mythic quests for new worlds of consciousness, nightmarish initiations into the mysteries of meditation. Gibson learned the art of poetic narration from his grandmother's prophetic tales, his father's visionary sermons, his mother's passionate gossip, from the Bible and Buddhist sutras, and from the poetry and prose of Walt Whitman, William Butler Yeats, James Joyce, Sherwood Anderson, Franz Kafka, Paul Goodman, and perhaps most of all, Kenneth Rexroth. Gibson's theory and practice of fiction, as of poetry, has been shaped by Zen and Tantric Buddhist thought and meditation, especially by his life in Japan (1975-1979), when he taught at Osaka University and married a Japanese poet, Keiko Matsui.

Major publications other than short fiction
POETRY: *Our Bedroom's Underground*, 1963; *Mayors of Marble*, 1966; *Stones Glow Like Lovers' Eyes*, 1970; *Dark Summer*, 1977; *Wakeup*, 1978; *Speaking of Light*, 1979.
PLAYS: "Madam C. I. A.," 1968; "Strongroom," 1970.
NONFICTION: *Kenneth Rexroth*, 1972.

SANDRA GILBERT

Born: New York, 1936

Principal short fiction
"The Noisemaker," 1968; "Weeping," 1970; "Waiting," 1970; "Sleepers Awake," 1972; "Heaviness," 1974; "Selvia," 1975.

Analysis
Sandra Gilbert writes stories of isolation, lovelessness, and incommunicative silence in which she tries to explore what Donne called "defects of loneliness"—the sometimes subtle, sometimes melodramatic or bizarre deformations of the solitary personality. Her tales are often realistic, in the mode of case histories, but occasionally she draws on the techniques of fantasy and fairy tale in order to examine surrealistic states of consciousness and apparently "impossible" events. As a fiction writer, she has been influenced both by her work as a poet and her activity as a critic/teacher.

Major publications other than short fiction
POETRY: *In the Fourth World*, 1979.
NONFICTION: *Acts of Attention: The Poems of D. H. Lawrence*, 1972; *The Madwoman in the Attic: The Woman Writer and the Nineteenth-Century Literary Imagination*, 1979 (with Susan Gubar).

ELLEN GILCHRIST

Born: Mississippi, 1935

Principal short fiction
"Rich," 1978; "The President of the Louisiana Liveoak Society," 1978; "The Famous Poll at Jody's Bar," 1979; "Traveler," 1980.

Analysis
Ellen Gilchrist plucks her stories from thoughts that occur to her and dog her until she commits them to paper. Sometimes she interprets the thoughts into poetry, but often the thoughts continue to plague her until she writes them down in prose. A friend who reads the story gives advice on changes that should be made. If the story is characterized by the element of verisimilitude, readers think it pertains to each of them, and Gilchrist considers it a success.

Major publications other than short fiction
POETRY: *The Land Surveyor's Daughter*, 1979.

JOHN GILGUN

Born: Massachusetts, 1935

Principal short fiction

Everything That Has Been Shall Be Again: Reincarnation Fables, 1980.

Analysis

John Gilgun's fables are based upon the premise that an individual can die and be reincarnated in the body of an animal with the full power of recollection of his previous lifetime and the ability to comment upon it. Each fable is a first-person narrative. The voice emerges from the body of the creature speaking with complete physical knowledge of what it feels like to be encased in that body. The fables contain a metaphysical view of human and animal existence embracing sex, death, metamorphosis, God, and nature. They owe a great deal to Gilgun's understanding of Western and Oriental philosophy, particularly to Buddhism. The fables were written to be presented at formal readings, and Gilgun has delivered them to audiences consisting of children and adults many times since he began them in the summer of 1975. They have been described, by the artist Larry Holmes, as "both funny and touching, too." Each animal has a different "voice," because these are performance pieces as well as stories to be read in a book.

JAMES P. GIRARD

Born: Oregon, 1944

Principal short fiction

"Carpe Diem," 1973; "The Boy, the Bear, the Ragged Man," 1975; "Something's Coming," 1975; "The Empty House," 1975; "The Alternates," 1976; *Changing All Those Changes*, 1976; "September Song," 1978; "In Trophonius's Cave," 1979.

Analysis

A natural novellaist, James Girard writes short fiction which tends more toward the complexities of the novel than toward the traditional unities of the short story, and which is highly compressed, largely to accommodate publishing standards. To deal with events over long periods of time in his characters' lives, Girard frequently employs such devices as revery, flashback (often telescoping one within the other) and quick "cinematic" cuts between scenes not connected chronologically. Girard gives great attention to precision in the use of verb tense, and it is this trait that typically provides the unifying structure in his serious work. Although a careful craftsman, Girard's principal concern is with story rather than form, and he strives chiefly to convey experience fully and truly, primarily in sensory terms and in language as simple and direct as possible, trying, as William Stafford has said, "not to say the simplest thing, but to say it in the simplest way." Girard's protagonists, typically, are characters whose sensory apprehension of the world has come to be at odds with their cognitive understanding of it, forcing them to reorder that understanding in order to survive. They are often adrift in the attempt to construct a coherent biography out of what seem chaotic bits of memory and experience. Girard's stories are set, almost exclusively, in Kansas and evoke a sense of place largely through tactile images, especially the interplay of weather and time. Reviewing Girard's novella, Greil Marcus described Girard's style as "a measured, toneless voice that in its deceptively artless rhythms recalls [the] prairie stillness." Girard's science-fiction stories lean on the social sciences and time travel because of his lack of background in the natural sciences.

ISABEL JOSHLIN GLASER

Born: Alabama, 1929

Principal short fiction
"The Duel," 1970; "On the Line," 1971; "Sweet Beckie's Wedding," 1973; "The Corset," 1975; "Harold Again," 1975; "A Night of Honeysuckle," 1977; "The Best Place to Meet Someone Nice," 1979.

Analysis
Isabel J. Glaser believes that a good short story is short only in length when compared to a novel; that a story should not have less meaning than a novel, nor should its action be less complete. Glaser's short fiction is concerned with exploring the human condition and often concentrates on the problems of poor Southern whites. Both place and characterization play important roles in these stories. Following more or less traditional forms, she introduces fresh images and brings the characters to life through action as well as through use of narrative detail, preferring, as a rule, the specific (concrete) word to the general. Dialogue is that of the characters' society (Southern, lower class), its distinctiveness suggested through tone rather than through literal reproduction.

Major publications other than short fiction
POETRY: *Old Visions . . . New Dreams*, 1977.

ADELE GLIMM

Born: New York, 1937

Principal short fiction

"Cultural Exchange Program," 1971; "To Build a Dream," 1972; "When We Have Enough," 1973; "A Woman's Heart," 1973; "Child of the Heart," 1973; "The Way Things Happen," 1974; "A Day to Be Cherished," 1974; "If I Could Tell You," 1974; "Spirit of Me," 1974; "Taking Flight," 1975; "People Are Hard to Fix," 1975; "Road Signs," 1976; "The Amateur," 1976; "Ways of the Heart," 1976; "Music from the Heart," 1976; "A Matter of Confidence," 1977; "Come Back, My Love," 1977; "My Daughter Is Seventeen," 1978; "The Surprise Party," 1978; "Only Love Never Changes," 1978; "To Be with You," 1978; "Love Match," 1979; "Unlimited Views," 1980.

Analysis

Although a few of these stories have male protagonists, most deal with conflicts in the lives of contemporary women. Conflicts between conventional characters and "breaking out" characters exploring new life styles are frequently explored, as are conflicts between the generations. These themes overlap with the themes of loss (of employment, of love through divorce or death, of outgrown life roles) and of change (characters struggle with such new roles as step-parent, adoptive parent, female worker in formerly male job). Underlying almost all the stories is the theme of individualism: the protagonist seeks to grow and develop, to remain uniquely herself despite society's pressures and expectations. The main character of each story is usually insightful and introspective: she analyzes her own feelings and behavior. Minor characters tend to be quirky, to do and say surprising things, to shake up the world of the story, to force the protagonist to work for whatever measure of growth and harmony she can attain by the story's end. A few stories are surrealistic; most are realistic in tone and technique. The world of each story is created more through the drama of human relationships than through physical or sociological detail. In some stories the atmosphere of a particular place—a Danish town in winter, a suburban house during a burglary, a San Francisco park—becomes a character in its own right, influencing human mood and action.

Major publications other than short fiction

NOVEL: *Richard's Wife*, 1968.

NONFICTION: "The Life and Death of Story Characters," 1975; "Emotional Value in Fiction," 1978.

THOMAS GLYNN

Born: Canada, 1935

Principal short fiction
"Except for the Sickness I'm Quite Healthy Now, You Can Believe That,"
1968; "Flo," 1972; "King Zamp," 1974; "The Monkey," 1975; "Needle," 1975;
"The Afterbirth," 1975; "Bo & Be," 1977; "Dog Star Man," 1979.

Analysis
Thomas Glynn's stories are too varied to fit under a single spectrum, but
many of them approach reality as a blind man approaches busy traffic—with
fear and trepidation. As the critic Jerome Klinkowitz said in *Innovative Fiction, Stories for the Seventies*,

> The artist of Thomas Glynn's story "Except for the Sickness I'm Quite Healthy Now, You
> Can Believe That" establishes this rapport in his expanding painting, which enables man
> to imaginatively experience the initiation rite of Einstein's Fourth dimension. Having
> disavowed the outmoded conventions of an earlier, three-dimensional world, writers such
> as Barthelme, Coover, and Glynn have struck beyond the limits of comfortable, decorous
> existence into the imaginatively strange and vile. Anything else is submemorable, and,
> in terms of the universe, physically dead. Man seeks life. After making a morass of modern
> life by delaying facing it with the meaningful forms of understanding, everyone, as Glynn
> understands, "wants to fall in my painting." Misfits, derelicts, and bums flock to his studio;
> placed in the new form, initiated into the fourth dimension, they live.

Major publications other than short fiction
NOVELS: *Temporary Sanity*, 1976.

LESTER GOLDBERG

Born: New York, 1924

Principal short fiction

"Natural Selection," 1972; "The Reckoning," 1973; "The Cavalryman," 1973; "Joshua in the Rice Paddy," 1974; "The Unthinkable," 1974; "The Sticking Room," 1974; "The Witness," 1974; "The Love Song of J. Paris Wladaver," 1974; "Happy Times in Ohio," 1975; "Sleeping," 1975; "Disorder and Desire," 1976; "Drop Dead, You Dummy," 1976; "One More River," 1976; "Semper Fidelis," 1976; "Paw Paw: Cousin John," 1976; "The Survivor," 1976; "The Early Train," 1976; "Cornstalks," 1976; "Testimony," 1976; "Last Train from Tottenville," 1977; "Shy Bearers," 1978; "May They Find Favor in Thine Eyes," 1978; "The Beast in the Walls," 1978; "Mating Habits," 1978; *One More River*, 1978; "In Siberia, It Is Very Cold," 1979; "After the Ice Age," 1979; "Who Shaves the Barber," 1979; "The Wrestler," 1979.

Analysis

Lester Goldberg's great strength in short fiction comes out of his working-class Jewish origins. In this world, all bruises are real and painful. Honest pain, honest hunger can teach, among other things, when it is not necessary to be fancy or clever, when it is possible for the writer to stand aside and allow the characters to be, to suffer and rejoice on their own.

Goldberg probes his Jewish past amid a cast of losers so painfully ordinary that they become memorable. The Jewish kid working in the pig slaughter-house, the factory worker deliberately burning himself as the Rosenbergs die, the mugged good Samaritan scribbling checks for worthy causes—Goldberg's people combat the overwhelming contradictions of their lives with small, defiant gestures. The interplay of public event and private trouble is Goldberg's theme and strength: the Depression, the Rosenberg execution, La Causa, Vietnam. Sometimes the connection seems humorous ("our kids haven't tasted grapes in eight years!"), sometimes tragic, as when young Joshua dies in a Vietnamese rice paddy. Always the unstated problem haunts: how to be human in a society that passes off causes and rituals as authentic social life. Goldberg worries the issue in restrained, elliptical prose. When a fellow named Israel becomes a silent witness, lurking in courtrooms to send vibes (Innocent!) at the jury, his stepson speculates that "since my mother and I have led such ordinary lives, this Israel, who is inflicted on us, must be an ordinary lunatic."

JEANETTE ERLBAUM GOLDSMITH

Born: New York, 1942

Principal short fiction
"Sadie," 1972; "Apocalypse," 1973; "Grand Passion," 1976; "The Stranger," 1979; "Pieces," 1979; "Saturday Afternoon," 1979.

Analysis
Jeanette Goldsmith's dynamic short fiction encompasses a variety of styles, including naturalistic, surrealist, and subjective prose. She employs cinematic juxtaposition, whimsy, and satire. Many of her first-person stories are characterized by a gently self-mocking character. Character, dialogue, and humor are her fortes. She favors the "open-ended" story with a subtle organic plot. Her subjects include marriage, apprenticeship, dependency, betrayal, sacrifice, and art. Although she eschews the "happy ending," she is a member of the "affirmative" school, relying, despite her better judgment, on the ultimate goodness and perfectability of humankind.

N. V. M. GONZALEZ

Born: Philippines, 1915

Principal short fiction

Seven Hills Away, 1947; *Children of the Ash-Covered Loam and Other Stories*, 1954; *Look, Stranger, on This Island Now*, 1963; *Mindoro and Beyond: Twenty-One Stories*, 1979.

Analysis

Mindoro and nearby islands in the Philippines have provided N. V. M. Gonzalez, as Lucien Stryk has written, with ". . . people to care about over those 7,000 islands of his. . . ." Here, indeed, are "farmers, fisherfolk, traders, teachers, and civil servants" to whose "life rhythms," Alfredo Salanga suggests, Gonzalez has intended "to be faithful. . . ." When *Children of the Ash-Covered Loam and Other Stories* first appeared in 1965, David Martin, writing for *Meanjin*, found "a peculiar inner rhythm" in the stories "which quite tenably one associates with the literature of the East and South East Asia and which, in recent years, has provided a unifying bond." In any case, Gonzalez has drawn from a world "attentively and lovingly observed," according to Francisco Arcellana. "In children and plain women," wrote Leonard Casper, "he has found his finest center of sensibility." A retrospective collection, *Mindoro and Beyond* has been described as "a landmark . . . with [a] sharply exact view of worlds fast changing." Indeed, the book covers some forty years of work, and perhaps behind the stories is an idea that evolved of itself: that in the imagined, as opposed to the actual, life is more real and meaningful.

Major publications other than short fiction

NOVELS: *The Winds of April*, 1941; *A Season of Grace*, 1956; *The Bamboo Dancers*, 1960.

ROBERT GOVER

Born: Pennsylvania, 1929

Principal short fiction
"Where the Music Is," 1965; "George Decides," 1967; *Getting Pretty on the Table*, 1976.

Analysis
By distorting what he calls "media reality" Robert Gover aims for "the tall tale told tongue-in-check." His protagonists are easily recognizable American types. The theme of his stories is usually a character's relationship with money, or the lack of it. As in his novels, characters scheme, scam, steal, or sweat for whatever they suppose an acquisition of dollars will bestow. This attitude propels them through conflict, sex, rape, murder, or moments of insight that create whole realms of argot-laden awareness. His bittersweet satires on the "American Way" have earned Gover mixed critical reaction. His style and perspectives have gained him wide translation of his work. The best of his short fiction, "Victor Versus Mort," is available only in translation, and even his successful novel, *One Hundred Dollar Misunderstanding* (1960), was roundly rejected in the United States until it became popular in French translation. It then appeared on American best-seller lists during a New York citywide newspaper strike. At his best, Gover writes with a belief that prodding the sacred cows of the national consciousness is good, clean fun.

Major publications other than short fiction
NOVELS: *One Hundred Dollar Misunderstanding*, 1960; *The Maniac Responsible*, 1963; *Here Goes Kitten*, 1965; *Poorboy at the Party*, 1967; *J. C. Saves*, 1968; *Going for Mr. Big*, 1972; *To Morrow Now Occurs Again*, 1976.

ROBERT GRAVES

Born: England, 1895

Principal short fiction
The Shout, 1929; *Collected Short Stories*, 1964.

Analysis
Robert Graves is known as a poet, historical novelist, autobiographer, mythologist, biographer of Lawrence of Arabia, but seldom as a writer of short stories. He has disclaimed any gift for original plots. His novels are based on history or myth; his short pieces, which he calls "stories," are usually anecdotes suggested to him by soldiers or by his own experience. He has written, however, an excellent Gothic tale, an ambiguous story of love, jealousy, demonic destruction, and fractured personality. "The Shout," published in 1929, might be interpreted either as a madman's fantasy or a supernatural tale; it is certainly related to the psychological story of the double. In spite of the story's fantastic elements, Graves has identified himself with the character Richard. Besides demonstrating Graves's craftsmanship as a storyteller, it transforms imaginatively one of the most shattering emotional upheavals of Graves's life.

Major publications other than short fiction
NOVELS: *I, Claudius*, 1934; *Claudius the God*, 1934; *Count Belisarius*, 1938; *Sergeant Lamb of the Ninth*, 1940; *Proceed, Sergeant Lamb*, 1941; *The Story of Marie Powell, Wife to Mr. Milton*, 1943; *The Golden Fleece*, 1944; *King Jesus*, 1946; *Seven Days in New Crete*, 1949; *The Island of Unwisdom*, 1949; *Homer's Daughter*, 1955; *They Hanged My Saintly Billy*, 1957.

POETRY: *Collected Poems*, 1938; *Collected Poems, 1914-1947*, 1948; *Collected Poems*, 1955; *New Poems*, 1963; *Poems, 1965-1968*, 1968.

NONFICTION: *Poetic Unreason and Other Studies*, 1925; *Lawrence and the Arabs*, 1927; *A Survey of Modernist Poetry*, 1927 (with Laura Riding); *Goodbye to All That*, 1929; *The White Goddess*, 1948; *The Common Asphodel—Collected Essays on Poetry*, 1949; *The Greek Myths*, 1955; *The Crowning Privilege*, 1955; *5 Pens in Hand*, 1958; *Steps*, 1958; *Food for Centaurs*, 1960; *Oxford Addresses on Poetry*, 1962; *Mammon and the Black Goddess*, 1965.

Katherine Snipes

RICHARD GRAYSON

Born: New York, 1951

Principal short fiction

"Reflections on a Village Rosh Hashona 1969," 1976; "Summoning Alice Keppel," 1976; "Talking to a Stranger," 1977; "Where the Glacier Stopped," 1977; "Understanding Human Sexual Inadequacy," 1977; "Cross in the Water," 1978; "The Bridge Beyond the Pleasure Principle," 1978; *Disjointed Fictions*, 1978; "Early Warnings," 1978; "I, Eliza Custis," 1978; "The Greatest Short Story That Absolutely Ever Was," 1979; *With Hitler in New York and Other Stories*, 1979.

Analysis

Since his first story appeared in 1975, Richard Grayson has published more than 150 pieces of short fiction, mostly in little magazines. Critics have remarked on the range and diversity in his work; Grayson has published straightforward narrative, children's stories, stories using experimental techniques such as pastiche, fragmented snatches of dialogue, questions, and answers, parodies of fan magazines and television programs, allusive academic puzzles, and slice-of-life stories that revolve around a New York Jewish milieu. Grayson's forte seems to be humor, from outrageous one-liners and puns to the more subtle and poignant comedy that appears in his stories of contemporary family life. Celebrities and the media tend to populate Grayson's fiction; the presence of television is always evident. The autobiographical element in his fiction is often so compulsive that, in the words of one critic, "there is less (but also much more) here than meets the eye."

GEOFFREY GREEN

Born: New York, 1951

Principal short fiction

"Kaddish for Rubin," 1971; "Police Report" 1973; "Puskaya," 1974; "Union," 1975; "The Retirement," 1976; "Premonitions," 1977; "Telaka Remembers," 1978; "*Nichevo?*/Nothing: A Russian Fantasy," 1978; "She Wore a Yellow Ribbon," 1979; "Peace," 1980.

Analysis

Readers who had first encountered Geoffrey Green's fiction through such early stories as "Kaddish for Rubin" (the naturalistic account of the reunion of brothers in a hospital where one of them has been a patient for sixteen years) or "Puskaya" (a son's narrative of the life and death of his Trotskyite father and of the guilt his father's unbidden political legacy imposed upon him) would have had considerable difficulty anticipating what lay ahead. Among Green's more recent publications is "*Nichevo?*/Nothing: A Russian Fantasy," in which an original Russian tragic narrative conceived in the Constance Garnett manner is provided with a fully transcribed score, allowing those who read music the opportunity to sing the doleful tale as they read it; there is also a pre-*Jaws* meditation upon the relationship between man and shark called "Union," a story which presents not only the perspective of shark-detesting, shark-desiring humans, but which also incorporates for good measure—and for considerable effect—an approximation of the shark's perspective upon the relationship. Green is not the only contemporary writer to have served his literary apprenticeship working with materials normally associated with the realistic tradition of the American Jewish novel—Stanley Elkin is another whose fictional voice was discovered through the employment of these materials. What is remarkable about Green's fiction is the extent to which it is able to meld the affective possibilities of that familiar genre with the innovative and intellectual potentials of experimental or fabulist fiction.

Peter Bailey

ALVIN GREENBERG

Born: Ohio, 1932

Principal short fiction
"Delta q," 1977; "The Serious World and Its Environs," 1978; *The Discovery of America and Other Tales of Terror and Self-Exploration*, 1980; "Game Time," 1980.

Analysis
A reviewer in *World Literature Today* describes Alvin Greenberg as someone who

> obviously knows Brautigan and Barthelme as well as Borges and Poe, but he is less sentimental than the first, less apprehensive than the characters of the second, more relaxed than the third, and more ironic about his inventions than the last. A bookish writer whose reading is a natural part of his world, Greenberg creates a narrative persona neither whining nor insistent, Midwestern American but neither complaining nor anathematic, confused but not nonplussed.

If that confusion stems from a view of the world as infinitely precarious, where trust—even in one's own perceptions—is hard to come by, then the quality of the nonplussed attained by his narrators/protagonists comes from a willingness to continue their journeys, their quests for value, in the face of such confusion and precariousness: to create value and meaning, like some knowledgeable but still naïve Beckett, by that very choice to continue. They seem to sense, however dimly at times, that so long as they believe in possibility then the world, for all its potential to undermine both belief and action, still remains a place of possibility: for the discovery of self and the creation of value on whatever minimal or purely comic levels. Formally the stories mirror this precarious optimism—where there are no finalities, only slowly growing awarenesses of the levels of possibility—by balancing great tightness of structure and economy of language against the confusions of both realistic action and the concerns of postmodern, self-reflexive fiction.

Major publications other than short fiction
NOVELS: *The Small Waves*, 1965; *Going Nowhere*, 1971; *The Invention of the West*, 1976.

POETRY: *The Metaphysical Giraffe*, 1968; *The House of the Would-Be Gardener*, 1972; *Dark Lands*, 1973; *Metaform*, 1975; *In/Direction*, 1978.

BARBARA L. GREENBERG

Born: Massachusetts, 1932

Principal short fiction

"Golden Worms," 1969; "Death Marks," 1972; "Didn't We Meet at Dachau?," 1976; "Settlements," 1976; "Fire Drills," 1977; "Important Things," 1978; "A Matched Pair," 1979; "A Show of Hands," 1979; "The Blind Boy," 1980; "Food Stamps," 1980; "Wolfprints," 1980.

Analysis

"I was somewhere between a dream and a state of emergency." The opening line of "Fire Drills" would serve as well for most of Barbara Greenberg's short fictions. The predictable concern of her stories is to locate the psyche of the central character in the context of real events (deaths, illnesses, mishaps) or, as in short pieces such as "The Blind Boy," through metaphoric encounters. In the absence of conventional story lines, tensions are situational and stylistic. Greenberg writes a poet's prose, intense and cadenced. The voice is a curious mix of passion and irony.

Major publications other than short fiction

POETRY: *The Spoils of August*, 1974.

PATRICIA BROWNING GRIFFITH

Born: Texas, 1940

Principal short fiction
"Brief Legacy," 1967; "Night's at O'Rear's," 1969; "The Liberator of East Texas," 1970; "Dust," 1974; "Orlando," 1975; "Zapata, Moro," 1979; "Marie," 1979; "The Coffee Break Killer," 1979; "Moons," 1980; "Still Life," 1980; "Mysteries of the Marine Monument: Or, The Colonel's Wife Who Becomes a Saint," 1980.

Analysis
Some of Patricia Griffith's stories are set in the East Texas country towns her childhood knew; others (including a number of her more recent ones) are set in the polar opposites of those Texas towns—the disoriented rootless urban worlds of New York and Washington. Yet in all Griffith's fiction, the sensibility is one formed from the quotidian habit of precise observation, nurtured on an infinite variety of Southern social distinctions, responsive to minute gradations in cultural texture, informed with the acerbity and wit that come from knowing everyone's place in the scheme of things. In the early stories, the sensibility manifests itself in the almost leisurely techniques of regional realism. In much of her later work, the sensibility emerges in startlingly authentic images of the banal, studding an increasingly condensed and elliptical prose. Griffith's characters often yearn for the kind of McLuhanesque pop culture glamour or notoriety that passes for achievement in the global village. If they cannot hope to be saints or heroes, they can at least try to become celebrities (a radio singer, a media-covered civil rights leader, a recording star, a Kilgore Rangerette, a composer of a new national anthem, a fantasy victim of a television-hyped murderer). Griffith knows well the tragic ironies inherent in such quests, but her sympathetic heart is kept in check by her sardonic eye.

Major publications other than short fiction
NOVELS: *The Future Is Not What It Used to Be*, 1970; *Victor Gollancz*, 1971; *Tennessee Blue*, 1981.

A. J. Griffith

STAN HAGER

Born: California, 1946

Principal short fiction
Lunatics and Other Lovers, 1972.

Analysis
There are many ready-made phrases which one might use to describe the short stories of Stan Hager, words of praise that might as easily be applied to works of numerous genuine craftsmen in the genre of short fiction—such phrases as "well-crafted," "image-centered," "skillful use of fast and slow time," or "development of significant dramatic tension." Such phrases, with others of a similar nature, would be appropriate, for Hager is a master of the short story. As a tale-teller, he is a modernist, an experimentalist, one of a kind. More important, however, are the themes and the certain sense of identity which the characters achieve within the framework of that which is Western American, in the best sense of the term. The stories in *Lunatics and Other Lovers*, as well as the significant body of hitherto uncollected work, project an extremely masculine world, with Animus in search of Anima on both the interior and exterior levels, the Wounded Prince in search of the Grail of self. The settings may range from a California campus in the 1960's to a small backwoods town in the Sierras to the dark forests of the high ridges, with chainsaws snarling in the background. The male heroes tend to be figures of powerful complexity, fiercely independent and hence often agonized or disoriented in dreamlike quests for their own identities.

Bill Hotchkiss

JAMES BYRON HALL

Born: Ohio, 1918

Principal short fiction

"By the Distaff's Hot Astonishment," 1952; "Estate and Trespass," 1954; "A Session of Summer," 1954; "The Fall and the Twilight," 1957; *15 x 3*, 1957 (with R. V. Cassill and Herbert Gold); "The Fish Camp Under the Snow," 1958; "Up in Her Room," 1958; "But Who Gets the Children," 1960; "The World Is a Hubcap Spinning," 1960; "The Race in the Afternoon," 1960; "The Omophagists," 1964; "Letters Never Sent," 1964; *Us He Devours*, 1964; "Getting Married," 1967; "While Going North," 1968; "God Cares but Waits," 1969; "I Like It Better Now," 1969; "The Other Kingdom," 1970; "The Executive Touch," 1973; "The Architect's Wife," 1974; "Foss," 1974; "The Rock Pool," 1975; "My Work in California," 1978; "The Valley of the Kilns," 1978.

Analysis

Characteristically, James B. Hall's short fiction is compressed, suggestive, and rises to psychological and/or mythic suggestion. Thus the stories bear rereading and have a long fictional "lifespan." With some accuracy, he has been called "One of America's most anthologized short story writers." If this is an assertion not open to verification, it still suggests high artistic quality and a high percentage of resonant, effective stories published regularly over the past twenty years. Structurally the stories are strong; scenically the stories are extremely "visual" and owe much to the influence of modern painters, especially the Expressionists. The poetic quality is closely associated with the highly wrought, poetic language. In certain early stories this language was rhetorical in places; in the middle and later stories the language is under absolute control. The uses of language are at one with a lofty concept of the short-story form. This multivalent concept of form is an obvious link to modern masters on the Continent.

The materials show range and variety. A half-dozen stories treat the artist, the writer's life in America ("The Gambler: A Portrait of the Writer," "The Claims Artist"); another group examines institutions such as the American academies or the world of business ("Inside a Budding Grove," "The Executive Touch"); still other stories recapture the author's formative years in the Midwest and in the United States Army. Of especial interest is a group of stories which deals with extreme situations: these stories present a world which is familiar but which is beyond precise identification ("God Cares, but Waits," "My Work in California"). Typical of this last and most complex group is the modern classic, "Us He Devours." In general, Hall's stories, novels, and poetry are of a piece. Taken together they represent a rich body of work which is generally underestimated at the present time in America. At the least, James B. Hall is one of the most accomplished writers working in the form today.

Major publications other than short fiction
  NOVELS: *Not by the Door*, 1954; *Racers to the Sun*, 1960; *Mayo Sergeant*, 1967.
  POETRY: *The Hunt Within*, 1973.

Wirt Williams

NANCY HALLINAN

Born: England

Principal short fiction

"The Fourth Dream," 1948; "Limbo," 1950; "Mr. Sweeney of Bagdad," 1955; "Fever of Unknown Origin," 1979; "Voting Day and the Art of Love," 1979; "Women in a Roman Courtyard," 1979; "Labor Day Saturday," 1980.

Analysis

Nancy Hallinan's stories are both contemporary and, at the same time, timeless. They deal with love and its complications: men and women, women and children, generations. Children speak up with piercing clarity; adolescents rebel in bewildered ignorance; adults fall in love in the language of poetry. Hallinan's vision of life is mixed. There is the tragedy of character and destiny ("Mr. Sweeney of Bagdad"), the comedic complications of adultery ("Fever of Unknown Origin"), and an impish humor ("Voting Day and the Art of Love"). Harding Lemay has written, "Miss Hallinan examines with wit and poetic insight the many masks which shield our vulnerable illusions about ourselves." Lionel Trilling has called her "A highly gifted writer" who has "grace, and an ingratiating wit, not merely of phrase but of perception and feeling . . . an unusual implication of emotional space." Orville Prescott has referred to her "mastery of language which adds an extra dimension through the suggestive magic of words."

Major publications other than short fiction

NOVELS: *Rough Winds of May*, 1955; *A Voice From the Wings*, 1965; *Night Swimmers*, 1976.

ABIGAIL ANN HAMBLEN

Born: Pennsylvania, 1916

Principal short fiction

"Speak, That I May See Thee," 1955; "The Cross," 1955; "Beloved and Most Kind-Hearted Friend," 1956; "The Father," 1956; "The Loveliest Season," 1956; "Pris," 1956; "The Vocation," 1956-1957; "Brahmin Belles Lettres," 1957; "The Afternoon of the Embroidery Club," 1958; "The Realm of Gold," 1958; "The Need Is for Heaven," 1958; "Love Game," 1958; "The Common Fact," 1959; "The Good Boy," 1959; "Happiness and Miss Grundmuller," 1960; "A Bad Day for Lloyd," 1960; "The Wedding Gown," 1961; "The Inheritance," 1961; "Invitation to a Ball," 1961; "The Parents," 1962; "Brother's Keeper," 1962; "Voice of the People," 1963; "The Bruised," 1964; "The Pal," 1967; "The Room," 1970.

Analysis

The work of Abigail Ann Hamblen is not wide in scope, but it is lighted with a pure sincerity. Hamblen writes of "unimportant" people and "average" people; she seldom deals in grotesques. She is incapable of depicting a hero. Her stories, however quietly told, are often shot through with passion—the passion of love, of envy, of grief, of frustration. Her people suffer in corners, as it were: there is no dramatic violence, yet their agony is often intense. For example, Hamblen frequently deals with adolescents, as in "Voice of the People," which shows the hurt rage of a son whose idolized father loses an election; or in "The Pal," which depicts the pain and feeling of guilt suffered by a youngster whose best friend is killed. "The Room" tells of a boy's terrible anquish at discovering his goddess has feet of clay. Although there is no sensationalism in Hamblen's fiction and it is unfashionably free of clinical sex, one is conscious that here is a writer who understands the drama and passion, the lusts and delights, that are part of every "normal" life. In her work she is saying that pathos and suffering, love and hate, are not limited to the "disadvantaged" any more than joy and serenity are the province of the well-to-do. She is saying simply that there is no such thing as a dull human life.

Major publications other than short fiction

NOVELS: *Agatha on Stage*, 1966; *Magic Summer*, 1967.

NONFICTION: *The New England Art of Mary E. Wilkins Freeman*, 1966; *Ruth Suckow*, 1979.

JOSEPH HANSEN

Born: South Dakota, 1923

Principal short fiction
"Surf," 1976; *The Dog & Other Stories*, 1979.

Analysis
The characters in Joseph Hansen's stories are survivors, not in the currently fashionable use of the word but with an implicit understanding that survival is a universal human condition. The events survived in the stories range from a slight operation to the loss of youth, the loss of hope, and the death of someone loved. Hansen's antitheses are the beautiful and the unbeautiful, the young and the old, not the male and the female. Homosexuality, as is true of his novels too, appears in most of the stories, not as crux of the drama but as background, like one of the human seasons. In *Enking*, with his sense of contemporary youthful mores which he employs melodramatically in his detective novels, Hansen presents the subtle interplay between an aging professor of English and an outrageous young visiting poet. In *The Bee*, the events being told, and even the main characters, a dead husband and a missing daughter, are offstage, underlining that Hansen's emotion is centered in what is missing, gone, what is being survived. *Mourner* is almost all loss, bewilderment, flight. A young boy escapes from the sorrow of his mother's death into a passionate interest in Indians. He releases an Indian prisoner from jail when he is staying in the sheriff's house. The final paragraphs, as the boy's life in a small prairie town comes to an end, give a source to the tone of voice in all Hansen's stories, a key to the author's understanding.

Major publications other than short fiction
NOVELS: *Fadeout*, 1970; *Death Claims*, 1973; *Troublemaker*, 1975; *Stranger to Himself*, 1977; *The Man Everybody Was Afraid Of*, 1978; *Skinflick*, 1979; *A Smile in His Lifetime*, 1981.
POETRY: *One Foot in the Boat*, 1977.

Donald Windham

DONALD HARINGTON

Born: Arkansas, 1935

Principal short fiction
"A Second Career," 1967; "Down in the Dumps," 1967; "Artificial Respiration," 1968.

Analysis
Donald Harington's stories, like his novels, subtly combine the everyday concreteness of reality and the philosophical themes fundamental to fiction. One such theme explores the voyeuristic desire to participate, from a distance, in the lives of others. This participation, the stories imply, often leads to a confusion in the characters' minds between the actual and the imagined. The fullest delineation of this theme is seen in "Artificial Respiration," where a man, like the one in "Down in the Dumps," lives his most meaningful existence in dreams and finds them nearly reality. Fiction, Harington maintains, is a double vision that can, at times, unite the real and the imagined. Its doubleness is seen both in plot—in the character confusing the actual and the dream and in his being at once observer and actor—and in language, especially in the duplicity of word play. The man in "Down in the Dumps" is metaphorically "in the dumps" because he suspects his wife of infidelity and literally "in the dumps" in order to spy on her by sorting through the debris of her life. It is the title, "Artificial Respiration," however, that epitomizes Harington's view of fiction. Artificial respiration, like fiction, is a man-made means, an art, of breathing new life, another life, into us. Its two bodies emblemize the reader and the writer, who, through the sharing of breath, of the Word, connect, momentarily at least, the dualities of human existence.

Major publications other than short fiction
NOVELS: *The Cherry Pit*, 1965; *Lightning Bug*, 1970; *Some Other Place, the Right Place*, 1972; *The Architecture of the Arkansas Ozarks*, 1975.

Larry Vonalt

CURTIS HARNACK

Born: Iowa, 1927

Principal short fiction
Under My Wings Everything Prospers, 1977; "Creating and Destroying," 1980; "A Tuscan Perspective," 1980.

Analysis
Writing in *Newsweek* (June 27, 1977) Robert Towers cites Curtis Harnack as being "among the few writers of the literary short story who see themselves as tellers of tales, willing to follow the evolutions of a situation *through time* until a real closure has been achieved. His best tales, though realistic, are in the vein of American Gothic, depicting lives pinched and contorted into grotesque postures within the puritanical confines of rural or small-town America. At his gentlest Harnack brings to mind the pathos of Sherwood Anderson and Willa Cather; but he is fully capable of Faulknerian horror as well. . . ." The short-story form figures prominently throughout his work, beginning with his first novel, *The Work of an Ancient Hand*, (1960), which is constructed out of interrelated stories with a single setting: a small town in Iowa. Both of his memoirs, *Persian Lions, Persian Lambs* (1965) and *We Have All Gone Away* (1973), are made up of a series of narrative personal essays joined by interlocking themes. George Garrett describes Harnack as "master of a modest, soft-spoken style, a gentle wit, and a sense of the rhythm and texture of many lives . . ." who possesses a "sensitive, imaginative capacity to create male and female characters who are wholly other than (it seems) himself."

Major publications other than short fiction
NOVELS: *The Work of an Ancient Hand*, 1960; *Love and Be Silent*, 1962; *Limits of the Land*, 1979;
NONFICTION: *Persian Lions, Persian Lambs*, 1965; *We Have All Gone Away*, 1973.

PENNY HARTER

Born: New York, 1940

Principal short fiction
"Mosaic of the Holy Place," 1978; "Weather," 1978; "Pomegranate," 1979; "The Tidal Wave Dream Baby," 1979; "Shadows," 1979; "Parakeet," 1980; "The Devils of Honesty," 1980; "Meat," 1980; "God's Virus," 1980.

Analysis
Penny Harter's stories range from the seemingly aimless musing of daydream, as in "Mosaic of the Holy Place," through stories in which a deadly realistic ordinariness traps the protagonist with nightmarish intensity (for example, "Shadows," "Meat"), to full-blown surrealistic nightmares. Of the latter, "Sacrifice" and "Fish Festival" demonstrate her ability to create a coherent world in fewer than a thousand words, and capitalize on our expectations with a sense of timing akin to Alfred Hitchcock's. These same tightly organized worlds expand to frame a myth in "God's Virus," or to give us a glimpse past Armageddon in the recently completed longer tale called "Games of the Wind," soon to be produced as a play by one of New Jersey's dynamic young professional theater organizations.

Once we accept the world of a Harter story, the action follows its only natural path, or so we feel, having finished reading; and the worlds in which she sets us, whether the middle-class suburban home of "Weather" and "Pomegranate" or the ocean beach of "The Tidal Wave Dream Baby" or the inner-city basement apartment of "Parakeet," convince, convince as utterly as any we might wake to in sweat or tears. As she said in a brief essay called "Why Write in the Eighties?," "The 'apocalypse' does not just come all at once. It comes in bite size pieces day by day. And we are swallowing it." Want to know what we are swallowing? Harter's stories are the ingredients label.

Major publications other than short fiction
POETRY: *House by the Sea*, 1976; *Used Poems*, 1978; *Lovepoems*, 1981.

William J. Higginson

GERALD HASLAM

Born: California, 1937

Principal short fiction
"The Trinket," 1966; "Chapter One," 1968; "Buck Hunt," 1972; "Hawk's Flight," 1972; "Rite of Passage," 1972; *Okies: Selected Stories*, 1973; "Wild Horses," 1973; "Marineman," 1973; "The Bard of California," 1973; "Wild Horses," 1975; "Someone Else's Life," 1975; "The Killing Pen," 1975; "Marineman," 1975; "Widder Maker," 1975; "Buck Hunt," 1976; "Dust," 1976; "Last Chance," 1976; "Home to America," 1976; "Chapters," 1976; "Survivors," 1976; "Happily Ever After," 1976; "Hawk's Flight," 1977; "The King of Skateland," 1977; "Home to America," 1977-1978; "The Prophet, or Virtue Unrewarded," 1978; "Dust," 1978; "Last Chance," 1978; "Man of the Year," 1978-1979; "The Daciano," 1979; "Flesh and Blood," 1980.

Analysis
Primarily a short-story writer, Gerald Haslam brings contemporary techniques and perceptions to material set in the American West. He writes about "the real West, actual situations and complications, not the fantasy West," developing characters as diverse as aging black cowboys, hippie revolutionaries, and urban winos. He has worked especially at converting oral literary patterns into writing, leading *Publishers Weekly* to observe, "Haslam has a real gift for dialect." Formally, his stories range from traditionally plotted to miasmic, for he seeks to unite subject and structure. Despite such diversity, Max Westbrook perceived a pattern in some of Haslam's stories: "Typically, Haslam begins with an innocent situation which catches the reader immediately, because of the remarkably concrete and effective style. Internal monologue, for example, is often used very skillfully to establish character and motivation while the plot continues to move along swiftly. Soon, . . . the threat of violence or evil arises. The threat will be mythic in character but not in personality. Haslam does not go to books or to other cultures to find a latent power: the threat of evil or violence is always home grown." Indeed, everything about Haslam's writing, save his willingness to experiment with form, is home grown, with a profound sense of place. Tom Pilkington called Haslam "a distinctive new voice in Western fiction," and asserted that "he is destined, I believe, to create a body of writing that will be recognized as a major achievement in our region's literature."

Major publications other than short fiction
NOVEL: *Masks*, 1976.
NONFICTION: *William Eastlake*, 1970; *Jack Shaefer*, 1976.

MARIANNE HAUSER

Born: France, 1910

Principal short fiction

"The Colonel's Daughter," 1948; "The Rubber Doll," 1951; *A Lesson in Music*, 1964; "Mimoun of the Mellah," 1966; "The Seersucker Suit," 1968.

Analysis

Regional diversity, "uniqueness of style," and refusal to identify with literary schools or cults make Marianne Hauser a maverick among story writers. Her short fiction, "structured, yet fluid," affects us cinematically. Her "offbeat characters, the truly contemporary complexities of her superimposition" address themselves to "a new generation trained to imagery by the film." Anaïs Nin compares the impact of Hauser's writing to the "erratic course of an emotional seismograph meticulously recorded, with all the shadings of a Bergman film." Attentive readers may discover that "a double lens was used, one for intricate close-ups, another for distance, range; and thus the personal and the symbolic are wedded." Interaction between men and women, dream and wakefulness are "carefully balanced. Marianne Hauser achieves sensitivity without sentimentality, irony without loss of humanity." Her portraits have "a crystalline transparency." Mysteriously, she folds "complete macrocosms" into small containers. Through haunting, multiform plots or themes, she weaves a spell where the comic and the tragic are part of the human drama, projecting details "almost as afterthoughts so the most astonishing events occur with a majestic calm as in a dream from which there can be no escape."

Major publications other than short fiction

NOVELS: *Monique*, 1934; *Shadow Play in India*, 1937; *Dark Dominion*, 1947; *The Choir Invisible*, 1958; *Prince Ishmael*, 1963; *The Talking Room*, 1976.

LESLIE WOOLF HEDLEY

Born: New Jersey, 1931

Principal short fiction
In the Beginning: The Tallest Jewish Basketball Player in the World.

Analysis
The short story is an art of condensing the essential. Leslie Woolf Hedley creates short fiction using every possible technical magic to communicate human and cultural paradox; but newness for display is mere consumerism. He employs art of the sentence to explore the human condition on various levels. Every line may be a scalpel cutting through the norm of banality. Satire is a necessary instrument, a microscope under which one enlarges the nakedness of people acting upon people. Black humor must bite to be effective. To entertain is not enough. Plot is what people do or do not do. Words become electric current and tonality, and characters exhibit themselves shamelessly as acts of selfish free will. In this, Hedley uses the heuristic principle. He smells Buchenwalds around us, and refuses to mask that reality. Most people are stereotypes without an honest mirror. Some of these teeth-gritting characters people his stories intentionally. The universe consists of clichés which are the counterfeit of exchange. Hedley's prose structure is built to house his view of existence. He wants to render truth and terror of his time. Life is a lament, a grotesque shriek day or night. Hedley shows the triumph of injustice, inhumanity, power, and money. Critics suggest that his work makes people uncomfortable. He asks: "What kind of people?" Some of his work has been censored or blacklisted. Hedley still insists upon being free from formal institutions and political sects.

STEVE HELLER

Born: Oklahoma, 1949

Principal short fiction

"The Red Dust of Lanai," 1977; "The Rainbow Syndrome," 1977; "A Matter of Style," 1978; "The Auteur," 1978; "The Summer Game," 1978; "The Player and the Giant," 1979; "Postcard from Lahaina," 1980; "The Rainbow Man," 1980.

Analysis

Steve Heller's published stories are set in the Hawaiian Islands, where he lived for a year, studying literature and writing, but, within this common *milieu*, Heller's fictions treat a rich variety of social and psychological types—the young and old, simple and sophisticated, male and female. Beyond this versatility of characterization, his stories differ interestingly with respect to style, tone, and theme. Steve Heller's craft reveals an accomplished talent, one still emerging and developing in the direction of ever-greater complexity and precision. "The Auteur" and "The Player and the Giant" exhibit Heller's ability to make the restrained employment of fantasy yield insights relevant to the real world. In the former story, the metaphor of film (and the bizarre character of the film freak, who slips in and out of the narrative) stands for the evasive substance of human memory and understanding; in the latter, the story's surreal premise—that the Pacific Ocean has suddenly gone dry—triggers the symbolic depiction of individual human striving for self-realization. The most excellent "The Summer Game" portrays an ordeal of maturation in the context of the annual sugar cane harvest. In "A Matter of Style" and "Postcard from Lahaina," Heller flourishes lyric description and delicate sensibility in the evocation of troubled human psychologies. Collectively, these stories of Hawaii present a concrete and particular sociological comment, their themes attaining a universality and profundity transcending locale. Heller's achievements argue that his storyteller's craft is not limited by time or place.

Gordon Weaver

JIM HEYNEN

Born: Iowa, 1940

Principal short fiction
The Man Who Kept Cigars in His Cap, 1979.

Analysis
The short short stories in *The Man Who Kept Cigars in His Cap* have been compared to the fiction of Sherwood Anderson. Although the sensitivity to small-town and rural American scenes invites this comparison, Jim Heynen's whimsy is more akin to Mark Twain and his treatment of human foibles to Geoffrey Chaucer, while elements of the macabre are reminiscent of some of the darker fairy tales from Europe. Tales, anecdotes, fables, legends, prose poems, allegories, parables—the short short stories in *The Man Who Kept Cigars in His Cap* hint at a variety of native American, American, and European oral forms, often deceptively familiar and yet defiantly evasive in both structure and sentiment. As a *Booklist* review put it,

> The time-honored art of storytelling revives in Heynen's country vignettes. His earthy wit, deadpan deviltry, and love for the eccentric prod the unique 'character' locked inside everyday people. . . . Marvel at these come-along riddles, come-uppances, leg pullers, fables, tricks and surprises, sad secrets and tall tales . . . bawdy, down-on-the-farm read-alouds.

Major publications other than short fiction
POETRY: *Maedra Poems*, 1974; *Notes From Custer*, 1976; *The Funeral Parlor*, 1976; *How the Sow Became a Goddess*, 1977.

DICK HIGGINS

Born: England, 1938

Principal short fiction
"Tender Tinderslide," 1969; *Legends & Fishnets*, 1976; *Cat Alley*, 1976; "Appearances and Disappearance," 1977; *The Epickall Quest of the Brothers Dichtung and Other Outrages*, 1978; "The Truth About Sadie Mee," 1979.

Analysis
Dick Higgins' characters exist in the environment of his language, which is highly unconventional (often composed by chance operations, like the music of John Cage) and strongly pictorial in the sense of a mimesis imitating what the mind sees or knows rather than what it has been or what it remembers— thus his characteristic strings of participles in place of the indicative mood of verbs. Characters, however, rather than metaphysical statements or themes or arguments, are what one is left with after reading a Higgins story. The focus is, evidently, on building an appropriate language environment for the character, but not on environment-building for its own sake. Events occur— the narrative element is always present—but they are subservient to the process of revelation of character, and are thus presented at breakneck speed in order to get on with the discovery of the character and the environment. The American Library Association's *Booklist* (July 15, 1977) states, "Higgins is one of the best and most original interpreters of language writing today."

Major publications other than short fiction
NOVELS: *A Book About Love & War & Death, Canto One*, 1965; *A Book About Love & War & Death, Cantos Two and Three*, 1969; *A Book About Love & War & Death*, 1972.

POETRY: *foew&ombwhnw*, 1969; *amigo*, 1972; *For Eugene in Germany*, 1973; *Modular Poems*, 1975; *classic plays*, 1976; *Everyone Has Sher Favorite (His or Hers)*, 1977; *some recent snowflakes (and other things)*, 1979; *The Colors/I Colori*, 1980.

NONFICTION: *What Are Legends*, 1960; *Towards the 1970's*, 1969; *Gesehen, Gehört und Verstanden*, 1973; *George Herbert's Pattern Poems: In Their Tradition*, 1977; *A Dialectic of Centuries: Notes Towards a Theory of the New Arts*, 1978.

Camille Gordon

JAMAKE HIGHWATER

Born: Montana, 1942

Principal short fiction
"Golden Gate Park," 1977; "The Sweet Grass Lives On," 1979; "Imaginary New Mexico, 1925," 1980; "The Ancient Ones," 1980; "Gallup, New Mexico," 1980.

Analysis
Native American concepts of time and personality are alien to classical/Western precepts but remarkably similar to certain post-Joycean elements in prose, in which "reality" is holistic and pluralistic. On the other hand, the poetic imagery so inherent in Indian languages is highly remote from most contemporary Western prose style. Jamake Highwater has attempted to produce a metaphoric language in English which conveys some of the focus, feeling, and essential mentality of the primal background of a Blackfoot and Eastern Cherokee Indian. The result, according to John Gardner, is

> a clean, clear voice, a story-telling method that's inextricably ancient and ultramodern. The parts of (Highwater's) stories, that is character, setting and action, are so mysteriously fused into one driving force that one is tempted to give up the modern word, storyteller, and go back to the grand old Indian word, legender.

Major publications other than short fiction
NOVELS: *Mick Jagger: The Singer, Not the Song*, 1973; *Anpao: An American Indian Odyssey*, 1977; *Journey to the Sky*, 1978; *The Sun, He Dies*, 1980.
NONFICTION: *Indian America: A Cultural and Travel Guide*, 1975; *Song From the Earth: American Indian Painting*, 1976; *Ritual of the Wind: North American Indian Dances and Music*, 1977; *Many Smokes, Many Moons: A Chronology of American Indian History Through Indian Art*, 1978; *Dance: Rituals of Experience*, 1978; *The Sweet Grass Lives On: Fifty Contemporary North American Indian Artists*, 1980; *The Primal Mind: Vision and Reality in Indian America*, 1980-1981.

CATHERINE HILLER

Born: New York, 1946

Principal short fiction
"Chesterlyme Rushes," 1976; "The February Fantasy," 1976; "The Perfect Aphrodisiac," 1979; "Monogamy: The Last Taboo," 1979; "Sexenders®," 1980.

Analysis
Catherine Hiller's short stories are sensuous, witty, and "very well-written"—praise which she often laments. "The highest qualities in fiction are perception and compassion: I don't want to be known for my style." Nevertheless, the style is graceful, rhythmic, seductive. Hiller's stories often focus on a single theme—courage, sickness, love, memory. The protagonists arrive at a real or fancied understanding through a series of events; patterns are, perhaps, perceived. Recurrent visits sometimes structure the stories: Simone's trips to the isolated dump in "Chesterlyme Rushes," Gerbson's visits to his dentist in "N_2O," and Carola and Tom's marital dramas on the old courts in back of the high school in "Tennis Mania." Her main characters tend to be intelligent, quizzical, and over-sexed. Hiller has written a number of satires, mainly sexual in subject and chaste in tone. These pieces, which have a strong narrative line, satirize current social trends and forms. "The Perfect Aphrodisiac," a spoof on LSD, is written like an academic journal article; "Monogamy: The Last Taboo" is a term paper of the future, complete with teacher's comments; "Sexenders®," which mocks behavior modification, begins with an advertisement urging people to come to an Introductory Class so they can eradicate lust from their lives. In recent stories, such as "Monkey Suit" and "Nursing Mother," Hiller seems to be moving toward a simpler style and greater emotional power. In all of her fiction, she aspires to lyric precision and to the truths which hide in the clutter of ordinary lives.

Major publications other than short fiction
NOVEL: *An Old Friend from High School*, 1978.

GEORGE HITCHCOCK

Born: Oregon, 1914

Principal short fiction
Notes of the Siege Year, 1974; *Collected Stories & Poems*, 1980.

Analysis
The work of a writer who is primarily a poet, George Hitchcock's stories are remarkable for their wit, intensity of visual imagery, and variety of psychological portraiture. Many are markedly surrealist in both source and structure.

Major publications other than short fiction
NOVEL: *Another Shore*, 1971.
PLAYS: *The Counterfeit Rose*, 1976; *The Devil Comes to Wittenberg*, 1980.
POETRY: *Poems & Prints*, 1962; *Tactics of Survival*, 1964; *The Dolphin with a Revolver in Its Teeth*, 1968; *A Ship of Bells*, 1969; *The Rococo Eye*, 1970; *Lessons in Alchemy*, 1976; *The Piano Beneath the Skin*, 1978; *Mirror on Horseback*, 1978.

GEARY HOBSON

Born: Arkansas, 1941

Principal short fiction
"An Attitude of Dignity"; "The c. o."; "Marlene."

Analysis

Geary Hobson's fiction reflects both his Native American background, as in "Marlene," "The Last of the Ofos," and "Daughters of Lot," and his experiences in the United States Marines, as in "The c. o." and "The Odor of Dead Fish." An important theme in his work appears to be the alienation, and even madness, often found in many aspects of city life, as in "An Attitude of Dignity," "Kyrie Eleison!," "Marlene," and "A Christmas Story." Alienation of a different sort plays an extremely important role in Hobson's "The Last of the Ofos," in which the principal character is the last speaker of his tribal language (and, in a more complete sense, the last member of his tribe) who, when confronted with the constant demands of anthropologists and linguists, retreats to the point that he remains completely silent for the last ten years of his life. This theme, which the author calls the "Ishi theme" (after the famous Yahi Indian who was "discovered" in California in 1911), appears in a strong form in Hobson's novel-in-progress, *The Desert*. Hobson has stated that he deeply resents the cultural blinders of many non-Indians who continually think of Native Americans as "creatures of the nineteenth century, and earlier," and he tries to combat these damaging images by dealing with Native Americans in a contemporary world.

Major publications other than short fiction

POETRY: *The Road Where the People Cried*, 1980; *Deer Hunting & Other Poems*, 1981.

EDWARD D. HOCH

Born: New York, 1930

Principal short fiction

The Judges of Hades, 1971; *City of Brass*, 1971; *The Spy and the Thief*, 1971; *The Thefts of Nick Velvet*, 1978.

Analysis

Edward Hoch is one of the few American authors today who makes his living almost entirely through the publication of short fiction. Although he has written every type of crime-suspense story, including some set in the past and in the future, he is probably best known among mystery readers for his detective stories built around several distinct series characters. Captain Leopold, a middle-aged police detective in an unnamed Connecticut city, has appeared in more than sixty stories, including Hoch's Edgar-winner, "The Oblong Room," chosen as the best short story of 1967 by Mystery Writers of America. The most popular of his characters is undoubtedly Nick Velvet, a thief who accepts assignments to steal unusual and valueless objects, and generally becomes a detective during the course of each adventure. Hoch's earliest series character, Simon Ark, is a mystical sleuth who solves crimes which seem to involve the supernatural. Other series characters include Jeffery Rand, a retired British cipher expert, and Dr. Sam Hawthorne, a country doctor who solves locked-room mysteries in New England during the 1920's. Although character development is often limited by their length, Hoch's detective stories are intricately plotted tales, often introducing unique variations on the classic mystery themes. His writing style is simple and somewhat cinematic, perhaps accounting for the fact that more than a dozen of his stories have been successfully adapted for television.

Major publications other than short fiction

NOVELS: *The Shattered Raven*, 1969; *The Transvection Machine*, 1971; *The Fellowship of the Hand*, 1973; *The Frankenstein Factory*, 1975.

ROLAINE HOCHSTEIN

Born: New York

Principal short fiction
"Child of Delight," 1966; "Some Girls Like Gray Dresses," 1967; "The Affirming Flame of Ardith Manners," 1969; "What Kind of Man Cuts His Finger Off?," 1972; "Sinclair's Wife," 1972; "True Blue and the Seven Dropouts," 1973; "The New Boy," 1974; "Charge!," 1974; "In a Very Low Voice, Words That Can Hardly Be Understood," 1975; "Emile Zola and His Friend, Paul Cezanne," 1975; "Cousin Della," 1978; "The Man Who Wanted Things Nice," 1979; "The Mother," 1979; "I Play Tennis," 1980.

Analysis
Rolaine Hochstein's stories are oblique, carefully composed, vividly set, and told in voices as varied as the subjects. Often, as in many paintings by Degas and his followers, the main action is seen through the eyes of an audience in the forefront. Often there is an offstage narrator who tells the story from a point of view that sets up a tension against the reader. For example, the impassioned narrator in "Emile Zola and His Friend, Paul Cezanne" repeatedly announces that he is being carried away by his imagination; the narrator of "What Kind of Man Cuts His Finger Off?" reminds the reader that she is only guessing at the facts of her story. Likewise, in the first-person stories the "I" is an active character who is revealed as much in the telling as by the events of the story. The dilettante housewife in "David Kissed Me" and the reluctant editor in "The Mother" are both emotionally threatened by the people they try to help—the former, an alcoholic poet and the latter, the tragic mother of a suicide. The experience of life as "thin ice" both physically and morally is a theme that pervades the work. In the first published story ("Child of Delight") and a recent one ("The Man Who Wanted Things Nice"), the events of a lifetime (and half a lifetime) lead to disaster: both the upper-middle-class darling and the lower-class street kid who becomes a gangster have taken easy ways, unquestioningly following a course laid before them. Both fools in paradise are unprepared for the abrupt realities that interrupt their joyride. "Cousin Della," on the other hand, steers her course so carefully to avoid unpleasant realities that she ends up in a closet life. The headlong teenager in "The New Boy" might be taking her first lesson in "reality avoidance." There is struggle and cruelty in all of these stories, and also human affection and a lot of edgy laughter.

Major publications other than short fiction
NOVEL: *Stepping Out*, 1977.

JULIUS HORWITZ

Born: Ohio, 1920

Principal short fiction
The City, 1953.

Analysis
New York—the city that is America and the world in the second half of the twentieth century—has been at the heart of the New York short stories and the philosophical novels of Julius Horwitz. There is no tradition for the philosophical novel in American writing; and in Europe, the novels of Horwitz have been acclaimed as philosophical novels of action. Horwitz's World War II novel, *Can I Get There By Candlelight* (1964), is viewed by critics in England and America as one of the outstanding novels to come out of the war. Horwitz's examination of marriage in *The Married Lovers* (1974) was given a major review in the London *Times Literary Supplement.* Although found outside the tradition in America, Horwitz's novel *Natural Enemies* (1975) was read in Europe as a major philosophical novel of action. Always employed at a nine to five job, writing his novels in the evening, after work, on weekends, drawing on subjects that haunt and confuse modern man, Horwitz has captured in his work the deepest fears and the most sublime hopes of modern man.

Major publications other than short fiction
NOVELS: *The Inhabitants*, 1960; *Can I Get There By Candlelight*, 1964; *The W. A. S. P.*, 1967; *The Diary of A. N.*, 1970; *The Married Lovers*, 1974; *Natural Enemies*, 1975; *Landfall*, 1977; *The Best Days*, 1980.

DAVID HUDDLE

Born: Virginia, 1942

Principal short fiction
"One Thing I Can't Stand," 1973; "Carlton Morris, His Wife Julie, and the Fragmentation of Contemporary Life," 1973; *A Dream with No Stump Roots in It*, 1975; "Gartley's Door," 1976; "Underwater Spring," 1978; "The Undesirable," 1978; "Sketching Hannah," 1978; "Poison Oak," 1979; "Dirge Notes," 1979; "Double Zero," 1979;. "The Wedding Storm," 1979.

Analysis
David Huddle's stories are conventional narratives written in clear, direct, occasionally graceful prose. His early pieces were mostly about the Vietnam War, although they had little to do with combat; his later ones have been strongly reminiscent accounts of small-town family life. Romance, sex, and marriage are also among Huddle's thematic concerns. The development of his fiction has been toward more sophisticated characterization, less violence, and more lyrical prose. His strongest story to date is probably the novella-length "The Undesirable," published in the Winter, 1978, issue of *Ploughshares*.

Major publications other than short fiction
POETRY: *Paper Boy*, 1979.

ALYCE INGRAM

Born: Minnesota, 1914

Principal short fiction
"Snow," 1973; "The Circle of Love," 1976; *Blue Horses*, 1976; "to March 15th Inclusion," 1977.

Analysis
Alyce Ingram's short stories deal intricately with interfamily relationships. She has an uncanny ability to assume the perspective not only of the women in her stories, but also that of the men and that of the children. The result is a compounding of insights and intuitions leading to a deeper understanding of the roles played within the family structure.

John Bennett

DONNA IPPOLITO

Born: Illinois, 1945

Principal short fiction

"Secrets," 1974; *Erotica*, 1975; "Solitudes," 1978; "The Shaman," 1977-1978; "The Gardener," 1977-1978; "The Builder," 1977-1978; "The Seeker," 1977-1978.

Analysis

Donna Ippolito's short fiction is concerned more with language and its power to evoke, stir, embody what is not yet fully known than with plot and character. Her forms evolve from the exploration of image and language rhythms as well as the attempt to create an intensity of experience in which the reader participates (as opposed to allowing the reader to remain detached, analytical, observing). She attempts to extend language beyond the mundane, narrative function into a realm where language itself becomes the organ of discovery, of *knowing*. Her themes very often touch on the erotic in a unique fashion. Ippolito broadly defines the erotic as a state of intense relationship rather than limiting it to the experience of personal sexuality. She uses sexuality as a metaphor for an "erotic" approach to experience itself. In her repeated explorations of this theme, particularly in *Erotica*, she seeks to create a language for states of being that generally have been considered either beyond the power of language or which have been completely vulgarized by a pornographic use of language.

Major publications other than short fiction

NONFICTION: *Uprising of the 20,000*, 1980.

JOHN H. IRSFELD

Born: Minnesota, 1937

Principal short fiction
"They Come in Threes," 1969; "Ambivalence Hardy Fire," 1974; "Stop, Rewind, and Play," 1974; "Finders Keepers," 1975; "Have You Knocked on Cleopatra?," 1976; "The Horse Fountain," 1976; "The Tourist," 1976; "A Rusted Lantern," 1978.

Analysis
Terse, sparse, clean, in a vein often reminiscent of Ernest Hemingway, John Irsfeld's style mirrors the philosophic intent of his fiction. His characters, cast-offs, society's unwanted, must act in a world not so much naturalistic, but one exorcised of even the cultural props that the modernist antihero still has to cling to. Stripped of reality touchstones, the crutch of close relationship, the chimera of success, and the tangible perspective of things which his predominantly desert settings disallow, in Irsfeld's fiction we find ourselves as readers involved with characters on the cutting edge of being with the ultimate question of existence before us: why act? Irsfeld shows us that the cause is inherent in the condition itself—of being—of being human—even a human on the fringe of his society. Irsfeld's characters, like Ambivalence Hardy Fire, the black soldier in the story of the same name, "Do their best." There is no Achilles among Irsfeld's menagerie of outcasts; thus, their persistence glows all the more heroic, and we know that once again a writer has accepted William Faulkner's challenge: there is reason to endure.

Major publications other than short fiction
NOVELS: *Coming Through*, 1975; *Little Kingdoms*, 1976.
POETRY: "Bach Upon Waking," 1973; "For a Place Called *Beer*," 1977.

Robert Dunkle

JOSEPHINE JACOBSEN

Born: Canada, 1908

Principal short fiction

A Walk with Raschid, 1978; "At the Edge of the Sea," 1978; "The Gesture," 1978; "The Sound of Shadows," 1979; "The Ring of Kerry," 1980; "Sunday Morning," 1980.

Analysis

Josephine Jacobsen's fiction can perhaps best be described by pointing out what she has not done. She has not involved her work with any clique, school, or group. She has tried not to force any story into an overall concept of "how to write fiction," when it should be left to create organically its individual style. She has not been content to repeat what she has already accomplished, or to establish any stance which would limit the flexibility of discovery. She has not confused technical innovation, however interesting, with originality or intensity. Jacobsen has not used fiction as a social or political lever; nor conceded that any subject matter, any vocabulary, any approach, or any form is of itself unsuitable to the uses of fiction. Her chief energizing concern is with the human character—its devastations, maneuveurs, emotions, great and mean adventures, effects on others, and breathtaking changes. Fundamentally, she is not interested in writing fiction which ignores identity or is indifferent to communication. Nancy Sullivan, writing in *New Letters*, says, "Jacobsen's language is always perfectly wedded to her subject matter and to the circumstances of her diversified characters. It is controlled, yet emotionally vivid, real yet surreal, factual and informative, yet provocative and resonant . . . Josephine Jacobsen is a master story teller, who writes in a masterly way."

Major publications other than short fiction

POETRY: *The Human Climate*, 1962; *The Animal Inside*, 1966; *The Shade-Seller: New & Selected Poems*, 1974.

NONFICTION: *The Testament of Samuel Beckett*, 1966; *Ionesco & Genet, Playwrights of Silence*, 1968.

DAVID JAUSS

Born: Minnesota, 1951

Principal short fiction

"The Post Office," 1975; "October Reunion," 1976; "A Document Concerning Apotheosis," 1976; "The Package," 1978; "Gentle Reader," 1978; "Sister Anastasia's Birthday," 1979.

Analysis

At their best, David Jauss's stories play a game of chicken with melodrama—they come as close to crashing as possible without actually doing it. Their subjects are people who are living "on the edge," where what matters is most dangerously apparent: a husband and wife in the midst of a destructive quarrel and an even more destructive reconciliation; a nun awaiting a death that will not come, no matter how much she desires it; a sixteenth century monk acquiescing to a pagan ceremony that makes him a god; and so on. The stories vary as widely as their principal characters. While other writers seem obsessed with finding voices they can patent as their own, Jauss wants to find his characters' voices. For him, fiction is an exploration of the alien, the other. Hence the stories differ in style, form, content, and theme. Some are "traditional," some "experimental," and some—most notably "A Document Concerning Apotheosis"—are both. In the civil war between traditionalists and experimentalists, Jauss is somewhat of a double agent, but not out of indecision or confusion. Rather, he seems to be trying to fuse the best qualities of both approaches to the craft of fiction.

JOE JOHNSON

Born: New York, 1940

Principal short fiction
If I Ride This Train.

Analysis
Joe Johnson's collected short fiction, *If I Ride This Train*, demonstrates the basic sources and rich complexities of Afro-American linguistic rhythms. His work is primarily intended to be read aloud. Currently his short stories are being published over the air (WBAI listener-sponsored radio in New York City). Since the ear as well as the eye is necessary to alert Johnson's audience to the culture (myth, logic, and ethos) of his characters, the stories are scored in poetic forms. The characters who people his work are revealed through their language, a conscious dreamscape of the Afro-American experience, which taps the collective unconscious of universal myth and folklore.

Major publications other than short fiction
POETRY: *At the West End*, 1976; *Hot*, 1977; *Rhythm and Blues*, 1977; *Tight*, 1978; *Radio*, 1981.

THOMAS JUVIK

Born: Washington, 1947

Principal short fiction

"Loitering in Lodi," 1972; "The Family," 1973; "High Tide," 1974; "What You Have to Be," 1975; "Falling Dreams," 1976; "Repossessions," 1976; "The Killing," 1977; "Accidents," 1979; "As You Can Imagine," 1980.

Analysis

Although his stories have yet to appear in a collection or as chapters in a published novel, it is clear from the few stories Thomas Juvik has had published that he is building toward something larger in the Faulknerian sense of creating a microcosm. In general, Juvik's stories capture a changing America of the 1960's and the dispirited America of the 1970's, revealing that there is nothing that lends itself so wholly to an examination of this America as a traditional American family in flux. Although his protagonists often assume a strong, traditional posture surrounded by all the trappings of masculinity, they are kept off balance by the shifting values of social change. Somehow there is adaptation and understanding, and the essential goodness of the individual survives because Juvik's characters are, indeed, survivors. One comes away from such stories appreciating the short story as it was meant to be written in America, wondering if Ernest Hemingway or John Steinbeck or John Dos Passos might not have written it this way if they had watched American life evolve through Woodstock, Vietnam, and Watergate. Jubik's stories find their strength not only in their characters but also in their dialogue, which is real and distinctive. Like his mentor, Jack Cady, Juvik works toward the lean and powerful phrasing with a resounding and clear voice. To those expecting the next literary Renaissance to issue from the Pacific Northwest, it is not entirely unexpected that "one of Washington's most promising young writers" will be there.

ROBERTA KALECHOFSKY

Born: New York, 1931

Principal short fiction

"To Light a Candle," 1958; "Monkey on My Back," 1972; "An Apostrophe to the Long Dark Street," 1973; "The Wind," 1973; "My Mother's Story," 1974; "1492," 1974-1975; "Cry, Baby," 1975; *La Hoya*, 1976; *Solomon's Wisdom*, 1978.

Analysis

The distinguishing theme of Roberta Kalechofsky's stories is the interpenetration of history and religion. She frequently creates characters whose religious consciousness, not necessarily schooled, shape their personalities and actions and create the motivating tension in the story. In a larger and more specific context, she is concerned with Christian and Jewish thought and modes of consciousness as they express themselves historically. Many of her stories assiduously cultivate a "historical climate" or era, and her writing is rich in the evocation of historical detail. A subliminal irony underlies her juxtaposition of the "past" with contemporary times, however, because, from the point of view of religious consciousness, all time is present time: for example, the Crucifixion or the Exodus. Religious time is not in harmony with historical time, but neither is it irrelevant to it. Thus, it would be wrong to regard her as a historical writer in the traditional sense. She is concerned with explicating our double consciousness of time, expressed through history and religion, and her techniques are the seemingly disparate methods of realism and allegory. She renders the realities of time and place, even to the point of using maps and trail routes, but an allegorical intention lies behind the carefully constructed social and geographical reality. Great literature, she believes, combines social scope, density of detail, historical reality, and magnificent language, qualities which pervade the best of her writing. Her stories have been included in several prestigious anthologies, and Kirk Polking of Writers' Digest has described her ". . . as possibly one of the best writers in the country."

Major publications other than short fiction

NOVELS: *Justice, My Brother*, 1973; *Stephen's Passion*, 1975; *Orestes in Progress*, 1975; *Bodmin, 1349*, 1980.

FRANZ KAMIN

Born: Wisconsin, 1941

Principal short fiction

Ann Margret Loves You & Other Psychotopological Diversions, 1980.

Analysis

The collection *Ann Margret Loves You & Other Psychotopological Diversions* spans about ten years and contains a wide variety of prose works as well as a few poems. None of these works can absolutely be viewed as "fiction" because Franz Kamin has had little interest in inventing characters in order to have them run around inside neat little plots. Thus, the only "character" exposed is that of the author, and the only "plot" is that of his own experience (which he may or may not be inventing as he moves along). Structurally, the pieces are often in the form of "confessional abstracts" wherein the emotional, conceptual, and physical bric-a-brac of one's life is used as construction material in the formation of some abstract structure which on occasion may also have a musical or mathematical base. Because of the fact that some of the stories (which appear initially to be quite different from one another) eventually intersect in areas of the same concern, they might be viewed as cells from some larger work not yet in evidence. Several of the pieces (such as "A Ritual Embedding of the Spider's Risk into non-Hausdorff M-Space" and "KCCK") were originally constructed as programming devices for various musical and/or multimedia works. These segments tend to stand alone as prose or poetry, even though their auditory, visual, and performance aspects are not available to the reader. In general this collection represents Kamin's more conventional side.

BERNARD KAPLAN

Born: New York, 1944

Principal short fiction

Prisoners of This World, 1970; *Obituaries*, 1976.

Analysis

Bernard Kaplan's short fiction is experimental but not self-referential, difficult but not obscure. Kaplan aims at that fictional territory where opposites collide and then reconcile. Humor and terror, fantasy and reality, colloquialisms and eloquence blend in each of his stories to produce particular worlds. Kaplan's stories are not novelistic. They offer the story form as a world complete unto itself, a world which offers by suggestion what the novel offers by minute delineation. Often, Kaplan's stories cover whole lives rather than moments in time. These lives are most often those of self-obsessed characters living in universes where private vision collides with or even eclipses the "normal" world. Kaplan's characters run the spectrum from "uneducated" workers to overeducated educators. For each of these people Kaplan attempts to craft a fictional form which correlates with the reality revealed.

Kaplan's stories do not render explicit judgment on the private worlds of their characters. It is clear, however, from the great grief that befalls most of his characters that Kaplan's vision, despite his humor, is a bleak one. Sometimes his characters manage to reach heavens, literal or otherwise. These heavens offer little relief from earthly hells. Sometimes his people attempt to bury themselves in permanent hells. These characters find that heaven itself cannot be easily shaken from the human experience, that heaven itself is part of the baggage we bear.

BEL KAUFMAN

Born: Germany

Principal short fiction

"La Tigresse," 1948; "Episode," 1949; "The Life and Death of James Philpotts," 1949; "A Present for Joel," 1949; "The Grass Is Greener," 1954; "From a Teacher's Wastebasket," 1962.

Analysis

Although Bel Kaufman is known as a novelist, both of her novels originated as short stories, *Up the Down Staircase* (1965) grew out of a short story in the *Saturday Review*, which a publisher asked her to expand. In *Love, Etc.* (1979), the novel-within-a-novel is composed of brief vignettes that can stand alone as short stories. (While she was writing this book, an irrepressible minor character kept taking over; she had to pluck her from the manuscript and star her in a separate short story before she would play her assigned role in the novel.) Kaufman began as a short-story writer; it was her training for her craft. In Russia, where she spent her childhood, she was brought up on the short stories of Anton Chekhov, who has remained her model. Kaufman's stories are short, tinged with irony, and basically sad. They are stories of character under stress, ending in a dart of insight, a moment of illumination suggesting a larger truth about the human condition than does the apparent story itself. She must select, from an infinite number of choices, the exact word, the evocative phrase, and the telling detail. Kaufman's writing consists of rewriting: a paragraph into a sentence, a sentence into a word. Before she writes her first line, she knows what her last line is going to be; and she swims toward that line as toward a life-saving raft, with an inexorable breast stroke, pushing everything extraneous aside. To make the reader feel at the end of the story both surprise and recognition is the challenge—and the reward.

Major publications other than short fiction

NOVELS: *Up the Down Staircase*, 1965; *Love, Etc.*, 1979.
POETRY: "Elegy Written in an English Classroom," 1966; "Epitaph," 1975.

TAMARA KENNELLY

Born: Illinois, 1946

Principal short fiction
"A Little Family Room," 1975; "Nails," 1975; "The Third Wheel," 1977;
The Woman Who Was Glass Inside, 1980.

Analysis
Vigorous and densely woven, Tamara Kennelly's stories explore the tensions and cushions of family life in a sometimes grotesque pinball-machine world that flashes, rocks, tilts, and sometimes lifts the characters beyond themselves. Striving always to penetrate the human heart, her prose opens inward through the cracked mirror of the self. Moving by way of indirection, it explores the chameleon, serpent, and peacock in the self; the manliness of a girlish heart; the incursion of the will on the boundary of the other; and the leap of love. Composed of sections that are often nonsequential, her stories use textured language, incremental imagery, layering techniques, and juxtaposition of scenes on a cancerous yet beautiful urban canvas.

Grenfall Fields

JASCHA KESSLER

Born: New York, 1929

Principal short fiction

An Eyptian Bondage & Other Stories, 1967; "A Blessing," 1974; "Casanova at Seventeen: Some Pages from His Bronx Diaries, May 1948," 1976; "Corinth," 1977; "Epiphenomenology," 1977; "Transmigration I," 1977; "Transmigration II," 1977; "Transmigration III," 1977; "Existentialism," 1977; "Poetry I," 1977; "Poetry II," 1977; "Poetry III," 1977; "Poetry IV," 1977; "James Joyce," 1977; "William Faulkner," 1977; "T. S. Eliot," 1977; Ezra Pound," 1977; "A Tourist," 1977; "Saul of Tarsus," 1977; "Bacchae," 1977; "Orpheus," 1977; "The Bird Cage," 1977; "Valley," 1978; "Eschatology," 1978; "Medea," 1978; "Proteus," 1978; "Sphinx," 1978; "Jacob," 1978; "Mentor," 1978-1979; "Maya," 1979; "The Young Muse," 1979; "The Old Muse," 1979; *Bearing Gifts*, 1979; "Genius Loci," 1979; "Cheiron," 1979; "Asklapios," 1979; "An Eden of Sorts: 1948," 1979; "Aeaea," 1979; "Rhadamanthys," 1979; "The Foundation," 1979; "Ikaros," 1979; "Apocalypse II," 1979; "Poetry V," 1979; "Perceval," 1979; "Exodus," 1979; "Teiresias," 1979; "Poetry," 1980; "Afrodite," 1980; "Esau," 1980; "Courtly Love," 1980; *Transmigrations*, 1980; *Death Comes for the Behaviorist & Other Stories*, 1980.

Analysis

A review in the *Los Angeles Times* states that Jascha Kessler "is both the experiment and the experimenter . . . it is a measure of Kessler's work that he never offers the easy prescriptions of instant solutions. His experience is individual; his evocation universal. . . . The secret theme is love, not the facile illusion of love which salves and redeems, but the complex connection between one human and another, man and woman, man past and woman past, parent and child, teacher and student. Redemption, salvation, change, growth are never easy matters." One can say that his stories almost always present themselves through a rich, harmonic, vivid, exactly detailed, and yet translucent prose narrative; his characters are people who have walked through our lives, in city and country, and who speak as individuated persons in the language of ordinary experience. Almost all of his work, the stories that are novella length, and those that are as short as prose poems, from 1952 on, are also always resonant with history: there is an aura about each story that shimmers with archetypes, with the recurrent lives of mythical personae, both pagan and prehistoric, as well as Judeo-Christian—although such flickering lights are not always visible, even to the reader sensitized to James Joyce's methods. Kessler's narratives are, for lack of better words, transcendental and numinous, mysterious at the same time as they are experienced easily in the American here and now.

Major publications other than short fiction
NOVEL: *Rapid Transit*, 1980.
PLAY: *Perfect Days*, 1966.
POETRY: *American Poems: A Contemporary Collection*, 1964; *Whatever Love Declares*, 1969; *After the Armies Have Passed*, 1970; *In Memory of the Future*, 1974.

DANIEL KEYES

Born: New York, 1927

Principal short fiction
"The Trouble with Elmo," 1958; "Flowers for Algernon," 1959; "Crazy Maro," 1960; "The Quality of Mercy," 1960; "A Jury of Its Peers," 1963; "The Spellbinder," 1967.

Analysis
Daniel Keyes's best known short story, "Flowers for Algernon," provides an insight into his fictional concern with the complexities of the mind. His stories and novels reveal a technique that blends character and idea into a structural movement of cumulative effect. In reviewing the novel developed from the short story, critic Eliot Fremont-Smith pointed out that the title "does not convey Daniel Keyes's love of problems."

Major publications other than short fiction
NOVELS: *Flowers for Algernon*, 1966; *The Touch*, 1968; *The Fifth Sally*, 1980.

STEPHEN KING

Born: Maine, 1946

Principal short fiction

"The Glass Floor," 1967; "The Reaper's Image," 1969; "Suffer Little Children," 1972; "The Cat from Hell," 1977; "The Gunslinger," 1978; *Night Shift*, 1978; "The Crate," 1979.

Analysis

Since the film version of his first novel, *Carrie* (1974), projected Stephen King into prominence in 1976, he has established himself as America's most successful author—commercially and probably artistically—of horror fiction. Like many novelists, King initially developed his talents by writing short fiction, which he published in "mystery" and "men's" magazines, especially *Cavalier*. In an article appearing in *Writers' Digest* (November, 1973), King stated that his ideas come from "my nightmares. Not just the night time variety . . . but the ones that hide just beyond the doorway that separates the conscious from the unconscious." What lifts King above most other workers in the genre, beyond basic writing ability, is his emphasis on character and his use of concrete contemporary materials in his stories; both his people and his evils are thoroughly modern and physically visceral. Hence, the malevolent force in "The Mangler" is a laundry mangle that thirsts for human blood; the ghosts in "Sometimes They Come Back" are three vengeful teenage hoods; and the aliens in "I Am the Doorway" stare out at the world through eyes set in the fingers of the story's astronaut protagonist. At the same time, it is the emotional weakness and indecision of the characters themselves, and the dissention between them, that makes them vulnerable to their awful fates. King's place as the foremost exponent of "dark fantasy" in the 1970's was well deserved, and his best work transcends the genre to rank with the better fiction being currently written.

Major publications other than short fiction

NOVELS: *Carrie*, 1974; *Salem's Lot*, 1975; *The Shining*, 1977; *The Stand*, 1978; *The Dead Zone*, 1979.

Keith Neilson

MARGARET KINGERY

Born: Indiana, 1934

Principal short fiction
"The Whirlwind," 1976; "The Joy of Evolution Toward Discomfort," 1977; "Kate's Happiness," 1977; "Tunneling," 1977; "Witness Before Apocalypse," 1978; "On the Half Shell," 1978; "Breathing Out," 1978; "The Terms of a Devil," 1978; "Wanting," 1978; "Banjo," 1978-1979; "Masuko," 1979; "Jesus Eats: Tendersweet Fried Clams," 1979; "On a Path," 1980; "A Study in Child Abuse," 1980; "About Zenta," 1980; "Suffering Machines," 1980; "The Power of Plain, Ordinary, Human Gentility," 1980; "Working Your Way to the Curb," 1980; "Born Teacher," 1980; "In Dulci Jubilo," 1980; "Dear Mr. Nader," 1980.

Analysis
Frequently alluding to myth, legend, and Christian tradition, Margaret Kingery's stories generally take place in the Midwestern prairie (reaching back in time) or in contemporary suburbia in a tension of assiduous consumerism and emotional vacuity; but her fiction qualifies neither as polemic nor as social criticism. For Kingery, "character is plot," and it is her love of character that combines with the raw power of subject matter to produce stories with hard surfaces—stories in which power is partially achieved through length and sheer accumulation of detail. Thematically, the fiction considers the fundamental dualism of all life and the universal human yearning toward reunion with an inexhaustible life-source. Characters move back and forth between the "dark world" and the "light world," in a resulting chiaroscuro effect which suggests that the dichotomies of the universe and the polarities within the self may be less opposites than coordinates. The action may be raised to the level of the comic or played out at the level of the terrifying. Her work is presented as straightforward narrative in which characters grope toward some kind of redemption that may or may not occur within the story but gives the illusion of occurring when "flesh becomes word." Trusting word and narrative—via which she achieves a classic prose style as opposed to the experimental or cinematic—Kingery, nevertheless, takes one beyond story, beyond word, so that the end result is a fictive process which appears to continue into actual life and thus becomes "a link back to life."

W. P. KINSELLA

Born: Canada, 1935

Principal short fiction

Dance Me Outside, 1977; "Illianna Comes Home," 1977; *Scars*, 1978; "The Sense She Was Born With," 1978; "Fata Morgana," 1979; "Indian Struck," 1979; "Pretend Dinners," 1979; "Fence & Ermine," 1979; "The Chicken Dancer," 1979; *Shoeless Joe Jackson Comes to Iowa*, 1980; "Buffalo Jump," 1980; "I Remember Horses," 1980; "The Runner," 1980; "The Sundog Society," 1980; "Goldie," 1980; "Suits," 1980; "The Killing of Colin Moosefeathers," 1980; "Weasels and Ermines," 1980; "Born Indian," 1980; "Strings," 1980.

Analysis

W. P. Kinsella's most successful, most unforgettable stories are those whose characters he portrays as human beings, not as propaganda vehicles. "These stories glimmer with the revelation that Indians can laugh, cry, reason, hate, eat, drink, covet, and love," according to *NeWest ReView*. *Dance Me Outside* is "soaked warm with life," and, according to *Quill and Quire*, "offers a refreshing and uncontrived glimpse of Canadian Indian Reserve life . . . a unique combination of uproarious humor and simple philosophy." This humor, apparent in *Scars* as in *Dance Me Outside*, is possible through Kinsella's view of the obligation of history to inform the present. He accomplishes this goal, without nostalgia but with humor to relieve the tension, by stressing "the complexity of relationships between Indian and Indian, and between Indian and White, in a world marked by the overwhelming fact of oppression," as noted in *The Gazette*. Kinsella's realistic portrayal of character continues in his most recent collection, *Shoeless Joe Jackson Comes to Iowa*. His characters, states critic L. Kessenich, "exude a warm glow. They are so real, so vulnerable, so good, that they remind us of that side of human nature which makes living and loving and striving after dreams worth the effort." Kessenich admits to coming away from the stories with a "delicious smile on my face and a soft little tear in my eye. . . ."

NANCY KLINE

Born: New York, 1941

Principal short fiction
"Games," 1966; "The Harbormaster," 1971; "Leavings," 1974; "Population Explosions," 1975; "Cutoff," 1981.

Analysis
Language, in all its aspects, humor, and imagery dominate in the short fiction of Nancy Kline. Densely textured and highly metaphorical, hers is an American voice with a slight French accent. Europe is less explicitly a theme in her short stories than in her novels. Modern European literature, however, has clearly influenced Kline's short-story technique, especially in the three interconnected, experimental stories, "The Harbormaster," "Leavings," and "Population Explosions," wherein echoes of such French New Novelists as Robert Pinget and Claude Simon may be distinguished. The major concern of these and other more traditionally structured stories, such as "Cutoff," is communication, our understanding and misunderstanding of one another, the naming of things and relations. The sense of loss and distance between Kline's characters is counterbalanced by their humor and by those moments of intense contact which they carry away with them, internalized, as they revert to their necessarily separate solitudes.

Major publications other than short fiction
NOVEL: *The Faithful*, 1968.
NONFICTION: *Lightning: The Poetry of René Char*, 1981.

CLAUDE KOCH

Born: Pennsylvania, 1918

Principal short fiction
"Winter Term," 1962; "A Matter of Family," 1962; "Persistence of Memory," 1963; "Clayfoot," 1963; "The Summer House," 1963; "Snowshoe," 1963; "Certain Conclusions," 1964; "Gift for Poseidon," 1964; "Look Up! Look Up!," 1968; "Artist at Work," 1968; "The Things of Spring," 1968; "Birtha," 1968(?); "Blainey," 1968; "You Taught Us Good," 1969; "Adventures in Moving," 1970; "Countermarch and Ride About," 1974; "Reverie and Departure," 1974; "The Block Collection," 1975; "Love," 1978; "Uncle," 1978; "Mother," 1979; "Aunt," 1980; "Grandfather," 1980.

Analysis
Claude Koch's short stories dramatize ways in which an individual affects the lives of others. Like Flannery O'Connor, whose Catholic background he shares, Koch takes a sacramental view of life: people and events are seen as outward signs of the workings of God's grace.

Koch's training as a poet and a teacher of Renaissance literature shows in his remarkably evocative style. The diction is allusive and imagistic; the mode usually explores allegorical possibilities. In the treatment of familiar subjects like sports, family life, and academe there are frequent overtones of myth. The stories always have a symbolic dimension as well as a literal one. "The stories all begin," writes Koch about his own work,

> with a desire to celebrate some remembered characteristic or circumstance or thing or place. The making is an act of love, not for the craft alone but—more importantly—for aspects of life that I desire to endure in the imagination (though totally metamorphosed).

Major publications other than short fiction
NOVELS: *Island Interlude*, 1951; *Light in Silence*, 1958; *The Kite in the Sea*, 1964; *A Casual Company*, 1965.

John Keenan

EDITH KONECKY

Born: New York, 1922

Principal short fiction
"The Sound of Comedy," 1961; "Charity," 1963; "The Power," 1963; "The Chastity of Magda Wickwire," 1965; "The Day the Wedding Ended," 1968; "Ralph," 1970; "The Box," 1970; "Love and Friendship," 1971; "Death in New Rochelle," 1973; "Lessons," 1976; "The Place," 1976.

Analysis
Edith Konecky's finely crafted, beautifully written stories deal with the contemporary concerns of sensitive and intelligent people, particularly with their quest for identity and need for definition in the particular context of their lives. Konecky's psychological insight and perfectly tuned ear catch the humor and pathos of her subjects from deep inside their own points of view, be they men or women, adults or children, wherever she finds them and whatever they happen to be doing.

Major publications other than short fiction
NOVEL: *Allegra Maud Goldman*, 1976.

HENRY KORN

Born: New York, 1945

Principal short fiction
Exact Change, 1974; "Candystand," 1977; "John Chancellor," 1978; *A Difficult Act to Follow*, 1980.

Analysis
In the seven years since the publication of his first collection, Henry Korn's style has shifted from a "spatial form," with development via juxtaposition, to a more hard-edged direct narrative. Yet his basic technique—the injection of fantasy into an ironically perceived reality—has remained the same, and so have his basic concerns. Korn is preoccupied with history, including the present moment, and with finding a place in it for innocence, truthfulness, friendship, and heroism. Such a place is not easy to find. Modern life, as Korn perceives it, is chock-a-block with glossy trash: designer jeans, wraparound sunglasses, diet mayonnaise, theme parks. For this modern junkyard, Korn has divided feelings. On the one hand, he betrays a popster's affection for such things as cars and candy and derives from them some of his finest comic and lyrical effects. On the other hand, he shows a pressing worry about the survival of clear perception and decent behavior in a world dreamed up by Madison Avenue, and this political passion, when aroused, lends his creation a sheen or menace. The political/moral concern, however, never outstrips the imagination. Korn's world is fully objectified in images of crisp clarity which give his alternately lyrical, comical, and satirical visions their unquestionable power.

Major publications other than short fiction
NOVELS: *The Pontoon Manifesto*, 1975; *Proceedings of the National Academy of the Avant Garde*, 1975.

NONFICTION: *Muhammad Ali Retrospective*, 1976 (stories, essays, and articles).

RICHARD KOSTELANETZ

Born: New York, 1940

Principal short fiction
Short Fictions, 1974; *Openings & Closings*, 1975; *Constructs*, 1975; *Numbers: Poems & Stories*, 1976; *Foreshortenings*, 1978; *Constructs Two*, 1978; *Inexistences*, 1978; *And So Forth*, 1979; *More Short Fictions*, 1980; *Epiphanies*, 1980.

Analysis
Most of Richard Kostelanetz's fictions are based upon intentionally radical formal experiments: stories with only one word to a paragraph, or two words; single-sentence stories that are either the opening sentences of hypothetical stories that might follow or the closing sentences of hypothetical stories that might have come before; single-sentence epiphanies of hypothetically longer stories; and stories composed entirely of numbers or entirely of line-drawings that metamorphose in narrative sequences that are sometimes, as in his "constructivist fictions," rigorously systemic. Whereas the aim of these strategies has been the use of radically alternative materials for printed fiction, the other direction of his creative work is making literature in media other than printed pages—not adaptations in the slick sense but genuine intrinsic translations that exploit the singular capabilities of each alternative medium and yet preserve the integrity of the original literary text. Thus, the constructivist fictions have also appeared as films. A final concern of Kostelanetz's creative work has been the essential differences among short fictions, novellas, and novels and between poetry and fiction, even at the avant-garde edges.

Major publications other than short fiction
NOVELS: *In the Beginning*, 1971; *Ad Infinitum*, 1972; *Extrapolate*, 1975; *Modulations*, 1975; *One Night Stood*, 1978; *Tabula Rasa*, 1978; *Exhaustive Parallel Intervals*, 1980; *Symmetries*, 1981.

MARILYN KRYSL

Born: Kansas, 1942

Principal short fiction
Honey, You've Been Dealt a Winning Hand, 1980; "Looking for Mother,"
1980.

Analysis
Marilyn Krysl's short fiction is made in a language that not only sparkles but also causes the reader to make constant adjustments and readjustments to fresh and vivid perceptions of reality. Each sentence is clean and sharp, like an imaginative black and white photograph of, for example, an old face or a storm gathering over a distant hill. Her vision of the human condition is emphatic: the twitches and unspeakable moments between mother and daughter, the subtle exchange and conflict between male and female lovers, the tenderness and pain between teenage friends, the mystery and power members of an older generation represent for a younger one. Krysl's command of form, style, and content shows the mature writer performing an impressive resuscitation act on the American language.

Major publications other than short fiction
POETRY: *Saying Things*, 1975; *More Palamino, Please, More Fuchsia*, 1980.

Clarence Major

HERBERT KUBLY

Born: Wisconsin, 1915

Principal short fiction
Varieties of Love, 1958.

Analysis
The sixteen stories in *Varieties of Love* were written over a period of ten years with no thematic relationship intended. When it came time to collect them into a book, however, it became clear that the stories shared a common theme of love as communication and the increasing absence of both love and communication in contemporary life. A majority of the stories were haunted by the tragic loneliness of human beings and their desperate and futile efforts to pursue compassionate human relationships. It is a theme that is pervasive also in Herbert Kubly's novels, *The Whistling Zone* (1963) and *The Duchess of Glover* (1975). His concern has not been specifically with romantic love but with a larger spectrum of all interhuman sensibilities. Suffering from the insecurities, fears, and guilts which are the conditions of our scientific and materialistic civilization, the characters in Kubly's stories grasp at one another like drowning men. Not finding sustenance in one another they part and continue their struggles alone. Identifiable characters and situations draw readers easily into seemingly naturalistic stories in which evocative settings, sometimes assuming catalytic roles, help move the plots toward fearsome images and fateful resolutions. A variety of moods and settings is present for readers of the tragic "A Quiet Afternoon" and "The Wasp" (Switzerland), the wildly comic "Rallye of Rotary" (France) and "Divine Ecstacy" (Italy), and the surrealist-imaged "The Merry Dance" (New England) and "The Unmarried Bartender" (Italy).

Major publications other than short fiction
NOVELS: *The Whistling Zone*, 1963; *The Duchess of Glover*, 1975.
PLAYS: *Men to the Sea*, 1944; *Inherit the Wind*, 1948; *The Virus*, 1973; *Perpetual Care*, 1975.
NONFICTION: *American in Italy*, 1955; *Easter in Sicily*, 1956; *At Large*, 1964; *Gods and Heroes*, 1969; *Life World Library: Italy*, 1971; *Life World Library: Switzerland*, 1973.

HERBERT KUHNER

Born: Austria, 1935

Principal short fiction
Broadsides & Pratfalls, 1976.

Analysis
Herbert Kuhner's literary intelligence—conveying psychological insights with cool precision, poetic verve and old-European wit—is deployed and displayed in his novels, *Nixe* (1968) and *The Assembly-Line Prince* (1980). He is a master of the short story—naturalistic fables—where he reveals a keen awareness of the neuroses beneath the veneer of civilization. Kuhner is also an accomplished poet, his main theme being sexual and emotional disillusionment, which he documents without self-pity and often self-mockingly.

Major publications other than short fiction
NOVELS: *Nixe*, 1968; *The Assembly-Line Prince*, 1980.
PLAYS: *Four One-Act Plays*, 1973.

Anthony Rudolf

A. J. LANGGUTH

Born: Minnesota, 1933

Principal short fiction
Jesus Christs, 1968; *Wedlock*, 1972.

Analysis
Critics have often remarked on A. J. Langguth's control over his material; this sense of craft imposed on options and choices he treats gives a sense of moral sifting and judgment to his work. In *Jesus Christs*, the character of redeemer is viewed in 130 short fragments, moving in and out of historical time but always united by a taut and witty style. In *Wedlock*, eighteen characters drift through relationships, again exploring many kinds of love and attraction, their confusions and human error held in check only by the narrator's cold and rational treatment. In both cases, the result is an acknowledgment of life's chaos, with a hope that through the hard lines of art it can momentarily be contained.

Major publications other than short fiction
NOVEL: *Marksman*, 1974.
NONFICTION: *Macumba*, 1975; *Hidden Terrors*, 1978.

Joe Saltzman

CHARLES R. LARSON

Born: Iowa, 1938

Principal short fiction

"Up from Slavery," 1969; "Upstairs in the Zoo," 1974; "Forgetting Mrs. Pfitzer," 1974; *Academia Nuts*, 1977; "New Hope for the Dead," 1977; "Hydrotherapy/Hydrophobia," 1977; "Invitation to a Wedding," 1977.

Analysis

A central image of much of Charles Larson's short fiction is the decline of service—the collapse of modern amenities once taken for granted. His settings range from Africa to academia to contemporary urban living; his conflicts often focus upon adult children still working out their problems with parental authority.

Major publications other than short fiction

NOVEL: *The Insect Colony*, 1978.

NONFICTION: *The Emergence of African Fiction*, 1972; *The Novel in the Third World*, 1976; *American Indian Fiction*, 1978.

NORMAN LAVERS

Born: California, 1935

Principal short fiction
"I Hate Everybody," 1971; "A Samish Island Calendar," 1973; "Dreams of Failure Fears of Dying," 1974; "The Divorced Mother," 1976; "Story," 1977; "The Whole Universe Goeth Coupld," 1979; "Environmental Impact Statement," 1979; *Selected Short Stories*, 1979; "Rumors," 1980; "The Navigator," 1980.

Analysis
Norman Lavers does not accept the old saw that every writer should strive to have his own "voice." Instead, he believes that each story he writes is a unique event, and determines, through inner necessity, its own voice, structure, technique, and theme. He feels that if he has done his work properly, each of his stories will appear to have been written by a different author. Nonetheless, there are some common features to his work. He often includes journals or letters in his stories, as he is interested in the way character reveals itself through idiosyncracies of spelling and writing style. Lavers is a lifelong naturalist who has published scientific papers and has studied and photographed birds and other wildlife in many parts of the world. This fact profoundly influences his writing, which often includes highly textured exotic landscapes, and which generally places man firmly in nature. Within this context, those of his characters who are the most conscious of the swift passage of time, of their aging, of the constant possibility of death or disabling injury, still contrive to be joyful. Indeed, if there is an overriding theme in his best work, it is that for the limited amount of time we have on earth before pain and sorrow and death overtake us, it really is not all that difficult to be happy.

Major publications other than short fiction
NONFICTION: *Mark Harris*, 1978; *Jerzy Kosinski*, 1981.

TODD S. J. LAWSON

Born: Minnesota, 1940

Principal short fiction
"The Village Crank," 1967; "Herbie and I," 1969; "The Absurd Letters of John Kowalski," 1976; "Best Underground Folktales of San Francisco," 1979.

Analysis
Todd S. J. Lawson's early fiction is marked by a rather rigid structure utilizing flashbacks; but by 1969 he had adopted a highly unique satirical, existential style, and by the early 1970's *Pacific Coast Times* stated "Todd S. J. Lawson has been described as 'Kafka with a sense of humor.' True." His fiction continues to be best described by respected publications such as *The San Francisco Review of Books*: "Lawson's humor is fierce and funny. He is a Dadist in attitude." Using contemporary themes which somehow seem to repeat themselves through generations, his stories humorously attack social institutions. *Booklist,* magazine of the American Library Association, characterizes his work: "Beloved sterotypes flip-flop. Nothing is Sacred. Pot shots are taken at presidents, consumerism, Arabs, peach trees, and 'midgetminded jerks' everywhere! Lawson delivers his scatological rabbit punches with the abandon of an underground cartoonist and the vigor of a Lenny Bruce." Lawson's short stories are masterfully controlled, and with characters such as Helen Hogborn, Igor Flatass, Merlin Waggs, and Marshmellow Mozambique, he is considered one of the more colorful of contemporary fiction writers.

Major publications other than short fiction
NOVELS: *The 69 Days of Easter,* 1977; *Best Underground Folktales of San Francisco,* 1981.
POETRY: *Patriotic Poems of Amerikkka,* 1971; *Pacific Sun Poems,* 1973.
NONFICTION: *The Empire of Howard Hughes,* 1975 (with Joe Davenport).

Maurice Custodio

JANE LAZARRE

Born: New York, 1943

Principal short fiction

"Forgiveness," 1975; "A Tale of Love and Sex," 1976; *Some Kind of Innocence*, 1980.

Analysis

In Jane Lazarre's work, intellect and idea are exemplified and skillfully transformed by the re-creation of experience so that the reader is enabled to absorb the idea viscerally. In that way, her writing does not remain on the level of logical or analytical prose although she consistently is moved by ideas. Involved in Lazarre's description of experience one always senses the truths gleaned from one's own experience. Much of the action in Lazarre's fiction takes place in the characters' minds, yet they describe their feelings with such immediacy that the reader feels a great deal has "happened." It is this quality of experience used as example that makes her work unique.

Lazarre stops at nothing in her quest for personal truth. Her experience is told with love, hatred, beauty, ugliness, and always with passion, so that the reader senses events rather than thinks about them. She writes about what concerns her as a woman, artist, mother, daughter, feminist, wife— about family relationships, love, friendship, ambivalence, betrayal and death—all those ordinary, enormous things which concern all human beings. Although a fine craftswoman, Lazarre's concerns rest with passion and truth rather than tastefulness, spareness, and technique. She never avoids what might be painful or difficult for a reader. In reading Lazarre's work, one should be prepared to be disturbed as well as entertained or enlightened.

Major publications other than short fiction

NONFICTION: *The Mother Knot*, 1977; *On Loving Men*, 1980.

Lynda Schor

MARIA BERL LEE

Born: Austria, 1924

Principal short fiction

"A Sunday Morning Drive," 1956; "The Escapade," 1970; "And Each Man Kills," 1973; "Love Story," 1973; "The Liberation of Laura," 1974; "Gouadeloupe Is for Grass Widows," 1975; "A Ticket for Tomorrow," 1975; "The Rivals," 1975; "Beer, Max and Solitude," 1975; "Frogs, Bonds and Box Tops," 1977; "Flight from Glasses," 1977; "New World Adventure," 1978; "A Tale of a Whale," 1978; "Gas Poisoning," 1979; "Rough Road Home," 1979; "The Creature," 1980; "A Bridge to Cross," 1980.

Analysis

Maria Berl Lee is remarkable through the sheer variety expressed within her writing. Her short fiction ranges from powerful, compressed tales of tragedy to autumnal, sensitive accounts of the griefs of "little" people—a lonely janitor losing the one being he loves, a Czech waiter adrift in a strange country—to tales of riotous fun. She is also unusual in that in addition to English works she writes in German and occasionally in French. The thread running through these variegated forms is their sheer readability. Don Heinrich Tolzmann (*Books Abroad*, Winter, 1976) calls her writing "magical, brittle and strikingly fresh." Each piece exhibits a strong intuitive perception of the people, problems, themes, and settings it creates. While the stories usually have believable characters who spring alive for the reader, together with a wider theme or point, the intuitive element lifts them beyond the traditional and imbues them with unusual cohesiveness, resonance, and credibility. Her geographical settings, from Prague of the 1968 spring to Mexico to New York's financial district, carry intense authority and conviction. Professor Ralph West has called her short fiction "varied, insightful and well-written" (*Schatzkammer*, Fall, 1978). Versatility and intuitiveness are paired with a sense of human incongruity, whether in absurdity and imperfections leading to tragedy, or in a candid and ironic humor in the comic tales. Underlying the stories is an appreciation of human courage, love, sacrifice, and imagination, or of the fateful consequences of their lack.

Major publications other than short fiction

NOVEL: *Postskript Für Lydia*, 1976.

PLAYS: *Ein Tag der Überraschungen*, 1966-1967; *Bombe im Tor*, 1970; *Don't Rock the Waterbed*, 1975; *The Case in Question*, 1977.

JOHN LEGGETT

Born: New York, 1917

Principal short fiction
"The Girl Who Lived in a Tree," 1947; "The Lie," 1955; "Stalking the Muse on Publisher's Row," 1965; "You Take the Easy Road to Success in Writing," 1966; "Little Flames of Genius," 1967.

Analysis
John Leggett's reputation as a writer rests on his novels and biography of the two novelists Ross Lockridge and Thomas Heggen, *Ross and Tom* (1974). Although his short fiction is sparse, his stories do reflect his interests and may be seen as experiments or sketches which he later developed in longer fiction and biography. "Little Flames," for example, is concerned with the effects of early success upon writers, those effects which lead to self-destructiveness and which make the drama of *Ross and Tom*. Similarly, Leggett's two stories about publishing which appeared in *Harper's Magazine* reflect the interests which culminated in his novel *Gulliver House* (1979).

Major publications other than short fiction
NOVELS: *Wilder Stone*, 1960; *The Gloucester Branch*, 1965; *Who Took the Gold Away*, 1969; *Gulliver House*, 1979.
NONFICTION: *Ross and Tom*, 1974.

FRITZ LEIBER, JR.

Born: Illinois, 1910

Principal short fiction

Night's Black Agents, 1947; *Two Sought Adventure*, 1957; *The Mind Spider and Other Stories*, 1961; *Shadows with Eyes*, 1962; *A Pail of Air*, 1964; *Ships to the Stars*, 1964; *The Night of the Wolf*, 1966; *The Secret Songs*, 1968; *Swords Against Wizardry*, 1968; *Swords in the Mist*, 1968; *Night Monsters*, 1969; *You're All Alone*, 1972; *The Book of Fritz Leiber*, 1974; *The Best of Fritz Leiber*, 1974; *The Worlds of Fritz Leiber*, 1976; *Swords and Ice Magic*, 1977.

Analysis

In a career that spans four decades, Fritz Leiber has written important works in more genres and garnered more awards than any other modern science fiction/fantasy writer. His first published short story, "Two Sought Adventure" (1939), introduced the characters of Fafhrd and the Gray Mouser, who became the protagonists of one of the most respected and popular of "Sword and Sorcery" sequences yet produced (he is, in fact, credited with having coined the generic label). Comprising six novels and short-story collections to date, the Fafhrd and the Gray Mouser series has been favorably compared with J. R. R. Tolkien's *The Lord of the Rings* cycle and Ursula K. LeGuin's *Earthsea Trilogy*. The best-known story in the group, "Ill Met in Lankhmar" (1971), won both the Hugo and Nebula Awards. In addition, Leiber has authored many provocative fantasies—especially "dark fantasies"—in modern dress, notably "The Automatic Pistol" (1940), about a gun that does its own killing; "Smoke Ghost" (1941), featuring a grubby modern-day specter; and "Gonna Roll the Bones" (1968), in which a compulsive gambler casts dice with the Devil. The near futuristic setting of the last story illustrates the way in which Leiber's fantasies blur into science fiction, a genre in which he has also produced a body of memorable material. Some of the stories—"Try and Change the Past" (1958), "Damnation Morning" (1959), "The Oldest Soldier" (1960), "When the Change Winds Blow" (1964), "Knight to Move" (1965)—involve the "change war" series, a number of narratives about a prolonged galactic war that is fought in time as well as space between two factions, "Spiders" and "Snakes," who both possess weapons capable of altering the past in attempts to influence the present. The best of Leiber's science fiction lies outside that sequence, in such masterful tales as "The Ship Sails at Midnight," in which a beautiful alien provokes homocidal jealousy in four contrasting earthmen; "A Hitch in Space," where the madness of a crewmember dooms them all; and "Catch That Zeppelin!," a vivid parallel-worlds story, one of Leiber's few ventures into hardcore science fiction. Writing for the most part during times when few science-fiction authors interested themselves in literary style, Leiber has always written with a careful, precise, yet ebullient style that is rich in imagery and suggestion.

Major publications other than short fiction
NOVELS: *Gather Darkness*, 1950; *Destiny Times Three*, 1952; *Conjure Wife*, 1953; *The Sinful Ones*, 1953; *The Green Millennium*, 1953; *The Big Time*, 1961; *The Silver Eggheads*, 1961; *The Wanderer*, 1964; *Tarzan and the Valley of Gold*, 1966; *The Swords of Lankhmar*, 1968; *A Spectre Is Haunting Texas*, 1969; *Our Lady of Darkness*, 1977.
POETRY: *The Daemons of Upper Air*, 1969.

Keith Neilson

MEYER LEVIN

Born: Illinois, 1905

Principal short fiction
"The Love Note," 1937; "The System Was Doomed," 1940.

Analysis
The biblical parable, accented by irony, characterizes Meyer Levin's favorite stories; but his range is from early Chekhovian mood pieces to crafted fiction for the "slicks." His most effective tale, thematically, was the first in *Collier's*, in 1937, *The Love Note*. It concerns an imaginative reform-school girl, spied on by a supervisor who finally sees her drop a note into a tree-hollow. The supervisor extracts the message; it reads, "To Whoever Finds This Note, I Love You." Levin wrote with the *Menorah Journal*, *Story*, *The New Yorker*, and *Esquire* during the 1920's. He became an editor, and he "discovered" Eudora Welty, among others. Discouraged by constricting outlets, Levin concentrated on novels. He has published no collection; however, there is a book that does not properly classify as his own: his retelling from Yiddish of Hassidic folk tales. First published as *The Golden Mountain* in 1932 and now in Penguin Books as *Classic Hassidic Tales*, this work is widely anthologized. It has influenced younger writers, as well as some of Levin's own fiction, such as his Jerusalem novella, *The Spell of Time*.

Major publications other than short fiction
NOVELS: *Reporter*, 1929; *Frankie and Johnny: A Love Story*, 1930; *Yehuda*, 1931; *The New Bridge*, 1933; *The Old Bunch*, 1937; *Citizens*, 1940; *My Father's House*, 1947; *Compulsion*, 1956, 1957; *Eva*, 1959; *The Fanatic*, 1964; *The Stronghold*, 1965; *Gore and Igor: An Extravaganza*, 1968; *The Settlers*, 1972; *The Obsession*, 1975; *The Spell of Time*, 1976.
PLAYS: *Compulsion*, 1959, 1960; *The Diary of Anne Frank*, 1975.

DAVID M. LEVINE

Born: New York, 1949

Principal short fiction
"The Medievalist," 1968; "Prolegomena," 1969; "Untitled Prose," 1970; "September Sequential," 1970.

Analysis
The short fiction David Levine has thus far written and published has been, in great part, an extension of his work as a lyric poet. In fact, it is not unusual for his prose to scan with some regularity and even to become, quite without warning, "poetry" when there is sufficient rhetorical or dramatic pressure. There has always been a marked schizoid element; on the one hand, he thoroughly accepts the Western tradition of love for love's sake while, at the same time, a good deal of exposure to modern psychology has allowed him to see that "pure love" cannot exist without an element of pure self-regard. His poetry and prose deal with this split, and he has used the prose to examine the more subtle permutations of individual situations that demonstrate this split. Since Levine's interest in the use of short prose work is largely psychological and self-revelatory, he has deliberately eschewed such considerations as plot development, "round characters," elegant beginnings, and satisfying endings (since, as Ezra Pound says, "there is no end of things in the heart . . ."). History for him is both completely mutable and never changing. People, although they may have changed since an incident he is examining, do not change during that brief incident he makes his subject, which is almost inexhaustible if he decides to examine it from the point of view of everyone involved. Levine does not believe that the establishment of sympathy held by the reader for one particular character is at all necessary, and he even goes to lengths to render the character representing him as unsympathetic as possible. Beside the situations that Levine's stories concern, he believes very strongly in the use of mythic and historical parallels wherever relevant, and he refuses to allow any crucial differences to separate the ancient bard and the contemporary narrator—in that sense he is old-fashioned, believing in omniscience. Levine's prose work is about the relationship of language to life and vice-versa, especially how the confusion of one for the other creates painful and sometimes insoluble problems for the people directly involved in the confused situation. He is eager to utilize any kind of experimentation he hears about, and much of his work has been cut up and reassembled at random. Levine is fond of writing dialogue which he tries to render as accurately as possible. Shorter prose grants him a rhetorical freedom that he does not allow himself in his epigrammatic verse, as well as allowing him to

dig deeper into actual causes and motives which intrigue him as they would intrigue any disciple of Kenneth Burke.

CLAYTON W. LEWIS

Born: Washington, D. C., 1936

Principal short fiction
"After the War," 1969; "The Search for Prester John," 1970; "What Happened Is," 1972; "Hallelujah!," 1972; "The Celebration," 1972; "Nina," 1973; "In the Fields of Time," 1974; "Movie Time," 1975; "Sons of Esau," 1976; "In Battlefields," 1976; "The Goat," 1978; "Memory's End," 1980; "American Dreams," 1980.

Analysis
Born of Southerners who left large traditional families (in North Carolina, in Oklahoma-Mississippi) for the modern cities of the east in the 1920's and 1930's, Clayton W. Lewis writes stories which typically portray characters who have lost traditional ties with family and place, and who have fallen into a world in which rushing events have little human meaning—are not part of ongoing history as much as they are simply terrible and chaotic. The technique of these stories blends stream of consciousness, biography, and history. The central effect of these stories is ironic and tragic; the reader sees how the character lives in the absence of tradition, in the rush of painful personal happenings and equally painful public-historic events (Vietnam, assassinations, riots). Rod Cockshut (*Charlotte News and Observer*, February 1972) says: "Lewis writes in a confident, unobtrusive stream of consciousness mode which injects you subtly but surely into the (characters') psyches." Eugene Garber in 1979 described the "relentless narrative pace," and the dramatization of "strange destructive forces that compromise the medium of the characters' lives—yet do not destroy those lives." In "The Goat," which is autobiographical, and in technique more traditional, the central character similarly falls into violent participation in the world when he is driven to the point of attempting to kill an officer while he is undergoing Marine bootcamp training. Lewis' work has been influenced by William Faulkner, but differs from the master in that it is centrally concerned with the children of the first generation to leave the South for the golden promise of modern eastern cities—with that dislocation and alienation. More recently Lewis has begun to deal with these themes in an unusual autobiographical mode which apparently derives from Vladimir Nabokov's *Speak, Memory* (1966), and in a less direct way from Erik Erikson's *Life History and the Historical Moment* (1975). In this work personal experience, memory, and recovered past are combined with vigorous foreground "design-making"; in this way the making of the fiction becomes the author's way of making living connections with ongoing historical processes and restoring, in a limited way, his own lost sense

of a traditional past. These autobiographical fictions have appeared in *The Southern Review* and *The Texas Quarterly*.

Major publications other than short fiction
NOVEL: *Violations*, 1981.
NONFICTION: "Style in Jefferson's *Notes on the State of Virginia*," 1978.

JANET LEWIS

Born: Chicago, 1899

Principal short fiction
The Wife of Martin Guerre, 1941; *Good-bye, Son, and Other Stories*, 1946.

Analysis
One of the many remarkable aspects of Janet Lewis' fiction is its breadth of appeal. Donald Davie has said of her work, "the narratives of Janet Lewis exemplify an art of literature which happily, though not humbly, collaborates with, and yet transcends, the disciplines of responsible scholarship." Ellen Killoh, who approaches Lewis' work from a feminist perspective, says,

> Janet Lewis' work offers more than a lament for an order whose social, economic, and intellectual underpinnings are being swept away. Her heroines have a strength admirable in any age, and Miss Lewis' own clarity of style, serenity of mind, and dispassionate modulation of voice can serve as reminders of what can be regained, on the other side of change, when self-conscious women writers have explored the stylistic and psychological difficulties coincident with any realignment of sexual roles.

Lewis concerns herself with the difficulty, both historical and modern, of trying to preserve culture and tradition. Her method in *The Wife of Martin Guerre* is to dramatize such an attempt not with familiar, heroic figures but with an ordinary yet stoic heroine involved in a domestic crisis of far-reaching proportions which transcend the immediate locale and speak for the kind of moral strength and honesty which Lewis sees in an older order. The settings of Lewis' short stories are in the 1930's and early 1940's. They are regional and intensely alive with her sympathy, insights, and vivid details.

Major publications other than short fiction
NOVELS: *The Invasion*, 1932; *Against a Darkening Sky*, 1943; *The Trial of Soren Qvist*, 1947; *The Ghost of Monsieur Scarron*, 1959.
POETRY: *The Indians in the Woods*, 1923; *The Wheel in Midsummer*, 1927; *The Earth-Bound*, 1946; *Poems 1924-44*, 1950; *The Ancient Ones*, 1979.

LUCY R. LIPPARD

Born: New York, 1937

Principal short fiction
"Cocteau at the Pentagon," 1971; "Waterlay," 1972; "The Romantic Adventures of an Adversative Rotarian, or, Allreadymadesomuchoff," 1973; "An Intense and Gloomy Impression for a Woman in the Nineties," 1974; "Caveheart (for Charles)," 1974; "Touchstones," 1975; "New York Times II," 1975; "New York Times I," 1976; "First Sight, or New York Times III," 1976; "Three Short Fictions: The Cries You Hear, Into Among, Headwaters," 1977; "Projections," 1977; "Stonesprings," 1978; "Photodialogue IV," 1978; "Hiding," 1978; "Rose Atoll," 1978; "Plateaus," 1978; "Excerpts from I See/You Mean," 1978; "New York Times IV," 1979; "The Artworld," 1979.

Analysis
Lucy Lippard's fiction is a collage; life (especially a woman's life) comes in fragments, and people's whole lives, rather than any more restricted notion of plot, is always her subject. Her first novel, *I See/You Mean* (1979), written in 1970, was influenced less by any other experimental fiction than by avant-garde visual art, with which she has been deeply involved for many years. This is perhaps even truer of the short than the long fiction. Lippard's characters tend to emerge from somewhere and then live their lives almost autonomously. She asserts her control over them through structure, in the organization of the material. She juxtaposes times, places, different "first persons," found material, stream of consciousness, dialogue, and description. As a result, the narrative is constantly shifting focus, sometimes harshly, sometimes sensuously. Out of the raw material provided by her characters emerges composite reality which she supposes to be her own view of life. The short fictions are potential fragments of unwritten longer fictions; the long fictions are potentially shattered into short ones. Lippard uses experimental techniques in both to provoke a dialogue with her readers. She likes to leave holes, or dotted lines, or spaces into which the reader can fall with her or his own associations and experiences. When these are combined with hers and those of her characters, the fiction becomes a trialogue. It changes with each new reader and each new juxtaposition, not like a chameleon (since each piece keeps its own identity) but like patchwork.

Major publications other than short fiction
NOVEL: *I See/You Mean*, 1979.

GERALD LOCKLIN

Born: New York, 1941

Principal short fiction
"An Xmas Carol," 1971; "Four Women," 1973; *Locked In*, 1973; "Six Blackbirds," 1974; "The Continuing Saga of Bruce," 1975; "The Tales of Roger Hotspur," 1975; "For Whom the Bells," 1976; "A Portrait of the Artist in His Declining Years," 1976; *The Four-Day Work Week*, 1977; "Prolegomena to Any Future Reflections on Violence in American Society," 1977; "Jonathan Billingsley's Car Won't Start," 1978; "The Requirement," 1978; "Sleepwalker," 1978; *A Weekend in Canada*, 1979.

Analysis
Gerald Locklin's stories are invariably accessible yet challenging in that they elude facile, conventional circumscription in regard to theme, subject, matter, tone, and form. A prolific poet, Locklin admits that some of his poems are "close to essays," but in his fiction the "priority is the story first and the idea second." The reader need only prepare for a variety of form and content and to remember André Gide's admonition about trying to understand someone too quickly. The persona seems intensely autobiographical here, whimsically objective there. The result is a robust range from the satiric and darkly humorous to the winsome and near-tragic; the stories are always comical, elegiacal, and tragical, but never pastoral or bathetical. The style is direct and unmannered; however, Locklin sprinkles his prose with allusions to motion pictures, literature, and sports that are deeply ingrained in the themes. His metaphoric playbook is well stocked. Narrative modes include both the traditional and the experimental. He has alluded to Jorge Luis Borges' success at showing that "fiction and exposition can successfully cross each other's borders." Locklin's tendency is to subsume the philosophical in the aesthetic, just as he has a tendency to subsume the personal in the aesthetic. Never coldly impersonal, the narrator leads the way through a world both fatal and farcical. No one is guilty. Some suffer; others lead lives of blissful assimilation. Love is not always the first player out of the huddle; but there is the feeling that teamed with compassion, friendship, alcohol, or memory, it can mount a drive against absurdity or effect a goal-line stand—scoring even an occasional upset.

Major publications other than short fiction
NOVELS: *The Chase*, 1976; *The Cure: A Novel for Speedreaders*, 1979.
POETRY: *Sunset Beach*, 1967; *The Toad Poems*, 1970, 1976; *Poop, and Other Poems*, 1973; *Son of Poop*, 1973; *Tarzan and Shane Meet the Toad*, 1975;

Toad's Europe, 1975; *The Criminal Mentality*, 1976; *Toad's Sabbatical*, 1977; *Frisco Epic*, 1978; *Pronouncing Borges*, 1978; *Two Summer Sequences*, 1979.

JOHN LOGAN

Born: Iowa, 1923

Principal short fiction
"The Picture for the Publisher," 1957; "The Bishop's Suite," 1957; "The Last Class," 1958; "Fire," 1959; "The Relic," 1961; "Panic Round," 1961; "The Loss," 1961; "The Cigars," 1965; "The Success," 1972.

Analysis
Writing in *Alone with America*, Richard Howard speaks of the burdens of John Logan's poems as being "the transfiguration of life not in immortality, but in the living of it." Life also undergoes such transfiguration in Logan's short stories—stories which are less well-known than his poetry, but no less serious or skillful. Logan's short fiction is related to his poetry in several ways. It is full of precise imagery, both of the natural and dream worlds. Dreams play an important role, projecting his fictional protagonists' inner conflicts upon a screen larger than life. His stories are enacted upon several fields at once—reality, dream, history, literature, and myth. Like his poetry, Logan's fiction is often in the autobiographical mode, tales of people becoming, as best they can, what they will become. His themes are imagination, lost opportunities, the burdens of tenderness, rituals of manhood, and myths of life. His stories are quests of identity, often stressing disorientation: the poet in the mechanistic world, the man of feeling in an unfeeling universe, the athlete in the classroom, the layman in the Church. Logan's ultimate message is, however, one of hope and compassion.

Major publications other than short fiction
POETRY: *Cycle for Mother Cabrini*, 1955; *Ghosts of the Heart*, 1960; *Spring of the Thief*, 1963; *The Zig Zag Walk*, 1969; *The Anonymous Lover*, 1973; *Poem in Progress*, 1975; *Aaron Sisskind, Photographs/John Logan, Poems*, 1976; *The Bridge of Change*, 1978; *Only the Dreamer Can Change the Dream: Selected Poems*, 1981; *The Bridge of Change: Poems 1974-1980*, 1981.

NONFICTION: *The House That Jack Built*, 1974; *A Ballet for the Ear: Essays, Reviews & Interviews*, 1981.

Robert Phillips

ROBERT EMMET LONG

Born: New York, 1934

Principal short fiction

"Trains of Another Time," 1969; "The Destination of Timothy Neill," 1969; "Farewell to Joey," 1969; "Champion," 1979, 1980.

Analysis

Robert Long's stories have thus far been concerned with patterns of initiation, and are often set either in New York City or in small towns of upper New York State. Certain stories involve humor that becomes grotesque or borders on actual hallucination, and have some affinity with Kurt Vonnegut and Jerzy Kosinski. Generally, however, the stories are traditional, spare in form, sensitive to nuance, and capture luminous moments of self-recognition. His work-in-progress, *The Gallagher House*, a cycle of interrelated stories about an Irish-American boyhood in upstate New York during World War II, deals with a boy's outward experiences and inward consciousness from the ages of six to twelve. A family saga, it depicts the boy's struggle to come to terms with a rich family tradition at the moment of its disintegration. The novelist Brian Burland has characterized Long's stories as "intimate," "confidential in voice," and "lyrical."

Major publications other than short fiction

NONFICTION: *The Achieving of 'The Great Gatsby': F. Scott Fitzgerald, 1920-1925*, 1979; *The Great Succession: Henry James and the Legacy of Hawthorne*, 1979.

GRANT LYONS

Born: Pennsylvania, 1941

Principal short fiction
"The Reef," 1971; "The New Smile," 1971; "In the Shadow of the Pines,"
1973; *4-4-4*, 1977; "A Matter of Metaphor," 1977; "The Cat," 1977; "Disputed
Territory," 1979; "The Sniper," 1980.

Analysis
Grant Lyons is a young fiction writer whose roots are in the American
South and Southwest, in Louisiana and Texas. His stories are authentic poems
of that climate and of the people who live and work under those broad, hard
skies. Lyons is, however, more than a regionalist. His characters live, whatever the apparent setting, in that inner territory where each of us tries to
transcend his limitations, to be a hero, if only momentarily, and if only on
the smallest, most local scale. Lyons' small-scale heroes struggle in a hostile
environment against apathy, despair, contempt for the original or unusual,
against their own limitations of will or strength or intelligence. We wish them
well; we care what happens to them; we hope they go on trying in the years
after the story closes behind them. Lyons, once a student of philosophy at
Tulane and at Northwestern Universities, has become a maker of fictions that
illuminate the oldest of philosophical questions: What shall we make of our
littleness, and of our mortality?

Richard A. Blessing

ANDREW NELSON LYTLE

Born: Tennessee, 1902

Principal short fiction
"Old Scratch in the Valley," 1932; "Alchemy," 1942; *A Novel, A Novella and Four Stories*, 1958.

Analysis
Andrew Lytle's career as writer, teacher, editor, and critic has been distinguished by his unsparing attention to the craft of fiction and his vast knowledge of Southern history and mores. Following the tradition of Gustave Flaubert and Henry James, he has perfected the rhetoric of "rendering" an action through the use of the five senses to evoke an "immediate sense of life" and through restricting the point of view to the mind of the protagonist—a mind not always equal to the occasion. Locating in his milieu "archetypal" actions, Lytle, like other writers who participated in the "Fugitive" and "Agrarian" movements, relates the Southern historical experience to "post-Edenic existence." Classical allusions enrich that vision of decline which finds strength and hope engendered by defeat. One must suffer knowledge of the fallen human condition in order to love. Flight from or conquest of the world will not serve. Lytle's subject is familial and spiritual inheritance which brings to crisis the tension between freedom and responsibility, adolescence and maturity, and—in most of his fiction—man and woman. The protagonist of "Jericho, Jericho, Jericho" discerns two "spirits" at work in her world. One is life-sustaining, "equal to the trials of planting, of cultivating, and of the gathering time"; one is not. The spirit that denies cannot long endure the trials of life. Responsible participation in the human community demands a large measure of sacrifice and charity, qualities that not only can regenerate the physical inheritance but that also can define the Christian.

Major publications other than short fiction
NOVELS: *The Long Night*, 1936; *At the Moon's Inn*, 1941; *A Name for Evil*, 1947; *The Velvet Horn*, 1957.
NONFICTION: *Bedford Forrest and His Critter Company*, 1931; *The Hero with the Private Parts*, 1966; *A Wake for the Living*, 1975.

Thomas M. Carlson

THOMAS MCAFEE

Born: Alabama, 1928

Principal short fiction
Whatever Isn't Glory, 1980.

Analysis
Tom McAfee is in many ways a traditional storyteller, interested primarily in character and scene. His characters often tell their own stories, revealing themselves through anecdote and incident. McAfee's own voice always sits behind these characters and directs the reader's attention and sympathies by way of a quick detail or a precise, descriptive phrase. The distance he maintains between his own voice and his character's point of view provides a texture which controls the material without stopping the scene or flow of time to editorialize. This is perhaps his most distinguishing characteristic. His prose is lean and precise in its attention to objective details: he puts down exactly what he sees, keeping exposition to a minimum. In this way, his technique can be described as cinematic. His sense of timing and phrasing has been learned not only from motion pictures but also from poetry, which he also writes. His subject on one level is often the South, but his interest is to cut through to "whatever isn't glory," to reveal the difficulties of character with both an unblinking toughness and a compassion for the pain he often finds there.

Major publications other than short fiction
NOVEL: *Rover Youngblood*, 1969.
POETRY: *Poems and Stories*, 1960; *I'll Be Home Late Tonight*, 1967.

Greg Michalson

DOROTHY MCCARTNEY

Born: Pennsylvania, 1914

Principal short fiction
"Straw Hat," 1932; "Doll House," 1935; "How the Swans Saved Their Nest," 1952; "Trailer Fever," 1952; "Ole Pete and the Phosphate Bag," 1975.

Analysis
Dorothy McCartney's stories are quiet tales about little people in little situations. Characters are presented "warts and all" without judgments. The settings are small-town or rural, usually; but the dilemmas are universal. The author gently scrutinizes the slices of life she chooses to put on the slides of her microscope. No great dramas appear here . . . just poignancy and the day-to-day struggle for simple dignity.

Major publications other than short fiction
POETRY: *Lemmus Lemmus and Other Poems*, 1973.

CAROLE SPEARIN MCCAULEY

Born: Massachusetts, 1939

Principal short fiction
Six Portraits, 1973; "Monty Montgomery Knorr, I Don't Love You Any More," 1979.

Analysis
Carole Spearin McCauley's fiction is concerned with a passion for human survivial, and who survives or fails and why, as in "Cage," "Ruby Wins," and *Happenthing in Travel On* (1975), a novel which deals with a women's commune on a winter mountainside. McCauley has a passionate interest in evolving the lives of contemporary women as in "Z and We" and *The Honesty Tree* (1977), a novel about a lesbian couple in a New England town. She experiments with the literary computer—the machine used as a tool, where appropriate, to make character portraits, dialogues, parable, satire, and parody significant to the twentieth century instead of the eighteenth. Feminist critic Andrea Dworkin wrote of *Happenthing in Travel On*: "This is a book about the struggle to survive—*in* the environment, not against it as its enemy. McCauley looks at things with an underlying ethic, a sense of justice. She sees the way women at our most whole do see: with compassion, without sentimentality. . . . This is an adventure story rooted in women's consciousness." Other critics have noted her meticulous grounding in reality, willingness to tackle sexual and political content usually avoided (lesbianism, bisexuality, politics of big money cancer research), and her ability to produce meaningful, even delightful work from an unlikely source of formal experimentation: the computer.

Major publications other than short fiction
NOVELS: *Happenthing in Travel On*, 1975; *The Honesty Tree*, 1977; *Cold Steal*, 1980.

NONFICTION: *Computers and Creativity*, 1974; *Pregnancy After 35*, 1976; *Surviving Breast Cancer*, 1979.

JOHN A. MCCLUSKEY, JR.

Born: Ohio, 1944

Principal short fiction

"The Pilgrims," 1971; "Nairobi Night," 1973; "John Henry's Home," 1975; "Forty in the Shade," 1978; "Winter Telltale," 1978; "Whatever Happened to Red Garland?," 1980.

Analysis

John McCluskey once stated that "as a writer I try to achieve that level of creative excellence so ably personified by artists as diverse as Ralph Ellison, Romare Bearden (painter), and Miles Davis (musician)." He still subscribes to that notion which strongly implies influences from a variety of art expressions. He attempts to utilize the rich and broad Afro-American vernacular in working what he hopes are precise and compressed statements about humanity. Although most of his few published pieces employ a basic and optimistic realism, he has experimented with the blending of individual and communal points of view to enhance his statement. McCluskey attempts narrative strategies that speak as broadly as possible, strategies rooted in and informed by a tradition familiar to him and in a tradition (often oral) that has been barely mined. Drawing upon his listening to Afro-American classical music / (jazz) and folklore, he views a multitude of thematic and structural possibilities.

Major publications other than short fiction

NOVEL: *Look What They Done to My Song*, 1974.

JAMES MCCONKEY

Born: Ohio, 1921

Principal short fiction

Night Stand, 1965; "Fireflies," 1977; "Mythology, Art, and the Farming Life," 1977; "The Tale of the Lucky Fisherman," 1977; "The Idea of Hawk," 1978; "The Man Who Couldn't Cry," 1978; "Bodiless Guests," 1980.

Analysis

A majority of James McConkey's short fiction is based on autobiographical materials. What gives fictional nature to such work, enabling it to extend beyond the memoir, is the degree to which events from an actual life achieve a universality which relates to the experiences of the reader while implying the relationship of those experiences to something beyond them. The "I" is representational, whatever the personal identification with the author. His stories, although self-contained, are part of a projected three-volume work, an autobiographical novel in which each story's present moment is one with the author's at the moment of writing, and from which the past, altering in interpretation as the author moves through time, can be viewed. The first volume of that work, *Crossroads* (1968), contains, in addition to the first-person stories in *Night Stand*, material written exclusively for it as well as the following, originally published as stories: "Every Day Requires an Atlas and More" and "In Praise of Chekhov." The second volume, planned for publication in 1981, will include several already-published stories.

Major publications other than short fiction

NOVELS: *Crossroads*, 1968; *A Journey to Sahalin*, 1971; *The Tree House Confessions*, 1979.

NONFICTION: *The Novels of E. M. Forster*, 1957.

HOWARD MCCORD

Born: Texas, 1932

Principal short fiction
"The Layman's Guide to Castration," 1965; "The Brigadier and the Nephew," 1968; *The Arctic Desert*, 1975; *The Arcs of Lowitz*, 1979; *The Great Toad Hunt and Other Expeditions*, 1980; "In That Act," 1980.

Analysis
The chiaroscuro energy in Howard McCord's fiction involves juxtaposition of characters against a strong geography: deserts, mountains, and wildernesses figure as metaphoric matrices defining the characters' situation and resolution. The sensual integrity of natural process provides an interface where interdependent development is inevitable. The excitement of the challenge is that some information is implied, luring the reader to make associative leaps and establishing rewarding conditions of complicity. His stories, varying in length from the poetically terse and compact "one-page novels" to full-form traditional narratives, recurrently involve a powerful, mysterious woman moving near a male narrator defined as both flawed and searching. If the female figure is not present, that absence itself is crucial as informational counterpoint, in the way that silence is used for emphasis in modern music. This is another important access to McCord's work: musicians and musical forms give compressed structural clues; present are such artists as Cecil Taylor, Archie Shepp, and Coleman Hawkins, placed near Kepler and Lowitz and alongside Greek and Asian classical figures. Neural resonances are produced by inevitable caesurae. In an interlock of physics and metaphysics ("Kundalini" and "The Kabbalah" exquisitely defined in *Eight Dreams*), there is the intense clarity of a personally observed and applied spirituality. The vocabulary moves from "kylix" to "psalter," the time-zone from Cenozoic to Yamabushi; the reader moves with Stéphane Mallarmé, Socrates, St. Thomas Aquinas, and Virginia Woolf through a varied landscape. The structuring of the prose itself is as elegant as music; human behavior is perceptibly entwined with earth-process, in history.

Major publications other than short fiction
POETRY: *Maps*, 1971; *The Diary of a Lost Girl*, 1972; *The Old Beast*, 1975; *Perfecting an Unspeakable Act*, 1975; *Selected Poems*, 1975; *Peach Mountain Smoke Out*, 1978.
NONFICTION: *The Life of Fraenkel's Death*, 1970 (with Walter Lowenfels); *Gnomonology: A Handbook of Systems*, 1971; *Some Notes to Gary Snyder's Myths & Texts*, 1971.

Carol Berge

WALTER MCDONALD

Born: Texas, 1934

Principal short fiction
"The Prodigal," 1972; "Snow Job," 1975; "The Track," 1976.

Analysis
  Most of Walter McDonald's stories come from his experiences as an Air Force jet pilot, or (better) from pilot-lore and what he observed and imagined. Realistic, terse, they focus on ordinary men caught up in the extraordinary experiences of flight and of war (usually the Vietnam War). Several of the stories come from a novel about the last Air Force fighter squadron in Vietnam, *Mayday*, scheduled for publication by a regional press.

Major publications other than short fiction
  POETRY: *Caliban in Blue*, 1976; *One Thing Leads to Another*, 1978; *Anything, Anything*, 1980; *Working Against Time*, 1980; *Burning the Fence*, 1981.

COLLEEN J. MCELROY

Born: Missouri, 1935

Principal short fiction
"The Lemon," 1974; "Ageless," 1974.

Analysis

Colleen J. McElroy's stories cover a remarkable range, both of subject and technique, from the seemingly effortless country-ballad flow of "A Brief Spell by the River" to the richly mysterious urban family memoir, "Look for You Yesterday and Here You Come Today," to the quiet doom of her Jason Packard and the Felliniesque hopeful despair of her Imogene. It is hard to think of another writer—black or white, male or female—who could have written both the deceptively underplayed, whipcracking shocker "Farm Day," and that astonishing science-fiction story "Wulfen," which deals with an Earth woman's passion for a truly alien being. Steadfastly resisting categorization of any kind, McElroy is as much at home in the moonscape of madness ("Under the Equinox") as with the struggle to cling to some form of sanity under impossible conditions ("The Simple Language of Drones"). She is a traditionalist in the sense that her work is most deeply concerned with *story*, *character*, *voice*, and especially *place*—she can call back a long-gone landscape as economically and rightly as she can summon up one that no one has yet seen. She made her first reputation as a poet; and her adventurousness, her willingness to experiment, is that of a poet, as is her understanding of texture and juxtaposition.

Major publications other than short fiction
POETRY: *The Mules Done Long Since Gone*, 1974; *Music from Home*, 1976; *Winters Without Snow*, 1980; *Lie and Say You Love Me*, 1981.

NONFICTION: *Speech and Language in the Development of the Preschool Child*, 1973.

Peter S. Beagle

MARY MACKEY

Born: Indiana, 1945

Principal short fiction
"The Feel of the Smell Itself," 1970; "Inside My Purple Python," 1970; *Immersion*, 1972; "Nadine, Honey Is That You?," 1974.

Analysis
Like her longer works, Mackey's short stories deal with questions of memory, time, and the interface between sensation and intellect. Underlying this is a recurrent concern with the position of women in American society. Often her works have a surreal quality which is reminiscent of Kafka or Bulgakov. A man awakens, for example, to discover that his girl friend has taken his body and left him hers, or a woman suddenly sees the world as an ant would see it and discovers that colors have their own particular smells. Mackey herself has long advocated a more plastic application of the traditional literary conventions, and in a recent interview she stated that she was working on a voice which she called "first person insane," a mode which would allow her to develop omniscient first person narrators. Her style, hence, is often humorous, but beneath the laughter she has placed numerous literary allusions, patterns of symbols, complex social and political questions, and experiments with the English language itself. As one reviewer put it, "Mackey reminds us of James Joyce on laughing gas."

Major publications other than short fiction
NOVEL: *McCarthy's List*, 1979.

FLORRI MCMILLAN

Born: Minnesota, 1939

Principal short fiction
"The Gun Lady," 1978; "Hollyhocks," 1978; "Daily Acts," 1978; "Services Are Private," 1978; "Petites Lecons Francaises," 1978; "The Elms," 1979; "The Lummox," 1979; "Statement," 1979; "Animus," 1979; "The Bereaved," 1980.

Analysis
In a relentless exploration of the human condition, Florri McMillan's stories reveal the inevitability of man's heroism. She employs a variety of fictional structures and a rich diversity of narrative voice to expand and dramatize her basic theme. The most common critical response is to her command of language and the facility of her prose. Authentic, unusually paced dialogue, and use of "the telling detail, often as image" are characteristic of her short fiction. Both her stories and familiar essays are scenic in design. Distinctions between the two genres are purposely blurred for maximum effect, as in "The Gun Lady" and "Petites Lecons Francaises." The influence of literary existentialism is evident in McMillan's fiction ("Daily Acts," for example) and has led her in her most recent work to a thematic exploration of psychological time. Moving forward from Jean-Paul Sartre's circular interpretation, she has presented in her novel *Harriet* (unpublished) an interior vision of concentric, rather than spiraling, levels of time. McMillan's conception of psychological time is most explicitly displayed in her short story, "The Survivor's Path."

Major publications other than short fiction
POETRY: "Spectrum," 1978.
NONFICTION: "An English Party," 1978; "The Head Table," 1978; "Mid North Reverie," 1980; "Confessions of a Menopause Maiden," 1980; "Maria Tallchief," 1980.

EUGENE MCNAMARA

Born: Illinois, 1930

Principal short fiction

Salt, 1975; *The Search for Sarah Grace and Other Stories*, 1977; "Midwinter," 1978; "Bright, Agile, Impassable and Subtle," 1979; "Pushing Fifty," 1979; "The Art of the Novel," 1979.

Analysis

Eugene McNamara is a talented writer who is a successful editor and poet as well as a fiction writer. His short fiction is accessible and easily absorbs the reader into its structure, which is niether deep nor multilayered but always effective and disturbing. Dermot McCarthy describes McNamara's short stories as "structures linking various dualities or polarities of character, time, and place." He goes on to say,

> Points of view, times settings, moods change, alternate. Moreover, McNamara's fictions are structures under stress; paradoxically, held together by the very tensions that threaten to pull them apart. . . . Character, time, and place are always divided or on the point of breaking up, as if some dooming fault runs through all experience. McNamara blends realism and romance in the manner of the ghost story and his best stories haunt the reader for some time afterwards.

Major publications other than short fiction

POETRY: *For the Mean Time*, 1965; *Outerings*, 1970; *Love Scenes*, 1970; *Dillinger Poems*, 1971; *Hard Words*, 1972; *Passages*, 1972; *Diving for the Body*, 1974; *In Transit*, 1975; *Screens*, 1977.

DAVID MADDEN

Born: Tennessee, 1933

Principal short fiction
"My Name Is Not Antonio," 1960; "Hair of the Dog," 1967; "The Master's Thesis," 1967; "Nothing Dies But Something Mourns," 1968; "A Voice in the Garden," 1969; "On Target," 1969; "The Day the Flowers Came," 1969; "Home Comfort," 1970; "Frank Brown's Brother," 1970; "The House of Pearl," 1970; *The Shadow Knows*, 1970; "Traven," 1970; "No Trace," 1971; "The Cartridge Belt," 1972; "A Secondary Character," 1972; "A Part in Pirandello," 1972; "The Spread-Legged Girl," 1972; "Looking at the Dead," 1972; "The Day the Flowers Came," 1972; "Night Shift," 1972; "The Singer," 1972; "Lindbergh's Rival," 1973; "Here He Comes! There He Goes!," 1973; "Wanted: Ghost Writer," 1973; "The World's One Breathing," 1973; "Hurry Up Please, It's Time," 1974; "The Hero and the Witness," 1974; "Second Look: The Rape of an Indian Brave," 1975; "Call Herman in to Supper," 1976; "In the Bag," 1977; "Putting an Act Together," 1980.

Analysis
David Madden's fiction consists of two major strains, the Southern and the non-Southern subject matter, rendered with a diversity of oral and literary styles and techniques that are inseparable from his recurring theme: the isolated individual copes with reality through various uses of the imagination, transforming himself and affecting others. Madden consciously uses techniques that activate emotions, imagination, and intellect to make the reader a collaborator in the creative process. Madden was first influenced by his grandmother's storytelling and the charged images of radio drama and motion pictures. The Appalachian storytelling tradition gives form to such stories as "God Proud," "The World's One Breathing," and "Home Comfort." The storytelling voices of young and old, male and female, are almost audible, creating a "pleasure-dome." Later influences were literary: Thomas Wolfe, James Joyce, Albert Camus, Wright Morris. Style and technique are more literary in "The Master's Thesis," "No Trace," and "The Day the Flowers Came." His novels also reflect this dual approach: *Cassandra Singing* (1969) and *Bijou* (1974) often dramatize the oral storytelling process itself; *The Suicide's Wife* (1978) is very much in the purely literary tradition. His experimental techniques are experienced more directly in "Looking at the Dead," "The Singer," and "Second Look: The Rape of an Indian Brave." Although most of Madden's fiction is written from the third-person point of view, he improvises upon various oral storytelling devices in his first-person stories. In his novel *On the Big Wind* (1980), Madden skillfully combines seven short stories, consciously making use of oral, literary, and experimental techniques

and styles, with a single central character as the motivating force, to make the episodes interact.

Major publications other than short fiction
NOVELS: *The Beautiful Greed*, 1961; *Cassandra Singing*, 1969; *The Shadow Knows*, 1970; *Brothers in Confidence*, 1972; *Bijou*, 1974; *The Suicide's Wife*, 1978; *Pleasure-Dome*, 1979; *On the Big Wind*, 1980.

PLAYS: *Cassandra Singing*, 1957; *The Day the Flowers Came*, 1975.

NONFICTION: *Wright Morris*, 1964; *The Poetic Image in Six Genres*, 1969; *James M. Cain*, 1970; *Harlequin's Stick, Charlie's Cane*, 1975; *A Primer of the Novel*, 1979.

Peggy Bach

RACHEL MADDUX

Born: Kansas, 1912

Principal short fiction

Turnips Blood, 1936; "Mother of a Child," 1938; "We Are Each Other's Children," 1938; "The House in the Woods," 1945; "Final Clearance," 1956; "Overture and Beginners," 1957; "The Clay Pigeon," 1959.

Analysis

At first glance, the stories of Rachel Maddux appear to be almost simple, folksy tales. They frequently involve a husband and wife or a pair of lovers as major characters; they speak in familiar terms and act familiar scenes of what life is all about. Each story, however, has far deeper implications that lead the reader to a universal understanding of the world that used to be, or, at least, ought to be—or never was. Many of the stories appear to be based on incidents from real life, but each situation is placed in a larger context which gives meaning to all such incidents, regardless of time and place. Life in (and around) the Army in World War II comes to be a representation of the struggle for freedom—for anyone; a delightful and poignant ghost story is actually a satire on bureaucracy and the red tape of government; a young girl with her dolls and teddy bear serves as a reminder of the life that we all had to learn (the hard way) not to expect any longer. There is, however, in her fiction the hope and the persistent struggle to keep alive the dream that out there somewhere is an attainable perfection. Such themes and plotting can lead to sentimentality; but Rachel Maddux knows the limits there, too. Her stories (and her longer works) are deftly plotted and philosophically concise, which may account for the several adaptations of her works to the stage, television, and film.

Major publications other than short fiction

NOVELS: *The Green Kingdom*, 1957; *A Walk in the Spring Rain*, 1966.
NONFICTION: *Abel's Daughter*, 1960; *The Orchard Children*, 1977.

Thomas D. Lane

CLARENCE MAJOR

Born: Georgia, 1936

Principal short fiction
"Ulysses, Who Slept Across from Me," 1957; "District: A Chapter from a Novel," 1959; "Girl in a Boat," 1960; "Church Girl," 1967; "Excerpts from a Novel in Progress," 1968; "From *The Faerie*," 1968; "Surviving Every Step of the Brutal Way," 1971; "Going Home Again," 1971; "The Future," 1972; "Sue & Tee," 1972; "A Life Story," 1972; "Dossy O," 1972; "Early Grave," 1972; "Eli," 1972; "Drama in Flames," 1973; "Realism: A Dark Light," 1973; "Resurrection," 1973; "Ten Pecan Pies," 1973; "The Father Surrogate," 1974; "Just Think: Survival," 1974; "An Area in the Cerebral Hemisphere," 1975; "All-American Cheese," 1975; "Fish, Tomatoes, Mama & Book," 1975; "Social Work," 1975; "Escape the Close Circle," 1975; "The Invention of Lubin," 1976; "Inlet," 1976; "Action," 1977; "Art," 1977; "Hitch," 1977; "Emergency Exit," 1977; "The Adventures of Maria Sinus: Or, The Return of the Action-Packed Adventure Story," 1978; "Fun and Games," 1978; "Marilyn," 1978; "Number Four," 1978; "The Vase and the Rose," 1978; "Maggie: A Woman of the King," 1979; "Da," 1979.

Analysis
Clarence Major's short stories mirror his deep concern for the art of fiction writing and the times. Similar to his longer fictions, Major's writing is experimental and does not follow the typical or standard techniques of plot and character development. Doug Bolling describes Major's works in "A Reading of Clarence Major's Short Fiction": "Rather than a concern for the 'form' . . . we see that this fictionist works with 'process,' with open forms, with the inconclusive, and with the interplay of formal and nonformal tensions." Bolling goes on to say:

> Clarence Major shows us how his fiction may bring its strengths to bear on the confusions and compromises of American culture while at the same time preserving its integrity as an art form and its right to break through the conventions of the academy in order to create new and potent rhythms, shapes, and perceptions.

Major publications other than short fiction
NOVELS: *All Night Visitors*, 1969; *No*, 1973; *Reflex and Bone Structure*, 1975; *Emergency Exit*, 1979.
POETRY: *The Fires That Burn in Heaven*, 1954; *Love Poems of a Black Man*, 1965; *Human Juices*, 1966; *Swallow the Lake*, 1970; *Symptoms & Madness*, 1971; *Private Line*, 1971; *The Cotton Club*, 1972; *The Syncopated Cakewalk*, 1974.
NONFICTION: *Dictionary of Afro-American Slang*, 1970.

MICHAEL PATRICK MALONE

Born: Illinois, 1951

Principal short fiction

"Inning," 1974; "On the Old Roman Special," 1975; "Nebraska, Outside," 1975; "Ice Cream Waltz," 1976; "I Was Charlie Manson," 1977; "Pilgrimage," 1977; "Kennedy Is Killed/A Father Drinks and Drives," 1977; "Stall #4," 1978; "Grandfather's Guests," 1978; "Reflection of Crying Brides," 1979.

Analysis

The characteristic stories of Michael Patrick Malone are set in Chicago's still strongly ethnic Irish neighborhoods, and depict an urban subculture that has lost its traditional vitality. The characters who people his fictions are torn between the disintegrating social and moral bonds of the past and the uncertain futures that loom for men and women inadequately prepared to imagine new ways of thinking and feeling. Malone's stories thus show affinities with the work of earlier authors such as James T. Farrell, but his themes are neither so sentimental as Farrell's, nor are his ironies as blatant and simplistic. In, for example, "The Old Roman Special," in which a city bus driver takes his young son on an all-day outing to Comiskey Park to watch the Yankees play the White Sox, Malone captures the warmth and humor of Chicago's working-class Irish; the dialogue that creates the scenes in a tavern is memorable. The ambiguous relationships between father, mother, and son in the matriarchal family are rendered with effective and economical particularity. Beyond this urban local color that exists to some extent for its own sake, there is a striking revelation of despair haunting the father's stunted life, and, further, of the shadow this casts across the sensibility of his impressionable son. Michael Patrick Malone is more than an urban local colorist; he is a regional writer in his work to date, but one who dramatizes with great skill the broader moral implications of a variety of slices of contemporary life.

OSCAR MANDEL

Born: Belgium, 1926

Principal short fiction
"A Conversation with Ossian Lhermite, Ph. D.," 1959-1960; *The Gobble-Up Stories*, 1966; "Three Tales," 1967; "Water from an Italian Pump," 1972; "The Lucky Pebble," 1972; "Two Blind Men," 1976.

Analysis
Oscar Mandel's fictions belong to a species that has become exceedingly rare; namely, the classical fable—in other words, the fable which is timeless in its choice of immediate subject, timeless in its theme, and timeless in its diction. The classical fable is patrician art, and Mandel is clearly enamored of the lapidary tradition: "Presently the Greeks built the horse (there was no one like Odysseus for the handling of hammer and nails) and soon thereafter Troy was captured and sacked to the last footstool." Some of these fables are friendly enough, but in most of them Mandel is faithful to the classical tradition again in successfully fusing charm and cruelty. The very title—*Gobble-Up Stories*—exhibits this fusion, for it is at once cozy and indicative of the death-struggles to come: "The ibis had become extremely rich by working hard, and the thrush had remained poor, also by working hard." These fables are like richly jeweled daggers, whose destination is either and both the museum for decorative arts and the bloody battlefield.

Major publications other than short fiction
NOVEL: *Chi Po and the Sorcerer*, 1964.
PLAYS: *Collected Plays*, 1970-1971; *The Patriots of Nantucket*, 1976.
POETRY: *Simplicities*, 1974.
NONFICTION: *A Definition of Tragedy*, 1961.

MARVIN MANDELL

Born: New York, 1927

Principal short fiction
"Narcissus," 1968; "The Aesculapians," 1971; "King David," 1973; "Paradise Lost: J. J.," 1976; "Love, Work, and Knowledge," 1976.

Analysis
"Anyone can make a yellow ball out of a sun," Picasso is reported to have said; "but to take a yellow ball and make a sun out of it—*that* is art!" Marvin Mandell believes that art should magnify, not trivialize, man. It should also magnify his language. In this age of dehumanization—of joylessness, of anomie, of alienation—art's purpose of celebrating life is crucial, perhaps sacred. The artist should not abdicate this calling. He should strive to show death-in-life without becoming dead himself or allowing his language to become so. He should also at least suggest the vital beneath the mask. "God has showed me a fair city," Villon wrote; surely that city is as real as the world in which we find ourselves.

FREDERICK MANFRED

Born: Iowa, 1912

Principal short fiction

"Child Delinquent," 1944; "Horse Touch," 1945; "Lord Grizzly," 1954; *Arrow of Love*, 1961; "Judith A Fragment," 1962; *Apples of Paradise*, 1968; "The Voice of the Turtle," 1973; "Sleeping Dogs," 1975; "The Founding of the Rock River Church," 1975; "Splinters," 1977; "Free," 1979; "Hijinks with the Minister's Sons," 1979.

Analysis

Frederick Manfred's short fiction retains the strong regional tenor of his novels. The stories are primarily rooted in Manfred's self-designated, but now popularly accepted, "Siouxland Territory," the intersecting locale of Iowa, Minnesota, and South Dakota. Farm, suburbia, college town; all are settings for these tales. The range of the stories, from rollicking comedy to moving tragedy, is similar to the novels, and revealing of Manfred's fictional skill. Several of the tales make use of Manfred's autobiographical character Thurs Wraldson (also called Alfred "Free" Alfredson in two recent novels). Two of the stories, "Arrow of Love," and "Blood Will Tell," are critically esteemed as among the best American short stories.

Major publications other than short fiction

NOVELS: *The Golden Bowl*, 1944; *Boy Almighty*, 1945; *This Is the Year*, 1947; *The Chokecherry Tree*, 1948; *The Primitive*, 1949; *The Brother*, 1950; *The Giant*, 1951; *Lord Grizzly*, 1954; *Morning Red*, 1956; *Riders of Judgment*, 1957; *Conquering Horse*, 1959; *Wanderlust*, 1962; *Secret Plume*, 1964; *The Secret Place*, 1965; *King of Spades*, 1966; *Eden Prairie*, 1968; *The Manly-Hearted Woman*, 1975; *Milk of Wolves*, 1976; *Green Earth*, 1977; *The Wind Blows Free*, 1979.

POETRY: *Winter Count*, 1966.

John H. Timmerman

JEANNE MARINA

Born: Michigan, 1941

Principal short fiction

"I am a Sisseton-Wahpeton Sioux," 1974; "You'd Like My Brother, He's a Cement Truck Driver," 1976; "Helvi's Sarena," 1978; "Grass Fires," 1979; "A Small Death," 1979; "The Blanket," 1979.

Analysis

Jeanne Marina is an unknown writer from the Middle West. She writes realistic fiction with internal monologue. She describes process in people's lives, and how process interacts with product. Thus, she shows how time, chronologically, does not matter, except as incident. Her working-class Finnish background laces her work.

MARION M. MARKHAM

Born: Illinois, 1929

Principal short fiction
"The Last Surprise," 1970; "Rain Violets," 1972; "The First One's the Hardest," 1972; "What Really Happened to Scrooge," 1973; "Almost There," 1974; "The Mother Planet," 1977; "The Ultimate Weapon," 1977; "A Study of Shadows," 1978; "The Man of Her Dreams," 1978; "Strangler's Hands," 1979; "Night Convoy," 1979; "The Handy Man," 1980.

Analysis
Each of us lives in a private world that no one else can fully understand. That is the theme of one of Marion Markham's short stories, the essential thread running through much of her fiction. She writes of alienated individuals in alien worlds. The quintessential problem is that their own private worlds are no less alien to them than the larger one. Their quest, then, becomes a universal: to find the continuum; to make meaning of the fragments of their lives. "Strange," says one of her characters, ". . . how the most unexpected things (happen) to the most ordinary people." Markham is a craftswoman whose lean, lucid style points up the ironies of life and its subtle connections. (Knowledge of another can be the ultimate weapon against oneself. The apple tree, shelter for lovers, bears the seeds of destruction. The heat from a tenement fire affects the pictures on a suburban wall.) Her stories, whether mystery, fantasy, or romance, evoke moods which transcend the final periods. With a light, sure touch, she unveils the mundane trappings of our lives to reveal the deeper, often horrifying, meanings they possess. Her insight, like Flannery O'Connor's, is slightly askew. She will give you the key; but—watch out—she may change the lock.

Carol Adorjan

JACK MATTHEWS

Born: Ohio, 1925

Principal short fiction

Bitter Knowledge, 1964; "Another Story," 1970; "On the Shores of Chad Creek," 1972; "The Burial," 1975; "A Questionnaire for Rudolph Gordon," 1977; "Who Is Who and When Will We Be Real?," 1978; *Tales From the Ohio Land*, 1978; "Muerte, Nada and Bradley Jones," 1979; "Tableau with Three Ghostly Women," 1979.

Analysis

For Jack Matthews, the writing of a short story is a heuristic act, a particular kind of hypothesis whose terms (beyond certain conventions of form, tempo, and distancing) are not formulated. The story itself provides the formulation by which it is to be judged. The direction of his probe is toward the inner life; it is by nature exciting, superficial, inflammatory, and empty. Thus, the "relevant narrative art of our time." Fiction can do more and achieve greater subtleties. Matthews' own intent being centripetal, he tries to articulate the realities that are implicit in being human, often as they are revealed in outwardly drab, reduced, "minimal" characters. Thus, the intent and movement of his fiction is opposed to most contemporary work; and he is content with this fact; he believes the art of fiction is too noble an enterprise to settle for thrills and sensations of plot (as in popular fiction) or those of imagery and radical juxtaposition (as in "literary" work). Even though he delights in experimentation, Matthews despises the current habit of viewing literature as a virtuoso performance, and finds talk about "new modes for new realities" both brainless and hateful. The traditional short story is a magnificent art form, conducive to humanity. It is no more exhausted as an art form than the eight-tone scale or old recipes for baking bread. The mystery stories which have always been celebrated are still very much intact (and in need of celebration), and the variations upon old themes provided by a changing world are theoretically infinite.

Major publications other than short fiction

NOVELS: *Hanger Stout, Awake!*, 1967; *Beyond the Bridge*, 1970; *Tale of Asa Bean*, 1971; *The Charisma Champaigns*, 1972; *Pictures of the Journey Back*, 1973.

POETRY: *An Alamanac for Twilight*, 1967.

NONFICTION: *Collecting Rare Books for Pleasure and Profit*, 1977.

JANE MAYHALL

Born: Kentucky, 1921

Principal short fiction

"The Darkness," 1947; "The Men," 1949; "The Game," 1951; "Mrs. Crutchfield," 1954; *Ready for the Ha-Ha*, 1967; "Gertrude Stein, Things as They Are," 1972; "The Enemy," 1973; "Sweets to the Sweet," 1978.

Analysis

Jane Mayhall's stories exhibit well-crafted, structural awareness and an approach to human conflict dramatically on target, and revealed in various aspects—brought into a narrative focus. Mayhall has been called both "saturnine" and "compassionate." Basically, she is neither. Her work is opposed to academic shufflings and stacking the decks in terms of preconceived ideas. Her characters, as in "The Enemy" and "Sweets to the Sweet," are not drawn from literary or sociological concepts. She is out to debunk the mystique of collective mediocrity, frivolous horrors, and sentimental violence. What remains are real people and their individual experiences which do not fall into stylistic slots. Her major interests in subject are New York streets and the poor enclaves of the Kentucky working class. Gustave Flaubert, Anton Chekhov, August Strindberg (his rare stories, not so much plays), and Doris Lessing have suggested intensities for the rendering of subtle or overt conflict. A lifetime can be communicated in four pages, with the swiftness of time and underlying profundities. In the use of dialect, spoken dialogue, and descriptive passages the metaphors always flow from natural sources, matching words with event.

Major publications other than short fiction

NOVEL: *Cousin to Human*, 1960.
POETRY: *Givers & Takers 1*, 1970; *Givers & Takers 2*, 1973.

IB MELCHIOR

Born: Denmark, 1917

Principal short fiction

"Fraülein Hannelore," 1947; "Sleeper Agent," 1948; "The Vidiot," 1956; "The Winner and New . . .," 1956; "The Racer," 1956; "A Christmas to Remember," 1956; "Nicole," 1957; "The Community Mind," 1958; "The Story of a Loaf," 1977; "Leif the Lucky," 1978.

Analysis

Ib Melchior writes and lives by a motto remembered from a Scandinavian short story of years ago: *"There is always a third way out."* The characters in his stories are often placed in seemingly impossible situations with an apparent "either-or" solution—with both choices disastrous. Melchior has them look for that third way out. Suspense; tight, logical plotting; imagination; vivid description; and complete authenticity and attention to detail are the hallmarks of Melchior's work. Coupled with characterizations in depth that offer remarkable insight this has prompted reviewers worldwide to observations about his work, he has been called "one of the masters of adventure fiction" in England, and the Danish Press called his work, "remarkable in its suspense, style and psychological insight." His work is now published in twenty-five countries. Melchior believes that an author must have a thorough, firsthand knowledge of his subject matter in order to sound accurate and authentic. He believes a reader will instinctively know if the author is *not* authentic—and, conversely, will respond to authenticity. Both his short fiction and his novels have, therefore, been based in many cases on his own experience as a United States counter intelligence agent in World War II. When he feels he lacks the personal experience, he goes out to get it.

Major publications other than short fiction

NOVELS: *Order of Battle*, 1972; *Sleeper Agent*, 1975; *The Haigerloch Project*, 1977; *The Watchdogs of Abaddon*, 1979; *The Marcus Device*, 1980.

PLAY: *Hour of Vengence*, 1962;

PAUL METCALF

Born: Massachusetts, 1917

Principal short fiction
"The Doll," 1963; "Indian Game," 1963; "A Good Appetite," 1974; "The Straw Hat," 1976; "Bourbon and Tomatoes," 1976; "The Assassination," 1976.

Analysis
Although the short story has not been a form to which Paul Metcalf has devoted major attention, certain ideas or impressions that have been valuable to him have found expression through no other mode. Some are discrete stories, some are excerpts from novels, and some are recorded dreams, the latter being formally structured, as though with conscious attention. In many cases the stories are less than ten pages and might more properly be called *vignettes*. It is the challenge of this method to gain a sharp impression of a single character, or to gain access, perhaps, to a complex idea through the juxtaposition of two or more unlikely characters—all this with the maximum clarity and economy of language.

Major publications other than short fiction
NOVELS: *Will West*, 1956; *Genoa*, 1975.
POETRY: *Patagoni*, 1971; *The Middle Passage*, 1976; *Apalache*, 1976; *Zip Odes*, 1979.

ROBERTA METZ

Born: New York, 1943

Principal short fiction
"Models," 1978; "Friends," 1978; "The Loved One," 1978; "Mother & Child," 1979; "Triple Exposure," 1979; "The Weightlifter," 1979; "Mandalay," 1979; "Blow-up," 1979; "Joanna," 1979; "Sunny," 1979; "Coming of Age," 1979; "Tuti," 1980; "Son Days," 1980; "Butterfly," 1980; "Some Ducks," 1980.

Analysis
The short fiction Roberta Metz writes takes texture from her poetry and experimental prose. Although lyrical, she strives for a clean, controlled style. Believing there is enough mystery within the "household," she avoids being elusive and unnecessarily oblique. What remains constant is the struggle to fuse personal experience into the universal one. When images make their slow march down the page, they are meant to give clues, not cloak or distract. Metz's stories have compelled both sexes to comment that these fictions impart a feeling of fresh air, vitality, tenderness, and sensuality, and that they radiate real joy. With a slightly missionary attitude, Metz has attempted to take "erotica" out of the literary ghetto and stress that this genre need not be written in one color: blue.

Major publications other than short fiction
POETRY: *Woman the Children the Men*, 1979; *Private Parts*, 1979.

LEONARD MICHAELS

Born: New York, 1933

Principal short fiction

Going Places, 1969; *I Would Have Saved Them If I Could*, 1975.

Analysis

The stories of Leonard Michaels tend to be about psychosexual relations in urban settings, particularly New York, and they vary a great deal in structure, style, and mood. They can be playful, grim, shocking, funny, lyrical; they range from long to short to very short. Most generally, the style is quick, very terse, and precise, with strong images, all controlled by the momentum of actions. A few of the stories are surrealistic, but none is unintelligible or without dramatic effect. Some characters reappear in several stories, especially a man named Phillip Leibowitz, his mother, friends, lovers, and antagonists. Through different incidents, which are the focus of different stories, some sense of Leibowitz's life, from childhood through early middle-age, begins to emerge. Most of the stories concern other characters—a college girl, a rabbi, a taxi driver—and certain historical figures; among the latter are Lord Byron and Leon Trotsky. Michaels' *The Men's Club* develops from a long short story by that name and contains numerous stories that parallel one another and overlap, exhibiting moments of erotic intensity in the lives of seven men who, in their relations with one another through a long night of talk and violence, discover themselves.

HEATHER ROSS MILLER

Born: North Carolina, 1939

Principal short fiction
A Spiritual Divorce and Other Stories, 1974.

Analysis
Heather Miller's stories convey realistically the multidimensional feelings that people have for one another and why these feelings change. Archetypes and symbols are delicately woven into the stories giving them a universal meaning. Miller further enlightens her readers to the psychological bonds that hold her characters together. Emma in "Little Orlando" has a strong wife-to-husband relationship with Roger. She describes him as "so strong and unafraid." When she is in his care, she feels warmth and comfort. Miller incorporates numerous archetypal symbols into "Little Orlando" giving deeper meaning to the story. In "Maria Is Hurt," a mother insists on washing her sick daughter's hair. "A child is clean and sweet. The most beautiful thing about a child is its innocence." Yet Maria's haunting fever dreams and flashback memories have already driven away innocence forever. The characters in *A Spiritual Divorce and Other Stories* range from an exotic foreign wife brought home by "crazy" Uncle Buck to an old woman who talks to her furnace; but major emphasis is placed on children. Miller states, "I do not always sympathize with them, but I think their positions in life (down under and always looking up) give them excellent views on adults who control life." Through her use of characterization, archetypes, and symbols, Miller leads her reader to a better understanding of these complex relationships.

Major publications other than short fiction
NOVELS: *The Edge of the Woods*, 1964; *Tenants of the House*, 1966; *Gone a Hundred Miles*, 1968; *Confessions of a Champeen Fire Baton Twirler*, 1976.
POETRY: *The Wind Southerly and Other Poems*, 1967; *Horse Horse Tyger Tyger*, 1973;

Elaine Parker

JIM WAYNE MILLER

Born: North Carolina, 1936

Principal short fiction

"The Lily," 1958; "There Sat We Down," 1960; "The Face and the Stone," 1961; "Brothers," 1963 (three related stories entitled "The Betrayal," "The War Games," and "Chinquapins"); "A Separation," 1963; "We Didn't Stop Running," 1966; "A Chicken in Every Pot," 1966; "The Man Who Feared a Lot," 1966; "A Card to Ruthie," 1967; "The Disrespectful Savages," 1967; "The Trade," 1967; "The Taste of Ironwater," 1969; "Shoeshine," 1969; "Steeltrap," 1969; "Devil's Due," 1969; "Going to the Mountains," 1969; "Run Under the Moon," 1970; "Clay People," 1970; "What Money Buys," 1974; "Little Birdie," 1977.

Analysis

Blending sophisticated and self-conscious storytelling with a folk mode found in the oral traditions of Appalachian America, Jim Wayne Miller's stories are clear and well ordered, carefully crafted, yet the antithesis of dense and difficult fiction in the arabesque mode. Characters and conflicts reflect contemporary Appalachia, where two worlds—the traditional and modern, with their "old-timey" and "outside" ways, their different values, viewpoints and rhythms—exist in stark and ugly juxtaposition and occasionally blend in interesting and harmonious accommodations. Miller writes of mountain men and women whose children have been scattered by the demands and entice-ments of business and industry, or who live on among a younger generation which has neither time nor inclination to follow the old ways. He writes of young people who shuttle back and forth between work places and places they consider home, or who struggle to break out of a way of life they consider morose, lacking in joy and affirmation. The story of a man who has lost children and grandchildren to contemporary America is told quietly in "Going to the Mountains," a representative narrative reminiscent of Chekhov's "The Lament." The Appalachian region and its people entered American fiction through the work of late nineteenth century local colorists who emphasized the quaint and exotic. At its best this fiction tended to be superficial; at its worst, it offered "rubberneck tours of rural slums." Miller's stories, like those of James Still, Harriette Simpson Arnow, and Gurney Norman, allow the reader to live with people who have, too often, only been looked at.

Major publications other than short fiction

POETRY: *Copperhead Cane*, 1964; *The More Things Change, the More They Stay the Same*, 1971; *Dialogue with a Dead Man*, 1974; *The Mountains Have Come Closer*, 1980.

WARREN C. MILLER

Born: Texas, 1924

Principal short fiction

"Wrap," 1973; " 'Or Only Asbury Park?', " 1974; "Knot," 1975; "Fabricator," 1977; "The Gulf's Message," 1978; "Learn and Tell," 1978; "Like It Was," 1979; "Gone with the Grits," 1979; "Essence," 1980; *A Small Town Is Best for Waiting and Other Stories*, 1980.

Analysis

Three of Warren Miller's stories, which have been appearing since 1971, have been cited in *The Best American Short Stories*: " 'Or Only Asbury Park?', " "Fabricator," "Like It Was." Laurel Speer states that Miller "writes with a combination of precision and warmth, controlling detail and building a complex, layered picture of his predominantly Southern landscape. Present is juxtaposed with past in a fluid movement of sound, rhythm, and repeated phrase. Every effect is subtly achieved, built word on word, image on image, so the reader is left in possession of fully fleshed characters in a context of both emotional and physical settings. The two elements are inextricable and skillfully intertwined." Warren Keith Wright states that "he incisively delineates personae trapped between what they recall of the past and what they fear of the future. Miller's is a completely imagined real world, where unbearable dreams impinge upon inescapable realities, and adaptation, however gallantly undertaken, does not always succeed. Miller's humor is a punchy propulsive madness." According to Betsy Feagan Colquitt, "Miller has written a series of stories about Lone Star, his fictive southeast Texas town. The authenticity of Miller's fiction is commendable as is his style, touched often with a gallows wit that adds complexity and irony to his themes." Miller's art is subtle, displaying his artistry through hilarious remarks and vivid imagery, which bring for the reader spontaneous laughter and satisfaction.

JOAN MILLMAN

Born: Massachusetts, 1931

Principal short fiction
"The Effigy," 1976; "Diminishing Returns," 1977; "Esau's Legacy," 1977; "Custody," 1980.

Analysis

Joan Millman's stories fall into two categories: treatments of first generation Jewish-American genre reminiscent of early Bernard Malamud, and acute commentary on contemporary suburbia. The former draws from her childhood which brought her close to the immigrant experience. In the latter, her caustic view of the middle-class woman dealing with mid-life crisis is drawn from her most immediate role, the wife/mother attempting to give house room to her muse. Millman's peculiar syntax evokes an ethnic irony patterned by the conversations of her youth. One might call her a Jewish John Cheever. All of her work is an attempt to explore the blandness of the assimilated life. Her fiction damns the mechanistic society which stamps out the most idiosyncratic among us. Her style is rambling, perhaps hyperbolic; lyric, but always grounded in the cynical or sardonic. Characters do not necessarily change or improve their lives. In "Diminishing Returns," for example, a doctor's wife can no longer find her image in the mirror, and in "The Effigy," an illiterate widow comes to grip with a still heavier handicap, her imposed sterililty. "Custody" cuts across family sentiment to indict the anonymous death banks, America's nursing homes.

EDITH MILTON

Born: Germany, 1931

Principal short fiction
"Singing Birds at Large," 1976; "Snapshots," 1976; "Codes of Honor," 1979.

Analysis
Edith Milton wrote her first piece of fiction as an antidote to some scholarly work she was doing on Charles Dickens. It started out, conventionally enough, as a detective story, but she found herself more and more interested in the paradox between the narrator's need to arrange his life in logical, progressive sequences, and the fact that that life took place largely in a mental hospital, where he worked, and where logic and progression were not the most obvious elements of the environment. When she turned to short fiction, seven or eight years ago, she worked on more sophisticated, less narrative-bound, variations of that same antithesis. Milton seems to find satisfaction in contrasting her characters' need for emotional and moral coherence with the random and insignificant arrangement of their actual lives. Most of her stories are autobiographical, in one way or another: there is a wonderful fictionalizing, organizing principle implicit in the act of remembering which not only illustrates her theme but also forms its subject matter.

Major publications other than short fiction
NOVEL: *Corridors*, 1967.

JOHN R. MILTON

Born: Minnesota, 1924

Principal short fiction

"Fire to Compassion," 1954; "An Inner Disquiet," 1955; "Once More Again," 1957; "The Walkaway," 1962; "A Small Betrayal," 1968; "The Inheritance of Emmy One Horse," 1968; "Come Back in Autumn," 1969; "La Bruja Who Missed," 1969; "Beginnings," 1972; "The Poet and the Moths," 1972; "We Think They Are Mad," 1973; "Emmy," 1974; "No Last Name," 1977; "An Inner Disquiet," 1979.

Analysis

Rhythmic and imagistic in style, with strong visual emphasis, John Milton's stories often seem to be tonal, impressionistic, and photographic rather than plotted entirely like traditional narratives. Fulfillment is more important than chronological progression, and symbols occasionally substitute for plot. Insight and vision take precedence over detailed development of character and story line. Milton is a poet and photographer as well as a fiction writer, and his prose style and sense of structure have been influenced by the elements of the poem and the photograph. While the stories are realistic on the surface, they are deceptively uncomplicated. Underlying most of them is a somewhat mystical attitude toward "place" and the relationship between character and the natural environment.

Major publications other than short fiction

NOVEL: *Notes to a Bald Buffalo*, 1976.

VALERIE MINER

Born: New York, 1947

Principal short fiction
"The Hopelessness of the Long Distance Peace Marcher," 1973; "They All Grew Up in Cabbagetown," 1974; "Deutschemarks and Venetian Blinds," 1979; "Sisterhood," 1979; "Joan Crawford Revival," 1980; "Class Reunion," 1980; "Cultured Green," 1980; "Aunt Victoria," 1980; "They Burn Witches, Don't They?," 1980; "The Giants Haven't Won a Pennant Since '62," 1981.

Analysis
Valerie Miner's stories are an original, witty and respectful look at the predicaments of contemporary women. "Literary," "intellectual," "political" are the three words often used to describe her work. She writes with a keen sense of feminism and of working-class culture. Her styles range from lush stream of consciousness to stark social realism. She is particularly interested in experimenting with form. In sum, her stories are delicate excavations into contemporary life.

STEPHEN MINKIN

Born: New York, 1944

Principal short fiction
"Jonathan," 1971; "The Man Who Found His Place," 1972; "The Story of Wholely Holy Woodrow and Iceberg Sleek," 1972; "We, the Students," 1973; "Natural Numbers," 1974; "Word Power Made Simple," 1980; "Natural Numbers," 1981.

Analysis
Stephen Minkin's short fiction to date comprises a diverse and highly eclectic collection. "Word Power" is a pseudo-scholarly satire on "material philology," "Natural Numbers" is a romance, and a philosophical dialogue about reason and passion in the form of an exchange of moves in a postal chess game; "We, the Students" is a relatively conventional tale about a schoolboy adventure; "The Story of Wholely Holy Woodrow and Iceberg Sleek" is a bawdy farce; and "The Man Who Found His Place" is surreal and nightmarish. Wide-ranging though the styles of the various stories are, all show the traditional concerns of the storyteller for a good tale that holds the reader's interest. The stories are simple in their overall shapes, but the characters that populate them tend to be intellectually and emotionally complicated. Humor is one of the author's strongest talents, and all of his work is rich in wit and comedy. Some of Minkin's short fiction shares with his longer work an ongoing interest in the problems of presenting the thinking or contemplative man as hero.

Major publications other than short fiction
NOVEL: *A No Doubt Mad Idea*, 1979.

STEPHEN MINOT

Born: Massachusetts, 1927

Principal short fiction
"Three-part Harmony," 1974; "Phang Song," 1974; "A Sometimes Memory," 1974; "Ghost/images," 1975; "Grubbing for Roots," 1975; *Crossings*, 1975; "A Passion for History," 1976; "Aye," 1976; "Reading the News—Keeping Informed," 1977; "See You Around," 1979.

Analysis
Partly through the influence of Jean-Paul Sartre, Stephen Minot tends to develop his characters more through the decisions they make and the actions they take or fail to take than by reflective dialogue or exposition. He is drawn to those moments when a character finds that he cannot choose not to choose. An admirer of Joseph Conrad, Minot frequently makes strong use of setting, drawing on rural New England and other areas not as ends but as means of developing tone. Occasionally a storm at sea, the tide, or winter ice takes on the force of a character. His themes often draw on the interplay between generations—the conflict and the reshaping of values which occur when individuals at different stages of life interact. His characters are frequently tested morally and psychologically, and although they occasionally fail, they suggest through their efforts an affirmation of the human spirit. Minot sees fiction as an extension of the reader's experience, a means of growth, and ultimately a celebration of life.

Major publications other than short fiction
NOVELS: *Chill of Dusk*, 1964; *Ghost Images*, 1979.
NONFICTION: *Three Genres, The Writing of Poetry, Fiction, and Drama*, 1972.

URSULE MOLINARO

Principal short fiction
"Candied Desire," 1963 (in Italy); "Desire Game," 1966; "Eating Melon in Marseilles," 1970 (in France); "Sweet Cheat of Freedom," 1971; "The Chemistry of Miracles," 1979; *Bastards: Footnotes to History*, 1979-1980.

Analysis
Ursule Molinaro's stories are the product of a rich and complex personality. This storyteller is also a painter, poet, dramatist, essayist, a translator from at least six languages. She is fascinated by the theme of *la danse macabre*—death whose presence can always be felt in the background of her work. Like Jean-Paul Sartre, an enemy of what he calls *la mauvaise foi*, she hates impostors and impostures. Aware of the tragic dimension of existence, she tells of unshared loves, of stifling mothers, of dull mediocre husbands, of women who suffer from infidelities and lies; she tells with compassion and sympathy of unhappy people. Her writings, however, contain strong elements of humor. She uses puns and charades, anagrams, repetitions, alliterations, parenthetic asides and clever footnotes. In the eyes of this writer, gifted with a true linguistic virtuosity, style cannot be separated from content, thought and expression must always coalesce. In her telling of events, real or suprareal, she uses a certain cadence, a certain rhythm, and succeeds in communicating that rhythm, that heart-beat, while, at the same time, remaining "involved" in character, setting, and theme. Molinaro's work may well be making a lasting contribution to the narrative art, in that her work is highly original, personal, and deeply human. Once read, her stories are hard to forget.

Major publications other than short fiction
NOVELS: *Green Lights Are Blue*, 1967; *Sounds of a Drunken Summer*, 1969; *The Borrower*, 1970; *Encores for a Dilettante*, 1978; *The Autobiography of Cassandra, Princess & Prophetess of Troy*, 1979.
PLAYS: *The Abstract Wife*, 1961; *Breakfast Past Noon*, 1977.
POETRY: *Mirrors for Small Beasts*, 1960.
NONFICTION: *The Zodiac Lovers*, 1969; *Life by the Numbers*, 1971.

Pierre E. Brodin

ELIZABETH GRAHAM MONK

Born: New York, 1939

Principal short fiction

"The Pony," 1961; "Heroes," 1963; "The Enemy: Love," 1965; "A Mother," 1974; "A Cure for Death," 1975; "Is Eating Necessary?," 1980.

Analysis

Elizabeth Monk's tightly crafted stories form widening circles of disenchantment with life's rules—both mythical and real. The early stories are of children questioning the omnipotent myths of the adult world through the events of daily life. In "A Mother," a "powerful and convincing" story, a young woman finds her isolating experience of tending her young baby too bleak to reconcile with her dreams about motherhood. In the two stores, "A Cure for Death" and "Is Eating Necessary?," which crisscross between reality and almost fantasy, the performer-heroine, Gun-Marie, has come to realize that no one is in charge of the rules and myths of life, and she simultaneously plunges into the resulting chaos, while she retains a cool, sardonic eye for its absurdities. In "Is Eating Necessary?," called "a damned good story, unflinching, powerful, and exquisitely written," Gun-Marie is stung by the hypocrisy, tenseness, and self-infatuation of most of the guests at a dinner party, while she is concerned about a guest who is a victim of cancer. In her mind she jibes ruthlessly at the conversation and posing of the guests. In the background is cancer; it is incurable and no one is to blame. Gun-Marie acts to help the cancer victim, she steals a small painting from the hostess, and accepts her errant husband back. She preserves herself with her relentless wit and her commitment to the view that what *is* must not be merely settled for, but must be cherished and enjoyed. The early stories are told in very conventional narrative styles. In "A Mother" the effect is "stark, almost too real." The Gun-Marie stories are told entirely from the interior of Gun-Marie's mind in breathless, emotionally charged monologues. The thought processes jump from subject to subject and with each jump the mood changes. The technique conveys a comically absurd view of the world without ignoring the pain.

MARION MONTGOMERY

Born: Georgia, 1925

Principal short fiction
"The Ties That Bind," 1953; "Mr. Wilson and William Shakespeare," 1957; "On a Sunday Afternoon," 1957; "Wayfaring Stranger," 1957; "Swanling's Way," 1958; "Always the Pig Got Out," 1958; "I Got a Gal," 1958; "The Bear Paw," 1959; "Vote for Whom You Please," 1959; "Tomorrow and Tomorrow and Tomorrow," 1960; "Epilogue for Three Innocents," 1960; "Willie Joe and the Ten Dollar Watch," 1961; "Graduation Snapshots," 1962; "A Breath of Air," 1962; "The Birthday Party," 1962; "All Our Cars Are Fords," 1963; "Chicken Chats," 1964; "The Strangers and the Watertank," 1964; "A Private, Simple Act of Charity," 1964; "Uncle Lebius and the Eagle," 1964; "Kingdom by the Sea," 1965; "A Visitation," 1965; "A Mess of Pardiges," 1966; "The Return," 1967; *Ye Olde Bluebird*, 1967; "Vacation," 1969; "The Decline and Fall of Officer Fergerson," 1970; "The Front Porch," 1974.

Analysis
Marion Montgomery's short stories show his working toward the larger form of the novel, exploring inherited techniques, modifying, and adapting them to his thematic concerns—comedy, irony, pathos of the individual's encounter with family and community history. In "The Strangers and the Watertank," there is a vestigial presence of the frontier tall tale. Many stories center upon the ancient engagement of the sexes in friendly and unfriendly wars within the confines of family and community pieties; others treat the wars between generations. "The Ties That Bind," "I Got a Gal," and "Kingdom by the Sea" reflect the first; "Graduation Snapshots," "A Visitation," and "The Decline and Fall of Officer Fergerson" treat the second. Some of his stories summon pathos out of a character's endurance of life in a world where no evil can be clearly localized as antagonist, as in "Always the Pig Got Out" and "The Birthday Party." In all of them hovers the presence of the past as it challenges the individual to discover an ordinate accommodation of his individuality to the demands of family and community.

Major publications other than short fiction
NOVELS: *The Wandering of Desire*, 1962; *Darrell*, 1964; *Fugitive*, 1974.
POETRY: *Dry Lightning*, 1960; *Stones from the Rubble*, 1965; *The Gull and Other Georgia Scenes*, 1969.
NONFICTION: *Ezra Pound: A Critical Essay*, 1970; *T. S. Eliot: An Essay on the American Magus*, 1970; *The Reflective Journey Toward Order*, 1973; *Eliot's Reflective Journey to the Garden*, 1979; *Poets and the Prophetic Poet* , Vols. I-III, 1980-1981.

RAYLYN MOORE

Born: Ohio, 1928

Principal short fiction

"Death Is a Woman," 1954; "They All Ran After the Farmer's Wife," 1970; "Out of Control," 1970; "A Different Drummer," 1971; "If Something Begins," 1971; "Lobster Trick," 1972; "Trigononomy," 1973; "Thaumaturge," 1973; "Windfall," 1973; "Where Have All the Followers Gone?," 1973; "Poverello," 1973; "Mars Black," 1973; "Shoes," 1974; "Fun Palace," 1975; "The Milewide Steamroller," 1975; "Valentino, Bogart, Dean & Other Ghosts," 1975; "The Castle," 1976; "Fair Eleanor Is Dead," 1976; "Life Among the Anthropologists," 1976; "A Modular Story," 1976; "Man Volant," 1977; "Strix," 1977; "Getting Back to Before It Began," 1977; "The Ark Among the Flags," 1978; "A Certain Slant of Light," 1978; "The Way Back," 1978; "No Left Turn, No Right Turn, No Thorofare," 1978; "Standoff," 1979; "The Recycling of Ardella Rudneff," 1980; "Falling," 1980.

Analysis

Raylyn Moore is considered a category writer by many publishers and critics since most of the stories seem to fit into one or more of the contemporary definitions of fantasy—not the mainstream of the fantasy genre, however, for in most of the stories no so-called natural laws are violated, nor do the conventions of traditional fantasy appear. The themes build around the overlapping of the two half-worlds of everyday life: the accountable and the unaccountable, using the perfectly natural events and characters that seem (and sometimes are) strange, or the bizarre events and situations that seem (and sometimes are) perfectly natural. Charles L. Grant, in his anthology *Shadows* (1978), says Moore ". . . tilts what we know to be so into something that we're not quite sure of."

Major publications other than short fiction

NOVELS: *Mock Orange*, 1968; *What Happened to Emily Goode After the Great Exhibition*, 1978.

NONFICTION: *Wonderful Wizard, Marvelous Land*, 1974.

RUTH MOOSE

Born: North Carolina, 1938

Principal short fiction
"Angel of the Lord and the One-Eyed Cow," 1970; "One Woman's War Against Drunk Driving," 1974; "A Biography of Seven Lives," 1978.

Analysis
Tightly controlled, superbly crafted, and densely layered, Ruth Moose's stories and people have a definite sense of place and who they are in their space of time. The reader sees through character the lives, past and future, of these people. From the evangelist preacher in "Angel of the Lord and the One-Eyed Cow" to the woman in "A Biography of Seven Lives" a landscape of lives appears both on and off the page. In brief space they are presented, yet remain, enlarged and enlarging.

Major publications other than short fiction
POETRY: *To Survive*, 1980; *Finding Things in the Dark*, 1980.

WILLIAM MOSELEY

Born: Kentucky, 1935

Principal short fiction

"Voices," 1967; "The Preacher and Margery Scott," 1967; "Old Solitaire," 1969; "Strong Is Your Hold O Mortal Flesh'," 1969; "Wild Geese," 1972; "Apology," 1972; "The Touch of Little Will," 1976.

Analysis

Lately William Moseley has concentrated more on playwriting but considers his short stories to be an important part of his whole work. Most of these stories are set in Kentucky, although they are not "regional," and he has made deliberate efforts to avoid the restrictions which the term "regionalism" implies. Moseley's characters are "small" people in "small" places—but the places could be anywhere humans live. Each story is built around that moment when a character (child or adult) comes to recognize the essential aloneness of the individual human life. For the child characters, it is a condition they have inherited with no way of understanding it; for the adult characters, it is no longer so much an inherited condition as it is one they themselves have made and cannot now unmake. Moseley writes slowly, with a great deal of concern for craftsmanship. His style is basically impressionistic, but without departing far from traditional storytelling. He wants each story to briefly open and close for the reader a peephole into that type of experience possible only in the world of fiction: a momentary glimpse of the true inner being of another self.

Major publications other than short fiction

PLAYS: *Winter Funeral*, 1978; *Blocks: An Absurd Play for Children*, 1978; *Jealousy*, 1979; *Strays*, 1980.

ROSE MOSS

Born: South Africa, 1937

Principal short fiction
"Party for the New Year," 1957; "A Tanglewood Tale," 1966; "Exile,"
1970; "The Shopping Trip," 1972; "The Birthday Present," 1973; "The House
Is Full of Cars This Morning," 1973; "Sina," 1974; "Gifts," 1974; "Spenser
Street," 1974; "Twice Her Size," 1976; "Networks," 1978.

Analysis
How is the kingdom of heaven with us?, Rose Moss's stories ask. They
scrutinize incidents of everyday life and apparently sudden actions to see how
the reader's inner states, dreams, and constructions of reality shape our lives.
Some stories read as naturalistic vignettes; in some, a slight incident ripples
outward to imply "an enormous dimension of meaning" through language
whose images, allusions, ironies, and wit become the substance of the fiction;
in some, highly focused, direct, and dramatic episodes ring clear and enigmatic. Many stories present separation, exile, an inarticulate loss, an unattainable garden, a longing that can hardly find words, and an inchoate
excursion in search of a new world. In current nonfiction Moss is exploring
how literature creates the writer and becomes an instrument of individual
autonomy. Moss's stories and novels have received prizes and awards. Critics
comment on brilliance, subtlety, mastery, humor, and compassion and invoke
comparisons with James Joyce, Vladimir Nabokov, and Henry James.

Major publications other than short fiction
NOVELS: *The Family Reunion*, 1974; *The Terrorist*, 1979.
POETRY: *Prometheus*, 1953.

ALICE MUNRO

Born: Canada, 1931

Principal short fiction

Dance of the Happy Shades, 1968; *Something I've Been Meaning to Tell You*, 1974; "Home," 1974; "Accident," 1977; "Connections," 1978; "The Stone in the Field," 1978; "Moons of Jupiter," 1978; "Honeyman's Granddaughter," 1978; *The Beggar Maid*, 1979; "Wood," 1980; "Dulse," 1980; "Prue," 1980; "The Turkey Season," 1980.

Analysis

As deceptively bare at first glance as Western Ontario's broad landscape, the scene of many of her short stories, Alice Munro's fiction probes profoundly into human behavior. Munro often focuses upon brief retrospective episodes in seemingly ordinary "lives of girls and women," evoking an unusually powerful sense of place and an equally intense although objective analysis of character. In the precision of her images and the psychological accuracy of her seriocomic portrayals, Munro often captures the essence of mid-twentieth century life in North America, with all its bewildering gaps between technological achievement and the human condition, society at large and the individual. In *The Beggar Maid* (1979), Munro's ten stories of Rose and her stepmother Flo are interwoven, as John Gardner suggested, into "a new kind of novel," with deft shapings of fictional time and sudden, sadly funny illuminating shifts in the perception of personality. Munro's *Dance of the Happy Shades* and *The Beggar Maid* have each received Canada's highest literary prize, the Governor-General's Award.

Major publications other than short fiction
NOVEL: *Lives of Girls and Women*, 1971.

Mitzi M. Brunsdale

MICHAEL MURPHY

Born: Wyoming, 1930

Principal short fiction
Friends of Frobisher & Other Enemies of Complacency, 1972.

Analysis
Michael Murphy's stories represent several variants from the conventional plotted story to the vignette, with strong emphasis on humor and irony. His earliest stories were extremely subjective and generated through prolonged and detailed analysis of dream experiences. His later stories reflect a mixture of irony, humor, and concern with the world of fantasy and absurdity in the human experience. Variants from the earlier and later stories include strong psychological studies of human behavior in fictive renderings that encouraged empathy in the reader.

Major publications other than short fiction
NOVELS: *The Will Rides the Wind*, 1962; *One of the Twelve*, 1967; *The Big Squeeze*, 1968; *A Wisp of Straw*, 1969; *Hemingsteen*, 1978.

NONFICTION: *Chicago Literary Movements*, 1965; *Main Street: 1970*, 1970; *A Tale of the Fire, Told by the Fire*, 1971; *Hemingway: Rod and Gun*, 1972; *The Will That Became a Legend*, 1974; *The Best of What He Had*, 1974; *Heritage*, 1975; *In Memoriam, Vincent Starrett*, 1975; *Write-No-More's Last Stand*, 1976; *Bad King John*, 1978; *Starrett Versus Machen*, 1978; *The Iroquois Theatre Fire*, 1978.

GEORGE MYERS, JR.

Born: Pennsylvania, 1953

Principal short fiction
NAIROBI, 1978; "An Apartment of Modern Art," 1979.

Analysis
Metafiction is playfulness. George Myers' *NAIROBI* gives readers the contemporary mode of understanding human life and the world as "texts" which require hermeneutic "unpacking." The loosely aphoristic and third-person point of view of the book leads the reader to see human life itself as a literary mode in which man writes the text of his own life as he goes, writes himself into a book that is his life. Generally, it is the specific "writer's condition" that is at the center of literature, be the writer a cartographer, a translator or censor (whose points of omission are the tales he tells) or "the poet assassinated." According to *A Critical Assembling* (1980), Myers "tells an untruth (fiction) without betraying his subjective authenticity. He profitably dons many disguises. . . ." *NAIROBI* is filled with Myers' telling adventures gained while living in East Africa in 1973. *Twentieth Century* (forthcoming) is a historical retelling of this century, like Guy Davenport's *Da Vinci's Bicycle* (1979), with an accent on the brief vignette and false interpretation of events in simple people's lives, events whose retelling creates history.

Major publications other than short fiction
POETRY: *Angels in the Tiring House*, 1975; *An Amnesiac on the Verge of Heaven*, 1976; *Tonal Odes*, 1981.

NORMAN NATHAN

Born: New York, 1915

Principal short fiction
"Another Man," 1946; "Safety for One," 1948; "Universe for One," 1958; "Shelved," 1960; "Embers," 1963; "Minimum of Things," 1964; "Diary of an Immigrant," 1966; "A Time Out of Time," 1967; "Happiness," 1968; "The Promise," 1969; "Buy Something," 1970; "The Girl Who Had Almost Everything" 1970; "By Telephone," 1970; "The End of the Honeymoon," 1971; "Why God Made the World," 1973; "Pot Luck," 1977; "Pretty and the Satyr," 1979; "Altered Ego," 1980.

Analysis
Norman Nathan's short stories divide into two categories: those that resemble science fiction and fantasy and those that, in a conventional format, explore the nuances of the wide variety of male-female relationships resulting from a conflict in personality. The former group revolves around eschatological situations: "Why God Made the World," the ultimate in solitude, reincarnation that includes the same personality and awareness, living with only the sensation of taste, two men in an environment that can support only one, how to get along in heaven. . . . The latter group concerns four women and their differing emotional problems as each one reflects herself against a variety of men. Trying to maintain a style using quick strokes, Nathan avoids the modern tendency of delineating a multitude of details in fleshing out a character. He pares away unneeded words amd makes frequent use of metaphor and symbol.

Major publications other than short fiction
POETRY: *Though Night Remain*, 1959.

OPAL NATIONS

Born: England, 1941

Principal short fiction
Sitting on the Lawn with a Lady Twice My Size, 1976; *The Tragic Hug of a Small French Wrestler*, 1979.

Analysis
On the whole, Opal Nations' books deal with the great archetypes, the same figures found in *Gulliver's Travels* (1726-1727), François Rabelais, and Wyndam Lewis' *The Childermass* (1928). These dramatic personae, however, have undergone a change unlike anything they have ever experienced before. Nations' actors have been reduced to their simplest elements and filtered through the screen of the commodity culture. The new culture forges a Rocky and a Rocky II from Ulysses; the Homeric Poet is confused with Flash Gordon *sans* Flesh Gordon; and instead of the Thin Man one gets Nations' "Mr. Skinny" in the story "Muscle by Mail." The jestor/author's characters of Varlot-Zeya, Princess Apollonaire, and Sly Chanbury—the mortician-priest who likes to marry his corpses to each other—all revolve in a roundtable of charlatans, actors, and commodity canaille. Nations stirs these characters up into a crazy soup, disassociates the elements, and uses what's left to create a vast social nightmare. The central theme of Nations' fiction is the author's need for distance versus what Nathaniel Hawthorne called the "magnetic chain of humanity." The tension may never be resolved. Like some of the odd characters of William Faulkner's novels, Nations' characters grow more heroic in the measure that they reveal their weaknesses. She is one of the most original writers of the 1970's and 1980's.

Major publications other than short fiction
NOVELS: *A Pen, Some Paper, A Pen and Some Paper*, 1976; *The Marvels of Professor Pettingruel*, 1978.

George Myers, Jr.

ANDREW NEIDERMAN

Born: New York, 1940

Principal short fiction
"Duke Has His Day," 1967; "A Very Special Student," 1968; "The Pupil
Who Was Punished for Being a Student," 1968; "The Rats in Congress,"
1969; "The Closest to Eden," 1970; "The Crumbling Wall," 1970; "The Weight
of Education," 1975.

Analysis
Disarming in their simplicity, Andrew Neiderman's stories illustrate a range
of style and development characteristic of a writer who is continually exploring
with form and style. Regardless of the themes and plots, Neiderman's stories
are always set in the Catskill world which he has inhabited since early childhood. "A sense of place must permeate character and theme. We are affected
by the environment in more ways than we know," Neiderman has said in
recent media interviews. His characters struggle against forces within themselves. According to Neiderman, "the solutions call for deeper understanding
of the human personality and that seems to be the most perfect goal of
literature." His style is simple, almost Hemingwayesque, yet Neiderman's
experience with poetry gives his language a delicate irony and vivid sense of
imagery. Readers detect an eerie underlying tone to much of his work. He
has an eye for the bizarre; and yet, he keeps his stories sufficiently within the
borders of reality to make the reader question what they see themselves and
what they see in themselves. His range of characters and plots have taken
him from publication in the most literary of magazines to the most
"commercial."

Major publications other than short fiction
NOVELS: *Sisters*, 1971; *Weekend*, 1980; *The Death of Pinocchio*, 1981.
PLAYS: *The Interview, Voice*, 1971; *The Box, Voice*, 1972; *The Girl in the
Cage, Voice*, 1975; *Quicksand, Voice*, 1971; *Fantasyland U. S. A. and Other
Plays*, 1976.
NONFICTION: *The Sesquicentennial History of Fallsburg*, 1976.

KENT NELSON

Born: Ohio, 1943

Principal short fiction

"Instants," 1973-1974; "To Go Unknowing," 1974; "The Clay Urn," 1974; "Incident in the High Country," 1974; "The Solitaire Player," 1974; "The Vacant Lot on Pearl Street," 1974; "Rising Star," 1974; "The New World of Harmony," 1974; "The Only Safe Place," 1975; "Looking into Nothing," 1975; "The Saint of Illusion," 1975; "The Humpbacked Bird," 1975; "One Turned Wild," 1976; "A False Encounter," 1976; "Spring Calf," 1976; "A Small Deception," 1976; "By the Way of Dispossession," 1976; "Bits of Broken Glass," 1977; "The Time and Manner," 1977; "Coming to Terms," 1978; *The Tennis Player and Other Stories*, 1978; "Light and Rain," 1979; "Wind Chimes," 1979.

Analysis

Kent Nelson writes with a spare, disciplined style, often about Western settings. Using landscape as mood, Nelson creates characters who are intimately bound to their surroundings. The conflicts which underlie Nelson's fiction resonate not only through the lives of the protagonists but also in our own consciousness, for they are fundamental: how to live honorably in a deceitful society; how to endure compromise and the gentle lies of promises and kindness; how to act simply and directly in the presence of darkness, ambiguity, chaos, and cruelty. Nelson's images possess a haunting, open-ended quality so that they reverberate beyond the last sentence. Characters linger in transparent silences, pinioned by or struggling with their dilemmas, and sometimes crippled by a painful sense of beauty and conscience. To try to reach what they seek, Nelson's characters oscillate between the opposites in their natures: they seek apartness and union, flight and safety. They ache for a life with the intensity of dreams, a life both pure and immediate. Often they need the encumbering closeness of family, friends, and love, while still yearning for invisibility, solitude, and freedom. It is not happiness they seek, nor ease, but, rather, transformation. They drive themselves to the edge of spiritual and sometimes physical endurance to discover instants beyond the world of appearances. To read Nelson's stories is to experience just such echoing instants.

RODNEY NELSON

Born: North Dakota, 1941

Principal short fiction
"Glorio," 1973; "Breidablik," 1974; "A Fine Green Bubble," 1974; "Gunnar Speaks to Ingrid," 1975-1976; "Legend," 1976; "Welcome to Riotwheel," 1976; "John Root Is Gone," 1977; "Labor Day," 1977; "Mads Abell," 1977; "The Movement," 1977; "Karl Iversen," 1979.

Analysis
Rodney Nelson's stories fall into two broad categories: regional and "other." He writes either of the Red River Valley of the North and the rich Scandinavian-American culture subsisting there, or of an often unidentified "other" place which resembles the American West but is in fact the materialization of a time: now. For Nelson, time and setting are one. Thus in "Breidablik" he can evoke centuries of tradition because the past is visibly *present* in a Norwegian-American resort community, while in "Welcome to Riotwheel" he can depict the horror of a town from which all signs of tradition have been removed, leaving its occupants faceless. Nelson loves words, and his prose tends to luxuriate. As David Madden says of "John Root Is Gone," "The lyrical, slightly formal, elegiac, sometimes excessive style perfectly expresses the narrator's attraction-repulsion relationship to the great self-destructive poet. . . ." In *The Boots Brevik Saga* (1978), Nelson combined his regional and "other" tendencies and the result was unexpected: humor.

Major publications other than short fiction
NOVEL: *The Boots Brevik Saga*, 1978.
POETRY: *Oregon Scroll*, 1976; *Vigil*, 1979; *North Farm*, 1980.
NONFICTION: *Edges of a Doctrine*, 1978.

JAY NEUGEBOREN

Born: New York, 1938

Principal short fiction
"My Son, the Freedom Rider," 1964; "Connorsville, Virginia," 1969; *Corky's Brother*, 1969; "My Life and Death in the Negro American Baseball League: A Slave Narrative," 1973; "The Place Kicking Specialist," 1974; "An Orphan's Tale," 1976; "Monkeys and Cowboys," 1976; "Uncle Nathan," 1978; "A Worthy Cause," 1978; "His Violin," 1978; "Kehilla," 1978; "Star of David," 1979; "The St. Dominick's Game," 1979; "Jonathan," 1980; "Poppa's Books," 1980; "Bonus Baby," 1980; "Noah's Song," 1980.

Analysis
A traditional writer, Jay Neugeboren's exceptionally well-crafted stories reveal his concern with social action. They engage the reader directly and lead him to a point where reader and story merge. Neugeboren's characters and the significant social statements they make are recognizable. Moreover, since his characters (for the most part Jewish, Black, and Spanish) exist in a social vacuum—not necessarily as outlaws but rather on the periphery of mainstream society—he centers the reader directly in situations where "normal" rules do not always hold. Neugeboren's sense of place is very important. A teller of tales of the inner city, of racial and religious conflict and *détente*, of social behaviour based on athletic codes, he captures the sensory and intellectual pulse of real places. As a realist, he relies on observed details and heard dialects, yet because the reality he presents often seems hallucinatory or surrealistic, dramatic action supports both tone and form. For example, the life of the poor, of street gangs and basketball courts, and of the culturally different is treated without sentimentality, without a reformer's condescending compassion. Neugeboren's stories suggest his closeness to his characters and their surroundings, and sports often become a partial answer to social fragmentation and alienation. Indeed, Neugeboren's somewhat cynical attitude in his autobiographical *Parentheses* (1970) becomes in his fiction a more optimistic faith in the ability of humans to communicate with and understand one another. He shows in the end the souls of his characters and their environments.

Major publications other than short fiction
NOVELS: *Big Man*, 1966; *Listen Ruben Fontanez*, 1968; *Sam's Legacy*, 1974; *An Orphan's Tale*, 1976.
NONFICTION: *Parentheses: An Autobiographical Journey*, 1970.

Vincent D. Balitas

J. E. NIGG

Born: Iowa, 1938

Principal short fiction
Four Stories, 1960; *A Glimpse of Proteus*, 1975.

Analysis
    J. E. Nigg's short fiction attempts to combine within single unified forms elements that for lack of more precise terms must simply be called realistic and romantic. The realistic Nigg associates with the world of common day, the romantic with the world of imagination, romance, myth, archetype. The shape-shifting figure of Proteus can be metaphorically useful to a writer with such intentions, for Proteus affords the writer a way of fusing the realistic and the romantic within a single story. A character can have a glimpse of Proteus, who is a shape from the world of the imagination appearing on the landscape of the mundane. The archaic meaning of *glimpse* is "a brief flash of light," as in the manifestation of a god, an epiphany. A character's glimpses of awareness of the common can, of course, take place anywhere; within the total context of a realistic landscape, however, metaphorical Proteus is likely to appear just beyond the edge of patterned experience. The stories are about characters who, looking beyond the usual patterns of home and work, are themselves changed by their glimpses of the changing shapes of things.

LARRY NIVEN

Born: California, 1938

Principal short fiction

"By Mind Alone," 1966; *Neutron Star*, 1968; *The Shape of Space*, 1969; *All the Myriad Ways*, 1971; *The Flight of the Horse*, 1973; *A Hole in Space*, 1974; *Tales of Known Space*, 1975; *The Long ARM of Gil Hamilton*, 1976; *Convergent Series*, 1978; "Spirals," 1978 (with Jerry Pournelle); "The Locusts," 1979 (with Steven Barnes); "The Green Marauder," 1970.

Analysis

A master of "hard" science fiction, Larry Niven launched his career as the New Wave hit its stride. Niven eschewed stylistic experimentation and the exploration of character—characteristics of the New Wave—when they worked to the detriment of extrapolation, background, and storytelling. As a result, his only competition came from Robert Heinlein, Poul Anderson, Hal Clement, and the like—the very people he wanted for his peers. Throughout his career, Niven has continued an old tradition: the extrapolative story, in which ideas are tracked to expose their implications for the future and their effects on human society. He did one thing, though, few others were doing. He learned his projected societies so thoroughly that he could see the humorous parts. Niven's primary goal, he says, is to tell an entertaining story, although he admits to being a "compulsive teacher." He would like to train his reader to play with ideas for the sheer joy of it. He wants him to dream in color and three dimensions, with sharp edges and internal consistency. Niven's fiction is rich in ideas. To Niven, the ideas most worth writing about are those that nobody has yet used. They are also the hardest to get across to the reader. Niven tries to use the simplest, clearest language possible. Literary experiments, he argues, are for people with nothing to say.

Major publications other than short fiction

NOVELS: *World of Ptavvs*, 1965; *A Gift from Earth*, 1968; *Ringworld*, 1970; *The Flying Sorcerers*, 1971 (with David Gerrold); *Protector*, 1973; *The Mote in God's Eye*, 1974 (with Jerry Pournelle); *Inferno*, 1976 (with Jerry Pournelle); *A World Out of Time*, 1976; *Lucifer's Hammer*, 1977 (with Jerry Pournelle); *The Magic Goes Away*, 1978; *The Ringworld Engineers*, 1980; *The Patchwork Girl*, 1980.

Jeffrey M. Elliot

STANLEY NOYES

Born: California, 1924

Principal short fiction
"The Taste of the Sea," 1956; "Ceremony," 1957; "A Flag for Independence Day," 1960; "The Last True Cowboy," 1976; *Western*, 1980.

Analysis
Although Stanley Noyes has written stories, he is more comfortable with the lyric or the novel. Technically his stories are straightforward. They rely on a strong narrative line, accurate dialogue, and the selective use of visual detail to create an impact. Their themes, as in his novels, are concerned with violence around and within the individual, especially when seen in the light of the traditions, legends, and fantasies of the American West.

Major publications other than short fiction
NOVELS: *No Flowers for a Clown*, 1961; *Shadowbox*, 1970.
POETRY: *Faces and Spirits*, 1974; *Beyond the Mountains Beyond the Mountains*, 1979.

TOBY OLSON

Born: Illinois, 1937

Principal short fiction
"The Girl with the Profile of a Shark," 1969; "The Sixth Column, The Fourth Entry," 1969; ". . . Shrinks Hemorrhoids Without Surgery," 1970; "The Nature of Discovery," 1974; "The Bird," 1975; "Uncles & Aunts," 1975.

Analysis
Toby Olson's stories all deal, in their way, with individuals who find themselves confronted with an aspect of the world that has gone slightly mad, and this aspect is almost always found in their own pasts. They had thought their lives had at least one solid base, the base that comes with understanding through memory. What they discover is that memory has played them false. Their pasts (and often their understanding of communal history as well) is incorrect; they are now forced to readjust their view of themselves and of their present lives. The presentation of this "new" past is most usually handled through image and visual emblematic moment, but the stories present no system of symbols. The reader is asked to see the images as they work on the understanding of the central character, and the task of drawing conclusions is left to him. The story in which this view of things is best examined is "The Nature of Discovery." The shorter piece, "Uncles & Aunts," handles the issue in a lighter, more humorous way. Each of the pieces was, in a sense, preparation for the writing of the novel, *The Life of Jesus* (1976), a "fictional autobiography." The author's own discovery is that all lives, through the selections and alterations of memory, are in their way fictional.

Major publications other than short fiction
NOVEL: *The Life of Jesus*, 1976.
POETRY: *Maps*, 1969; *Worms into Nails*, 1969; *The Brand*, 1969; *Pig/s Book*, 1970; *Vectors*, 1972; *Fishing*, 1973; *The Wrestlers*, 1974; *Changing Appearance*, 1975; *Home*, 1976; *Doctor Miriam*, 1977; *Aesthetics*, 1978; *The Florence Poems*, 1978; *Birdsongs*, 1980.

JOE OLVERA

Born: Texas, 1944

Principal short fiction

Voces de la Gente, 1972; "My Voice," 1976; "King Kong Raids Ice-Box," 1976; "Homme de l'Monde," 1977; "A Farmworker's Lament," 1978; "Marie the Turk," 1978; "In the Land of Allah," 1979; "Still Magic America," 1980.

Analysis

Joe Olvera is a Chicano writer whose stories reveal his early and continuing experiences amidst varying cultures. Written in a style influenced by a strong admiration for Jack Kerouac and the Beat Generation, his stories challenge the ordinary reader who will encounter not only English and Spanish but also Black English, Shakespearean English, and Pachuco Spanish. With these Olvera presents an honest portrayal of his world, including such diverse subjects as character sketches, domestic scenes, travels, sexual experiences, and childhood recollections. His manner of composition is generally spontaneous; his stories develop through association and are thus multileveled, as in "King Kong Raids Ice-Box" which relates the wide-eyed amazement of a Chicano boy who has saved fourteen cents shining shoes to see the 1933 movie version of *King Kong*. Besides the child's perceptions, the reader is continually aware of the mature narrator who sees King Kong as a symbol for the powerful potential of repressed and exploited peoples everywhere. Through such stories, Olvera seeks to transform the negative stereotype of the Chicano and replace it with portrayals that are realistic because they are based on real people who, like the protagonist in "King Kong Raids Ice-Box," view their multicultural and linguistic world with childlike amazement and mature circumspection. Olvera has published in several literary genres—poetry, nonfiction, drama, essays, and reviews—but it is his short fiction that brings into focus the witty, ironic, picaresque, urbanite writing creativity of Joe Olvera.

Major publications other than short fiction

NOVEL: *Book of Thailand*, 1980.

PLAYS: *Peyote Discount: 10% OFF*, 1977; *A Barrio Tragedy*, 1978.

James Gonzalez and *Teresa Duran*

GREG ORFALEA

Born: California, 1949

Principal short fiction
Fault Stories; "Out by the Scoreboard," 1975.

Analysis
Greg Orfalea's fiction is best characterized by its clarity and straightfor-wardness. Few, if any, stylistic and structural complexities mar the flow of narration; rather, his characters—which often include the narrator, even when the third-person point of view is used—move autonomously within the circumstances and setting of a particular plot toward some epiphany which has symbolically resonated throughout. It is perhaps Orfalea's lack of concern for the intellectual wranglings that are the province of much contemporary fiction which allows him the freedom to delve into the tensions that control and often overwhelm his characters. Never nihilistic, rarely despairing, his stories in the end affirm the human condition by celebrating the humanness of the people who inhabit them.

Major publications other than short fiction
POETRY: *Pictures at an Exhibition*, 1977.

Pablo Medina

CAROL ORLOCK

Born: California, 1947

Principal short fiction
"Passacaglia and Fugue," 1974; "The Calling," 1976; "Counting," 1978; "Your Daughter's Patchwork," 1980.

Analysis
In stories generally about women, but which transcend feminist rhetoric, Carol Orlock troubles both our intellect and imagination with her postexistential vision. As a product of the Cold War generation that did not create existentialism, but lived it, Orlock writes stories that point to form in chaos. They suggest that chaos can be greatly lessened if reader and writer are willing to engage fully with life. The narrative is often reportorial, never harsh; and sympathy, while apparent, is restrained. Compassion for the character never gets in the way of characters' actions. In Orlock's early publications, as well as in her current work, despair gradually gives over to a limited measure of hope and a larger measure of humanism. The reader never expects to discover mere kindliness here, but he does experience increasing joy as both writer and characters are freed by achieving even temporary order.

Jack Cady

CAROLYN OSBORN

Born: Tennessee, 1934

Principal short fiction
"The Land Man," 1962; "Eunice B.," 1963; "Ancient History," 1964; "Mrs. Jenkins, Mrs. Danforth, and Mrs. Jim Bowie," 1967; "The Last of It," 1971; "The New Dürer," 1974; "Having Cake and Eating It Sometimes," 1975; "Other People's Mail," 1976; "Dreamer When Last Seen," 1977; *A Horse of Another Color*, 1977; "Wildflowers I Have Known," 1977; "Running Around America," 1978; "The Circuit Rider," 1978; "Reversals," 1979; "Stalking Strangers," 1979; "The Gypsy on the Stairs," 1980.

Analysis
The stories in Carolyn Osborn's *A Horse of Another Color* reflect an artistry nurtured by three powerful influences. The first is modern Southern literature. Born in Tennessee, Osborn possesses a keen interest in kinship, family loyalties, and manners that recalls such superb Southern writers as Eudora Welty and Katherine Anne Porter. "G T T," for example, explores the emotional costs of a woman's having to leave her family in order to discover her own identity. An equally strong factor in Osborn's vision is the Southwest, especially Texas, where she has lived for more than twenty years. Stories such as "My Brother Is a Cowboy" gain their force from an ironic critique of Western myths of masculinity symbolized by the cowboy. The third influence is essentially one of technique. An admirer of such giants of the short story as Anton Chekhov and James Joyce, Osborn constructs stories with great care, involving her protagonists, often women, in crises of consciousness that result in hard-earned epiphanies. In her most recent work, formal experimentation is increasingly evident. Already with her first book Osborn has moved beyond being derivative, however; her concern for formal order, reinforced by a lean, witty style, places her work among the most interesting produced in the Southwest.

Don Graham

NANCY HUDDLESTON PACKER

Born: Washington, D. C., 1925

Principal short fiction

"Povera Baby," 1953; "One Man's Meat," 1962; "Giving, Getting," 1964; "The Man Who Hated Cigarettes," 1966; "Conversion and After," 1973; "Lee's Lieutenants," 1973; "The Man Who Loved the Scenery," 1976; "Lousy Moments," 1976; *Small Moments,* 1976; "Cousins," 1980; "The Women Who Walk," 1980.

Analysis

Nancy Packer's stories fall in the category of traditional, psychological realism. They deal with the small but significant moments in the lives of middle-class, well-educated and aware men and women, some old, some young. The tone is generally ironic and sophisticated.

JOSEPH PAPALEO

Born: New York, 1927

Principal short fiction

"Resting Place," 1955; "The Kidnap," 1959; "Graduation," 1959; "On the Mountain," 1960; "Nonna 11," 1963; "Nonna," 1969; "New Flesh," 1975; "The Company," 1976; "Tony," 1980.

Analysis

Although the stories of Joseph Papaleo are part of the realist tradition of the 1950's, they resemble all ethnic writings in that they are generally careful, and respectful of their subject matter, usually a minority group unknown to the readership. Most of Papaleo's stories concern the characterological conflicts of Italian Americans moving into the middle class in pursuance of the "American-reward-dream." The interaction of group identity and personal identity is always central to his work. His characters are caught in modern urban middle class neurotic dilemmas. The style is generally spare and slightly lyrical. The view is antistereotypical in that the group he writes about is so universally known for a few stereotyped traits as to censor the normal variety inherent in these people. Papaleo feels that it is the fate of ethnic writing to be both known and limited by the prevailing beliefs about the ethnic group rather than the elements and qualities of the fiction.

Major publications other than short fiction

NOVELS: *Areté*, 1960; *All the Comforts*, 1968; *Out of Place*, 1972; *The Nice Boy*, 1980.

ROBERT PARHAM

Born: Maryland, 1943

Principal short fiction
"Angels and Gods," 1963; "Down by the Riverside with You, My Love, with You," 1967; "No Tickee, No Trickee," 1968; "The Blue Mobile," 1970; "The Secret of Wilbur Wilmott's Success," 1975; "The Last Days of Dideon Thunder-Ten," 1975.

Analysis
Although Robert Parham's work, like that of many contemporary writers, presents difficulties involving syntax and plot sequence, his theme remains accessible to the sensitive reader. Parham's published fiction defies conventional classification. Its surface content (science fiction and fantasy), its audiences (the readers of elitist literary journals and soft-core men's magazines), and its thematic tenor (a harried protest against the vitiating effects of the materialistic, sexist, and militaristic goals which, in our eager pursuit of them, have betrayed our civilization and alienated us from our feelings)—all these aspects of the author's work seem somewhat incongruous with one another. Without the arrogance or stridency of a D. H. Lawrence, Parham entreats his readers to renounce the costly false security of the anachronistic stable ego, to risk the adventures of genuine passion. Thus he is a progressive writer in the most vital sense of the word. If there is to be a "men's movement" in the literature of the 1980's, Parham's work belongs in the vanguard.

Major publications other than short fiction
POETRY: *Sending the Children for Song*, 1974.

Christopher Gould

PAUL J. J. PAYACK

Born: New Jersey, 1950

Principal short fiction

A Ripple in Entropy, 1973; *Windows in the Stone*, 1974; *The Star-Tales Cycle: Solstice I* (1975), *Solstice II* (1976), *Solstice III* (1977); "Life of the Saint," 1976; "Computer Misprint," 1976; "Crack in the Cosmic Egg," 1976; "Music of the Spheres," 1976; "Found on a Misplaced Microdot," 1976; "Historia Calamitata," 1976; "Fabricating the Mythology," 1976; *The Unexpected Twist Series*, 1976; *The Black Lists*, 1977; *Mythomania*, 1977; "New Wisdom," 1977-1978; "On the Nature of History," 1977-1978; "Doe or Zho?," 1977-1978; "The Face of His Father," 1977-1978; "A Little Known Fact Number Four," 1977-1978; "The Intelligence Quotient," 1978; "Dreams to Ashes Turned," 1979; *Microtales*, 1979; *Mortality Tales*, 1979; *The Land of Orth*, 1980; "Polyethylene Wind," 1980; "Unexpected Twist Number Five," 1980; "Memory, Forgetfullness & Being," 1980.

Analysis

The genre in which Paul Payack works is called "Metafiction," although the *Kansas City Star* called his work "polyphonic prose" and *The Paris Review* labeled it "prose poetry." He is a member of the Science Fiction Writers of America, but he does not consider himself a science-fiction writer. His work is often compared with that of Herman Melville and Franz Kafka. One reviewer called his work "the closest writing in America to Borges," while another used it to demonstrate the evolution of contemporary literature as predicted by Edmund Wilson in 1938. Sylvia Berkman called him "a writer of great originality, seriousness and imaginative zest. . . ."

Payack shows immense concern for that limited stretch of continued existence, time. He attempts to place his tales in the everlasting, so to speak, to make them comprehensible to other times and societies as well as our own. He is particularly interested in language and the relationship of words to things, events, and ideas and how these evolve through time.

Major publications other than short fiction

NONFICTION: *A Short History of Chess*, 1979; *Upon the Birth of a First Child*, 1980.

RICHARD MYERS PEABODY, JR.

Born: Washington, D. C., 1951

Principal short fiction
"The John Ashbery Memorial Houseboat," 1979; "Lost Causes," 1980; "Atrophy," 1980; "Der Dreibeintanz," 1980; "Field Trip," 1980; *Monaural*, 1980.

Analysis
Sequential, chatty, and strictly twentieth century in subject and era, Richard Peabody's stories revolve around the life of the artist in a world of popular culture; Brian Eno, punk rock groups, and the literary Romantic are the *deux ex machina* of his machine-age prose. Peabody prefers scene to panorama, dialogue to drama, and plot to meditation. He appears to have successfully struggled against post-modernist tendencies in current fiction as well; characters are given the ability to grow and change where other authors' characters only become more textlike. Although the names of Peabody's female characters change, his personae respond to each of them similarly—with curiosity, disdain, remorse, love, and fear. His male characters appear emasculated in several stories (notably in *Monaural* and several uncollected pieces), like those of D. H. Lawrence, not because women have taken over a masculine role, but because as artist or musician dependent on the woman, Peabody is more sensitive to the external balance, or what Henry Miller calls "the social maladjustment of the artist in the world today." Humor abounds but only explicitly and in ways similar to J. D. Salinger's more famous novel about growing up. Peabody's characters are named Hedgehog, Buzz, Cricket, and they often appear in surroundings which have outgrown their youthful zeal—walking the darkened alleys near Wisconsin Avenue in Washington, D. C., in one of their fathers' large chairs, or lost on a freeway. Although the never-decreasing gap between family members and loved ones remains a strong theme in Peabody's prose, his primary topic is of what's lost when zeal and zest come of age in a malevolent world.

Major publications other than short fiction
POETRY: *I'm in Love with the Morton Salt Girl*, 1979.

George Myers, Jr.

DEREK PELL

Born: New York, 1947

Principal short fiction
Scar Mirror, 1978, *Morbid Curiosities*, 1980.

Analysis
Derek Pell's short fictions, often accompanied by his own collage illustrations, are an exploration into the absurd, pushing beyond the boundaries of social "sanity." In his series of stories known as "The Crater Chronicles" the author uses his protagonist, the missing Judge Crater, to puncture the myth of the American family through the use of the outrageous *non sequitur*. Capitalism, sex, and children's literature are demolished as well. Humor, often black and remorseless, is Pell's primary weapon in the war against conventional life; however, his prose often achieves a strange, poetic surrealism. His experimental fictions satirize and pervert existing forms and genres. For example, he has reconstructed short versions of the erotic novels *The Story of O* (1966), *The Image* (1968), and *Emmanuelle* (1974) with remarkable results beyond simple parody. So, too, has Pell dissected nineteenth century English morality and manners in his "Doktor Bey," books which seem a bizarre combination of Thomas Hardy and Terry Southern.

Major publications other than short fiction
POETRY: *Frozen Sunlight*, 1968; *The Invention of Style*, 1978.

MICHAEL PERKINS

Born: Michigan, 1942

Principal short fiction
Down Here, 1969.

Analysis

Michael Perkins' stories collected in *Down Here* attempt a composite portrayal of life on the Lower East Side of New York City in the late 1960's. By describing himself as a reporter to whom stories about hippies, Puerto Ricans, black militants, junkies, and criminals are dictated, the narrator can be both inside and outside the stories, some of which are formal and lengthy like "The Birthday Party"; most, however, are glimpses, anecdotes, and asides. This informal structure allows Perkins a fluidity and swiftness in narration, as well as the freedom to use a variety of techniques in different stories. First person, third person, participant, observer, documentor, and poet, the "reporter" hops from one aspect of life on the Lower East Side to the next, from tragedy to comedy, telling his stories in a mixture of surrealistic and naturalistic modes. Many of the stories include elements of eroticism and violence. Victimization of the helpless is a major theme, but a kind of mad gaiety suffuses even the grimmest incidents; affirmation is found in simple survival, and the pleasures of the poor.

Major publications other than short fiction

NOVELS: *Evil Companions*, 1968; *Terminus*, 1968; *The Tour*, 1968.
POETRY: *Blue Woman*, 1966; *Shorter Poems*, 1968; *The Persistence of Desire*, 1977.
NONFICTION: *The Secret Record*, 1976.

BETTE PESETSKY

Born: Wisconsin, 1932

Principal short fiction
"The Second Whirlpool," 1959; "The Cliffhangers: A Family Saga," 1978;
"The Hobbyist: A Scientific Examination," 1978; "Care by Women," 1978;
"The Theory of Sets," 1979; "The Encomiast," 1979; "Three Girls on Holiday:
A Play," 1980; "Kitchen," 1980; "Phylogeny and Other Spiritual Matters,"
1980; "The Autodidact," 1980; "Offspring of the First Generation," 1980;
"Stories Up to a Point," 1980.

Analysis
In Bette Pesetsky's tightly crafted stories, the real world is scrambled by
the special consciousness of one character. The stories are a mixture of fragments of past and present. The "good" are seldom rewarded in her fiction,
and, indeed, their only reward may be an understanding of the black humor
of their lives. Pesetsky creates a judgmental society in which hallucinations
and nightmares are as likely to be punished as acts of will. The stories are
often set in the form of scenes in which a few lines of dialogue may define
an entire life. The typical time span of a story covers decades in which the
characters pass from uprooting to renewal with growing links to the past.
These scenes may have actually occurred or may exist solely as part of the
interior life of the characters. In Pesetsky's fiction, the rules of society are
violated by people who want both perfection and love. They find the past
much richer than the present. The past is characterized as having more events
and thicker layers of emotions. Multisyllabic words are used to evoke the
past, and the characters have complex names. The revenge sought is against
the emotionally diluted present.

MARY PETERSON

Born: Minnesota, 1946

Principal short fiction
"Salt," 1976; "Coming About," 1976; "To Dance," 1976; "Travelling," 1978; "Crazy Lady," 1980; "Two Cats," 1980.

Analysis
In "Travelling," a 1979 O. Henry Award-winning story, Mary Peterson writes of a husband who copes with children and the complexity of his feelings when his middle-aged wife leaves for Nova Scotia for two weeks by herself: anxiety, pride in the way she's reared the children, admiration of her courage in leaving. After she returns, he leaves her for a night to go alone to the sailboat which he loves and she does not. There, he realizes that he wants her to feel as lonely as he did. He wants to punish her, and he's ashamed of this feeling. In the past year she has grown away from him, asserting now instead of asking. He feels abandoned, and yet he loves her energy, their differences. "So what is a man to do?" he wonders, sitting in the cockpit, alone that night. He discovers ". . . in going to what we love, we don't deny anything," and when he looks up, ". . . the boat had shifted in the tide so that the main mast seemed about to pierce the moon." Peterson deals with enormous complexity and ambivalence in all her stories. She can, in the Anton Chekhov phrase, ". . . speak briefly on long subjects." Her range is astonishing. She writes about men and women with equal insight and compassion. A husband discovers that his infidelities to his Japanese wife are known to her in "Two Cats." In the Pushcart Prize-winning story "To Dance," a woman who cannot dance moves in with an Arthur Murray dance instructor and learns the first step of love in masturbation. In "The Carved Table," a three-page story, a Midwestern woman marries into a rich New England family and discovers the terrible price of fitting in. In "Salt," which won the South Dakota Review Award, 1979, a teenager copes simultaneously with her father's death and her mother's alcoholism. Peterson's stories are marked by stylistic compression and emotional intensity. There are many moments of insight on each page of each story; and there is wisdom.

CATHERINE PETROSKI

Born: Missouri, 1939

Principal short fiction

"Out of the Question," 1970; "Exercise," 1972; "Creatures of This Place,"
1973; "Lines," 1974; "The Girl with the Naturally Curly Hair," 1973; "Tonight
Is New Year's Eve and I Am Decorating," 1974; "You and Me Claude," 1974;
"Fool Me Once, Fool Me Twice," 1975; "A Wild Lens," 1975; "Beautiful My
Mane in the Wind," 1975; "Austin," 1975; "Drawer," 1975; "Something to
Wear," 1975; "A Wrong Enough Thing," 1975; "The Pump," 1977; "Rings,"
1977; "sSs," 1977; "The Deposition," 1977; "The Taj Mahal," 1977; "The
Double Yellow Line," 1978; "Drinks," 1978; "The Dream Syllogism," 1979;
"John Gardner and the Summergarden," 1979; "Beginning," 1979; "The Ep-
ithet Maker," 1979; "Life as the Wife of Khan & Khan," 1980.

Analysis

Points of view as divergent as those of children, scientists, academic lions,
and a range of ex-urbanites and suburbanites mark a characteristic variety in
Catherine Petroski's short fiction, although her major concerns are a close
attention to language and the design of the piece of fiction, whether or not
such design reflects the traditional element of plot. Science, natural surroundings, and animals figure strongly among her images. The conflicts of heredity—
the means by which humans transmit or fail to transmit their qualities and
knowledge—has been perhaps her dominant theme, both as reflected in the
narrow sense of "family" and in broader terms. A highly visual quality and
a distinct sense of place are present in Petroski's stories, the settings of which
range from Texas and southern Illinois, to Chicago and New York, to locations
in several European countries.

FRED PFEIL

Born: Pennsylvania, 1949

Principal short fiction

"Skeeter's Last Reflections," 1975; "Holding On," 1976; "The Quality of Light in Maine," 1978; "Bev's Song," 1978; "Vet," 1978; "You, Fred Astaire," 1979; "The Idiocy of Rural Life," 1980; "Requiem," 1980; "Shine On," 1980; "Miss Olive's Retreat," 1981; "The Collected Works of Brown," 1981.

Analysis

To date, the most prominent characteristic of Fred Pfeil's stories may well be their variety. Formally, his writing ranges from the traditional realism of place, time, and character ("The Quality of Light in Maine") to the deliberately uncomfortable quasi-surrealism of "Miss Olive's Retreat" and "The Idiocy of Rural Life," in which both plot and character seem both fantastic and possible. Stylistically, his narrative may be as willfully quiet as "Holding On," as convoluted as "Shine On," or as encyclopedic in its juxtaposed styles as "The Collected Works of Brown." Pfeil's stories are as likely to be about the return of an old love to a lonely Pennsylvania farmer's life as they are to concern what would happen to Fred Astaire if Ginger Rogers ever ran off the set. Yet beneath this array of styles, forms, and subjects, a basic preoccupation emerges. Pfeil is above all concerned with the inadequacy of the conventions of realism and the "personal" to deal with the full imaginative complexity of social life today—life that is likely to be at least as publicly constructed, and as infused by mass mediated fantasy and propaganda, as it is quietly, privately signified and significant. Thus his stories tend to deal with characters who are coming to terms with this new reality, whether as farmers, janitors, schoolteachers, or factory workers. It is in this sense that one can think of Pfeil's fiction as political, even radical: these stories question old verities about low mimetic realism and the well-made short story (and are themselves whole stories, even plotted ones) just as the characters inside them are often forced, in one way or another, to question the truth and solidity of their own identities and selves.

LOUIS PHILLIPS

Born: Massachusetts, 1942

Principal short fiction

"The Black Messiah Cape," 1974; "Must I Weep for the Dancing Bear," 1975; "Herlihy's Guardhouse," 1976; "The Gorilla and My Wife," 1979; "What It Is Like to Be a Boston Red Sox Fan," 1980.

Analysis

Better known for his poetry and his plays, Louis Phillips has written numerous works of short fiction, stories collected under the general title *Must I Weep For the Dancing Bear*. These stories, many written in the first person by an unreliable or naïve narrator, center on young men growing up in the South or in a small-town atmosphere. Other stories by Phillips are more experimental in tone, mood, or subject matter. In "The Gorilla and My Wife," for example, a woman is given a post-hypnotic suggestion that when she sees her husband, she will see him as a gorilla. Given such a burden, the marriage falls apart. Such stories are, for the most part, humorous and/or satirical, but often tinged with a sad refrain.

Major publications other than short fiction

NOVEL: *Theodore Jonathan Wainwright Is Going to Bomb the Pentagon*, 1973.

PLAYS: *God Have Mercy on the June Bug*, 1973; *The Envoi Messages*, 1975.

POETRY: *Celebrations & Bewilderments*, 1975; *In the Heart of Quickest Perils*, 1977; *All the Natural Cruelty of Things*, 1979.

ROBERT PHILLIPS

Born: Delaware, 1938

Principal short fiction
"The Planting Time of Granny Falk," 1959; "Grounds for Divorce," 1969;
The Land of Lost Content, 1970; "Pigeon Summer," 1973; "A Brand New
Life," 1974; "The Girl with the Beautiful Clothes," 1975; "The Sleeve," 1975;
"Magic, Parsimony, & Wheels," 1975; "In the New World," 1978; "Children
of Old Booger," 1978.

Analysis
Lucid, linear, well-made, the stories of Robert Phillips have yet to be
sufficiently appreciated in this country—perhaps because his three poetry
collections, so well and widely reviewed, have cast him in the mold of "poet"
in the eyes of his many critics. This is unfortunate, because the best of his
stories are full of telling details, memorable characters, universal situations,
and they explode in small epiphanies or realization. Truth *and* consequences
could be a subtitle for his collected stories. In such stories as "Children of
Old Booger," still uncollected, the protagonist (and the reader) will never
quite be the same after reaching the natural and seemingly inevitable climax.
Readers looking for experimentation will have to look elsewhere; Phillips'
stories are more in the manner of Guy de Maupassant (to whom he has been
compared by more than one critic) than to Jorge Luis Borges or John Barth.
More often than not his stories take place in the fictional town of Public
Landing. His major theme, as of 1980, seems to be loss—loss of innocence,
illusion, identity, even ecology. Behind the peeling façade of Public Landing
lie the quiet and desperation of the lives of its people; within the trivia of
their everyday existences Phillips finds the nettle and, with a palpably strong
sense of drama and sharp clarity, exposes it. Like Elizabeth Bowen, he is
especiallly good at depicting the terrors of childhood. Above all else, in every
sense, he is a *story*teller.

Major publications other than short fiction
POETRY: *Inner Weather*, 1966; *The Pregnant Man*, 1978; *Running on Empty*,
1981.
NONFICTION: *The Confessional Poets*, 1973; *Denton Welch*, 1974; *William
Goyen*, 1979.

Tom Baker

FELICE PICANO

Born: New York, 1944

Principal short fiction
"Absolute Ebony," 1980; "Slashed to Ribbons in Defense of Love," 1980; "One Way Out," 1980.

Analysis
Fiction begins for Felice Picano when a specific consciousness enters the realm of the new, the unexpected, the suddenly altered, the extraordinary. This is not traditional "occult" or "horror" fiction by any means: although the instant acceptance of her work—especially shorter pieces—in this area is a sign of the genre's new expansiveness and its interrelation with other genres. Picano is not concerned with the inexplicable as much as with the mind's delicate balance in crisis, the ideal world splashing into the real, the obsession allowed to flower fully. Personal encounters and relationships are seen as potent fields of manipulation and power games; as entrapments and releases; as crucibles of change or bogs of stagnation. All emotions are suspect because so prone to sudden change, but experience and rationality are also useless as guides. The format of her novels and stories is usually conventional: scenes and action are suspenseful and quickly paced, and the unraveling of a central enigma often depends on the unraveling of the protagonist's psyche. These elements are in contrast with her use of odd or combination points of view and multiple perspectives viewing a single object, person, event, or situation. The narrative is a mixture of dialogue and description but is usually tied to almost stream-of-consciousness monologue. Picano's intention in all this is not to predigest or prejudge her characters and their actions, but to force her readers to reexperience key periods of their lives and thus to convey the immmediacy and complex mental patterning of human life. Critical attention so far has centered on the inherent controversy of Picano's themes (such as female sexuality, homosexuality, extraordinary desires and capabilities); on her unusual plots, milieus, and characters; and on her psychologically accurate dissection of states of thought during supercharged moments. Little note has been given to the more formal aspects of her work, such as structure, style, language, and so on.

Major publications other than short fiction
NOVELS: *Smart As the Devil*, 1975; *Eyes*, 1976; *The Mesmerist*, 1977; *The Lure*, 1979.
POETRY: *The Deformity Lover and Other Poems*, 1978.

FREDERIK POHL

Born: New York, 1919

Principal short fiction

Alternating Currents, 1956; *The Case Against Tomorrow*, 1957; *Tomorrow Times Seven*, 1959; *The Man Who Ate the World*, 1960; *Turn Left at Thursday*, 1961; *The Wonder Effect*, 1962 (with C. M. Kornbluth); *The Abominable Earthman*, 1963; *Digits and Dastards*, 1966; *The Frederik Pohl Omnibus*, 1966; *Day Million*, 1970; *The Gold at the Starbow's End*, 1972; *The Best of Frederik Pohl*, 1975; *The Early Pohl*, 1976; *In the Problem Pit*, 1976; *Critical Mass*, 1977.

Analysis

Since the early 1950's, Frederik Pohl has been a dominant figure in science fiction in a variety of capacities—as a fan, an agent, an editor, an anthologizer, and, most importantly, as a writer. During the 1950's, Pohl turned his deft satirical talents on the American economic and political system to produce a "consumer cycle" of stories, the best known of which is probably "The Midas Plague," in which the poor are punished by being forced to consume huge amounts of food and goods, while the rich can abstain.

In the 1960's Pohl's short fiction began to reflect the concerns of that turbulent decade, and aliens came to occupy a larger space in his work—reflecting the common assumption that science fiction frequently used the "alien problem" as a metaphor for America's own racial traumas. Four Martian "sketches" emphasized his best work in this area, "The Martian Stargazers," "The Day After the Martians Came," "Earth 18," and "Speed Trap." Shifts in sexual mores and practices were explored in "Day Million" and extended into the 1970's, perhaps grotesquely in "We Purchased People," a story that takes the theme of human manipulation to an extreme, violent conclusion. A new, more hopeful note also came into Pohl's fiction in his somewhat romanticized view of the youthful "counterculture" and the new "therapies" of the period. In two excellent stories, "The Gold at Starbow's End" and "In the Problem Pit," individuals "tuned in" to the contemporary scene combine to solve problems and chart new directions for mankind, violently in the first story, more peacefully in the second.

Major publications other than short fiction

NOVELS: *The Space Merchants*, 1952 (with C. M. Kornbluth); *Search the Sky*, 1954 (with C. M. Kornbluth); *Gladiator-at-Law*, 1955 (with C. M. Kornbluth); *Slave Ship*, 1957; *Woflbane*, 1959 (with C. M. Kornbluth); *Drunkard's Walk*, 1960; *The Reefs of Space*, 1964 (with Jack Williamson); *Starchild*, 1965 (with Jack Williamson); *Rogue Star*, 1969 (with Jack Williamson); *The Age*

of the Pussyfoot, 1969; *The Farthest Star*, 1975 (with Jack Williamson); *Man Plus*, 1976; *Gateway*, 1977; *The Starchild Trilogy*, 1977; *JEM*, 1979; *Beyond the Blue Event Horizon*, 1980.
NONFICTION: *The Way the Future Was: A Memoir*, 1978.

Keith Neilson

PATRICK VICTOR POWER

Born: Ireland, 1930

Principal short fiction
"Consolation," 1959; "The Station," 1960; "Grandstand," 1965; "The Bull-fight," 1970; "The Operation," 1970; "Threshold," 1971; "The Ragged Rascal Ran," 1974; "The Ashplant," 1975; "Lackendara," 1976; "The Imposition," 1980; "In the Town of Ballymuck," 1980; "Circle of Knives," 1980.

Analysis
Victor Power's fiction is set primarily in Ireland. The earlier stories though they ring clearly of Dublin caricature, concentrate mainly on rural Ireland and the "crazy relationships" among the less sophisticated Irish. Power's exposition is explicit about setting and character development. He knows the Irish. Change is the unifying theme in his work: Ireland's transition from agriculture to industry, from rural, pastoral values to urbanization, old outlooks contrasted to the new. Most obvious is the change in the attitudes of the people: the generation gap, the increased sophistication, the coming of technology releasing craftsmen from traditional roles, the secularization of a rigid, Catholic society, the galloping materialism and prosperity, the impact of television on a traditionally bent pastoral world. Power's work resembles painting; his ability to set a stage and introduce a reader to his strange universe, is remarkable. The tone of much of his work is that of a youth passing from innocence to enlightenment and experience. His narrator is often a child or adolescent, handled by the mature and experienced writer. Power deals also with the sophistication of upper-class city characters but his focus seems to lie with the qualities of Thomas Hardy's country people. He has captured their pub talk, the details of their settings, and he presents them vividly. Power's short fiction, as well as his drama, has changed since he became an American citizen; his subject matter is similar, but he has written more novellas than short stories. Regardless of length, the quality of the writing is excellent; the author's perception and story development are beautifully executed.

Major publications other than short fiction
PLAYS: "The Mudnest," 1969; "The Escape,"

NANCY PRICE

Born: South Dakota, 1925

Principal short fiction
"The Invisible Ones," 1968; "White Mouse," 1969.

Analysis

Nancy Price was a poet first, and a poet's care is evident in her work. She has commented that she finds it difficult to put any explanation, any writer's voice, between her story and the reader. Her aim is to make the story happen in the reader's mind, beyond any instrusion. Using the ordinary world we think we know, she turns it slightly so that it shows us another face that may, perhaps, change our way of seeing. *Publishers Weekly* wrote of her latest novel, "Her characters are unique, her story line is inventive and unusual. This is a moving, even terrifying novel with a rare richness, subtlety and depth."

Major publications other than short fiction
NOVELS: *A Natural Death*, 1973; *An Accomplished Woman*, 1979.

H. L. PROSSER

Born: Missouri, 1944

Principal short fiction
Dandelion Seeds, 1974; *The Capricorn*, 1974; *The Day of the Grunion*, 1977; *Spanish Tales*, 1977; *Goodbye, Lon Chaney, Jr., Goodbye*, 1978; *Summer Wine*, 1979.

Analysis
H. L. Prosser creates incisive, often biting portraits of a situation or circumstance in which one or more characters are forced to perceive and internalize their existence in the context of what is confronting them. The stories are complex, tightly structured, and terse. He creates within an existential framework of reality, making the everyday and common experiences one encounters deep voyages into the psyche of humankind. His themes range from joy and shared happiness, magic, madness, loneliness, sexuality, Christian existentialism, environmental struggle, to mysticism and love. At the root of his fiction is the central theme that all perception is paradoxical and often is not what the individual truly sees but imagines that he sees as a reality. His writings have been compared to those of Ray Bradbury, Nathanael West, William Faulkner, Henry James, Kawabata, and others. He has been called an existential mystic, a romantic, and a master of contemporary fantasy. There is an emphasis on color and characterization; and the end result is perfectly developed characters that realize or reach some internal conclusion about their existence, and regardless of what that conclusion may be, are left with the innate ability to cope and persevere.

Major publications other than short fiction
POETRY: "The Cymric," 1976; "The Alien," 1980; "Topoxte Island," 1980.

NAHID RACHLIN

Born: Iran

Principal short fiction
"Foreigner," 1978; "Poet's Visit," 1978.

Analysis
Nahid Rachlin's stories, written in English, with mostly Iranian characters, often deal with the shattering of dreams and the character's reactions. In Iran people are exposed to Western culture and ideas but cannot fulfill Western ambitions. Young men and women want to become actors, actresses, writers, painters, industrialists, and politicians. The culture of freedom is there but freedom is not there—neither under the Shah nor, despite rising hopes, under the present government. This sort of conflict has a terrible effect on people. Some of the stories are about people who escape, go to the United States, and see the chance to achieve their ambitions; but despite their dreams, they cannot adjust to the Western culture. Some give up and return home; some become more American than Americans; others turn into mere imitations of themselves.

The stories demonstrate that the conflict between East and West takes place inside individuals, not between them. Rachlin's characters are victims of dreams created by Western culture—books, films, and music. The conflict of the stories is mirrored in Rachlin's simple, terse, precise writing style, which contrasts with the ornate Iranian culture she is describing. This device, together with the presentation of the Persian idiom in the dialogues, lends clarity to scenes and people.

BURTON RAFFEL

Born: New York, 1928

Principal short fiction
Short Story, 1960; "Goodbye," 1960; "The Lady of the Lake," 1968;
"Twelve and No More," 1972; "The Butcher," 1978; "The White Desert,"
1979; "The Emperor at Elba," 1980.

Analysis
Short stories seem to Burton Raffel somewhat more like poems than do novels. The form is immensely variable: although his basic bent is for psychological analysis, the stories he has published range from what might be called straight realism ("Fatherhood") to realism tinged with a kind of interior horror ("Sicilian Vespers"), and from relatively straightforward science fiction ("Goodbye") to parodistic science fiction ("The Lady of the Lake") to a kind of meditative science fiction that has very little plot and no dialogue ("The White Desert"). Raffel finds his approach, in each case, in some clue or clues that seem to him inherent in the material. For example, two of the stories are about figures in professional sports, but although the boxing story ("The Butcher") is deeply serious, even grim, the baseball story ("The Emperor at Elba") is satirical to the point of nastiness. Raffel is determinedly nontheoretical about everything he writes: to the best of his knowledge he has never written a story for technical (nonsubstantive) reasons, nor has he ever written anything to prove or to disprove any approach. He writes because, simply stated, he has to, and he deals with his material on a case-by-case basis. He cares immensely about technique in general and about prose style in particular; he does not care for anyone's theories, including the occasional ones he finds and tries to ignore in himself.

Major publications other than short fiction
NOVEL: *After Such Ignorance*, 1980.
POETRY: *Mia Poems*, 1968; *Four Humours*, 1979.
NONFICTION: *The Development of Modern Indonesian Poetry*, 1967; *The Forked Tongue: A Study of the Translation Process*, 1971; *Introduction to Poetry*, 1971.

DAVID RAY

Born: Oklahoma, 1932

Principal short fiction

"Esse," 1964; "The Brawl + Two Burgers," 1964; "The 38 Page Letter F. Kafka Once Wrote," 1966; "A Tin Can, A Nosey Dog, A New Widow," 1968; "What Went Wrong," 1971; "Vahakn and Herr Hauptmann," 1971; "Mending Fence," 1971; "The Mulberries of Mingo," 1975; "Suffern," 1976; "Under the Clock," 1976; "The Devil and Henry James II," 1978; *The Mulberries of Mingo and Other Stories,* 1978; "Bert's House," 1979; "An Elegant Dinner in San Francisco," 1979; "And His Ox Babe," 1979; "A Visiting Lecturer," 1980; "A Convention Not to Speak," 1980; *The Lighthouse and Other Stories,* 1981.

Analysis

With the perfect cadence and economy of his best poetry, David Ray writes fiction about characters he knows and loves or those whose rejection he remembers and about which he grieves. The deeply buried sorrow in Ray's fiction blossoms forth in lines that are as clear and pure and (seemingly) as casual and unrehearsed as the lilies of the field. His fictional characters in *The Mulberries of Mingo*—an aunt, a grandmother, a grandfather, a sister— vibrate with feeling. Ray lets us know their dilemma in language as simple and alive as breathing. Always on the side of the poor, of the innocent victim, of the disinherited and of the orphaned, Ray is an author with his emotions in full control: he brings tears to your eyes while you think you are still laughing; he has a delightful and surprising gift for satire. His fiction, for a long while upstaged by his own achievements in poetry (he is winner of the 1979 William Carlos Williams Award from the Poetry Society of America for *The Tramp's Cup*), has yet to be fully recognized by the literary critics. In one of the few collections of his short fiction so far available, *The Mulberries of Mingo*, Ray brings to us the tragic burden of the oppressed in his wholly understated group portraits as delicate as Watteau or Fragonard.

Major publications other than short fiction

POETRY: *X- Rays*, 1965; *Dragging the Main*, 1968; *A Hill in Oklahoma*, 1972; *Gathering Firewood*, 1974; *Enough of Flying*, 1978; *The Tramp's Cup*, 1979.

Natalie L. M. Petesch

BARBARA REID

Born: New York, 1922

Principal short fiction
"Brothers," 1957; "The Old Lady," 1970; "The Meeting," 1972; "Bernice,"
1975; "A Bird of Passage," 1976; *The Tears of San Lorenzo*, 1977; "Accident,"
1978; "The Waltz Dream," 1979.

Analysis
Traditional in their construction, often complex, and extremely evocative,
Barbara Reid's short fiction has "the poet's concern with emotional truth,"
the revelations that come with profound and universal experience: Pain,
psychic and physical (illness), tenuous relationships, loneliness, death itself.
Increasingly her stories explore the theme of aging. The characters in these
stories, their memories sharpened by time, have the long perspective. She
feels this perspective is fascinating, and their last days unfold with an intensity
that is crystallized in scenes sometimes humorous, sometimes moving. She
believes with Eudora Welty that "writing is the response of love, that [the
writer] needs to write with love, with internal vision . . . to see and radiate."
She thinks of it as building a bridge between people, one of understanding,
filling the loneliness; it is, she believes, a bridge of love.

RANDALL REID

Born: California, 1931

Principal short fiction
"Detritus," 1972; "A Lecherous Poet Named Hench," 1973; "Sea Story,"
1976; "The Best," 1977.

Analysis
Often employing first-person narrators, Randall Reid's stories show a strong
concern for the sound and idioms of spoken language. Like his long fiction,
they also explore the ways in which people "really" tell stories—in journals
or letters or over a beer, whether talking to others or to themselves. He has
little interest in disguised autobiography, and his narrators seldom resemble
his own personality. They are instead rather like Geoffrey Chaucer's pilgrims—varied tellers of stories which, however complete simply as stories,
also reveal the person who tells them. His published stories are part of a
projected collection (now nearing completion) in which the individual stories
will implicitly comment upon one another. Although thematically related,
they employ contrasting tones and styles and, when read together, will establish a complex vision of Eros from different and often discordant points
of view. The stories are sometimes ribald, sometimes poignant, sometimes
chilling, sometimes "affirmative." Candid without being prurient, they examine the intricacies of human desire and love in ways which owe little either
to conventional mores or to current fashions.

Major publications other than short fiction
NOVEL: *Lost and Found*, 1975.
NONFICTION: *The Fiction of Nathanael West: No Redeemer, No Promised
Land*, 1967.

JEAN RHYS

Born: West Indies, 1894   **Died:** England, 1979

Principal short fiction
The Left Bank, 1927; *Tigers Are Better-Looking*, 1968; *Sleep It off Lady*, 1976.

Analysis
Jean Rhys's literary reputation rests on her largely autobiographical explorations of isolated womanhood. Her stories are impressionist *aperçus* of people and places almost entirely descriptive, with but a minimal plot to sustain a slight narrative flow. Characters, mainly women hovering at the brink of an emotional crisis, are skillfully sketched with very few strokes and delicately touched up with color and significant details. Her carefully polished, reticent style is almost translucent in its unemphatic simplicity and reminiscent of Anton Chekhov in economy and depth. There is a fragile equipoise of humor and compassion—irony and melancholy at times—in her prose which creates a peculiar suspense. Marvelous craftsmanship and exquisite artistic taste have suppressed all sentiments superfluous to a calculated effect. An exceptional "instinct for form" much praised by Ford Madox Ford, and the rhythmical flow of narration undistorted by reflections or intellectual abstractions make these stories vivid, passionate, and painfully true. Her themes are almost obsessionally narrow in their scope and of an ephemeral, elusive quality, which is put across rather through a suggestive arrangement of incidents than through a conscious narrative design. The freshness and haunting intensity of her images and her straightforward, almost casually clear tone never miss their aim, be it the exotic atmosphere of the West Indies or tenuous fragments of a solitary life adrift and vulnerable in an endlessly hostile world.

Major publications other than short fiction
NOVELS: *Quartet*, 1928; *After Leaving Mr. Mackenzie*, 1930; *Voyage in the Dark*, 1934; *Good Morning, Midnight*, 1939; *Wide Sargasso Sea*, 1966.
NONFICTION: *Smile Please*, 1980.

Marie-Antoinette Manz-Kunz

MARY ANN RISHEL

Born: Pennsylvania, 1940

Principal short fiction
"Nickel Dirt," 1977; "Staus," 1977; "Uncle Perk's Leg," 1979.

Analysis
The characters in Mary Ann Rishel's stories are working class Slovaks living in Pittsburgh. Traditional in structure, these stories are comic, especially through the language and plot; they move away from the comic as the quiet pain of the characters is revealed. The imagery is ethnic and domestic and comes almost exclusively from lower-class occupations. The dominant theme is strength, the characters' abilities to survive even though they are fully aware of their helplessness.

MARY ELSIE ROBERTSON

Born: Arkansas, 1937

Principal short fiction
"You Ain't Been Blue," 1960; *Jordan's Stormy Banks and Other Stories*, 1961; "The Horseleach Had Two Daughters," 1974; "Mothers," 1977; "Moonsong," 1978; "First Snow," 1978; "A Winter Story," 1978; "Witness," 1979; "Cold Comfort," 1979; "Drifting Out," 1981; "Secrets," 1981; "Smartest Kid in the Class," 1981.

Analysis
The best of Mary Elsie Robertson's short stories—for example "Secrets," "Witness," "First Snow," and "Mothers,"—work like poems. They are beautifully written metaphors of a power and depth that belie their apparent quietness. Her stories all have a vivid sense of landscape and weather of which her characters are a part. Her themes often concern women—the relationships between mothers and daughters, the ambiguities and ambivalences of intense, personal relationships, the moments of self-discovery. Her voice is unmistakably her own, but she combines melancholy and humor in the tradition of the best Southern writers. Her stories are subtle and powerful illuminations that readers are unlikely to forget.

Major publications other than short fiction
NOVEL: *After Freud*, 1980.

Peter Marchant

RALPH ROBIN

Born: Pennsylvania, 1914

Principal short fiction

"The Improbable Redemption of Donald Grenfell," 1949; "Pleasant Dreams," 1951; "Neither," 1952; "The Beach Thing," 1952; "Budding Explorer," 1952; "Rabbit Punch," 1952; "The Peeping Tom," 1953; "Jumping Bean Season," 1953; "Business for Lawyers," 1953; "Inefficiency Expert," 1953; "Mr. Prime," 1953; "Four Men and a Suitcase," 1953; "Open Ears," 1953; "A Great Day for the Amorous," 1953; "The Wrong People," 1953; "Mr. Pruitt," 1957; "Health," 1957; "Fountain of Folly," 1958; "Scott Burgess and His Friends," 1958; "Suitable Employment," 1958; "Such Are Kind Ideas," 1958; "The Hope of Man," 1959; "By and Large Happy," 1961; "Something Really Big," 1962; "Eddie," 1962; "You Don't Need No Mediator in a Two-Group," 1962; "Call Me Bromius," 1964; "The Heating and Ventilating Engineer Who Hates *Hamlet*," 1964; "Circumpromenadation of David and Natalie," 1964; "Lamina 96," 1966; "The Night Visitors," 1967; "When Everything Falls Apart Be Polite," 1967; "In Woods and Fastnesses," 1968; "Oh, I Had to Call Bayard," 1969; "The Last Monogamist," 1970; "Little Sister's Electric Finger," 1970; "Eric and the Incandescent Maiden," 1970; "Do You Play Checkers?," 1971; "The Good Doctor Bradford," 1977.

Analysis

The particular quality of Ralph Robin's short stories that is first apparent to the reader is their liveliness. His stories embody and invoke emotion. In language that is vigorous, resonant, and sensitive, he weaves patterns of feeling and thought. Some of Robin's writing has been called experimental. It is more accurate to say that his work is original, whatever form he chooses to employ. An element of fantasy is present in Robin's fiction. Of course there are the outright fantasies which appeared in science-fiction magazines and four imaginative stories which appeared in literary magazines: "Fountain of Folly," "Such Are Kind Ideas," "By and Large Happy," and "Call Me Bromius." But consider "Mr. Pruitt," Eli M. Oboler, reviewing *The Best American Short Stories 1958* in *Library Journal* (October 15, 1958), wrote: "Ralph Robin has perhaps the most memorable story in 'Mr. Pruitt,' a penetrating and mature study of a frigid woman." "Mr. Pruitt" is a realistic story; yet it has a magical atmosphere that links it to fantasy. As with fantasy, so with humor. In Robin's most serious stories there is humor, and in his most comical stories there is seriousness. So playful a story as "Budding Explorer," praised for its humor in *The New York Herald Tribune Book Review* (April 19, 1953), has penetrating things to say about politics; and so serious a story as "Eddie" has its bitter humor. Like his character Eddie, the author is a man who considers "the plain, downright comicality of being a human being." Robin's talent for blending realism with fantasy and seriousness with humor sharpens in the stories he published in the middle and late 1960's and in the 1970's.

Major publications other than short fiction
POETRY: *Cities of Speech*, 1971.

LEONARD WALLACE ROBINSON

Born: Massachusetts, 1912

Principal short fiction
"A Licence to Paint," 1942; "Prelude in 4 F," 1942; "All Their Lives Long," 1943; "Return of a Soldier to Mufti," 1943; "The Ten Funny Ashbarrels," 1943; "The Last Chance," 1944; "The Sin," 1945; "The Ruin of Soul," 1950; "A Small Tragedy in Manton," 1956; "The Decision," 1965; "The Practice of an Art," 1965; "Cement, Etc.," 1979.

Analysis
His first eight stories in *The New Yorker* revealed Leonard Wallace Robinson as a very strict realist in the Hemingway-O'Hara tradition. He used very short one-, two-, and three-scene events that ended in bitter, usually urban epiphanies characteristic of the so-called *New Yorker* magazine "casual" of the 1940's and 1950's. Gradually, Robinson's stories expanded in length and in aesthetic intent. They became richer psychologically, far more inward and subjective and more concerned with metaphysical and even religious themes. Robinson remained, however, well within the Mansfield-Joyce-Hemingway naturalistic tradition both in subject matter and in his manner of treating it. His latest stories, however, have become frankly experimental. They have broken out of the naturalistic tradition in his selection of subject matter while remaining within it in his formal treatment of the subject matter. His current stories are a blend of surrealism and naturalism. This new treatment is truly original and gives his stories a preternatural freshness, a curious closeness to pure poetry, which is his intention.

Major publications other than short fiction
NOVELS: *The Assassin*, 1968; *The Man Who Loved Beauty*, 1976.

Patricia Goedicke

DEBORAH ROBSON

Born: Illinois, 1948

Principal short fiction
"The Stained-Glass Butterfly," 1973; "A Woman's Walk," 1973; "Initiation," 1974; "If a Wizard Came Riding," 1975; "Carrie," 1976; "Eft," 1979; "Flight," 1980.

Analysis
Deborah Robson' stories aim to portray the elusive intersection between the individual and the cultural context—or, between freedom and determinism. This statement sounds extremely dry, and the stories are more like air-paintings, but the "analysis," if it must be stated, seems true. While using techniques borrowed from poetry—and thus devising nontraditional narrative methods—she intends her stories to be accessible, and she focuses on character as a means to that end.

LEON ROOKE

Born: North Carolina, 1934

Principal short fiction
Last One Home Sleeps in the Yellow Bed, 1968; *Vault*, 1973; *The Love Parlour*, 1977; *The Broad Back of the Angel*, 1977; *Cry Evil*, 1980.

Analysis
Leon Rooke's work roams wide and far, across city and country, from the densely psychological to the unsophisticated rural. He is "at home in all conventions, in all voices," nearly always with "technical wizardry" and often with genuine innovativeness. Frequently difficult because of "his disarming habit of showing so much by telling so little," his stories initially "ask to be misread because everything positive is paradoxically evoked by an assertion of its negative counterpart." "Truth is always presented as a shifting synthesis of opposites." He is not content to let the reader "locate a single point of view but rather to concentrate on the mysterious blending of several." Sometimes using real true-to-life characters routinely caught against a backdrop of "overpowering atmosphere," his stories inevitably force the question "why is this story being told *now*?" While this immediacy most often moves between the representational and the surreal, and while Rooke eschews place in the normal sense, unlike many modern and postmodern writers he remains faithful—deceptively so, at times—to the traditional concepts of plot and theme. A "unique stylist," as "comic as he is grotesque," his work consistently probes "the disintegration of self and of relationships," the struggle "to give and receive love," the "mating of hope with despair," and the "measuring of and search for *soul*, given each individual's self-recognized (and frequently self-achieved) fall from grace."

Major publications other than short fiction
NOVEL: *Fat Woman*, 1980.
PLAYS: *Krokodile*, 1973; *Sword/Play*, 1974.

RITA L. ROSENFELD

Born: Canada, 1936

Principal short fiction

"The Whistler," 1975; "The Letter Writer," 1975; "Michael Rode His Dream Aboard," 1977; "The Honolulu Sun," 1977; "Forever Dreaming," 1979; "Life's a Ball," 1979; "To Pass Through Honey," 1979; "The Innocence of Rasputin," 1979; "All Kinds of People," 1979; "Insect Collecting," 1979; "By the Eyes You Can Always Tell," 1979; "My Sister's Keeper," 1979; "Chrysalid," 1979; "I'd Have Kicked Her Out," 1979; "Friends of a Friend," 1980; "Old Friends," 1980; "Relations," 1980; "Leonara's Passion," 1980; "Moving with the Times," 1980.

Analysis

Rita Rosenfeld uses a universal theme centering on the loneliness of self, an alienated society, and the inability of people to communicate. The stories have careful character portrayals, dramatically incisive introspections of mind, and excellent background detail; there is no one particular style or format which they follow. Each story is a complete microscopic look at individual desires, perceptions, and often disappointments; each examines how people cope, endure, and survive. Despite a kind of unifying theme (isolation, alienation, desperation), each story has a life of its own and does not relate as a continuity to the others; the exploration of the thematic material is varied and wide in scope. Inherent in all the stories' themes is that most basic of human needs, a seeking after "belonging," love, and emotional security, and, reflecting our society, most often there is failure to attain those ends. There is incisive humour running as a thread throughout the stories, however, and hopelessness is not endemic to the writing.

CAROLE ROSENTHAL

Born: Illinois, 1941

Principal short fiction
"The Star," 1976; "Breaking," 1976; "Selected Short Subjects," 1976; "Cowboys," 1977; "The Independent Nose," 1978; "Snapshot," 1978; "Fusion," 1978, 1979; "A Specialist in Still Lives," 1979; "Inside, Outside," 1979; "The Baby Tooth," 1980.

Analysis
Carole Rosenthal's fiercely energetic and carefully crafted stories about male-female relationships are often surrealistic in both effect and plot as they explore contrasts and contradictions between the internal world of feelings and the external world of behavior. Funny, painful and passionate, the images tend toward the biological and the primitive. These images are juxtaposed against sharp contemporary social detail. The predicaments in which the characters find themselves reveal people trapped into apparently logical action by their verbal intelligence and psychological sophistication. Yet they are inevitably surprised that their actions have unforeseen and irrevocable consequences in the external world of event.

Major publications other than short fiction
NONFICTION: "A Degree in Enlightenment," in *Woman in the Year 2000*, 1975.

Lynda Schor

MORDECAI ROSHWALD

Born: Poland, 1921

Principal short fiction

"The Politics of Ratology," 1960; "Awakening Olympus," 1967; "Encounter at Interlaken," 1967.

Analysis

Short fiction has been only a marginal literary activity of Mordecai Roshwald. This literary medium is used to convey a certain social or political message. Yet, the moral purpose is not announced or preached; it is conveyed through a satirical tale, which also tends to be colored by fantasy or science fiction. In a way Roshwald follows the tradition of Jonathan Swift or Voltaire, which is also true of his published fiction to date.

Major publications other than short fiction

NOVELS: *Level Seven*, 1959, 1960; *A Small Armageddon*, 1962, 1976.
NONFICTION: *Man and Education*, 1954 (in Hebrew); *Humanism in Practice*, 1955; *Moses: Leader, Prophet, Man*, 1969 (with Miriam Roshwald).

NORMAN ROSTEN

Born: New York, 1914

Principal short fiction
"A Visit to Heaven," 1953; "Can I Play With Your Little Girl," 1954.

Analysis
Norman Rosten's first book of fiction, *Under the Boardwalk* (1968), began as a group of separate stories. Dealing with a single Coney Island summer (a childhood reminiscence), the effect is novelistic by virtue of reappearances of the same characters in different sections of the book, within a unity of time and place. There is no formal sense of plot. It may be the use of the "I" that is the truer unifying element, or perhaps the pattern of memory that guides the narrative. When published, critics approvingly called the work a novel, which category is acceptable to him. Rosten's second book, *Over and Out* (1972), also had its origins in a cluster of scenes and narrations, again in a first-person frame. This time, a plot asserted itself, however loosely.

In a third book, just completed, Rosten seems to have finally written a "pure" novel, with development of plot and character. The cohesion of the novel is as mysterious as that of any natural element, with the added human ingredient of the irrational. In Rosten's case, the short (story) form is the crucible in which the larger structure is shaped. His best efforts are literary—that is, in the writing style itself, the mortar rather than the architecture. Here, Rosten's background as a poet is expecially valuable to the good effects he achieves.

Major publications other than short fiction
NOVELS: *Under the Boardwalk*, 1968; *Over and Out*, 1972.
PLAYS: *Come Slowly, Eden*, 1966; *Mister Johnson*, 1969.
POETRY: *Return Again, Traveler*, 1940; *The Fourth Decade*, 1943; *The Big Road*, 1946; *Songs for Patricia*, 1951; *The Plane and the Shadow*, 1953; *Thrive upon the Rock*, 1965; *Selected Poems*, 1979.

MIRIAM RUGEL

Born: Pennsylvania, 1911

Principal short fiction

"The Venus," 1938; "Don't Marry," 1938; "Shakespeare and the Magic Sentence," 1938; "The Insufferable Fannabelle," 1939; "The Medal," 1950; "Flowers on the Table," 1951; "Do You Believe, My Darlings?," 1952; "The Gettysburg Address," 1952; "The Flower," 1953; "Let Me Tell You," 1954; "Success Story," 1954; "I Can Go Anywhere," 1956; "Whoever You Are," 1957; "The Sweet Forever," 1963; "The British Empire," 1964; "The Sapphire Door," 1968; "Paper Poppy," 1969; "The Golden Forest," 1972.

Analysis

Miriam Rugel does not write vertical poems, interpretations of myths, or crossword puzzles. She is uninterested in typographical design on the printed page. Her presentation is with people: what she sees them do, what she hears in a spontaneous line, the revelation in an isolated moment, a face with agonized eyebrows in a movie line. Rugel writes because it is the medium to which she was born and because she loves language as a tool. She communicates as directly and swiftly and with as much wily artfulness as she can command. She moves from the individual to the universal, reaching especially for clarity. Her work has been printed in Canada, England, Africa, Italy, Australia, and the United States.

ALBERT RUSSO

Born: Zaire, 1943

Principal short fiction

Incandescences, 1970; *Splinters of Malachite*, 1971; *Musaïque New Yorkaise*, 1975.

Analysis

Many of Albert Russo's stories are set in Central and Southern Africa where he spent seventeen years of his life. The themes are basically socioracial in context, and the style is intimistic and concise. Russo favors the shorter genre, and his novels are in fact long novellas. About *Splinters of Malachite*, Georges Sion of the French Goncourt Academy said: "Having read the whole book, one feels that the young author has a lot to say. . . . Endowed with a vast knowledge of languages, with rich experiences, with strong emotions which influence his style, Albert Russo should strive for peace of mind and simplicity. . . ." Russo writes in both English and French, and through his eclectic experiences—American, European, and Third Worldly—he evolves in directions which make it difficult for critics to classify him. His style has in turn been likened to that of Marcel Proust, Guy de Maupassant, Franz Kafka, and Peter Abrams. Yet, personally, he feels a stronger kinship with painters and musicians than with these writers, however much he respects them. Russo often uses flamboyant imagery and because of this he is, at times, taxed with being too lyrical. He cannot dissociate the words from the picture, the mosaic, or the fresco. Were it not for the fact that in both the Anglo-Saxon and Francophone literary arenas the novel predominates, Russo would expend most of his creative energy in the short story form. Recently, he has turned his attention to the realm of the absurd and the fantastic, including science fiction. Having also worked on a few screenplays, he finds the cinema an extremely rewarding alternative.

Major publications other than short fiction

NOVELS: *Splinters of Malachite*, 1971; *Devil's Peak*, 1973; *Triality*, 1976-1977; *Princes and Gods*, 1980.
PLAY: *Convalescence*, 1971.

BIENVENIDO N. SANTOS

Born: Philippines, 1911

Principal short fiction
You Lovely People, 1955; *Brother My Brother*, 1960; *The Day the Dancers Came*, 1967; "When Exiles Meet," 1978; "The Brief Education of Solomon King," 1978; *Scent of Apples*, 1980.

Analysis
Bienvenido Santos' short stories chronicle the varieties of pathetic frustration, the sense of abandonment associated with liberation from a colonial past, the wearing away of protective naïveté. They capture the infallible faith, the resilience, the resurgent dream of self-recognition and esteem, the folk endurance of a people partially immunized against despair by so long a history of dispossession. In all of Santos' fiction, this compulsion to belong consistently raises images of departure and provisional return, of loss and attempted recovery. He is less concerned with history perceived as ocean current or successive waves, than with culture as an entire archipelago of diverse islands in that stream. What he discerns is that any ethnic group consists of individual particles, no two of which are exactly identical, but all of which have declared their commitment to participate, as if in some consummate entity. The declaration of a common bond tends to be more perfect than uneasy coexistence may actually turn out to be. Nevertheless, it provides a measure of meaning even for those who pay it lip service only. This is the recurring theme in Santos' work: how hard it always is, yet how important, to be "Filipino" at heart, with all that that implies about human decency, good humor, and honor, consideration beyond courtesy, and putting both hands to a common burden; while at the same time trying to make a life out of being overseas Filipinos, Philippine-Americans, temporary "permanent residents" obligated to be buried "at home," or those assimilated beyond recovery of any heritage whatsoever.

Major publications other than short fiction
NOVELS: *Villa Magdalena*, 1965; *The Volcano*, 1965.
PLAYS: *The Bishop's Pets*, 1967; *A Long Way Home*, 1967.

Leonard Casper

SARA
Sally Blake

Born: Massachusetts, 1925

Principal short fiction
A House Divided, 1968; "In the Rear-View Mirror of Godseye," 1980.

Analysis
Sara (Sally Blake) demonstrates a sure touch for the simple drama of people's lives. Her characters evoke a compelling human sympathy for the loneliness, anguish, and despair in their stifling round of everyday activities. There is also humor, courage, and an unquenchable vitality of spirit in her work. Her stories reveal the crucial issues that lie behind the commonplace— the loss of innocence, the agony of parting, the inexorable forces of change. She understands the complicated web of emotions that haunts the human psyche, the aching love mixed with the feelings of frustration and inadequacy, the desire for one's own identity warring with the cultural pressures without and one's own insufficiencies within. She understands how actions with the best of intentions can turn out badly. Sara takes these universal themes and constructs from them stories of depth and poignancy. Her writing style, straightforward and clean, surges with emotional power. In her characters, very real and very human, we see mirrored something of our own selves, our own souls. Like us, they bear the wounds of sundered relationships, the scars of unsought experience. Like us, they skirt the edge of some great, possibly awesome, mystery. Like us, they know a great deal about life, and they have a great deal more to learn.

Major publications other than short fiction
NOVEL: *Where Mist Clothes Dream and Song Runs Naked*, 1965.

Louisa Arndt

GEORGE BRANDON SAUL

Born: Pennsylvania, 1901

Principal short fiction

The Wild Queen, 1967; *Carved in Findruine*, 1969; *A Little Book of Strange Tales*, 1969; *Liadain and Curithir*, 1971; "Four Tales from the Elf-Mounds," 1971.

Analysis

Carved in Findruine and "Four Tales from the Elf-Mounds" are efforts at "reincarnating," in personal tone and manner, and in the general tradition of James Stephens and Ella Young, ancient and medieval Irish story material. *A Little Book of Strange Tales* is precisely that, and is nourished by the Pennsylvania-Dutch and Philadelphia backgrounds of George Brandon Saul's youth, as well as by a marked interest in the macabre, although there is also one invention of Irish flavor. All of Saul's stories have something of the brevity and condensation—as well as the pace, freedom from clichés, and regard for structure—natural to a lyric, and in some cases a narrative, poet.

Major publications other than short fiction

NOVEL: *In Mountain Shadow*, 1970.

PLAY: *Hound and Unicorn Two Plays*, 1976.

POETRY: *The Cup of Sand*, 1923; *Bronze Woman*, 1930; *Unimagined Rose*, 1937; *"Only Necessity . . ."*, 1941; *Selected Lyrics*, 1947; *October Sheaf*, 1951; *Hound and Unicorn: Collected Verse—Lyrical, Narrative, and Dramatic*, 1969; *Candlelight Rhymes for Early-to-Beds*, 1970; *Postscript . . .*, 1971; *A Touch of Acid*, 1971; *Skeleton's Progress*, 1971; *The Stroke of Light*, 1974; *Adam Unregenerate: Selected Lyrical Poems*, 1977; *In Borrowed Light*, 1979.

PETER SCHNEEMAN

Born: Minnesota, 1937

Principal short fiction
"American Autumn," 1970; "God of Many Names," 1973; "Through the Finger Goggles," 1976.

Analysis
Peter Schneeman works by analogy in a very deliberate way. Sets of correspondences are related by association, natural and artificial. The example of Henry David Thoreau is a somewhat distant model. The style of the stories is tightly compressed and demanding; and, in all his stories published thus far, a chronological narrative in the "present" is intercut with remembered encounters, events, and the example of artists and writers. Schneeman is fond of incorporating into his text visual icons of modern culture such as boxcar insignia and rubbings from the Kennedy half-dollar. The actions, moreover, are played off against and through allusions to and quotations from modern writings; Wallace Stevens, Ezra Pound, and Henry Adams furnish epigraphs to the three stories. It is also significant that the author has written on Pound and William H. Gass, comparing the latter's method with Thoreau's. Of "God of Many Names," a reviewer commented, "Anyone who can link Pound and pudendums and protests and puberty rites and do it all in an entertaining style deserves a hand." While the subject matter is contemporary, 1960's contemporary, the material is under constant scrutiny by Zeno, Euripides, Robert Fludd, Piranesi, and others. Through all these analogical techniques, the stuff of everyday is urged toward transcendent meaning.

Major publications other than short fiction
NONFICTION: "3 Fingers of Figures for Gass," 1973; "Pound's *'Englischer Brief'*: A Look Toward Germany," 1978.

Alec Bond

LAWRENCE SCHNEIDERMAN

Born: New York, 1932

Principal short fiction
"Sequel," 1980; "Theda the Matchmaker," 1980; "Silence," 1981; "The Passover War," 1981.

Analysis

Terse, spare, Lawrence Schneiderman's stories concentrate on the human adventure, quick in passage, and on ubiquitous relationships. Quests in Schneiderman's fiction are for potency and intimacy. Even when the struggle is how to find a way through present or impending tragedy, the arena scrutinized is that of connections: father-son, grandparent-granddaughter, lover-lover (current, married, or ex). It is through the intense presence of another that the characters confront their own uniqueness and the core of their drive and dilemmas. In "Theda the Matchmaker," a Jewish academic from New York (who reads pornographic novels and recalls dropping condom water bombs on little girls) yearns for, yet is terrified by, the prospect of actual merger with a woman in the less inhibited sexual milieu of California. In "Silence," an accomplished author (obviously facile with words) cannot find the language to articulate the loneliness and the growing powerlessness that he feels in his marriage. In "The Passover War," a young Jew is destined to play out with his own offspring the geneology of arrogant pain inflicted upon him by his father. In "Sequel," a loving grandfather invents a parable to ease the lonely growing of a parentless granddaughter who must shortly lose to cancer the presence of this very special old man. Schneiderman's stories express the fact that everyone must struggle, that the struggle is both painful and funny, and that illusion and delusion, laughter and love are effective antidotes in the world of harsh realities. Through juxtapositions of the mundane, the serious, and the absurd, through brilliant descriptive detail and dialogue at once sparse and vernacular, readers become involved and concerned. Readers are touched—uncomfortably, perhaps—as they identify with one "who had stuffed himself with experiences without feeling them"—or hysterically and warmly—as they appreciate the specialness of the zanies, those for whom, supposedly, "maladjusted" moments seem the happiest, and with whom they feel magically akin.

Major publications other than short fiction
NOVEL: *Sea Nymphs by the Hour*, 1972.

Sandra L. Bertman

ARTHUR SCHNITZLER

Born: Austria, 1862   **Died:** 1931

Principal short fiction
Viennese Idylls, 1913; *The Shepherd's Pipe and Other Stories*, 1922; *The Little Comedy and Other Stories*, 1977.

Analysis
On the surface, the world of Arthur Schnitzler's stories is the Vienna of coffee houses, the opera, Strauss waltzes, and gracious, cultured living; but beneath the surface is a world of decadence and melancholy, a fear of nothingness, and terrifying loneliness. Schnitzler's stories are peopled with characters from the Viennese leisure class who are too weak to cope with their lives and are incapable of lasting attachments. Often they commit suicide or are killed in duels. Love and eros are important in Schnitzler's stories but the protagonists are often disappointed in love or are unfaithful to each other. Death is another of Schnitzler's central themes: even in the midst of the gaiety of Viennese life, death casts a shadow over all the characters. Yet death is not always viewed negatively; it can be the healer of human melancholy, an escape. In his stories Schnitzler depicts the transitoriness of life, life full of illusion, futility, and mortality. Many of his characters live in a world of dreams and illusions, where they play complex roles to escape from reality. Schnitzler shows the disintegration of life. He unmasks hypocrisy, showing the emptiness of convention and the false code of honor of his protagonists. Many of Schnitzler's stories evidence his interest in psychology and he often uses stream of consciousness as a narrative technique.

Major publications other than short fiction
NOVELS: *The Road to the Open*, 1923; *Fräulein Else*, 1925; *Beatrice*, 1926; *None but the Brave*, 1926; *Daybreak*, 1927; *Rhapsody*, 1927; *Theresa*, 1928; *Little Novels*, 1929; *Casanova's Homecoming*, 1930; *Flight into Darkness*, 1931; *Viennese Novelettes*, 1931.
PLAYS: *Professor Bernhardi*, 1928; *The Green Cockatoo*, 1977; *Anatol*, 1977.

Jennifer Michaels

LYNDA SCHOR

Born: New York, 1938

Principal short fiction
Appetites, 1975-1976; "My Strange Marriage," 1976; *True Love & Real Romance*, 1979.

Analysis
The body of the world is what Lynda Schor is interested in. She is entranced by the earthy, tangible, sticky, utterly demystified sensuality of life. As richly as Freud, her work asserts that every one of our abstractions, philosophies, wars, meaningful relationships, and works of art, is laced with the devilish smile of a sexual clown. Schor's way of connecting to us as an artist is not to tell us about feelings, but to force us to experience those very disturbing, contradictory, ambivalent emotions we like to deny we have.

Schor is deeply feminist in the sense that she reveals women's lives (ravenous hungers, frightened indifference, everyday jealousies, and mundane murderous fantasies) to be totally earthbound, uncomfortably real. Always well-structured, although sometimes unusually so, the impossible crazy situations she creates are as undeniably familiar as our chronic disappointments in love. In her stories the fantastic is embedded in what is most inescapably ordinary. The negative mark of the true romantic winds through all her work.

Lane Lazarre

RUTH WILDES SCHULER

Born: Massachusetts, 1933

Principal short fiction

"The Eyes," 1967; "The Dragon," 1976; "The End of the Honeymoon," 1977; "Admiral Byrd," 1977; "Of Porcupines and Death," 1977; "A Waddle in the Rain," 1977; "Reincarnation of Edward," 1977; "The Waiting Room," 1978; "Monologue from Mary," 1978; "Monterey Morning," 1978; "The Mission," 1978; "View from the Mound," 1979; "Cousin Francis Albert," 1979; "Frustration," 1979.

Analysis

Using tight and stark language, Ruth Schuler uses the technique of understatement. Her themes lean toward the dark side of life, exploding prejudice and death and portraying individual frustration and loneliness. Children are often used as protagonists with their experiences epitomizing the microcosm of this ever-larger universe; and the horror of the mundane is propounded when viewed through a more simplistic level. Characters are almost always victims whether it be deliberate or by chance. The physical landscapes of her stories are all encompassing of this nation, and they stretch from New England, through the South, and to the West Coast. Her stories reach across time from the early part of this century to the present.

Major publications other than short fiction

POETRY: *The Temporal Twilight*, 1974; *Daughter from the Other Side of the Drawbridge*, 1977; *Born of Buffalo Bone*, 1978; *Portraits of a Poet Passing Through*, 1978; *February's Child*, 1979; *An American Entering the Age of Aquarius*, 1980.

JOHN SCHULTZ

Born: Missouri, 1932

Principal short fiction
"Holy Unfeeling," 1967; *The Tongues of Men*, 1969.

Analysis
John Schultz's bold, ironic themes emerge from the interplay of the beginning catalytic image and strong sense of character and situation; character, theme, and action develop together. In fantastic and realistic stories, the catalytic image triggers, generates, predicts. In the satirical fantasy, "Custom," the salesman in search of a woman in a strange town while surrounded by unattainable women pacing on flowering balconies, foretells the ironic illusion of quest both personal and national; in "Morgan," Sfc Morgan's "accidental" killing of a Korean woman's baby with his jeep introduces themes of undeniable evil and the consequences of action. The most inventive of characters and situations are realized through the exhilarating, sometimes frightening, often furiously humorous and always compassionate art of the master storyteller. Never abandoning his reader, Schultz gives immaculate, imaginative attention to visual/palpable and psychological perceptions: Schultz tells the reader whatever he needs to know, straightforwardly from points of view of storyteller and persons within the scene. Imagery, stark or lush, is straight to the target, difficult to forget, yet exerts an expansive effect upon the reader. All pervading is the keen sense that the author is talking to us, has chosen us, for the unfolding of this very special (frequently mind-shattering) tale.

Major publications other than short fiction
NOVELS: *No One Was Killed*, 1969; *Motion Will Be Denied*, 1972.
NONFICTION: "The Story Workshop Method: Writing from Start to Finish," 1977; "Story Workshop: Writing from Start to Finish," 1978.

Betty Shiflett

HOWARD SCHWARTZ

Born: Missouri, 1945

Principal short fiction

A Blessing over Ashes, 1974; *Lilith's Cave*, 1975; *Midrashim: Collected Jewish Parables*, 1976; *The Captive Soul of the Messiah*, 1980.

Analysis

Howard Schwartz's stories are intended to work in the tradition of Jewish literature and folklore, as do the stories of I. L. Peretz, S. Y. Agnon, and Isaac Bashevis Singer. As Yann Lovelock has written: "Schwartz's parables are the result of studying and speculating upon old Jewish traditions and are a little reminiscent of the strange lore that Borges is notable for gathering together. Such familiar properties of dream and Jewish lore as rites, profound and mysterious books, magical speculation, flaming torches and secret caves return time and again. It is Schwartz's achievement to have made works of art from material common enough for us all to respond to but extremely difficult to make convincing." Building on traditional sources drawn from the Bible, the Talmud, the Midrash, the Kabbalah, and Hasidic lore, Schwartz's tales are in part original, in part re-creations of ancient legends, a conjunction of personal search and dreaming with mythical or timeless patterns or cycles. There is also a pronounced archetypal element in the tales, such as is found in the stories of Franz Kafka and Jorge Luis Borges, which makes it apparent that the influence of Jungian thought on Schwartz's stories has been considerable.

Major publications other than short fiction

POETRY: *Vessels*, 1975; *Gathering the Sparks: Poems 1965-1979*, 1979. NONFICTION: *Dream Journal*, 1974.

CAROLYNNE SCOTT

Born: Alabama, 1937

Principal short fiction
"The Map to Heaven," 1967; "The Eye of the Needle," 1969; "Far Bella Figura," 1970; "The Pearly Gates," 1970; "Goodbye, Hello Joe," 1975; "Far Bella Figura," 1980; *The Green and the Burning Alike*, 1981.

Analysis
Somewhat eccentric characters, such as the virginal Latin professor entrapped by militant Women's Libbers; the dwarf country boy in a tree spying on his mother's assignation; the elderly lady seeking release from a nursing home in hopes of resuming her homelife with two gay men, these are people of Carolynne Scott's fiction. All the stories are problematic and evolve out of some abiding belief on the part of the main characters. Dialogue is realistic, often humorous, and the exposition is revealed in the idiom of the main character (most often using a third person limited point of view). An attempt to underscore some moral frailty of society or the characters underlies but does not encumber the story's progression. A sense of place is often overwhelming, particularly in stories set in the mythical Templeton, a rural, small town in Alabama. Symbolism in the landscape often foreshadows the story's outcome.

Major publications other than short fiction
NONFICTION: *Country Roads: A Journey Through Rustic Alabama*, 1979.

ANNA SEGHERS
Netty Reiling

Born: Germany, 1900

Principal short fiction

Auf dem Weg zur amerikanischen Botschaft, 1930; *Die Kraft der Schwachen*, 1965; *Benito's Blue and Nine Other Stories*, 1973; *Sonderbare Begegnungen*, 1973.

Analysis

Anna Seghers' work can be divided into three major periods: her years in Germany up to 1933, the years she spent in exile from Nazi Germany in Mexico, and her life in the German Democratic Republic. Her work in the first period is characterized by her struggle with questions of form and aesthetics, especially the question of how to portray reality most effectively. In this period she experimented with such techniques as montage and stream of consciousness. In the second period she achieved a balance between form and content. In the third period her work was dominated by the principles of socialist realism. Seghers' protagonists are usually ordinary people who feel deeply and act intuitively rather than rationally. They are portrayed mostly in crisis situations. The world she depicts is one of illness, brutality, and fear in which people are lonely, hopeless, and persecuted. Common themes taken from her own experiences are exile, flight, suffering, and death. Another important theme is the struggle for social justice for the economically and politically oppressed, as seen from the Marxist perspective which she early espoused. In her stories Seghers records a history of Germany in this century: the fate of people in World War I, in the Weimar Republic, under Hitler, and finally in East Germany. Throughout this realistic chronicle of her age, Seghers stresses the importance of the individual, especially of the average person. This stress on the individual often sets her off from, and in opposition to, other Marxist writers of her time.

Major publications other than short fiction

NOVELS: *The Revolt of the Fishermen*, 1930; *The Seventh Cross*, 1942; *Transit*, 1944; *The Dead Stay Young*, 1950; *Die Entscheidung*, 1959 (*The Decision*); *Die Überfahrt*, 1971 (*The Crossing*).

Jennifer Michaels

HUBERT SELBY, JR.

Born: New York, 1928

Principal short fiction

"A Penny for Your Thoughts," 1963; *Last Exit to Brooklyn*, 1964.

Analysis

Rhythmical, energized prose in the American idiom, Hubert Selby's fiction is composed of a fabric of supernaturalistic utterance, making his work akin to contemporary morality plays. His characters often embody moral constructs, and in this sense he writes cautionary tales which are framed by biblical quotations. He once said that a literary work either changes one's life (meaning the reader and the author), or it is not art. The landscape of Selby's fiction has no middle ground; characters are polarized by experience and society, they are either in or out of control of their lives. One of the most remarkable qualities of his fiction is the fact that little physical description is used to reveal character, but instead the author evokes characters with intangible, highly emotional speech. The characters speak for themselves, and this talk in turn creates their ambiance and physicality. Selby also said recently that his first four works of fiction present pathologies without solutions and that subsequent writing will embody solutions, too. Selby's work often is referred to as being highly poetic, which is not to say ornamented or flowery, but rather informed by what William Carlos Williams called language charged with energy and emotion. In fact, Williams and Ezra Pound were early influences on Selby's writing, their poetic truths being transmitted to Selby from his life-long friend, poet and novelist Gilbert Sorrentino, to whom Selby's first book is dedicated. Selby's poetic sense of speech and honesty, however, goes back further to Dante and the Bible, two sources which constantly seem to inform his writing. Selby is a major influence on contemporary American fiction; he is now known internationally, and the academic community studies his works in that continuum which includes Herman Melville, Walt Whitman, and Edgar Allan Poe.

Major publications other than short fiction

NOVELS: *The Room*, 1971; *The Demon*, 1976; *Requiem for a Dream*, 1978.
PLAY: *Awake*, 1976.

Michael Stephens

VARLAM T. SHALAMOV

Born: U. S. S. R., 1907

Principal short fiction
Kolyma Tales, 1969, 1978, 1980.

Analysis
Suffused with the bitter cold of Kolyma, the vast Siberian prison complex in the U. S. S. R. where for seventeen years the author struggled to stay alive, Varlam Shalamov's "tales" both document and respond artistically to Stalin's systematic attempt to destroy the creative and intellectual talent of an entire generation. Shalamov's spare, intense prose works circulate in *samizdat* within the Soviet Union, while they appear in the West under a disclaimer of his responsibility, indicating his position with the Soviet government. Unlike Aleksandr Solzhenitsyn, who acknowledged Shalamov's depth of experience and literary gifts by offering him the coauthorship of *The Gulag Archipelago* (1973-1976), Shalamov professes to believe that the forced labor camps led not to spiritual ascent but to the ultimate corruption, the abandonment of that peculiarly Russian ennoblement of inner being achieved only through shared suffering: "The same frost that transformed a man's spit into ice in midair also penetrated the soul." That deathly isolation of the spirit pervades the *Kolyma Tales*, cruel as the Siberian winds that in one of Shalamov's fictional glimpses into hell drove his typically unnamed narrator to strip his dead comrade's body for its ragged underclothing: "Tragedy is not deep and sharp if it can be shared with friends." The naked fact of their creation, however, allows the *Kolyma Tales* to contradict Shalamov's public stance, claiming by their existence, like his *samizdat* poems, that even in Kolyma corruption cannot freeze the tiniest spark of humanity.

Major publications other than short fiction
POETRY: *Shorter Poems*, 1962.

Mitzi M. Brunsdale

EVELYN SHEFNER

Born: Illinois, 1924

Principal short fiction

"Monday Morning," 1955; "The Fourth-Floor Apartment," 1958; "The American Uncle," 1966; "In 7," 1967; "The Invitations," 1967; "Mary Johnson, I Know You," 1967; "Subway Roses," 1969; "Notes on a Water Crisis," 1969; "Sea-Changes: Their Variety," 1970; "Troubles of a Tattooed King," 1973; "The Answer Book," 1974; "An Easy Life," 1974; "Collage," 1974; "Dust," 1976; "What's New—Where's Everybody?," 1976; "Royal Bones: Part One," 1976; "A Hardened Case," 1979; "According to Need," 1979; "Corny and Becca," 1979.

Analysis

The stories of Evelyn Shefner fall roughly into the categories "realistic" and "lyrical-legendary." The pain, tension, and tenderness inherent in family living; reports from the man-woman battleground; the confrontation of German and Jew at a Maine summer resort are some subjects explored with fidelity to setting and realistic detail. Further removed from the "here-and-now," a series of fabulous tales include as their protagonists a tattooed showman-monarch, a seven-foot female overachiever, a lady stalled on a slow-moving train without a destination. This group is executed with greater attempt at formal control, patterning, and distancing. Straddling both categories, other stories open with ostensibly realistic incident, but arrive at grotesque or bizarre conclusions by way of heightened language. Within this "middle group," a tenant gratuitously surrenders her identity to a deranged landlady, a woman is harassed by the relentless hospitality of strangers, three sisters stick together by means fair or foul. In general, in Shefner's stories the effect is of dramatic immediacy, laced with a measure of ironic detachment. The language is more "worked" than otherwise, making use of imagery and precise description, employing dialogue that may be colloquial, intense, humorous, quirky, or lethal.

EVE SHELNUTT

Born: South Carolina, 1943

Principal short fiction
"Affectionately, Harold"; "The Past Is a Jealous Lover"; "An Appropriate Feeling"; "Timing"; "Sorrow"; "Driving with 'Raoul'"; "The Idea of Order"; "The Formal Voice"; "Indigo"; "Fable Without End"; "Allegro Ma Non Troppo"; "Prognosis"; "Ineffable"; *The Love Child*, 1979.

Analysis
Perspicacity of language and resourcefulness of form are the outstanding characteristics of Eve Shelnutt's writing. The stories seem to break down the distinction between prose and lyric poetry. The language is rooted in the union of sense, sensuality, and intelligence that is the source of metaphoric expression and poetic thought. The consciousness inhabiting the stories is marked by the absolute awareness and receptivity that is the imperative for modern fiction, but it is also marked by the withdrawn interiority of lyric impulse. Therefore, voice replaces conventional narration, rhythms of thought and feeling replace plot, inflection and implication replace authorial presence, the exact but discontinuous observations and reflections of a mind which is both self-absorbed and startlingly alert take the place of characterization and description. The stories are difficult and dense, subtle and nuanced, not because obscurity is an end but because these strategies are necessary to the tenuous balance of despairing knowledge and hopeful desire that is their motive. The reader who wishes to follow the development of thought and feeling in Shelnutt's work is well-advised to read all the stories with care and to consider them in relationship to one another.

Shirley Clay Scott

ALLEN SHEPHERD

Born: Massachusetts, 1936

Principal short fiction
"The Father of the Family," 1972; "One Evening for Pleasure," 1973; "All Alone," 1973; "The Bicycle," 1973; "The Flowers," 1973; "Judgment Days," 1974; "And the Head Dies," 1974; "Hill 218," 1974; "A True History," 1974; "A Little Game," 1974; "The Man Who Knew Henry Miller," 1974; "Fat," 1974; "The Man on the Stairs," 1974; "Somewhere in the Grass," 1975; "A Man She Was Doing Things With," 1975; "Cat," 1975; "Doing Things Right," 1976; "Mr. and Mrs. Bessette," 1976; "An Honest Man," 1977; "In the Tank," 1977; "Goodbye, Goodbye," 1977; "Giving Them a Sign," 1978; "Welcoming Back the Crumps," 1979; "In," 1979; "Nil Admirari," 1980.

Analysis
Most of Allen Shepherd's stories run to domestic or academic comedy, from grim to wry, in which typically the middle-aged male protagonist, imagining his back to the proverbial wall, attempts the liberating, defining act, only to find himself by story's anticlimactic end content with his old self and prospects. Character, not plot, is preeminent, style is semiformal and understated, and psychological penetration rather than philosophical depth is the writer's aim.

STEVEN SHER

Born: New York, 1949

Principal short fiction
"Spare Rib Park," 1977; "Woolen Pants," 1977; "The Fisherman," 1977; "Silverman's Tomb," 1979; "Beasts," 1980; "Sonny the Fruit Man," 1980.

Analysis
Drawing on his extensive skill as a poet, Steven Sher's use of language is particularly important in describing the beauty and bittersweet humor in much of what he sees. His personal glimpses of life are explored in a direct, detailed way as he questions personal power, the problems of aging, or racial and sexual confrontations. Sher's stories develop strong characters and play on the psychological interactions between them. He works short spans of the subject's life together, selecting scenes of building emotion to move the reader inside the story. His work stems from a deep love and understanding of the human ability to encompass both good and evil in the same person.

Major publications other than short fiction
POETRY: *No Longer Strangers*, 1973; *Nickelodeon*, 1978; *Persnickety*, 1980; *Caught in the Revolving Door*, 1980.

JUDITH JOHNSON SHERWIN

Born: New York, 1936

Principal short fiction
The Life of Riot, 1970.

Analysis
Deliberately, meticulously, relentlessly, the characters in Judith Johnson Sherwin's fictions pursue their own ends, observed with a deadpan intensity that suggests they may be figures in an allegory. As her people move step by step to a variety of extremes, Sherwin exhaustively details the mechanics of the processes, insists on their logic. She is not a storyteller interested in characters to whom things happen, but a creator and anatomist of images of human conditions, often grotesque ones. A poet, she says her stories derive from image/ideas. Strongly drawn pictures and contrasts, and play with techniques of approaching and distancing things, are perhaps evidence of early versions she writes as film scripts. The ear is not neglected for the eye: various formal and formulaic styles of language—Jonathan Swift's, a bureaucrat's—are mimed to insist in another way on the significance of imposed form.

Sherwin challenges the reader to imagine the forces that forge what can be seen and heard, to feel the passion of imagining implicit in their strength. Her isolated, bleak, wary, sometimes repellent characters are both willful, passionate creatures and creatures of passion and will: the elaborate machines for loving some of them devise, like the toneless voice in which their moves are described, make the connection between the mechanical and the emotional, the banal and the keenly felt. These stories, Sherwin says, are about wanting so much that one creates that which has not been given, in forms as elaborate as one's deprivation is extreme. The tension that accumulates as one reads is not, as in conventional narrative, a function of time and event, of plot, but instead of information accruing to push the reader to a brink or a breaking point of emotion. The clash of several kinds of data, of tone with content, of colloquial and lyrical styles, of seriousness and humor, creates exacerbating crosscurrents of tension.

The ingenious writer is moved, like her characters, to extremes. Bizarre sexual acts, observed as if they were office or kitchen routines, are strong, persuasive images of strong need and feeling. The connection between the deliberate, small, physical acts that make love and the fierce passion of loving preoccupies Sherwin: it is her supreme metaphor, evidence that the imagination and will create the shapes and the strength of desire. Sherwin's vision of a world of people driven by the implacable obligation to keep on passionately feeling is stern but not bleak: it is informed by a conviction, tenaciously held, of love's value, and a firm sense of what love is.

Major publications other than short fiction
POETRY: *Uranium Poems*, 1969; *Impossible Buildings*, 1973; *How the Dead Count*, 1978; *Waste: The Town Scold*, 1977; *Transparencies*, 1978; *Dead's Good Company*, 1979 (a three volume sequence).

Rachel Brownstein

BETTY SHIFLETT

Born: Texas, 1929

Principal short fiction

Phantom Rider; "After Christmas, Before Spring," 1968; "Sweet Lavender," 1968; "How to Melt, Blacken, and Break," 1968; "In a Foreign Land," 1976.

Analysis

In Betty Shiflett's stories, the storyteller's extraordinarily careful and vivid entrancement draws the reader into the situation and point of view of a character at a critical time in that character's life. With sensuous and sensual imagery, rich with perception of "common secrets," she presents scenes of the terrors, desperations, deceptions, loneliness, and pleasures of women, men, and children in kitchens, bathrooms, bedrooms, living rooms, yards and gardens and play areas, churches, and work areas. Bicycle trips, taken by the woman, go out from the house into an autonomous "foreign land" of reveries of death and desire, suggestions of lovers. Inventive forms, points of view, distinctness of voice, directness of address, and vivid verbs become instruments of exploration as well as realization of the entrancement. With the exception of one first-person story, and of first-person references in "Phantom Rider," Shiflett maintains flexibility by keeping overall third-person authority and access to the central character's point of view: this gives opportunity for dual points of view of wife and man in the family stories, for the distanced telling of the modern folktale, and the transformational tale, and for the play of the humorous fantasies. Throughout, the memories of a West Texas childhood reverberate hauntingly: early deaths of mother and father, and teenage orphaning. Because of the storyteller's full respect and deliberate seeking for the ambiguity of human relationships, her male and female characters come through with vivacity and strength. These techniques culminate in the novella-length play-story "Phantom Rider," in which a woman and a man, on silver bicycles, attended by an ominously playful stage mechanic, take a dream-and-memory journey by way of their own competitive games, in search of a house to buy, to an ending which combines sensual ecstasy with supernatural terror and the realization of the consequences of choices.

Major publications other than short fiction

NONFICTION: "Special Report," 1969; "Cairo U. S. A.," 1971; "Story Workshop as a Method of Teaching of Writing," 1973.

John Schultz

ANN ALLEN SHOCKLEY

Born: Kentucky, 1927

Principal short fiction
The Black and White of IT, 1980.

Analysis
Most of Ann Shockley's stories deal with the ways the lives of individual and coupled black heterosexuals and black and racially unidentified lesbians are short circuited by racism, sexism, and homophobia. There is a constant interface of intracouple tensions—those that exist between the partners in every relationship who choose each other yet need to define personal boundaries—and the tensions of shared victimization. Shared oppression and, in the case of lesbians, social invisibility make them more desperate for each other and less sure of each other, push them closer together than autonomous adults can stand to be, and give greater priority to their shared persecution and those attributes for which they are victimized than to those unique personal qualities that make or break relationships undertaken in greater freedom with social reinforcement. She documents the erosions of hope, the challenges to loyalty presented by threats to survival, the insecurities of those trapped in socially devalued categories, and the poisoning of love and intimacy by the invasions of bigotry. She writes of the personal and illuminates the political. As Barbara Smith characterizes her work, ". . . there are a handful of Black women who have risked everything for truth. Audre Lorde, Pat Parker, and Ann Allen Shockley have at least broken ground in the vast wilderness of works that do not exist." Shockley, in addition to short fiction and novels, writes scholarly essays and is a librarian at Fisk University.

Major publications other than short fiction
NOVEL: *Loving Her*, 1974.

Susan Koppelman

SHIRLEY SIKES

Born: Kansas, 1928

Principal short fiction

"Aaron's Brother," 1953; "Home Is the River," 1953; "The Harp," 1957; "The Rose-Petal Necklace," 1970; "Burial," 1970; "Pioneers," 1970; "The Saint," 1971; "The Birds of Sadness," 1971; "A Plains Spring," 1972; "The Death of Cousin Stanley," 1972; "Leroy and I," 1974; "*Apocalypse*," 1975; "Go Not Happy Day," 1976; "The Country of His Youth," 1977; "To the Manor Borne," 1978; "Annie and Mr. Spencer," 1979; "Saving Graces," 1979.

Analysis

At times easily accessible (but not shallow), at times abstruse, Shirley Sikes's stories reflect her belief that literature should be catholic, that it may vary from a voice of smoothness to a staccato sharpness. Beneath the surface of her stories, however, there is a narrowing of belief—a conviction: that human beings must face affliction with courage and hope—not because they do not recognize and receive the cruelty of the world, but precisely because they do. Harold Schneider, co-editor of the *Kansas Quarterly*, writes:

> Shirley Sikes's fiction is rooted in a time and place: the heart of America, mid-America but not Middle America, in the mid-twentieth century. She takes situations from ordinary family life—the kind we all know—and develops them with such richness of character and detail that what in another's hands would remain ordinary has been transformed into an experience as intensely observed as would be a visitor's sudden emergence in a foreign country. But it is not that, like say Flannery O'Connor, she invests the ordinary with elements of the bizarre; it is rather that she opens the inner life of her characters to the reader's eyes. Whether in her O. Henry Awards story, "The Death of Cousin Stanley," or the more recent "Saving Graces," she is always creating stories of quiet passion, and we know more about the experience of being fully human when we finish than we did before.

Major publications other than short fiction

NONFICTION: "The People and the Dam," 1952; "The Mariadahl Church," 1952; "To the Stars Through Difficulties," 1961.

LAYLE SILBERT

Born: Illinois

Principal short fiction

"Double Hook," 1971; "I Pledge," 1971-1972; "The Man from Harappa," 1972; "The Skywriter," 1973; "The Rout of Carpentier," 1975; "Exotic Flies," 1975-1976; "The Dancing Lesson," 1976; "The Corset," 1976; "Right on the Street," 1977; "The Bankers' Friend," 1977; "Potemkin Village," 1977; "A Hole in California," 1977; "Really Alice," 1978; "The Story of My Life," 1979; "The Bantu Mask," 1979; "Rich and Married," 1980; "Meeting Jews in Karachi," 1980; "The Tuning Fork," 1981.

Analysis

Layle Silbert's stories which proceed innocently in a realistic treatment often take a surrealistic turn, slip into dream or fantasy. An encounter by an American woman with a polygamous family in Pakistan turns into a speculative dream: what if her husband were to take another wife, too? Many of the stories concern children, small girls actually, and their concerns about their own lives, often the same as those of grown people. In a fugue from home, a school girl goes looking for material for a story she wants to write. In another story, this same character tries to arrange her own marriage. Traces of Silbert's travels in the Far East surface in such stories as "The Man from Harappa," which is based on an archeological metaphor, and "Exotic Flies," set in Calcutta. These influences meld in with those from Silbert's early life in Chicago in a Russian Jewish family with socialist leanings. These are not sunny stories; a strain of despair and disenchantment runs through them, tempered by humor, sometimes sardonic, sometimes with irony, as characters deal with death, marriage, widowhood, violence, and hypocrisy. The style of writing and the treatment of character and action make these stories accessible and readable.

ROBERTA SILMAN

Born: New York, 1934

Principal short fiction
"Years Later," 1976; "A View of the Mountain," 1977; *Blood Relations*, 1977; "Touchstone," 1980; "A Labyrinth of Love," 1980; "A Special Occasion," 1980.

Analysis
Roberta Silman's stories have for their themes the need for connections to nurture and sustain us while we survive, the difficulties and joys of family relationships, and the often bewildering distance between generations. While most of her characters appear quite ordinary, they often live rich inner lives; a few even take on obsessive qualities: an elderly widow whose son is sick drifts into shoplifting ("Lost"), a lonely social worker whose friends are people from the past finds herself in bed with a young hitchhiker ("Company"), a harassed young mother who wants to be a writer buys a painting and is then able to write about the silences which plague her ("Chairs for Angels to Sit In"). Memory is important to Silman: the memories of immigrant Jews as they learn the rituals of American life, the memories of parents who watch their children set out in the world, the memories of past loves, which may even be invented. The epigraph of *Blood Relations* is from Chekhov: ". . . we do not see or hear those who suffer and what is terrible in life goes on somewhere behind the scenes." Although she is not afraid to write about the horror of watching young children die ("Giving Blood" and "A Bad Baby"), Silman also knows about the wealth of humorous detail that clutters domestic lives.

The stories appear quite traditional, yet on close reading one sees that Silman uses rich, often unforgettable detail and, in the more recent stories, sharp images, a firm use of language, and what one reader-critic calls "spaces in which the reader can come to his own conclusions." These understated stories were compared in reviews to her master, Chekhov, to Willa Cather, and to some of the Southern writers (notably Eudora Welty) although Silman's people are mostly middle-class Jews who live near New York City. *Blood Relations* was runner-up for the P. E. N. Hemingway Prize and the Janet Kafka Prize.

Major publications other than short fiction
NOVEL: *Boundaries*, 1979.

BENNIE LEE SINCLAIR

Born: South Carolina, 1939

Principal short fiction
"Sisters," 1969; "The Heart of the Prodigal," 1971; "The Warwoman's Legacy," 1976; "Starlie," 1976; "Norma," 1978; "The Lesson," 1980.

Analysis
    Grounded in life, as in maturity of style, Bennie Sinclair's stories generate from her keenness of observaton and her unique perception. Often considered a "Southern" writer because of her understanding of the psychology, life-styles, and people of her native region, her subjects greatly range in scope, encompassing the universal. Her style is unmistakable, with a precision of language that may well engender from her writing of poetry. The character is the most important part of her short stories, with conflicts eliciting a powerful emotional response from the reader. A student of nature, her settings are carefully drawn and replete with nature imagery. While keeping her settings realistic and concrete, Sinclair begins with her characters where more conventional writers might finish, probing beneath the surface of what appears to be, seeking a greater reality. Her stories grow, she says, as she writes, reaching for their own resolution, often taking wing to speak for themselves. George Garrett noted the amazing "variety and range" of her work. Mark Strand acclaimed her as a writer whose work ". . . has a disarming directness about it. Passionate in its concerns, it engages the world with an odd mixture of innocence and authority."

Major publications other than short fiction
POETRY: *Little Chicago Suite*, 1978; *The Arrowhead Scholar*, 1978.

Lori Storie

HARRIET SIROF

Born: New York

Principal short fiction
"Fifty," 1971; "The Adventure," 1973; "In the Basement," 1973; "The Landmarks of My Youth," 1975; "The Price of Corrugated," 1975; "The Dinner Party," 1977; "Felicity," 1978; "Battlefield," 1979; "Fountain of Youth," 1979.

Analysis
Harriet Sirof's short stories catch the special moments that illuminate and reveal character. Whether the characters in her stories are a group of cousins playing a guessing game after a family funeral, a failed artist running his way out of an alcoholic episode, or an elderly man hiding in a factory basement, they are presented during moments when they must either face themselves or choose to look away. The stories are written in clear polished prose. They are tightly structured in the traditional mode, with a beginning, a middle, and an end. The story themes may also be regarded as traditional. The themes are concerned with people's efforts to make some sense out of their lives, to define their relationships with others, and to come to terms with the world in which they find themselves. This world is usually urban or suburban middle-class America. Sirof cares deeply about the "ordinary" people who live and struggle in this world, and she passes her caring on to her readers.

Major publications other than short fiction
NOVELS: *A New-Fashioned Love Story*, 1977; *The IF Machine*, 1978; *Save the Dam!*, 1980.
NONFICTION: *The Junior Encyclopedia of Israel*, 1980.

DON SKILES

Born: Pennsylvania, 1939

Principal short fiction

"No Electric Lights in Rome," 1977; "The Man Who Had Never Been in Tacoma," 1979; "All over America," 1979; "The Man Who Taught Nude Bicycling," 1980.

Analysis

Difficult to characterize, perhaps the leading mark of Don Skiles's stories is a humor that turns on the constantly changing uses of language in urban environments, the impact of the city on individuals, and the truly remarkable adventures of people living in modern cities. These "adventures" are often inner, and much of his stories' power derives from the conflict between the inner and outer scales of a character's life.

Some of Skiles's work is nonsequential narrative, but he has also written longer works in more traditional forms. Along with the unusual descriptive details of his stories, the characters themselves provide the chief interest; they are not mainstream characters, engaged in what are sometimes termed meaningful professions, but neither are they stereotyped fringe radicals, or outsiders. Many of them are practicing artists, and the theme of how the artist, and the artist-to-be, copes with contemporary American life is important in this work. Although Skiles is not a regionalist writer, a number of his stories are set in San Francisco and the San Francisco Bay area; they convey an excellent sense of the culturally diverse atmospheres of this area. Not a surrealist or symbolist, his key influences as a fiction writer have been Mark Twain, Henry Fielding, Laurence Sterne, F. Scott Fitzgerald, James Joyce, Tomasso Landolfi, and Italo Calvino.

CORDWAINER SMITH

Born: Wisconsin, 1913   **Died:** 1966

Principal short fiction

You Will Never Be the Same, 1963; *Space Lords*, 1965; *Quest of the Three Worlds*, 1966; *Under Old Earth*, 1970; *Stardreamer*, 1971; *The Best of Cordwainer Smith*, 1975.

Analysis

Cordwainer Smith was the pseudonym of Dr. Paul Myron Anthony Linebarger, Professor of Asiatic Studies at The Johns Hopkins University, military adviser and intelligence officer, expert in psychological warfare, world traveler, and godson to Sun Yat Sen—all of this unusual background finds its way into the stories, transformed by one of the most colorful, extravagant imaginations in or out of science fiction. In Smith's vision, which extends approximately fifteen thousand years into the future, the "Instrumentality," a vaguely defined group of priest-politician aristocrats, attempt to guide the destiny of mankind as they eliminate all pain, disease, and old age (everybody except the especially favored lives four hundred years), as well as supervising man's conquest of space in three great waves of exploration. Beginning with his first published tale, "Scanners Live in Vain," Smith peopled his stories with bizarre creatures (Scanners are humans with all nerves severed to protect them from the pain of space travel), incredible devices (space ships that use oysters in the walls to protect the passengers; other ships that are moved by giant sails like old-fashioned sailboats), grotesquely real landscapes, and truly exotic relationships (such as the "love affair" between a human male and a cat female in "The Game of Rat and Dragon"). These extravagant, romantic "tall tales" succeed brilliantly because Smith's elaborate, deliberately "archaic" way of telling the stories, influenced by his knowledge of ancient Chinese literature, gives the feeling of an oral history, even a legend. The future world Smith presents is, ironically, so extravagant and exotic, so unlike any logical extrapolation from our present society, that it seems possible, even familiar.

Major publications other than short fiction

NOVELS: *The Planet Buyer*, 1964; *The Underpeople*, 1968; *Nostrilia*, 1975.
NONFICTION: *The Ocean War*, 1937; *Psychological Warfare*, 1948.

Keith Neilson

R. E. SMITH

Born: Massachusetts, 1943

Principal short fiction

"Sparrow Fly Free," 1968; "And Be My Love," 1969; "Progenitor," 1970; "God Rest Ye Merry," 1970; "King of Beasts," 1972; "Rack," 1973; "The Angel on the Stairs," 1974; "Showdown," 1975; "The Gift Horse's Mouth," 1981.

Analysis

Robert E. Smith, Jr. is basically a traditional writer in that his stories depict clearly delineated characters and have beginnings, middles, and endings. Within his traditional approach, however, the characters and situations of his stories vary widely. Some stories feature realistic characters while others depict reclusive midget pool players or enigmatic angelic visitors. His use of time is often straightforward, but he also juxtaposes characters from different eras and shifts the narrative back and forth in time to achieve a desired effect. His style is more akin to that of Ernest Hemingway and John Steinbeck than it is to William Faulkner and Thomas Wolfe. In general, his characters reaffirm the human capability to create order out of life's chaos. Smith's family has been in Texas since before the Civil War, and his recent work has been concentrating increasingly on that area.

JOHN THOM SPACH

Born: North Carolina, 1928

Principal short fiction
"Jerusalem Fire Dept," 1972; "Riding the Moonbeam," 1977.

Analysis
Someone once said that all fiction is a search for the truth. In John Spach's case his search is for fun. He believes in writing to entertain—and to an exaggerated degree. If you let him, he will lead you up a path of laughter that continues to go higher with the unexpected but highly logical peak. Once he selects a premise, he carries it to a farce and from there to a riot. Such an ordinary American scene as a small town obtaining its first fire truck becomes under his pen a conflagration of the entire village in order to satisfy the zeal of the volunteer fire fighters. This North Carolinian who is native to O. Henry's home ground writes in a style and tradition similar to that master of short fiction. The spirit of Mark Twain is also present in his work. Spach covers a wide range of topics, all interjected with humor. His work is zany but within the range of possibility. Justice always triumphs. The pompous and haughty are the favorite targets of his jokes, but the jokes have no malicious intent. Spach's work is structured with purpose. The reader is uplifted, for the characters are believable and chosen from life. The vernacular is used with a captivating and entertaining result. His choice of vocabulary is comprehensible, not pedantic or stilted. He thinks people are funny; and the more seriously they take themselves, the more humorous they become. Spach is always looking for the good in people, not the bad. The plots in his works are structured in such a way that they build to a most improbable but possible height. Readers caught in the spirit of his work will often laugh out loud at the unexpected humor.

Major publications other than short fiction
NOVEL: *Time Out from Texas*, 1969.
PLAY: *The Road to Carolina*, 1975.

Frances A. Garvey

MURIEL SPANIER

Born: New York, 1925

Principal short fiction

"The Big Dream," 1961; "The Sweet Sound of Strings," 1962; "That Last Summer," 1965; "A New Kind of Love," 1965; "The Reception," 1971; "Virgil Man," 1977; "On the Water Tower," 1977.

Analysis

The characters in Muriel Spanier's stories are often locked in a private struggle with a harsh and arbitrary fate. Bewildered, temporarily immobilized, they move through landscapes, both exterior and interior, made all the more alien by the everyday mundanities with which they are forced to contend. Fantasy is used to good effect—a dream-balm of wish and image that supports and reinforces her characters in their challenge to an absurd and monstrous world. In "The Reception," a child is witness to the violent, senseless street death of his mother. At first he resorts to silence as an anesthetic. Not to speak is not to think is not to know or feel. He is speechless for months. Gradually moving from silence to contemplation of violence as depicted in television shoot-outs and blood-lettings, he acknowledges his own helpless rage. He reads of Che Guevara's death and loses himself in an imaginative rendering of the minutiae of that death. In the image of Guevara, the hero who is both yielding and defiant before a firing squad, the child sadly senses his own salvation. In "Virgil Man," Spanier deals with the conflicts of young people trying to come to peace with their families and society on one hand and their own heated yearnings on the other, sometimes with disastrous effect. In "Virgil Man," the young man, suffering a rejection not only of himself but also of the societal matrix from which he comes, strangles his beloved cat. Despite the often aberrational circumstances of Spanier's stories, there is usually an element of hope and affirmation on the part of her characters, a striving toward the conventional norm. Hopelessly isolated by overwhelming insecurity, they long to fit in. Although Spanier's stories are usually linear in structure, they are endowed with textural density, a brocade of introspection and imagery that in some instances, as in "The Sweet Sound of Strings," adds a phantasmagorical quality to her work.

RONALD SPATZ

Born: New York, 1949

Principal short fiction

"XCQWP BNKJVS FGHZTD," 1970; "The Cartographer's Whip," 1973; "Kabob," 1974; "The Startled German," 1975; "The Curator," 1975; "The Prostate Gland," 1976; "An Easy Dance," 1976; "The Cabbage Palm," 1977; "The Patrons," 1977; "Tricks of Finding Water," 1978; "The Office Visit," 1980; "A Long Farewell to Glittering Trifles," 1980.

Analysis

Condensed to the bare essentials, Ronald Spatz's stories are lyrical explorations of fragile, contemporary situations and characters. Objective reality is superceded by the vivid imagery of sensual and emotional discovery. Throughout Spatz's fiction, the reader is guided toward understanding by a trail of carefully controlled implications, precise language, and crystallized, interconnected imagery. Hence, the traditional narrative line is replaced by a "vertical structure," to illustrate better the multifaceted, psychological reality of the human experience. Therefore, the reader should focus on the descriptive development of situation without expecting a "resolution" of that situation. In general, Spatz portrays characters that reflect moods of isolation, rather than alienation, by synthesizing the darkly humorous with the poignant; all within the larger context of the contemporary rhythms of a crowded, computerized, but also, an often very lonely society.

CAROL SPELIUS

Born: North Dakota, 1919

Principal short fiction
"The Frigid Heart," 1968; "Apollonian Disorder," 1977; "Frannie's Failing," 1978; "The Wild One," 1978.

Analysis
Carol Spelius' home turf is the West, and she really knows the territory. To know it and to be able to write the territory into living, breathing prose that engages the reader are two different things, yet she succeeds admirably. Her language is spare and clear and, in action scenes, can fairly explode off the page. We are visually aware of what is happening at all times and can be left with such strong scenic memories of her stories that we want to read them again just to reexperience the moment when we were first imprinted with a lasting image we could not shake.

Because her language is lean and her characters seem true, we think as we read . . . "Ah, yes, we know these people. We know what's going to happen." We do not. She engages her fictional characters in conflict and then brings them out of it in ways we do not expect. When the last moment comes, we are not surprised as O. Henry might have surprised us, but rather reassured that these could have been—perhaps were—living people who lived through an expanded moment in their own way, providing their own solution. The stories seem organic, as if they sprang to life complete. Once the problem to be solved has been presented, there is no sense of an intrusive author. We move along, carried by our own interest in the outcome. The characters speak to one another, and we are fortunate to be able to listen. We care about the outcome, and even in those stories where the ending is tragic, there is a feeling of rightness as well as satisfaction for the reader.

Major publications other than short fiction
POETRY: "To Be or Not to . . . ," 1975; "Trees," 1976; "Cowbird," 1976; "Swimmers Chant," 1976; "Eye of Hurricane," 1977; "Life Guard," 1978; "Back Packer," 1978.

Edith Freund

ELIZABETH SPENCER

Born: Mississippi, 1921

Principal short fiction
Ship Island and Other Stories, 1968; *The Stories of Elizabeth Spencer*, 1981.

Analysis
Elizabeth Spencer's stories have developed along two distinct lines, one, a short, vivid scene or account, meant to seize upon an incident, event, or encounter which serves as an examined foreground for the unexamined—that is, for the larger history or substance or dramatic dilemma of the characters' lives, or for the social background, the panorama, in which they exist. Spencer's desire is to reveal the large by way of the small, as one flash of lightning can for a moment show a large landscape, otherwise dim or unknown. These stories may have little plot development, being too short, though as incident, they may portray character and admit of conflict and tension, while not attempting resolution. Her other form of story is the long, leisurely tale which comes to her naturally out of her heritage as a native Southerner. They unfold in a rather casual way, involve social conflict, character developed with some degree of elaboration and change, and are securely set in a particular time and place. Some of the stories Spencer has done fall between these two modes, but if her achievement in the short story is to be evaluated, such evaluation would have to be made by considering the two forms she has most successfully developed.

Major publications other than short fiction
NOVELS: *Fire in the Morning*, 1948; *This Crooked Way*, 1952; *The Voice at the Back Door*, 1956; *The Light in the Piazza*, 1960; *Knights & Dragons*, 1965; *No Place for an Angel*, 1967; *The Snare*, 1972.

PETER SPIELBERG

Born: Austria, 1929

Principal short fiction
Bedrock: A Work of Fiction Composed of Fifteen Scenes from My Life, 1973; *The Hermetic Whore*, 1977.

Analysis
The stories in Peter Spielberg's two collections are noted for the precision and brevity of their character portrayal. The situations which order their plot lines are generally mundane, but lifted by his technique into the realm of universality. According to Bruce Allen, Spielberg's stories in *Bedrock* "extend real situations into conditions of neurotic existential stalemate." His two-dimensional characters, states Barbara McDaniel, "convey the futility and emptiness of existence." Less pessimistic in treatment than the stories in *Bedrock*, Spielberg's stories in *The Hermetic Whore*, published four years later, "tend to be more broadly comic and topical," according to Larry McCaffery's review. Because of Spielberg's portrayal of the grotesque, however, elements of shock and crudity abound.

Major publications other than short fiction
NOVEL: *Twiddledum Twaddledum*, 1974.

LAWRENCE P. SPINGARN

Born: New Jersey, 1917

Principal short fiction
"Feeding Doves, Slender Vines," 1952; "Family Album," 1957; "The Ambassador," 1968; "The Vacuum," 1971; "The Duchess," 1971; *The Blue Door & Other Stories*, 1977; "The Black Cap," 1978; "The Lady with the Shears," 1980; *Moral Tales*, 1980.

Analysis
The fiction in Lawrence Spingarn's *The Blue Door and Other Stories*, starting from conventional themes of alienation, death, love, and old age, has a pervasive and unsettling aura of decay, as if the author were seeing the future unfold now. A girl abandoned by her feckless young husband, an elderly man humiliated by his alcoholic young mistress, a retired San Francisco stevedore confronting memory and desire in the person of a whore who shares his flat— these are wounded people armed only with a hope to endure but not always with the inner resources to live in dignity. Spingarn is a master at isolating characters who stand out against familiar or exotic backgrounds. They willingly pay the price for small mercies; their stories end on a note of compassion and understanding.

Moral Tales derives from the medieval *exampla* of Western Europe whose roots are found in Talmudic and Midrashic literature. Among the practitioners were Petrus Alfonsi and Cervantes, de Sade and Jarry, Firbank and Horace Walpole, and Ambrose Beirce in his *Tales of the Parenticide Club*. More than absurd, they are also fantastic and surreal. As the preface tells us, they "have a moral quality in that they reflect or imitate, in a Platonic sense, the chaos or senselessness of the real world in which we live, where substance and true significance become apparent, if at all, only by accident. . . . The moral . . . is indeed concealed within the triviality or the absurdity of the accidents" that each describes or narrates.

Major publications other than short fiction
POETRY: *Rococo Summer & Other Poems*, 1947; *The Lost River: Poems*, 1951; *Letters from Exile: Poems*, 1961; *Madame Bidet & Other Fixtures*, 1968; *Freeway Problems & Others*, 1970; *The Dark Playground: Poems*, 1979.

LES STANDIFORD

Born: Ohio, 1945

Principal short fiction

"Closing the Sarasota Road," 1973; "Guerin Returns," 1974; "Guerin's Ninth Life," 1975; "The Fan in the Beaver Coat," 1976; "Making Sheriff," 1977; "The Grandfather of Satchel Paige," 1977; "Guerin and the Sail Cat Blues," 1978; "Guerin's Voyage to Mars," 1979; "Guerin and the Sneeze of Death," 1980; "Guerin and the Presidential Revue," 1980; "Guerin Returns," 1980.

Analysis

Les Standiford writes stories which attempt to be familiar enough in their use of plot, characterization, and setting to engage the reader's initial attention. Beyond that, however, he tries to twist the reader's expectation to bend "normalcy" by some point in the story in order to elicit surprise, and, ideally, some awareness in the reader that small impossibilities might exist in his own "real" life. Standiford usually writes of characters who would ordinarily be considered unimportant, even unengaging—perhaps this enhances the sense of surprise. He employs quiet humor in his writing, preferring to have a subtle joke go absolutely unrecognized than to have a grand joke fall flat. He attempts to allow his characters some small act of will, feeling that tiny acts are heroism enough in such a world as we have. Walter Isle, writing in the *Houston Chronicle*, said that "The Fan in the Beaver Coat" combined "realism and fantasy in a marvelous portrait of seventy-year-old Guerin, who starts jogging and winds up a track star. Standiford moves from the everyday details of running to Guerin's final vision of new life and new meaning in a very effective story that is all fantasy and all true." Norman Lavers, in *The American Book Review*, called "Making Sheriff" a "fine quite understated human profile."

LORRAINE STANDISH

Born: Massachusetts, 1937

Principal short fiction

Alabama Prize Stories-1970, 1970; "In-Laws Or Out-Laws," 1974; "Horse-back Riding Is Fun If You're a Horse," 1978; "Kidnapped," 1978; "Someday," 1978; "The Halloween Husband Thief," 1978; "Metamorphology," 1978; "Marlane," 1980.

Analysis

Because Lorraine Standish is primarily a poet, her fiction has a lyrical quality which weaves and blends throughout her stories. Her humorous stories are light, tight, and well-structured. Her serious works of fiction succeed at involving the reader in a real emotional sense, into the inner workings of the human psyche. She is a creative writing teacher, and her advice to her students is always, "Show it—don't tell it. 'Hook' your reader in the very first sentence of your story. Keep it moving. Make the ending of your story just as interesting as the beginning, so that your reader will feel that your story was worth his time and trouble in reading it; and he will look for your name again the next time he wants to read a good short story."

Major publications other than short fiction

POETRY: "Melancholia," 1974; "Poltergeist," 1976; "Interloper," 1977; "Fragmented," 1978; "Lonely Road," 1978; "Epitaph," 1978; "Blackberry Winter," 1979; "The Creation," 1979; "My Garden," 1979; "The Amber Maze," 1979; "The Red Man," 1980.

NONFICTION: "A Matter for Common Scents," 1971; "Making Christmas Balls," 1977; "The Secret of Success," 1978; "Getting It Published," 1978; "Writing Poetry for Children," 1979.

DOROTHY STANFILL

Born: Tennessee, 1911

Principal short fiction

"Goodbye, Ocie May," 1967; "Destinies," 1974; "The Encounter," 1974; "The Albino," 1975; "Shades," 1977; *Katharine and the Quarter-Mile Drag and Other Stories*, 1978; "The Adversary," 1980.

Analysis

Dorothy Stanfill surveys the social scene through the medium of selected contrasts. The effect thus made to synthesize, by individual effort and choice on the character's part, such opposites as joy and grief, old and new tradition, love and hate, loyalty and temptation, mirrors a paradigm of the human condition. People are bound by time and place but always struggle never to give in to their limitations. Nowhere is this quality better illustrated than in the two stories, "From Darlene, With Love" and "Katherine and the Quarter-Mile Drag," in her short collection by the latter title. Katharine is a docile wife-all-but-widowed until she yields to the fascination of speed and the dynamic search for the unattainable in the drag race. Claire, in "From Darlene, With Love," a volunteer in a Head Start program with a history of breakdowns, attains a new adjustment through her relationship with an autistic child. In like manner, others in the collection affirm in various ways the meaning inherent in every human life. Her stories are set in the South, but she is not a regional writer; her style is eclectic, using a variety of techniques, reminiscent in turn, a critic says, of William Faulkner, D. H. Lawrence, and Edith Wharton. These stories, she states, "grow in meaning until they touch the lives of all men."

Major publications other than short fiction

PLAYS: *The Brunch*, 1968; *Faith*, 1976.

MARK STEADMAN

Born: Georgia, 1930

Principal short fiction
McAfee County, 1971; "Cast on the Waters and Raised on High," 1978; "Professions of Love," 1980.

Analysis
Mark Steadman's most satisfying stories deal with poor, uneducated, and inarticulate people. These characters are interesting because their lack of sophistication makes them more original than characters in the mainstream would be. Their inability to articulate their feelings compels them to action, and active characters suit the kind of stories Steadman wants to tell. Steadman cannot keep comedy out of his writing, although the author himself considers his stories as essentially serious. Rather than undercutting the seriousness, his humor serves to relieve and amplify the sadness of his fiction. Steadman writes simply and clearly, feeling that strong action and characters require no verbal hype. If there is an underlying theme in Steadman's fiction, it is the possibility of kind, humane, and interesting action in a life which is, at best, fundamentally and sadly neutral.

Major publications other than short fiction
NOVEL: *A Lion's Share*, 1976.

MAX STEELE

Born: South Carolina, 1922

Principal short fiction
"Grandfather and Chow Dog," 1944; "All the Wet Animals," 1945; "Ah Love! Ah Me!" 1945; "I Become a Mohammedan," 1945; "Chief Rainbow and the Kid in Paris," 1952; "Forget the Geraniums," 1953; "The Silent Scream," 1960; "Rock Like a Fool," 1967; "The Most Unbelievable Character I'll Ever Forget," 1968; "Color the Daydream Yellow," 1968; "The Ragged Halo," 1968; *Where She Brushed Her Hair*, 1968; "The Long Vacation," 1969; "My Mother's Night Out," 1976; "The Girl from Carthage," 1976; "About Love and Grasshoppers," 1977.

Analysis
Max Steele's prose is precise, graceful, richly suggestive, but his technical mastery is never cold, because he cares most for the people in his stories. He tends to be traditional in his storytelling methods, never experimenting for the sake of novelty. Many stories draw on his biography: growing up in the Piedmont South, and studying and writing in Paris, San Francisco, and North Carolina. His characters are sometimes eccentric, and a good many are children. Steele observes life from an angle that is fresh, even slightly askew. Always understated, the stories, comic or sad, deal with problems of innocence, and more often than not they deal with tentative forms of love. Longing—man for woman, child for parent—is often the issue, as is that love which leads to jealousy, hate, and even self-hate. Yet Steele is never disheartening. His characters are capable of love, humor, compassion, and courage, and perhaps most importantly they have imagination. As the working title of one story, "Fiction, Fact, and Dream," indicates, Steele is especially interested in the interplay of memory, experience, and daydream or fantasy. The interior life of his characters is always dynamic, and it has a real effect on the world outside. Dreams, as a result, often play a key role in the structure and plot of the stories. For the person who learns to use them, and especially for the artist, memory and dream are ways to confront the world's horrors—loneliness, fear, death. Through memory and dream, Steele has said, "even the soul pinched by despair may yet find fulfillment in this strange and sometimes delayed life."

Major publications other than short fiction
NOVEL: *Debby*, 1950 (retitled *The Goblins Must Go Barefoot*, 1966).
NONFICTION: "James Thurber," 1955 (with George Plimpton); "The Most Exciting Magazine," 1963; "Student Voices in Literature," 1968; "The Cool

Voice," 1968; "Teen-age Fiction," 1968.

Grady W. Ballenger

MICHAEL STEPHENS

Born: Washington, D. C., 1946

Principal short fiction
"Prospecting," 1971; "The Last Poetry Reading," 1973; *Paragraphs*, 1974; "Still Life," 1978; "Shipping Out," 1979.

Analysis
Michael Stephens is a writer of short prose—not necessarily short stories, but prose with a high focus on speech or "the spoken," and with the emotional burst associated with poetry. He believes the large novel to be a nineteenth century artifact which reactionary conglomerates refuse to let expire with dignity. His only commercial publication was a first novel, *Season at Coole* (1972); thereafter, all his books were done at noncommercial presses. *The New York Times Book Review* called his first novel "a poem that soars." Other works have not been reviewed commercially or by small press publications, although critic Jerome Klinkowitz devoted one chapter to Stephens' works in his book *The Life of Fiction*. His last story was published by *Tri-Quarterly* in 1973. His fiction is usually too long for magazine publication and too short for commercial houses, so small presses have taken up the slack. Influences have been Hubert Selby, Jr., Samuel Beckett, James Joyce, William Butler Yeats, Bertolt Brecht, and a host of twentieth century American poets too numerous to mention. Stephens is often erroneously associated with Irish Catholic writing. He is also a playwright, and he has translated Korean poetry.

Major publications other than short fiction
NOVEL: *Season at Coole*, 1972.
POETRY: *Alcohol Poems*, 1973; *Tangun Legend*, 1977.

ROSEMARY STEPHENS

Born: Georgia, 1934

Principal short fiction
"Cousin Meggy," 1968; "Pink Roses," 1971; "Horses," 1971; "The Animal,"
1972; "Christmas Come, Christmas Gone," 1972; "The Love Seat," 1973;
"Underfoot," 1973; "Elopement," 1974; "Politician in the Family," 1974;
"Elizabeth Jackson's Gingham Bible," 1976; "The Neighborhood," 1976;
"Remember Rowena," 1979.

Analysis
In Rosemary Stephens' short stories, people come to life and grapple with
problems (achieving maturity, gaining compassion, understanding one another, growing old) in a world familiar to the reader. Stephens' artistry encompasses subtle imagery, understatement, irony, and humor. Whether her
short stories deal with reality or fantasy, they usually result in strong reader
identification and remain in the reader's mind long after the magazine has
been put aside. Stephens has received a number of national awards for excellence in the writing of short stories.

Major publications other than short fiction
NOVELS: *Silver Dollar Mystery*, 1971; *Mystery of the Spider's Web*, 1975.
POETRY: *Eve's Navel*, 1976.
NONFICTION: *Nymph Imagery of Keats and Shelley*, 1971.

ELISABETH STEVENS

Born: New York, 1929

Principal short fiction

"Little Joey," 1951; "The Bride," 1957; "The Nurse," 1974; "Hospital Game," 1976; "Dirt Pile," 1978; "An Old Lover," 1980.

Analysis

Sensuous imagery and symbolic but believable situations predominate in Elisabeth Stevens' short fiction. The approach is that of the novel of manners, but the overtones are those of poetic fantasy. Precise, evocative visual descriptions harmonize with themes of realization and self-discovery. Stevens, who illustrates some stories with block prints and is also a poet, aims most of all for unity and wholeness. Vivid contemporary situations viewed through the eyes of varying characters are presented in imaginative but carefully thought out sequence like a series of sonnets.

WENDY J. E. STEVENS

Principal short fiction
"of similar thread," 1976; "in search of a lost woman," 1977; "this is the end," 1977; "taking back the night," 1978; "Only Fiction," 1979.

Analysis
Wendy Stevens' stories are woven from the many parts of people's lives that they carry with them at any moment. Her stories have their basis in collage—they are remnants of history, dreams, environment which emerge to create characters who still relish the idea of creating an order to the disarray of events. All of the stories are told from the first person perspective, because "women have had their stories told by others for too long." The author deals with time not as a chronological entity, but as a sequence of developing random vision reflecting off of the steady beating of the day-to-day world. More than anything, Stevens' stories have to do with process and the intricacies of each moment of being.

JAMES STILL

Born: Alabama, 1906

Principal short fiction
On Troublesome Creek, 1941; *Pattern of a Man*, 1976; *The Run for the Elbertas*, 1980.

Analysis
In 1979 James Still won the Majorie Peabody Award of The American Academy & Institute of Arts and Letters for his "continuing achievement and integrity in his art." This citation is the logical summation of a writing career which spans more than forty years, embodying poetry, the novel, juvenile works, and the short story. Since the 1930's he has lived and worked in Eastern Kentucky. From his life there he has depicted a fascinating folk in an especially poetic area of the South. Local idioms and vanishing folkways dot his creative landscape, but never do they intrude on the purity of his style. That style supports elements both universal and intensely regional. The voice which relates these tales remains distinctly his own. Walker Percy once noted that the works of Still are "extraordinarily moving, skillful and haunting." Martha Foley has reported, "A delight to read are James Still's warm-hearted stories of his Kentucky neighbors whom he depicts in an English language as unspoiled as when Chaucer and the Elizabethans first made it into glorious literature." In several ways Still's short stories are prose poems which evoke response from the reader by subtle delineation and deceptive simplicity. Subjects dealt with include topics as diverse as the imagination of childhood ("Mrs. Razor"), Freudian psychology ("The Nest"), the starkness of murder ("The Scrape"). This Appalachian-based artist has helped make his often-misunderstood area a little clearer for us all.

Major publications other than short fiction
NOVELS: *River of Earth*, 1940; *Sporty Creek*, 1977.
POETRY: *Hounds on the Mountain*, 1937.

William Terrell Cornett

ANTHONY E. STOCKANES

Born: Illinois, 1935

Principal short fiction
"Vandals," 1976; "At Rest and in Love with Fire," 1977; "Jerusalem House," 1978; "Gunderson's Oak," 1978; "The Milk-Glass Chicken," 1978; "The Murderer," 1978; "Mr. Eustice," 1979; "The Petition," 1979; "75," 1979; "A Simple Woman," 1979; "A Simple Dying," 1980; "At the Border," 1980.

Analysis
Anthony E. Stockanes is equally adept at writing in the comic and dramatic modes. His work has remarkable variety; yet it is always consistent in its control, its wealth of evocative detail, and its insight. The texture of language is always important (and impressively handled) in his fiction, but he is not a writer who substitues language or aesthetic theory for experience. No matter how wryly or bleakly his fictional world is presented, it is still recognizably our own world. The reader is conscious throughout of an author's perception and vision, but it never intrudes on our own very private absorption in what is read. His greatest skill lies in taking characters whose consciousness is perhaps intensely personal ("Vandals"), or perhaps chilling ("The Ivory Penguin's Wife"), and making their voices entirely believable, entirely universal. His stories are included in most of the outlets for serious short fiction today.

Jean L. Thompson

NANCY STOCKWELL

Born: Kansas, 1940

Principal short fiction
Out Somewhere and Back Again (The Kansas Stories), 1978; "Beaver Dams," 1980.

Analysis
"Several of these stories depend on violent resolutions. A white racist is crushed under a bus carrying blacks to a freedom rally. A typhoon (tornado) threatens retribution in another. The natural world tends to be noisy with omens and wonders. It is the kind of melodrama one also finds in Eudora Welty, Carson McCullers, Flannery O'Connor, though Nancy Stockwell also draws on the much more ordinary, seasonal, familial. She is writing in that rich tradition which has proved so daunting because in ways it is so beautiful a prison of family, of landscape, of social and religious custom, typical of both the South and the Midwest. Gifted women have had to forge a language of confrontation and transformation rather than escape. Nancy Stockwell is working toward a language not only for remaking Kansas but for remaking the world in our own image," according to Jane Rule, 1978. In a recent interview in Washington, D.C., Stockwell explained the frightening incidents and bizarre characters which one finds in *The Kansas Stories*: "People will go to extremes to learn the truth. And nature often aids them in that pursuit." Stockwell, whose reputation is supported in both the small and the feminist presses, is a tough writer who explains the complex searching out of truth and the discovery of love in simple settings and language, in straightforward, determined, plunging searches. She often combines this with exquisite descriptions of a part of the country which has had the reputation of being dull and ugly.

Major publications other than short fiction
NONFICTION: "Kate Millet: I'm Always in Love," 1975; "Women Monsters: Media New Jaws," 1975; "Sexual Junkyards: Massage Parlors and Prostitution," 1976.

Marianne Lester

ROBERT JOE STOUT

Born: Wyoming, 1937

Principal short fiction

"A Place of Need," 1965; "Machines," 1966; "Mote in the Pond's Eye," 1966; "Christmas at Aunt Sarah's," 1967; "Ah! Paris!," 1967; "Love That Spring Kills," 1967, "A Streak of Sun," 1967; "The Cage," 1967; "A Nice Young Man," 1967; "Ah! Middletown!," 1967; "The Little People," 1968; "The Almond Trees," 1968; "The Mythmakers," 1968; "A Stroll by the Sea," 1968; "The Choice," 1968; "The Surrender," 1968; "The Black Cong," 1968; "The Goddess," 1968; "A God for Thelma," 1968; "The Truce," 1968; "Big Daddy," 1968; "The Rebels," 1969; "Why Not Say You Loved Her?," 1969; "Hawaiian Teak," 1969; "The Storm," 1969; "The Wolf," 1969; "Run, Run, Run," 1969; "The King of the Yippies," 1969; "The Heirs," 1969; "A Letter to Orlando," 1969; "The Little Things," 1969; "Roots," 1970; "The Spanking," 1970; "The Arrival," 1970; "A Living Son," 1970; "The Great Emancipator," 1970; "The Cross," 1970; "Between Light and Shade," 1970; "The Mother," 1971; "Narahara's House," 1971; "The Shally," 1971; "Touching Games," 1972; "The Hero of Aberlleyn," 1972; "Different," 1972; "The Lost Animal," 1972; "The Dorchester Fist," 1972; "My Momma, My Daddy and Jesus Christ," 1973; "The Brave New Art," 1973; "The Victor," 1973; "The Coup," 1973; "The Wooden Elf," 1973; "McLamb," 1973; "The Mad One," 1973; "Wa-ne-go," 1974; "The Living, the Dead," 1974; "The Hourglass, 1974; "Dear Carol," 1975; "Medicine Creek," 1975; "Bandol," 1976; "You," 1976; "The Dark Side of the Moon," 1977; "Something Special," 1978; "The Way to Pinal," 1979.

Analysis

The characters in Robert Stout's short fiction are vulnerable, exposed, and embarrassingly real. They are seekers, determined to find more than their physical and psychological environment allows their personalities. The thematic injunctions that motivate and frustrate them reach back into myth, both Western and Eastern. They are, like most people in our country, spiritually incomplete; and it is in their striving toward completion that tensions, violence, and love arise. Stout's interest in Vedanta is apparent in the struggles of many of his protagonists to separate their eternal from their temporal existences. The crowded streets of Mexico City, the lonely plains of Southwest Texas, and the mountain communities in California's remote Sierras serve as settings for many of the more than sixty stories published during the late 1960's and early 1970's. Never a part of any academic literary movements or styles, Stout pulls his readers into the commonplace world of the clerk, the migrant worker, the small town journalist; and they become, like him, lone wolves forced to face the isolation of the human psyche in an alien and often destructive social and physical world.

Major publications other than short fiction
NOVEL: *Miss Sally*, 1973.
POETRY: *Moving Out*, 1973; *Trained Bears on Hoops*, 1974; *The Trick*, 1976; *Camping Out*, 1976; *Swallowing Dust*, 1976.

Joe Pires

LAWRENCE STURHAHN

Born: New York, 1928

Principal short fiction
"The Democrat," 1956; "The Fathers," 1958; "Remembrance," 1960; "Company D They Had a Dog," 1961; "The Horse That Got Caught in Barbed Wire," 1961; "The Intruders," 1962; "The First Spectator and the Last," 1971; "All the King's Horses and All the King's Men Couldn't Put Mr. Wilberforce Together Again," 1971; "Ask Alice," 1973.

Analysis
The majority of Lawrence Sturhahn's work is very much of its time informed by the conception that traditional short stories have a beginning, middle, and end; that the meaning (theme) is illuminated in a key moment, or epiphany; and that character is more important than action. The technique, which might be characterized as "dramatic realism," expresses the idea by which believable human behavior is represented through character interaction—pleasure, pain, success, and failure. Such single image stories are an efficient way of keeping a unity, a coherance. Another technique is that of dramatic irony; the point of view of the author is objective third-person. Literal images evoke the rich, ambiguous complexity of existence to engage a reader by hooking him/her to something familiar in life. The first six of these are linear stories, as opposed to what became the prevalent motifs and forms of stories of the later 1960's and 1970's—the impromptu or spatial. "Ask Alice" and "The First Spectator and the Last" are examples of that form, arising from the conception that the real horrors and inequities of modern life are beyond an author's straight telling and thus demand a certain "formlessness" which, of course, also became a form.

Major publications other than short fiction
NONFICTION: "North from Tucson," 1969; "See—the Phoenix Rising—," 1971; "Genesis of 'THX-1138': Notes on a Production," 1972; "Coni Beeson—Filmmaker," 1974; "Easter—1974—An Experience of Dying," 1976; "Harry Falk Talks About Directing The Streets of San Francisco," 1977; "Learning to Rely on Each Other," 1978.

WALTER SUBLETTE

Born: Illinois, 1940

Principal short fiction
"A Bridge to Nowhere," 1967; "The White of the Eye," 1967; "The Crossing," 1968; "Secret," 1975; "His Brother's Keeper," 1979.

Analysis
Disturbingly ironic, deeply angry, and by necessity sadly tragic, Walter Sublette's short fiction concentrates on the relatively unknown racial subculture that connects black society and white society in an otherwise racially polarized world. His characters are racially marginal people, people whose racial heritage is both black and white, whose experiences are as culturally mixed as their biological genes. Depending upon one's point of view, these characters may be seen as either very light-skinned blacks or very dark-skinned whites. Whatever the category, however, the social dilemma remains the same: individual lives are trapped in the no-man's-land between the races, where the dominating issue of personal identity is neither natural nor moral, but is usually consciously determined by choice, will, or practical concerns. Plot, setting, character, theme, and linear development arise naturally from the material, appearing as consequence within a given organic whole, basically acting to support the main focus, which is usually certain psychological repercussions to the individual, certain psychological consequences which cannot be separated from the sociological cause. Considering the unusual nature of the subject, human understanding is of imperative importance, which means the racial dilemma portrayed must be shown through the careful use of technique and craft, the enigma itself made strongly believeable in the context of realism. Final understanding is achieved through tones of rich poetic prose, boldly stated images that are taken from both black and white cultures. Alienation and social estrangement are of course inescapable conditions. The purpose of Sublette's short fiction is to inform and enlighten regarding complex matters of race, to show a certain subculture which has naturally evolved from the presence of the other two, a subculture which has by far been overlooked and neglected by the short-fiction writer. Critical response to the subject has shown surprise, uncertainty, and confusion.

Major publications other than short fiction
NOVEL: *Go Now in Darkness*, 1965 (pseudonym S. W. Edwards).
PLAYS: *In the Sleep of Wishes and Dreams*, 1974.
POETRY: *The Resurrection on Friday Night*, 1980.

SIDNEY SULKIN

Born: Massachusetts, 1918

Principal short fiction
"The Plan," 1947; "The Exile," 1949; "The Ship," 1952; "Old Man," 1969; "In Place of Parent," 1970; "Miserable Catullus," 1970; "Phil," 1971; "The Living Season," 1972; "The Secret Seed," 1975; "Hopefully Quotas Will Be . . . ," 1976; "The Undercover Man," 1977; "The Prophet," 1977.

Analysis
For the most part, although without conscious intent, Sidney Sulkin's stories cluster around a theme that in "The Undercover Man" is described as "the disorder and ugliness of exile, that universal sense of uprootedness and the anger that goes with it that simmers like an underground stream through the world and is perhaps the real world with the rest only a fantasy we others cling to in desperation and fear." Exile, internal or external, creates the visionary. Excluded from the "normal," Sulkin invokes a personal construct of the real, claiming for his separateness a kind of thaumaturgic distinction. Political exile, the ectopia of our time, produces its own distortions. In "The Exile," the moral imperative to return, to rebuild, is contradicted by the visceral yearning to have and to belong. In "The Undercover Man" and "The Ship," displacement is total; there is no return, nothing to belong to; reality itself has gone up in smoke. The Josh stories ("The Secret Seed," "Old Man," "Miserable Catullus") play the theme of voluntary internal exile; the Phil stories ("The Living Season," "Phil"), the motif of death the separator. Although grounded in realism, these stories war on the ordinary. Ewig, the accused prophet, notes on one of the innumerable pieces of paper that fill his shoebox: "Will spring come? Yes. How do we know? By hunger."

Major publications other than short fiction
NOVEL: *The Family Man*, 1962.
PLAY: *Gate of the Lions*, 1980.

STANLEY SULTAN

Born: New York, 1928

Principal short fiction

"And Jacob Called," 1948; "The Fugue of the Fig Tree," 1952; "An Early Autumn," 1955; "Feigenbaum and Mary Jane," 1976; "Ba'lawa," 1977; "The Hills of the Chankly Bore," 1979; "A Little World Made Cunningly," 1980.

Analysis

Stanley Sultan's characters are agents of their own cultural history. Ethnic experience—that accretion of communal attitudes and ancestral voices—battles the individual's short personal history for the rights of continuity over change. Each story focuses on an attempt to make human contact across the boundaries of community or the chasm of age. In "Fugue" and "Ba'lawa," middle-eastern Jewish immigrants face the compromises of deracination. In "Early Autumn," an imaginative boy resists initiation into the cult of unthinking adolescence. The protagonist of "The Hills of the Chankly Bore" sails away in the sieve of his supposed individuality and finds himself spiritually stranded. Sultan's careful attention to architectonic detail is all in the service of revealing cultural density. Here, as in James Joyce's *Dubliners* (1914), an economical style draws the hoard of significance from every name and object. The characters' voices, more than anything else, reveal the presence of an aggregate experience. The voices range from a flat American drawl to the counterpoint of earthiness and formality in Sultan's remarkable English renderings of Arabic and Hebrew. In nearly every story, the threat of loss sharpens the protagonist's sense of continuity. Frank Sylvester, in "The Hills of the Chankly Bore," is embarrassed by that continuity—he was originally Francisco Silvestro. Most of the characters, however, are able to express tenderness in a variety of relationships, with a warmth and respect untainted by sentimentality. Only those who cannot distinguish memory from mere nostalgia can exclude themselves from these ties.

Major publications other than short fiction

NOVEL: *Rabbi: A Tale of the Waning Year*, 1978.
NONFICTION: *The Argument of Ulysses*, 1965; *Yeats at His Last*, 1975; *Ulysses, The Waste Land, and Modernism*, 1977.

Bruce Herzberg

GLADYS SWAN

Born: New York, 1934

Principal short fiction
On the Edge of the Desert, 1979.

Analysis
The American Southwest. A young man drifts in search of a gypsy father. A spinster librarian, confronted by her barren past, feels remorse and rediscovers her terror of men. A quartet of conniving impersonators set upon one another like a pack of quarrelsome dogs. A roving folksinger is forcibly drawn into the whirlwind center of a blighted farm and bereft farmer. A woman returned to a town that was once her home, to a critically ill mother, and to the desert's magical tenacity. In these stories and others, Gladys Swan depicts individuals who discover the danger of the territory they inhabit and are forced to come to terms with the desert within and outside themselves. Arnold Lustig, author of *Diamonds of the Night*, said of her, "In her stories she is able to touch the undefinable border of beauty. . . . Her writing is remarkably wise and honest." George Gore, editor, *Sewanee Review*, remarked, "One feels and tastes her world's weather, sees its terrain, and becomes involved with its people. The author reminds me in some respects of Sherwood Anderson." Critics have praised Swan for her language, "pure and poetically clear." "Each recollection is evoked with a penetrating clarity and a certain quiet pathos."

BRIAN SWANN

Born: England, 1940

Principal short fiction
The Runner, 1979; *Unreal Estate*, 1980; *Elizabeth*, 1980.

Analysis
Brian Swann had written poetry for some time when he began to feel stifled by the restrictions of its form. As he expressed it, "I felt I had painted myself into a corner. . . ." He turned to short fiction in the form of prose poetry and thus found freedom to experiment. From his early "poems-in-prose," he moved to a novella, *Elizabeth*, a novel, *A Book of Voices* (1980), and then to poetry again, inspired anew by the prose techniques he had learned. What he has discovered in his fusion of poetry and prose, he says, he values as "something close to the bone, if not in the bone."

Major publications other than short fiction
NOVEL: *A Book of Voices*, 1980.
POETRY: *The Whale's Scars*, 1974; *Roots*, 1976; *Living Time*, 1978; *Paradigms of Fire*, 1980.

MYRON TAUBE

Born: New York, 1929

Principal short fiction
"The Bunny," 1962; "Epstein," 1964; "The Mess," 1964; "The King of Honor," 1965; "Heshy," 1965; "The Professional," 1965; "The Explosion," 1965; "Shelley," 1965; "Margaret," 1966; "Margo," 1966; "Mirror, Mirror, on the Wall," 1966; "The Kiss," 1966; "The Tree," 1967; "Bach Is for the Loving Kind," 1967; "The Confession," 1968; "The Smell of Heather," 1968; "The Student," 1968; "The Magician," 1968; "Just You Wait, Leonard Dorfman, Just You Wait," 1968; "The Lesson," 1968; "The Kaddish," 1968; "The Long, Hot Summer," 1969; "The Gift," 1969; "House Divided," 1969; "Him," 1969; "Perfect Lover," 1969; "The Cross," 1970; "One Summer," 1970; "On the Bridge," 1970; "The Investigation," 1971; "Esther," 1973; "The Mutt Killer," 1973; "The Ski Bum" 1974; "The March of the Saints," 1974; "The Obituary," 1975; "Max," 1975; "The Party," 1975; "The Goof-Up," 1975; "The Star," 1976; "Sam," 1978; "Fortunato's Confession," 1978; "The New Life," 1979; "The Callers," 1979; "The Stone," 1979; "Kiddush," 1980.

Analysis
Author of more than sixty uncollected, traditional stories, Myron Taube joins a tragic view of life with the comic perception that the ongoingness of life dissolves stark tragedy. Nature, society, and the family all support continuity and survival. Consciousness of one's own finite quality gives to life the dignity and honor and nervous edge that makes meaning. Taube's characters often search merely to find what has been deepest within them. Taube planned to use as an epigraph for one of his collections the words of Jorge Luis Borges: "Any life, no matter how long or complex it may be, is made up essentially *of a single moment*—the moment in which a man finds out, once and for all, who he is." His characters move in that narrow area where personal choice sums up a life. Man's existence, however, stretches out behind him in his cultural, historical, and biological continuity; and it reaches into the future in one attempt to overcome the darkness that ends one's personal consciousness. Rejecting the despair that comes of denial, and accepting the limitation that is inherent in human experience, Taube has created a wide range of human characters in a Chekhovian mode. His strengths are a good ear that catches the vitality and nuances of common speech, and an insight into the lives of ordinary men and women. Writing of his prize-winning story "Kiddush," Kay Boyle wrote:

The language of "Kiddush" for me actually reverberates on the page. It is heard loud and clear as well as being seen by the eye. And what is heard and seen, moreover, is not only humor, but compassion gentle and fierce enough to break the heart. It is a story that speaks out of that peculiar kind of courage that makes bearable our outrageous daily lives.

ROBERT TAYLOR, JR.

Born: Oklahoma, 1941

Principal short fiction

"The Death of Bird, Pres, and Billie Holiday," 1970; "Harrissy's Passion," 1970; "Night Crawlers," 1971; "Light My Fire," 1971; "A Selection from the Memoirs of Ferlin Tussaud," 1971; "Touching," 1972; "La Granada," 1973; "Up Against the Wall," 1973; "Vacant Houses, Empty Rooms," 1973; "Transfiguration," 1974; "A Woman in Ice," 1975; "A Message from Pancho Villa," 1976; "The Willows Letters," 1977; "Meditation," 1977; "Letters from the Great Valley," 1977; "Going to Casablanca," 1977; "The Hog-Eyed Man," 1979; "The Over-28 Club," 1979; "Later Phases of the Western Migration," 1979; "Where Are Our MIA's?," 1979; "Profligate Lives," 1979; "Staking Claims," 1979; "Union Street," 1979; "The Discovery of Oklahoma," 1979; "The Opening of Oklahoma," 1979; "Letha Posey's Husband," 1979; "The Selling of Quantrill's Bones," 1979; "Legends," 1979; "Loving Belle Starr," 1980.

Analysis

Robert Taylor's short fiction, while frequently forgoing linear plot, makes extensive use of time, place, mood, and character. At their best, these stories blur the distinction between poetry and fiction, achieving a kind of lyricism through rhythm and image. Recently Taylor has turned to the past for his "plots," taking his characters and their situations either from memory or from history. The history stories form a sequence, related by time and place (territorial Oklahoma) and by recurring characters who are either outlaws or the kin of outlaws (Belle Starr, Zerelda James). History stories and memory pieces are linked by theme, each in some way portraying a struggle for redemption, a decayed or decaying society.

STEVE RASNIC TEM

Born: Virginia, 1950

Principal short fiction
"The Assassination," 1976; "A Letter Written to Gabriel After His Death," 1978; "City Fishing," 1980; "Forward," 1980; "The Painters Are Coming Today," 1979; "Hideout," 1979; "At the Bureau," 1980; "Filmmaker," 1980; "Again, the Hit and Run," 1980; "Mechanic," 1980; "The Sound of Hawkwings Dissolving," 1980; "Boy Blue," 1980; "Morning Talk," 1980.

Analysis
Steve Rasnic Tem considers himself essentially a fantasist, his major interest being in a line of literary concerns, which he traces as Ovid's *Metamorphoses*, Kafka (particularly "A Country Doctor"), and such modern fantasists as Lord Dunsany, Italo Calvino, Jorge Luis Borges, Gerald Kersh, J. G. Ballard, Ramsey Campbell, Tom Disch, and Harlan Ellison. Tem's stories often actualize childhood fears, fantasies, and dreams as adult characters confront the unresolved elements in their lives. As Tem says in *Center 10* (1977):

> My characterizations are adapted from gestalt dream studies: each phrase, image, or other character considered as a projected aspect of the narrator or main character. I think such "dream" characterization began with myth, and continued in a significant way with Ovid, as an alternative way of seeing character psychology to the Homeric tradition. The structure of the story follows the structure of the character's dream states. Viewed this way, we see that Kafka's characters are not as one-dimensional as some have supposed; each element of the tale tells us something about Kafka's main character. Each element is a projection. The modern fantasy or horror tale, when written with this kind of consciousness, can be the most "human" of fiction, can tell us more about ourselves than the most "realistic" of tales.

WILLIAM THOMAS

Born: New York, 1912

Principal short fiction
"The Trinket," 1975; "The Way Ahead," 1976; "Plants Die When I Touch Them," 1978; "Where the Cool Is At," 1979; "When He Lies Asleep You Let Him," 1979; "The Devil's Apprentice," 1979; "The Winter Kind," 1979.

Analysis
To enter the world of William Thomas is to enter an ancient Greek world where Dike is distant, unpredictable, and powerful and where every creature—even cockroaches and retired cleaning ladies—play a part in the large scheme. His is the voice of the balladeer filling his stories with symbolic neon signs and red setters, bone-cracking cold, and cryptic nuns who recur in the stories like Delphic oracles and blind seers. An old Irish man in a great coat with a pocket big enough to hold his beer appears from nowhere and then disappears—a modern day Tieresias. The future of neighborhoods is as important as the survival of Troy in a world that swirls with interrelated but mysteriously unpredictable events. The characters, urban working class, batter their way through a hostile world of chance where policemen shoot each other by accident and are out on the take like everyone else. The world, however, does not feel urban. Even the buildings, signs, and cars crowding the streets seem as alive as Ulysses' wine-dark seas. Every person is a potential hero regretting the loss of the good days of the past and sometimes finding hope in recognizing familiar and predictable gestures of love—in the flushing of the toilet at the same time every night by a loved one—while he or she goes into the daily battle not knowing what the inscrutable plan of Dike will be today.

Major publications other than short fiction
POETRY: *Requiem*, 1978; *On Oliver Street*, 1979.

Jean Fawsett Atthowe

SANDRA THOMPSON

Born: Illinois, 1943

Principal short fiction
"Memoir, Cut Short," 1977; "The Baby in Mid-air," 1978; "Close-ups," 1978; "Montauk," 1980.

Analysis
Sandra Thompson's fictions are marked by an elegance of tone and style which make attractive, and nearly belie, their underlying threads of alienation, disorientation, and, at times, dissociation. Her characters find themselves mired in a world the workings of which—like the nature of undertow, geo-magnetism, and gravity itself—are unavoidable, perceivable, yet essentially undefinable, a world in which they know the meaning of much less than they experience. Her primary focus is on classic themes: the nature of love, the meaning of relationships, especially those of lovers, spouses, and parents and children. Her primary formal unit is the short scene in which, obliquely as often as directly, characters pursue their destinies either unconscious of their own motivations and the underlying meaning of their words and actions, or with only a sense that they are under the sway of forces which, although they can feel and even identify them to the point of dissection, exert an irresistible influence over them. Thompson's fictions have appeared in a number of small press publications, and her first collection of stories, *Close-ups*, was chosen as one of the final selections for review in the Associated Writing Program Award Series in Short Fiction.

Major publications other than short fiction
POETRY: "The Knife-Thrower's Girlfriend," 1976-1977.
NONFICTION: "Is Dr. Welby a Menace to Women?," 1973; "My House Husband—I Think I'll Keep Him," 1979; "Children Welcome—If They're neither Seen nor Heard," 1979.

Les Von Losberg

IRENE TIERSTEN

Born: New Jersey, 1940

Principal short fiction
"Anna," 1975; "Who Is Singing the Night Music," 1976; "Mr. Macho," 1977; "Dramatic Tension," 1977; "Women Are Fainting All over Manhattan," 1977; "Animal Crackers and Alphabet Soup: Or, The Shape of Lunch," 1978; "Rocks," 1978; "Nina," 1979; "Intruders," 1980.

Analysis
Irene Tiersten, who began her writing career as Irene Trachtenberg, is the winner of the Fels Award for Short Fiction in 1976. Her writings are of three types: realistic, even naturalistic; surreal; and experimental. In such stories as "Anna," "Intruders," and "Nina," the emphasis is firmly upon character, and the narrative line is linear and clearly developed. "Nina" is included in Red Clay's *Love Stories by New Women*, which has been reprinted by Bard/Avon in the United States and by The Women's Press in London. Some of Tiersten's prose is surreal and hallucinatory. "Mr. Macho," for example, and "Who Is Singing the Night Music" employ the imagery of dream from which to weave perplexing and haunting spells, leaving the reader puzzled but intrigued and stimulated.

The most interesting and sophisticated of Tiersten's writings, however, are the visual/verbal creations that combine either drawings and text or a variety of texts that are distinguished from one another by typology and spacing. These pieces achieve an effect of diversity of tone and of ironic interplay that is tinged with self-directed humor. In "Dramatic Tension," abstractly worded rhetorical questions and lists are used to set off the domestic humor of a woman's attempt to explain her divorce and choice of a new partner to her skeptical Jewish grandmother. "Rocks," whose technique may have been suggested by Virginia Woolf's novel *The Waves* (1931), employs descriptions of changing natural conditions on a beach as implied comments on the abrasive interaction between the principals. The wittiest of Tiersten's visual/verbal creations is "Animal Crackers and Alphabet Soup: Or, The Shape of Lunch," in which whimsical line drawings are interspersed with the text to make a deceptively simple statement about the problems faced by married women and mothers when they attempt to assume the obligation of disciplined creative work.

The range of modes in which Irene Tiersten writes gives her work an ingenious boldness; her writing is also extremely timely because her focus is on the changing patterns of family life today, especially the challenging new roles that women are creating for themselves.

Tiersten has recently been awarded a New Jersey State Council on the Arts Fellowship.

Major publications other than short fiction
NOVELS: *One Big Happy Family*, 1980; *From One to the Other*, 1980.
PLAY: *Connections*, 1977.

Sharon Spencer

CAROLINE B. TOTTEN

Born: Ohio, 1935

Principal short fiction

"Strangers When We Part," 1966; "Of Doves and Hawks," 1968; "The Case of the Winking Bride," 1968; "Who Will Cry for Gabor Doniska," 1974; "The Cave of Sighs," 1976; "Working My Way to Sunday," 1977; "Treasures in Your Trash," 1978.

Analysis

The release of the pure spirit and its struggle to survive and flourish in a corrupt world is the recurring theme in the fiction of Caroline Totten. The stories are often handled with poignant humor, and the characters have been described by critics as "utterly human, flawed and lovable." Although the characters dictate the story, the technique varies from experimental poetic prose, dense and layered with images, to simple, dramatic narratives. The symbolism is implicit and its literary purpose is revelation. An excerpt from "The Cave of Sighs" reveals the artistic intent of the author: "Whomever we meet . . . serves as a guide to our transcendence." Spiritual realism, not religion, flows in the undercurrent. As a result, it is only when the pure human spirit rises to the surface that one is capable of being in harmony with oneself.

Major publications other than short fiction

NOVEL: *River of the Sacred Monkey*, 1970.

MARTIN TUCKER

Born: Pennsylvania, 1928

Principal short fiction
"Suburban Transit Gloria," 1976; "The Chauffeur," 1978; "Snapshots," 1980.

Analysis
Traditional methods of craft are distinguished in Martin Tucker's stories, but his underlying attitude is often subversive of accepted canons of moral attitude. He employs humor to show that man somehow copes even when he is perceived as not coping. Thus the surface of his work is meant as a covering to be pierced for its deeper and sometimes paradoxical levels. His style is that of concision and imagery; his stories are often short for the length of action and detail they exemplify. As in his poetry, Tucker's stories are shaped for reverberating effects: the image suggests the hero's and heroine's conflicts and desires and involves the reader in the acceptance of questioning without the certainty of the question itself. His issues are philosophical issues, particularly those of assumptions and prejudgments, but they are clothed in the slipperiness of everyday occurrence.

Major publications other than short fiction
NONFICTION: *Africa in Modern Literature*, 1967; *Joseph Conrad*, 1976.

LEWIS TURCO

Born: New York, 1934

Principal short fiction

"The Book of the Black Heart," 1964; "Pleasant Dell," 1965; "The Catalogue Idea," 1968; "The Prison," 1968; "Salt," 1968; "The Man Who Invented Eternity," 1969; "The Scent of Honeysuckle," 1969; "One Sunday Morning," 1969; "The Master of Cerements," 1974; "The City of the Dead," 1978; "Cologne," 1978; "Shipmates: The Bo'sun's Story, The Yeoman's Story, The Gunner's Story," 1978; "The Unicorn Hunter," 1979.

Analysis

Although he published his first short story in 1949; Lewis Turco is known primarily as a poet. Like his poems, Turco's stories are variously written. Although his earlier pieces appear to be avant-garde, his tendency is to write the traditional "well-built" story. Some of the better of these, most of them in the "Horace" series, have been cited as "Distinguished" in Foley-Burnet for 1967, 1969, and 1970. A set of three short pieces titled "shipmates" is a continuation of *The Book of the Black Heart* which was conceived as a "prose poem epic" and abandoned when David French characterized it as a "novel"— one of these is a partial reworking of Turco's earliest published short story. In much of Turco there is a strong tendency toward fantasy, which works in his poetry quite often, but in his prose narration turns into supernatural or science fiction. The one book in which all these elements come together, including prose narration, is *The Inhabitant* (1970), ostensibly a book of poetry, of which Ray Bradbury has said,

> Lewis Turco and I share similar worlds. Everything in *The Inhabitant* is part of my own real or remembered world. I particularly like "The Porch" and "The Glider" to start with, but there are many riches. Reading the book is like going up in the attic on an autumn or summer night, to open trunks and fetch out strange images and treasures.

Major publications other than short fiction

POETRY: *Awaken, Bells Falling*, 1968; *The Inhabitant*, 1970; *Pocoangelini*, 1971; *The Compleat Melancholick*, 1981.

NONFICTION: *The Book of Forms*, 1968.

KEVIN URICK

Born: Michigan, 1952

Principal short fiction

"Among the Exhibits," 1976; "Planting the Seeds for a House of One's Own," 1977; *Seems Like Time*, 1977; "To Those Who Can Handle Success," 1977; "Portrait #1," 1978; "Portrait #2," 1978; "Portrait #3," 1978; "Portrait #4," 1978; "Portrait #6," 1978; "Portrait #8," 1978; "Portrait #9," 1978; *Nakedness*, 1979; "Clearing the Air," 1980; "A Simple Exchange," 1980; "Letters to the Editors," 1980.

Analysis

Kevin Urick has stated that, "I am mainly interested in the emotion I can put into my writings. . . ." What he is after in his fiction is the investigation and analysis of emotion and its relationship to character. By mapping out the borders of his characters' thoughts and feelings about the situations they enter, he is able to comment on universal types and our present day state of affairs. Detachment keeps the work from being ephemeral in the "trendy" sense, while Urick cuts to the bone in a terse, clipped prose that reveals the meat of our chameleon moods and selves. Women prove the most perceptive, complex characters. Plots often turn on their permutations. Devices are sometimes borrowed from other genre to stimulate moods and emotions. No matter how introspective the fiction appears, the landscape is never forgotten, and the accumulation of outside detail works symbolically to define and influence character development. Readers should expect to enter a world where the Marx Brothers, Monty Python, Jonathan Swift, and William Shakespeare hold equal sway.

Major publications other than short fiction

NOVEL: *The Death of Colonel Johns*, 1980.

Richard Peabody, Jr.

RONALD VANCE

Born: Connecticut, 1930

Principal short fiction
"George Henry Freedman," 1971; "Even in Spain, a Love Story," 1978; "Bruna Sevini," 1978; "CANOEing/Body Types, Rivers, Maryland," 1978-1979; "The Underrated Bestseller," 1979; "Say It's a Chair," 1979; "Field Notes," 1979; "Core Tune Ease," 1980; "Bad Cheat," 1980.

Analysis
Ronald Vance invites readers to shed their reading habits of memory and anticipation in order to experience reading-writing as a succession of instants. Working with existing texts, Vance engenders a text disengaged from story, theme, subjective mood (he does not take as his occasion for writing a mythology created out of his own psychology). Accumulation is one of his characteristic rhetorical devices: a Vance text grows in several directions, expanding rather than lengthening. Inconsistency is one way of articulating multiformity, and so is levity, which in Vance's work takes the form of using whatever paragraphs, sentences, phrases, words, syllables, phonemes come to hand/mind at the time he is writing. He thus incorporates in his texts the quirky, the accidental, the diverse, and he dissolves formal categories and distinctions such as that between verse and prose, fiction and nonfiction; and by so doing he deliberately accords things equal value with their opposites. Compression is another rhetorical device Vance uses, for summarizing several language events (connotation, association) in one charged instant or allowing one event to obscure another before the reader has a chance to name it (Vance undoes nomination). In his writing, it is assumed that an element of langue (grammatical, syntactical, lexical, a change of tense, a shift in sound or spelling) is in and of itself significant; what it communicates is in large part determined by the reader, and it is different with each reading.

Major publications other than short fiction
NONFICTION: *The Home Gardener's Guide to Bulb Flowers*, 1967.

HENRY VAN DYKE

Born: Michigan, 1928

Principal short fiction
"Ruth's Story," 1962; "Happiness in a Hotel," 1979; "Velma," 1979; "Not a Litany, Not a Blues," 1979; ‡u Côté de Chez Britz," 1979.

Analysis
Henry Van Dyke's work has the particular virtue of dealing with race relations as if they were ordinary human relations. A writer of individual character, of the hidden idiosyncrasies, he attempts to reveal that which is ordinary and human and pathetic in us all—but almost invariably through ironic and humorous means. In a mode which is generally pithy and witty, Van Dyke reaches in his work for an offbeat mixture of comedy and suspense.

Major publications other than short fiction
NOVELS: *Ladies of the Rachmaninoff Eyes*, 1965; *Blood of Strawberries*, 1969; *Dead Piano*, 1971.

RICHARD VETERE

Born: New York, 1952

Principal short fiction
"Maspeth," 1976; *Don John*, 1977; *The Last Detective*, 1978.

Analysis
Unlike the poetic naturalism of his plays, screenplays, and longer fiction, Richard Vetere's *The Last Detective* and "Maspeth" are stories told in a clean, dry, and unemotional voice. The main character of each piece is purposely nameless and the world the character inhabits is overwhelmingly banal. In this world, both the lonely, middle-aged man of *The Last Detective* and the bored, young boy of "Maspeth" have difficulty in dealing with their own emotional lives. Childish sex acts and awkward violence perpetuate the loneliness of their dull, working-class environments. As people they are friendless and familyless, relying on the extravaganzas of their own imaginations to help separate themselves from the meaningless landscape of their lives. In both pieces, it is only in the urban setting that we find the sensual and the poetic. The physical reality of an "empty alley" or a "bus stop" is more dramatic than the events of the characters' daily routines, no matter how extreme those events are. Both characters fail to show any resemblance of feelings that are not exaggerated or downright pitiful in their meager scope. As with all Vetere's characters, those of his short fiction are basically working-class people whose lives are counted in hours and who feel dispairingly the insignificance of their own experiences.

In a recent review, *The New York Times* said, "Mr. Vetere demonstrates an ability to mix the colloquial with the poetic," and *The Village Voice* commented that in his work, ". . . imagery and metaphor blend (often brilliantly) imparting beautiful word pictures." Vetere's short fiction is an essential element to any student of his work since in it his characters are not weighed down by particular or specific behavioral traits as found in motion pictures, plays, and longer fiction. Because of their purity and because of their distinct inability to identify themselves in their own world, they are closer to this young writer's vision and are more a comment on contemporary urban living, especially the late 1970's, than his more commercial pieces.

Major publications other than short fiction
NOVELS: *White Summer*, 1976; *The Capitalist*, 1980; *Maniac*, 1980.
PLAYS: *Paradise*, 1976; *Rockaway Boulevard*, 1978; *Johnny on the Pony*, 1979.

Sandra Ventura

SARA VOGAN

Born: Pennsylvania, 1947

Principal short fiction
Scenes from the Homefront, 1981.

Analysis
One of the prominent themes in Sara Vogan's fiction is the working out of relationships, whether between an individual and his surroundings, a parent and child, or lovers. The success or failure of these bindings often seems random, subject to influences over which one has no control—like death, love, or war. Vogan likes to deal with the choices made in modern society and the effects those choices reveal. Often good choices go awry and one must rearrange his life to accommodate the consequences. As a writer of short stories and novels, Vogan finds the story can often provide moments of awareness or opportunities for experimentation that would be overwhelmed in novel form. If a character's situation can best be illuminated in isolation, without the backgrounding a novel can provide, then the short story is the best form to use. The brevity of the story gives her the chance to present an idea, relationship, or choice as clearly as possible. Since the story is a short form, she feels more freedom to experiment. It challenges Vogan to write a story that covers a sixty-year time span or to write from the second person point of view. Not every idea or character, choice or relationship, needs the scope of the novel and the short story provides a showcase for those moments in time and experiments in form.

Major publications other than short fiction
NOVEL: *In Shelly's Leg*, 1981.

JOHN WALKE

Born: Pakistan, 1947

Principal short fiction

"Remember St. Lawrence's Road?," 1977; "Bringing It Home," 1978; "Night Bathing," 1979; "The Coal Dust Moon," 1979; "To the Mountains," 1980.

Analysis

In his Eurasian stories, John Walke pieces together the mosaic of the small, culturally and socially marginal Anglo-Indian community as seen from within, on its own terms and not those of the traditional British and Indian perspectives which have, in the past, ground their own axes. He does this through the eyes of Eurasian children in their social and sensual awakenings and aspirations as they discover the strengths and weaknesses of their community. Albert Callan (Editor, *Connecticut Fireside*) considers the "brilliant atmosphere and strong emotions," of his stories "evocative of India and Pakistan." His "rich imagery," (Howard Sage, Editor, *Pulp*) "beautifully descriptive, vividly written," (*Webster Review*) leads to "the evocation of heat, the feeling of time standing still, and the laziness an environment like that causes," (Valentino Ramirez, Fiction Editor, *Hawaii Review*). His occasional irony and complex motifs and themes reflect the culturally munificent environment that germinates them. Yet, by his sharp juxtaposition, midst the hot, timeless, lethargic ambience, of "so much energy, so many pictures, so much that needs to be written . . . I felt as if I were in a storm," (Ramirez). Walke depicts the internal conflict and ceaseless tension of a people whose inheritance through generations has drawn upon both East and West and demands a reconciliation. Though the stories can be understood independently, they acquire deeper resonances when read collectively.

KARL C. WANG

Born: Indonesia, 1950

Principal short fiction
"The Roommate," 1971; "Sojourn to a Western Mountain," 1975; *The Actress*, 1978.

Analysis
Control is essential for expertise on the subject matter of short-story writing, a view expressed by a gifted younger artist in possession of a unique background to Western Literature. Karl Wang's work is fresh, and not estranged from his own personality. His work is blunt, crafted by a new eye, and spoken in an honest voice, neither moribund nor tiresome. Short fiction proves most successful as a source of remedies for both the author and the reader; in spite of the kind of ailments the reader suffers, the short story is still indispensable as medicine. For the overgrown confusion in the fully industrialized nations category, Wang believes that fiction offers hope for humanity; and *he* is evidence that *art* lives, and like some of his contemporaries (perhaps only a handful in the world), he is truly involved.

Major publications other than short fiction
POETRY: *Chinaman*, 1976; *Unfinished Letters of an Opium Smoker*, 1976; *Palms & Armpits*, 1978; *Wielding Wires at Midnight*, 1979.

DAVID WATMOUGH

Born: England, 1926

Principal short fiction
Ashes for Easter, 1972; *Love & The Waiting Game*, 1975; *From a Cornish Landscape*, 1975; "Beyond the Mergansers, Above the Salal," 1976; "Terminus Victoria," 1976; "Ashes," 1976.

Analysis
All of David Watmough's fiction to date—novels, short stories, and mono-dramas—are concerned with his protagonist, Davey Bryant, and represent a concerted attempt to create the life and times of a single twentieth century man, beginning with his Cornish childhood, following him through wartime London and postwar France, to San Francisco, New York, and finally to the Canadian West Coast. The fictions are cast in an autobiographical form and are strongly confessional in nature. Speaking of Watmough's work the critic George Woodcock comments:

> So . . . with all its revelations of the general human fear of what reminds us of our inevitable ends, the past is closed off, from obligation, but not from memory, as the great corpus of Watmough's recollective stories and monodramas show, building up, as they do, into a kind of living novel whose very episodic structure guarantees its continuity as long as memory still fascinates David Watmough . . . in the end I suspect this yet-unnamed masterpiece of imaginative recollection . . . will become the most monumental work of fiction . . . that has been written on the Pacific Coast.

Major publications other than short fiction
NOVELS: *A Church Renascent*, 1951; *Names for the Numbered Years*, 1967; *No More into the Garden*, 1978.

LAWRENCE WATSON

Born: North Dakota, 1947

Principal short fiction
"Just A Minute, I'm Not Ready," 1975; "A Small Favor," 1975; "Where I Go, What I Do," 1977.

Analysis
Lawrence Watson's stories are of characters on the far edge of something—of society, of a relationship, of their own sanity—and these characters, who are more inclined to reflection than action, seem primarilly concerned with these questions: how did I come to be what I am; where am I; how do I behave under these circumstances. His treatment of the traditional elements of fiction, plot, character, setting, and theme is likely to be conventional. His fiction belongs to the tradition of realism. Although Watson's concern that language give his stories a texture that pleases the reader's senses, his first attention is to the clarity of the narrative. Finally, although he believes all of these statements to be true of his fiction at this moment, he would not want them to be binding; what he wants most to be open to in his writing are the limitless, miraculous, and always present possibilities for discovery and change.

Major publications other than short fiction
NOVEL: *In a Dark Time*, 1980.

ROBERT WATSON

Born: New Jersey, 1925

Principal short fiction

"The Itch," 1966; "My Great-Aunt Marion and My Mistress Charlotte," 1966; "The Plane from Marathon," 1975; "Tale of a Coat," 1977; "Tale of a Physician," 1977; "Tale of a Magician," 1977.

Analysis

For many years before Robert Watson wrote fiction, he was a poet. His fiction began when he discovered that some ideas simply would not lend themselves to poetic form. When he began to write short stories, he made a further discovery: although the stories were complete in themselves, he found that they were also part of something larger. The story "My Great-Aunt Marion and My Mistress Charlotte" thus became part of the novel *Three Sides of the Mirror* (1966). In a similar fashion, the three tales, "Tale of a Magician," "Tale of a Coat," and "Tale of a Physician," turned out to be parts of another novel called *Lily Lang* (1977). Now the story "Treasure Salvors" is part of a novel in progress. Most of Watson's stories concern people whose lives are ordinary, even very dull. Then circumstances beyond their control send them spinning off in another, frequently disastrous, direction. Most of his characters come from an invented city in Northern New Jersey called Rawpack.

Major publications other than short fiction

NOVELS: *Three Sides of the Mirror*, 1966; *Lily Lang*, 1977.
PLAY: *A Plot Against the King*, 1963.
POETRY: *A Paper Horse*, 1962; *Advantages of Dark*, 1966; *Christmas in Las Vegas*, 1971; *Selected Poems*, 1974; *Night Blooming Cactus*, 1980.

WINSTON WEATHERS

Born: Oklahoma, 1926

Principal short fiction
The Lonesome Game, 1970; "Brotherly Love," 1972; "The Costumes of Professor Mordecai," 1973; "The Wrestling Match," 1973; "Padre Island," 1974; "The Dancing Goat," 1975; "Now, Voyager," 1975; "Mortality," 1976; "The Man on Thin Ice," 1978; "The Staircase Man," 1980.

Analysis
Winston Weathers' short fiction deals most frequently with members of psychological, emotional minorities—people living in small Midwestern or Southwestern towns, those minor characters in society who are frequently waiting for "something to happen" and who create simple illusions in order to survive in an otherwise drab, meaningless world. Many of his protagonists are children or, as one reviewer has suggested, people who "are still children emotionally because of the desolation that place or circumstance or ignorance forces upon their lives." There is little of social criticism in Weathers' work and only a sparse kind of realism: the main thrust of the fiction is a sympathetic portrayal of those whose role in society is slight, tenuous, peripheral, and whose radical epiphanies go essentially unnoticed by the world around them. Weathers deals with a personal loneliness that becomes representative of something philosophically larger; as another reviewer wrote, "If life for Weathers is a lonesome game, bounded by darkness and tragic in nature, it is also filled with mysteries and strangeness which cannot be accounted for by simple categories and dogma, Christian or Freudian." As far as craft is concerned, Weathers' stories eschew any vivid realism and move toward stylized perceptions that have elicited such reviewer characterizations as "poetic," "intricately patterned," "haunting and beautifully achieved," "beautifully wrought," "finely wrought," and so on. Writing outside mainstream naturalism and its celebrations of rough sincerity and uncalculating honesty, Weathers works to effect the well-made piece that will reflect his belief that artifice is a valuable part of human experience and that fiction is essentially an imaginative achievement; each story is a "constructed" aesthetic object.

Major publications other than short fiction
NOVEL: *The Gifts That We Bear*, 1976.
POETRY: *Messages from the Asylum*, 1970; *Indian and White: Sixteen Eclogues*, 1970; *The Island: A Quadricinium*, 1975.

GORDON WEAVER

Born: Illinois, 1937

Principal short fiction

"Wadek," 1963; "The Bearded Lady," 1964; "Reasons I Insist You Call Me By My Right Name," 1968; "Neery Christmas," 1970; "Twist Ending," 1970; "Won't You Come Out, Crazy Dave?," 1971; *The Entombed Man of Thule*, 1972; "The Turning Clock," 1972; "Canavan's Knee," 1972; "Some Killers," 1973; "Flowers: *Memento Mori*," 1973; "Moving Back Into a House Again," 1973; "At Otto Pfaff's Inn," 1974; "Ghosts," 1975; "In the Dark of Summers Past," 1975; "My Brother and the Perfect People," 1975; *Such Waltzing Was Not Easy*, 1975; "Falling: Past, Present, Future," 1976; "Lewinski Agonistes," 1976; "Batterman: At the Center of Time," 1976; "Closing Time: The Red-granite Wisconsin Bowl-A-Go-Go," 1976; "Horse: Now," 1976; "Romy in Winter," 1977; "What Batterman Did in the Police Action/Conflict," 1977; "Dirt," 1978; "Learning Business," 1978; "A Small Buddha," 1978; "The White Elephant," 1978; "The Road as Metaphor," 1979; "Dreaming Ninety Years," 1979; "A Dialogue," 1979; *Getting Serious*, 1980; "Looking for the Lost Eden," 1980; "Self-Portraits," 1980; "Fearing What Dreams?," 1981.

Analysis

Two frequent settings for the stories of Gordon Weaver are lower-middle-class homes and bars of many types, from urban dives to resort lounges. The homes, often in Milwaukee or a small town in Illinois, are scenes of family conflict, more battlegrounds than havens. The bars are the surrogate family parlor of the lonely. Although Weaver's stories have many other locales, these places represent major thematic concerns in his fiction. His family stories depict, with resonant detail and dialogue, the dissolution of a family as seen by the youngest child, and his loss of family ultimately becomes a loss of self in "Oskar Hansen, Jr., Speaks to His Son," "Low Blue Man," "Granger Hunting," and "The Engstrom Girls," to mention a few. The narrative persona recaptures this family through storytelling, comes to see their weakness and courage in perspective, and through them, comes to understand human nature and himself. The isolation stories present a protagonist alone—in spirit if not in fact—one who must define himself by choice and action. A stoic tone, relieved and heightened by ironic humor, pervades these stories. If the protagonist acts, the effect is redemptive, but ironically, by committing himself he sacrifices the dark comfort of anonymity. Once he acts, there will be further expectations of him; thus the inevitable conflict develops between what he is and what others want him to be. This problem is variously treated in "Finch the Spastic Speaks," "The Entombed Man of Thule," "The Day I Lost My

Distance," "The Cold," and "Getting Serious."

Major publications other than short fiction
NOVELS: *Count a Lonely Cadence*, 1968; *Give Him a Stone*, 1975; *Circling Byzantium*, 1980.

James Curry Robison

BERNICE LARSON WEBB

Born: Kansas

Principal short fiction
"Harvest," 1963; "Lost and Found," 1968; "The Tomato Tree," 1975.

Analysis
Versatility in form, subject, and style is the forte of Bernice Larson Webb as writer, moving as she does among the genres of poetry, short story, essay, biography, and drama. Her characters may be ordinary people caught in events that temporarily overpower them, as happens with the Swedish-American farmer in "Harvest"; or her figures may be whimsical. In "Lost and Found" Mr. Easy, who absentmindedly leaves his wife in a roadside gas station in Last Chance, Colorado, must reach a moment of comic illumination before driving forty miles back to reclaim her. In "The Tomato Tree" fantasy is given lighthearted treatment when a middle-aged housewife is forced, for love of a man, into a strange rivalry with a jealous house plant. Contrasting to the earlier stories in its less tightly woven structure, its symbolism, its discrete layers of meaning, and its indefinite closure, "Love on Friday" can be interpreted as the story of a modern dilemma. Human beings, frustrated in their search, on the one hand, for spiritual signs and, on the other, for the "good life" promised by twentieth century technology, must accept an uncertain compromise.

Major publications other than short fiction
POETRY: *Beware of Ostriches*, 1978.
NONFICTION: *The Basketball Man: James Naismith*, 1973; *Poetry on the Stage: William Poel, Producer of Verse Drama*, 1979; *Lady Doctor on a Homestead: Mary Amelia Hay, Kansas Pioneer*, 1981.

FRANCES WEBB

Born: New Jersey, 1929

Principal short fiction
"A Great and Wonderful Death," 1970; "Them Good-Talking People What Only Know the Sun," 1973; "The Duet," 1974; "A Conversation," 1979; "The Indignity," 1979; "A Map of the Streets of the City of New York," 1979; "The Memoir Man," 1980.

Analysis
Fiction makes the inarticulate articulate. It gives voice. A writer listens for this voice constantly, and if he or she is lucky, it may come as an epiphany and become the beginning of the answer to a finally realized question. Themes, therefore, are afterthoughts. The stories of Frances Webb have themes only in so far as they are the resultant working through of an unknown. Many of the questions that have amorphously begun a story in an eruption of voice, words, and feeling, deal with such broad aspects of life as sanity, death, love, and friendship. Webb's stories range from the immediacy of stream of consciousness to the distance and objectivity of a third-person tale teller. In all cases, the narrator and/or narrator's voice is the primary "character" of the story. The minute actions and fragmented marginal thoughts are frequently the means of expression for the characters in lieu of verbalization or large-scale "plot." These actions and thoughts also become metaphorical underpinnings and move from the writer's unconsciousness to the reader's unconsciousness, and in this manner the reader responds in a feeling way rather than in a cerebral way.

Major publications other than short fiction
NONFICTION: "An Old Soldier's Return to France: 'There Were No Flowers in 1918,'" 1974; "Sentence Structure," 1977.

ROBERT WEGNER

Born: Ohio, 1929

Principal short fiction
"The Left-Handed Screwdriver," 1962; "The Woman with Concave Breasts," 1965; "How Lightning Shot Out of the Rat's Ass," 1966; "I'm Going Down to Watch the Horses Come Alive," 1970; "The Sentimentalist," 1970; "The Road out of Big Rapids," 1971; "Cleanse Me Cobalt, Let Me See Spring," 1975; "To Go Down Being Eaten," 1977; "The Enclosed Affair," 1977; "The Freshman," 1979.

Analysis
The prevailing motif of Robert Wegner's short fiction is the exploration of multiple and simultaneous awareness. The present becomes intense as it is invested with relevant memories and expectations. The structure of these stories is a familiar place or setting—a kitchen, a cobalt therapy room, a moving automobile—in which a narrator (or narrative perspective) is confined and from which awareness radiates, not only into the past but also into an anticipated or hallucinated future. Because the associations made are not "free" or arbitrary but triggered by a meaningful and crucial experience in the life of a recognizable human being, the narration retains a sense of the rational and coherent. Nevertheless, the stories, serious and humorous, unfold with emphasis less upon the linear than upon the expansion of emotional and psychological awareness.

Major publications other than short fiction
NONFICTION: *The Poetry & Prose of E. E. Cummings*, 1965.

RON WELBURN

Born: Pennsylvania, 1944

Principal short fiction
"The Nightsong of Dashieki Henry," 1970.

Analysis
Ron Welburn's stories, sketches, and tales attempt to bring the oral tradition of the black residents of Chester County, Pennsylvania to "fiction." The pieces approximate rural discourse, employing various points of view, interior monologue, and conversational language. Their literary antecedents include Washington Irving, John Neal, Nathaniel Hawthorne; their cultural antecedents, black and native American world views, and the lore of southeastern Pennsylvania. Character is secondary to theme, setting, mood, and experience, despite occasional first-person narrators in the peripatetic "Bosch in Devon." The best work avoids sleights of hand, self-conscious diction, and the grotesque for its own sake. Other fiction by Welburn involves blending of consciousness and voice, collage structure, techniques associated with the prose-poem, and occasionally those of the social realists. In all his fiction a strong metaphorical sense prevails.

Major publications other than short fiction
POETRY: *Peripheries: Selected Poems*, 1972; *Brownup & Other Poems*, 1977; *The Look in the Night Sky*, 1978.

PAUL WEST

Born: England, 1930

Principal short fiction

"A Slave to the Lyre-Bird . . . ," 1964; "How to Marry a Hummingbird," 1966; "The Season of the Single Women," 1971; "The Man Who Ate the Zeitgeist," 1971; "Life with Atlas," 1973; "Invitation to a Vasectomy," 1973; "Brain Cell 9,999,999,999," 1974; "Tan Salaam," 1974; "The Wet-God's Macho," 1974; "The Universe, and Other Fictions," 1975; "The Sun in Heat," 1975; "Short Life of Esteban Fletcher," 1975; "The Monocycle," 1975; "The Paganini Break," 1976; "Gustav Holst Composes Himself," 1976; "The Glass-Bottomed Boat," 1976; "*Captain Ahab*: A Novel by the White Whale," 1977; "Another Minotaur," 1978; "Klaus von Stauffenberg Reads the Palm of His Hand While Shooting Niagara," 1979; "The Basement of Kilimanjaro," 1979; "Stauffenberg's July," 1979; "Villa-Lobos in Winter," 1980.

Analysis

Several of Paul West's stylish, demanding, and fastidiously built stories reveal the same interest in science that shows in his novels: a brain cell talks, the sun yearns for the Trifid nebula, the steady-state universe babbles with the big-bang version. Yet, fond as West is of the extra-literary paradigm, he is fonder of operatic experiments in voice, experiments that succeed poignantly while the voices' minds break down: his novelistic White Whale, Arctic-exploring Gustav Holst, Jamaican shaman Toby Flankers, go down talking or chanting. The range of West's borrowed or invented entities is amazing: he mixes mythic primitives with Nazi colonels, and composers with vast underground vegetables. Often grotesque and expressionist, he is a writer consumed by emotions he does not so much analyze as vent while trying to accept the universe *in toto*. A voodoo of the imagination informs his stories, as Patricia Tobin discerns in her study, *Time and the Novel* (1978), associating him with Mario Vargas Llosa and Gabriel García Márquez for wanting to actualize "a plenitude of possibilities unrecognized in real creation . . . from Eden to Apocalypse."

Major publications other than short fiction

NOVELS: *A Quality of Mercy*, 1961; *Tenement of Clay*, 1965; *Alley Jaggers*, 1966; *I'm Expecting to Live Quite Soon*, 1970; Caliban's Filibuster, 1971; *Bela Lugosi's White Christmas*, 1972; *Colonel Mint*, 1973; *Gala*, 1976; *The Very Rich Hours of Count von Stauffenberg*, 1980.

POETRY: *The Spellbound Horses*, 1960; *The Snow Leopard*, 1965.

NONFICTION: *The Growth of the Novel*, 1959; *Byron and the Spoiler's Art*,

1960; *The Modern Novel*, 1963; *I, Said the Sparrow*, 1963; *The Wine of Absurdity*, 1966; *Words for a Deaf Daughter*, 1970.

Diane Ackerman

JOHN WHEATCROFT

Born: Pennsylvania, 1925

Principal short fiction
"Hero," 1963; "The Forfeit," 1963; "Kamikaze," 1963; "The Shadow of a Bear," 1963; "Sunday Breakfast," 1964; "Reunion of '03," 1965; "Image of Departure," 1966; "Honeysuckle," 1966; "Daffodils," 1966; "I Love You, Joe Gish," 1967; "The Lapse," 1970; "Letter from a Stranger," 1971; "The Appeal," 1974; "The Great Television Conspiracy," 1974.

Analysis
Exhibiting the economy and precision of language that characterize his poetry as well as the sensitivity to rhythm of speech that distinguishes his plays, John Wheatcroft's carefully crafted stories are most notable for the complexities of the ironies they dramatize. His protagonists—never stupid or insensitive—are aware of the ironies (often the hypocrisies) in their lives, but only partially, self-justifyingly aware. Within every irony the characters perceive lurks a further, larger irony as the deftly controlled, detached narrative voice implicitly mocks the narrow, self-serving limits of their perceptions. Nor does the process end there, for the subtly ironic narrative voice is itself subject to the scorn of an implicit voice behind the voice. What Wheatcroft thus achieves in his fiction is a kind of self-reflexive effect in which ironic vision is itself treated ironically and which ultimately forbids author and reader alike the pretension of awarenesses that may not themselves be viewed ironically from a broader perspective. Wheatcroft's stories tend to be symbolic rather than strictly realistic or allegorical, conventional rather than experimental in their employment of readily graspable plots and recognizable characters. The understated revelation of their shortcomings, as characters enact variations on the same theme of self-deception, is largely comic. Wheatcroft's satire, however, is more sadly accepting than savage. For the exposure of the varied ways in which his characters are found wanting is tempered by a deep compassion for the ludicrous shifts they (and all readers) resort to in striving to preserve an elusive sense of personal dignity.

Major publications other than short fiction
NOVEL: *Edie Tells*, 1976.
PLAY: *Ofoti*, 1970.
POETRY: *Death of a Clown*, 1964; *Prodigal Son*, 1968; *A Voice from the Hump*, 1977; *Ordering Demons*, 1980.

Dennis Baumwoll

JAMES P. WHITE

Born: Texas, 1940

Principal short fiction

"The Healing," 1966; "Tommy," 1967; "I'll Fetch Thee Brooks," 1967; "Sore Awake," 1967; "Make-Up," 1968; "The Campus," 1968; "Defeat at Shiloh," 1968; "Summer," 1971; "Late in the Evening," 1972; "Wives," 1973; "For Love or Money," 1973; "Domains," 1975; "The Apple of Louise Mann," 1976; "Spread," 1976; "The Patient," 1977; "First Love," 1978.

Analysis

James White is best known for his novel *Birdsong* (1977), but he has published a number of short stories. The short fiction has a quiet, clear tone, and usually a rural setting where somebody is up to something. Above all, the stories show a concern for language. In "Wives" the narrator, his grandmother, and his great aunt Nell successfully marry off a friend named Ella who weighs "two pounds under a cow." In "The Healing" the narrator is healed of some undiagnosed heartburn; "Late in the Evening" is the story of the marriage of the grandmother. "The Apple of Louise Mann" is a humorous portrayal of the grandmother and the great aunt competing with their flower gardens. In "Summer" the character Dewey has returned to the small town, Haskell, Texas, and sees his grandmother from a point of view in vivid contrast to that of his boyhood. Many of these rural stories depend upon a mood resulting from characterization and setting.

Major publications other than short fiction

NOVELS: *Birdsong*, 1977; *The Ninth Car*, 1978.
POETRY: *Poems*, 1978.

Ray Giguette

ALLEN WIER

Born: Texas, 1946

Principal short fiction
"Cobs and Robbers," 1971; "Eddie's Story," 1978; "Bill Bailey Call Home,
It's Not an Emergency," 1978; *Things About to Disappear*, 1978.

Analysis
Each of Allen Wier's stories is a finished thing; there is considerable variety
of tone and even style in his work, but throughout it there is nevertheless a
strong unity, especially in the eight stories collected in *Things About to Disappear*; what holds the work together is a wisdom rarely encountered in one
so young. The collection opens with "An Elegy," a recollection of a friendship,
paradoxically lifted from sentimentality by the blatantly literary device of
titling the story's sections with the traditional ingredients of the classical
elegy—"Invocation to the Muse," "A Procession of Appropriate Mourners,"
and so on. The tension between the facts of the friendship and the classical
echo is maintained through the final story, "Things About to Disappear," in
which the narrator, driving east through Texas, recalls his father's recent
death. He sees an accident, tries to help, and drives on, thinking of his father's
last days; and the reader recalls the end of "An Elegy," which is called "A
Consolation: Discovery of the Gate to a Higher Life."

Throughout these stories there are ordinary people with bizarre obsessions,
and bizarre people with ordinary preoccupations, all drawn with economy
and skill. "Cambell Oakley's Gospel Sun Shines on Roy Singing Grass" is a
flawless presentation of friendship and death; "Mr Ollie, Think of the Baseball" is a moving evocation of the small but precious joys and triumphs of old
age. Wier has a keen eye for the emblematic details of a life; combine that
with wisdom, and the result is storytelling of rare distinction.

Major publications other than short fiction
NOVEL: *Blanco*, 1978.

Henry Taylor

SYLVIA WILKINSON

Born: North Carolina, 1940

Principal short fiction
"Jimson," 1966; "A Maypop from Merton," 1969; "The Chosen One," 1974; "Journal of a Solitary Traveler," 1980.

Analysis
The fictional world of Sylvia Wilkinson is characterized by people who emerge from the pages and exist in their own right so convincingly that the reader feels the characters' reactions as surely as if they were his own. Skillful and unique dialogue lets the characters communicate directly with the reader, and a writing style that reveals the environment of the characters in intricate detail allows the reader to envision the setting. He knows where the cabbage is planted as surely as he knows the location of the plants in his own garden. Indeed, Wilkinson seems to remember everything that she has ever seen or felt, and such past experiences are combined with imaginary ones so that each scene is alive and vital. Recurring themes suggest a conflict between the expected conformity and generality (for the sake of efficiency) of the adult world and the freedom, individuality, and specificity of the child's world. This conflict plays a part in creating the pressures and insecurities of childhood. Then too, there is the conflict of the individual securing and adapting to his place. As novelist Fred Chappell wrote in "Unpeaceable Kingdoms: The Novels of Sylvia Wilkinson" ". . . if I had to choose the single most valuable quality of Miss Wilkinson's writings, I would choose the portrayal of the community of spirit between the natural world and those chosen few who know how to meet it."

Major publications other than short fiction
NOVELS: *Moss on the North Side*, 1966; *A Killing Frost*, 1967; *Cale*, 1970; *Shadow of the Mountain*, 1977; *Bone of My Bones*, 1980.
NONFICTION: *The Stainless Steel Carrot: An Auto Racing Odyssey*, 1973.

Lyn Walker

MARY LOUISE WILLEY

Born: Connecticut, 1929

Principal short fiction
"A Nonsense Story," 1965; "The Imprisonment," 1966; "The Mind's Eye,"
1976; "Weather," 1979.

Analysis
   Mary Louise Willey's earlier stories are more expansive and philosophical,
exploring the problem of the artist (in these cases a male artist) as a solitary
figure within the social structure. The artist's solitude, necessary but too often
pushed to extremes, eventually leads to both personal and artistic breakdown.
The protagonist of "The Imprisonment" is destroyed by an intricate combination of forces within himself and without, in society; in "A Nonsense Story,"
the narrator's experiments in "meaningless" language lead to his being declared insane. Technique is traditional, although settings are usually unspec-
ified and even almost surreal ("The Imprisonment"). More recent stories,
such as "Weather," explore relationships between the sexes from the female
viewpoint, in particular the connections between sex and anger, passivity and
aggressiveness. The emphasis here is on brief, highly charged scenes—the
intense, poetic recreation of specific moments.

JOHN ALFRED WILLIAMS

Born: Mississippi, 1925

Principal short fiction
"A Good Season," 1961; "Son in the Afternoon," 1962; "Navy Black,"
1966.

Analysis
Primarily a novelist and writer of nonfiction, John A. Williams has used
short narrative, both in expository prose and fiction, to test techniques and
themes in his longer fiction. "A Good Season" is one of the author's first
presentations of the international theme embodied in his most celebrated
novel, *The Man Who Cried I Am* (1967). "Son in the Afternoon," which has
been anthologized widely, rehearses the layered motifs of black and white
consciousness, of male and female, and of mother and son orchestrated in
Sissie (1963). "Navy Black," strongly autobiographical like much of Williams'
fiction, presents the black American military experience that the author would
elaborate fully in *Captain Blackman* (1972). Plotted traditionally, realistic in
method, and often naturalistic in its implications, Williams' fiction deals typically with various forms of exploitation—racial, sexual, economic—that define for the author the human condition. Creating one of the broadest
landscapes in contemporary literature, Williams in his short fiction, his autobiographical narratives such as "The Boys from Syracuse: Blacks and Jews
in the Old Neighborhood," and his novels explores the entire American
enterprise from the central perspective of race. Focusing on what he terms
"the politics of race," Williams has perfected a mode of fiction that projects
personality as the product of historical imperatives. Penetrating the black and
white mind on an international scale, Williams seeks those unique moments—
for example, the dropping of the atomic bomb on Hiroshima that frames the
action in "Navy Black"—in which race, history, politics, and personality coalesce. The tone of Williams' fiction thus is analytical and philosophical.
Williams is a moralist and fabulist exploring the ways that people attempt to
control their lives (typically through moments of love and commitment) in
a world that conspires against them.

Major publications other than short fiction
NOVELS: *The Angry Ones*, 1960; *Night Song*, 1961; *Sissie*, 1963; *The Man
Who Cried I Am*, 1967; *Sons of Darkness, Sons of Light*, 1969; *Captain
Blackman*, 1972; *Mothersill and the Foxes*, 1975; *The Junior Bachelor Society*,
1976.
NONFICTION: *Africa: Her History, Lands and People*, 1963; *This Is My*

Country Too, 1965; *The Most Native of Sons*, 1970; *The King God Didn't Save*, 1971; *Flashbacks*, 1973.

Gilbert H. Muller

THOMAS WILLIAMS

Born: Minnesota, 1926

Principal short fiction
"Waiting for the Moon," 1960; *A High New House*, 1963; "The Old Dancers," 1964; "The Survivors," 1965; "All Trades, Their Tackle and Trim," 1965; "The Snows of Minnesota," 1966; "Paranoia," 1970.

Analysis
Thomas Williams' fiction has generally been called "realistic," although he has said that he is not happy with the term, believing that all serious fiction is essentially unreal and necessarily experimental. *A High New House*, which was awarded a Dial Press Fellowship for Fiction and given the Roos/Atkins Literary Award in 1963, was praised by the judges of the latter prize (Herbert Gold, George P. Elliott, and Albert Guerard) for its compassion toward the human condition and its clarity of style. Granville Hicks, in *Saturday Review*, complained that the stories were too complicated and cerebral, while Alfred Chester, in *The New York Times Book Review*, objected because Williams' heroes were too gentle and did nothing to offend the reader. For one reason or another, Williams turned to the novel, and now only occasionally works in the shorter form, although certain of his novels, such as *The Hair of Harold Roux*, 1974, (National Book Award for Fiction, 1975), contain episodic units which might be called complete short stories.

Major publications other than short fiction
NOVELS: *Ceremony of Love*, 1955; *Town Burning*, 1959; *The Night of Trees*, 1961; *Whipple's Castle*, 1969; *The Hair of Harold Roux*, 1974; *Tsuga's Children*, 1977; *The Followed Man*, 1978.

BARBARA WILSON

Born: California, 1950

Principal short fiction
Talk & Contact, 1978; *Taking Sides*, 1981.

Analysis

Barbara Wilson's impartial narrative, familiar characters, and colloquial dialogue reflect the influence of writers she has always admired, notably Jane Austin for her ironic "landmine sentences." Some key stories are formally experimental, but the structure is usually traditional. The most captivating, entertaining stories often carry the most complex metaphor. "They are subjective, not autobiographical," says Wilson, as important a distinction as is her *feminist* perspective. Her emphasis on women is integral—thus avoiding dogma—and even though many stories explore relations between the sexes, the overriding sense of possibility between women is the provocatively dominant theme. *Talk & Contact*, her first short-story collection, explores the dilemma of growing up female in contemporary society. Her young heroines are unrooted, alienated, and seek ways to demonstrate the individuality they feel or yearn for. Heroines in Wilson's collection are still alone, but self-possessed adults, taking up the challenge of affecting their own futures. Some crucial syntonic component is missing from female/male relationships, however, even where the wisdom of compromise is an important revelation. The issue is still the extent of their polarity: he may see the apocalypse where she has a vision of the future and prepares to meet it.

Hylah Jacques

ROBLEY WILSON, JR.

Born: Maine, 1930

Principal short fiction
The Pleasures of Manhood, 1977; *Living Alone*, 1978; "Wasps," 1979; "A Fear of Children," 1980.

Analysis
From a range of experience that includes young manhood in Maine, Air Force duty in occupied Germany, marriage, writing poetry, and teaching college in the Midwest, Robley Wilson, Jr., has written realistic yet hauntingly mysterious stories of the lifescape W. H. Auden has called "the age of anxiety." A master of conventional narrative techniques, Wilson uses them in startlingly innovative ways. "The Pleasures of Manhood" sees past the soap opera of a love triangle to the imaginative qualities of sexuality itself. "Loving a Fat Girl: A Diary" is a deliberate challenge to imagine the unimaginable, to endure the unendurable; in Wilson's hands the story becomes a self-conscious test for his writing, just as his writing is a test for the rigors of his imagination, and as his imagination has in the first place been tested by the reader's dare. "A Stay at the Ocean" is a tour de force of realistic narrative art, as the scene of an eerily receding ocean is first domesticated by mood-setting description and detail, only to have its ending write itself as the truly terrifying sea returns in its awesomeness. "Saying Goodbye to the President," Wilson's most often reprinted piece, consists of seven parallel segments, each of which retells the story of a Chief Executive's departure from office—but in increasingly ridiculous circumstances. Because the particulars of each version differ, there is no compulsion to suspend disbelief; yet the form of each section toils away in solemn order, with no violations of mimesis or credibility. By such achievements Wilson has become an experimental realist, accomplishing the most innovative effects without ever abandoning the most traditional tools of fiction.

Major publications other than short fiction
POETRY: *All That Lovemaking*, 1961; *Returning to the Body*, 1977; *Family Matters*, 1980.

Jerome Klinkowitz

DONALD WINDHAM

Born: Georgia, 1920

Principal short fiction
"Rome," 1953; *The Warm Country*, 1960; *Emblems of Conduct*, 1963.

Analysis
Donald Windham writes in a clear and simple style which touches the innermost reaches of the human soul. In the "Introduction" to Windham's *The Warm Country*, E. M. Forster states that "the most important thing about him is that he believes in warmth. He knows that human beings are not statues but contain flesh and blood and a heart, and he believes that creatures so constituted must contact one another or they will decay." Windham does not, however, convey this warmth in his stories by using "slick," schooled writing techniques; instead, he utilizes precisely the right word or detail to produce the desired atmosphere or feeling. Jeremy Larner writes, "Donald Windham's sense of balance is infallible." He continues, "Everything is handled with a purity of language and emotion that moves the reader directly and without distractions to the unique anguish of each story's hero. Words are used carefully, but transparently, so that they never get between the reader and what Windham wants him to care about." A highly accomplished writer, Windham has written several well-received novels and has written a play with Tennessee Williams.

Major publications other than short fiction
NOVELS: *The Dog Star*, 1950; *The Hero Continues*, 1960; *Two People*, 1965; *Tanaquil*, 1978.
PLAY: *You Touched Me!*, 1945 (with Tennessee Williams).

HILMA WOLITZER

Born: New York, 1930

Principal short fiction
"Today a Woman Went Mad in the Supermarket," 1965; "Ending," 1969;
"The Sex Maniac," 1970; "Waiting for Daddy," 1971; "In the Flesh," 1971;
"Behold the Crazy Hours of the Hard-Loving Wife," 1974; "Trophies," 1975;
"Photographs," 1976; "Bodies," 1978.

Analysis
Hilma Wolitzer's stories, hilarious and solemn, emerge out of the devious
ordinariness of domestic life. Her housewife characters are adept at keeping
secret their profundity; they are embroiled in ordinary lives, but they are
more wise and good-natured than most, more eternally hopeful, more loving,
and surely a great deal funnier. In spite of all they perceive of tragic limitation
and foolish need, these women never act out of alienation or bitterness.
Wanting the things that "everybody" wants, they seem to make their objects
deserving by believing only the best of them. Most of the action of Wolitzer's
stories takes place in the kitchens and elevators, even the laundry rooms, of
New York City apartment complexes, but the seasons that overtake the
women and children in the playgrounds are the seasons of the speaker's (wryly
observed) soul. In "The Sex Maniac," her character's response to the news
that there is a molester loose in the apartment complex is typically unruffled:
"I thought, it's about time. It had been a long asexual winter." By the story's
end, she has managed to find sympathy for the maniac, the delivery boy, her
frustrated neighbors who need such passion to loosen them from "the icy
crusts of our hearts," and certainly for herself. Vengefulness is for others,
and so is derision. Everybody, Wolitzer seems to be saying in all her stories,
needs all the help there is. "Behold the Crazy Hours of the Hard-Loving
Wife," which was the origin of her second novel, *In the Flesh* (1977), is the
fullest development in story form of Wolitzer's amused, tolerant, and yet
deeply serious point of view. Wolitzer has a poet's capacity for conciseness
and irony, and her wit keeps her from grandiloquence. It is by virtue of this
complexity of tone that her work transcends the apparent smallness of its
world. "Who is it accuses us of safety?" the poet Linda Pastan asks, as does
Wolitzer, about "conventional" family life. "We have chosen the dangerous
life."

BRUCE P. WOODFORD

Born: Oregon, 1919

Principal short fiction
"The Necessary Illusion," 1947; "The Midwife," 1950; "A Young Hunter," 1953; "The Impertinent Dust," 1960; "The Dark Room," 1961; "The Other Ones," 1964; "Sound of Surf," 1975; "Early Harvest," 1975; "Blindweaver," 1976; "A Boatful of Flowers," 1976; "The Rock in the River," 1976; "Insulin," 1977; "Ivory," 1977.

Analysis
Bruce Woodford's stories range from simple classical plotting to a kind of imagist technique which puts the reader as close to the action as possible. There is strong visual focus and use of language in an almost tactile manner. In some stories the effort is simply to create a situation that a reader will not forget. Other stories use a counterpoint which may act as a forecasting of events or simply to add dimension to the narrative. From the premise that any story is an invention, it follows that any method—including asides, author intrusion, peripheral voices, or double narrative—is legitimate.

Major publications other than short fiction
PLAY: *The Prisoner*, 1958.
POETRY: *Twenty-one Poems and a Play*, 1958; *Love and Other Weathers*, 1966; *A Suit of Four*, 1973; *Indiana, Indiana*, 1976; *The Edges of Distance*, 1977.

AUSTIN WRIGHT

Born: New York, 1922

Principal short fiction
"Camden," 1968; "All That Racket and All That Water," 1979.

Analysis
Although both of Austin Wright's stories are excerpts from novels, they can also be read as independent wholes. Both stories emphasize a character's multiple and paralyzingly complex view of things in a very concrete situation in which he finds himself. Most of Wright's fiction is concerned, among other things, with ways in which people try to formulate their perceptions into words, into narratives, when those perceptions are intense and ambiguous.

Major publications other than short fiction
NOVELS: *Camden's Eyes*, 1969; *First Persons*, 1973; *The Morley Mythology*, 1977.
NONFICTION: *The American Short Story in the Twenties*, 1961.

SAMUEL YELLEN

Born: Lithuania, 1906

Principal short fiction
"Death of a Girl," 1930; "The Statisdemon," 1950; "The Gallic War and the Tired Elk," 1954; "Mr. Ozanne of Central High," 1955; *The Passionate Shepherd*, 1957.

Analysis
The stories are set mainly in Cleveland, where Samuel Yellen grew up, or in southern Indiana, where he has lived for many years. The characters are from various areas of life, from the academic to the rough street corner. Often the stories are told in first person by the chief character, creating an effect more like that of a short drama. The endings and the structure may remind some readers of Edgar Allan Poe and O. Henry. From the jacket of *The Passionate Shepherd*,

> Here is an author with a sense of the world around him, an incisive eye, a fine style, and gentle humor, who is also a craftsman in the short-story form. . . . Samuel Yellen writes of the recognizable stuff of everyday life, yet freights it with universal meanings, so that his stories, when one finishes them, have continuing echoes in the reader's imagination.

Major publications other than short fiction
NOVEL: *The Wedding Band*, 1961.
POETRY: *In the House and Out*, 1952; *New & Selected Poems*, 1964; *The Convex Mirror: Collected Poems*, 1971.
NONFICTION: *American Labor Struggles*, 1936.

LEE ZACHARIAS

Born: Illinois, 1944

Principal short fiction

"The Two-Bit Baby," 1972; "Time Out," 1974; *Helping Muriel Make It Through the Night*, 1976; "At the Feast," 1979; "Janie and Ben, June 6, 1964," 1980.

Analysis

Lee Zacharias' stories grow from the belief that art is a perfect and constantly changing balance between cruelty and nostalgia. In her shorter fiction, there is an emphasis on the cruelty, for it is cruelty, she believes, which makes structure, and structure is what makes the story, unlike the novel, work. A recurring motif in her short fiction is the character who takes a new name in a doomed, metaphorical effort to escape himself. The central conflict in many of her stories is the character's wish to be someone else, for the only conflicts worth writing about, she insists, are those deep wars within, whose progress is not made but measured by action. Action as a measure is her basic method, and her work is largely dramatic, relying heavily on scene and dark humor.

SUZANNE OSTRO ZAVRIAN

Born: Maryland, 1928

Principal short fiction
"Stills," 1973; "For the Iceman," 1974; "Excuse Me," 1975; *Demolition Zone*, 1976; "A Mystery Novel," 1979; "A Real Love Story," 1980.

Analysis
Suzanne Ostro Zavrian's work is an excursion into the meaning of language; of concepts of space, time, and the ambiguity of the senses; of the comedy of interpersonal relationships and the ironies of experience. Her work explores images of light, sound, and color; belonging and alienation; form and chaos. Throughout, there is the relativity of perceptions and experience, the everyday seen through the sensibility of modern physics, the phenomenological reconsidered, the commonplace refracted in its own perception. From early signs in the prose poem "For the Iceman," her work has evolved through a technique of collage into three-page multichaptered "novels" of love, hate, and the mystery in life. Trying to decipher the signs along the way, she is a Wittgensteinian Alice before the doors and signs of Manhattan; a child of John Barth on a journey through the labyrinth of life.

Daniel J. Kurland

ROGER ZELAZNY

Born: Ohio, 1937

Principal short fiction

Four for Tomorrow, 1967; *The Doors of His Face, the Lamps of His Mouth, and Other Stories*, 1971; *My Name Is Legion*, 1976.

Analysis

Roger Zelazny was one of the pivotal figures in that shift in science fiction during the 1960's that came to be known as the "New Wave." The "New Wave" approaches and techniques are most evident in Zelazny's impressive short fiction. His concern with inner space can be seen in the Nebula Award-winning novella, "He Who Shapes" (later extended and retitled *The Dream Master*, 1966), which tells the story of a therapist who actually enters and controls the subconscious of his patients—until his own weaknesses catch up with him. Like many of his predecessors, Zelazny favors the "hero" who intrudes to solve the problems created by lesser men; but his typical hero is almost the opposite of the usual muscular, technically competent, he-man space captain; Zelazny's protagonist, rather, reflects "counterculture" values: detachment, spiritualism, introspection, pacifism, "feminine" emotions. For example, Jerry Dark, hero of "The Keys to December," assumes a moral responsibility for the creatures he has been sent to dominate, rejects the technology of immortality, and lives out his life more like an Eastern guru than a science-fiction hero. Zelazny's ability to create sensuous, convincing landscapes, ingenious, fantastic situations, and believable, sympathetic characters, coupled with a prose style that is both highly poetic and stridently colloquial, makes him one of the most interesting, exciting talents of his era.

Major publications other than short fiction

NOVELS: *This Immortal*, 1966; *The Dream Master*, 1966; *Lord of Light*, 1967; *Isle of the Dead*, 1969; *Creatures of Light and Darkness*, 1969; *Nine Princes in Amber*, 1970; *Jack of Shadows*, 1971; *The Guns of Avalon*, 1972; *To Die in Italbar*, 1973; *Today We Choose Faces*, 1973; *Sign of the Unicorn*; 1975; *The Hand of Oberon*, 1976; *Deus Irae*, 1976 (with Philip K. Dick); *Doorways in the Sand*, 1976; *Damnation Alley*, 1977; *The Courts of Chaos*, 1978.

Keith Neilson

ANITA ZELMAN

Born: California, 1924

Principal short fiction
"Fooling with the Laws of Nature," 1966; "An Odd Bird," 1966; "The Sunshine Phone," 1973; "Traveling Jewish," 1974; "Tripping Them Up," 1974; "Anybody Else's Son," 1974; "Little Chincha," 1975; "The Bewitched Isles," 1975; "A Fun Paper," 1975; "Bad Guys Are Nice," 1975; "Second Aid," 1977; *Alone at Last*, 1977; "The Chasidah," 1977; "Manzanar," 1977; "Menudo," 1978; "A Monomaniac Is the Only Kind of Maniac to Be," 1978; "Just Whistle," 1978; "Move by Move," 1978; "Rami," 1978; "The Goddess Lives," 1979; "Money Matters," 1979; "The Last of Life for Which the First Was Made," 1980; "Without Tomato Aspic," 1980; "There Once Was a Union Maid," 1980.

Analysis
Anita Zelman's tightly structured short stories deal with concerns of girls and women faced with specific problems at specific times, not necessarily turning points or crossroads. The times may occur during the "muddling through" periods in a woman's life. Imagery is rarely used and when a story such as "The Goddess Lives" calls for it, Zelman keeps it to a minimum, using only those images that appeal to the senses: "The dark trees on our front lawn, which usually appear ominous at night, were beautiful now as the lines from the moon pierced the lace pattern of their leaves," leads to a scene in which a mother and daughter are reunited. Zelman's characters are intensely involved with living. When an occasional antiheroine takes over a story, she, too, is an affirmative person, in a negative way. There are humor and wit in these women, who are actors and not watchers. The settings are urban and urbane—a chess tournament, a woman-of-the-future's book-filled house in Jerusalem, a senior citizens' home turned into one for junior citizens in Los Angeles. Zelman does not linger on descriptions of the backgrounds. They are there as noncomplex stage settings for her women to make their moves when they have discovered their directions.

LLOYD ZIMPEL

Born: Minnesota, 1929

Principal short fiction
"Wrung Dry," 1971; "Sleeve," 1973; "The Scratching Cat Befriended,"
1969; "Eye and Axle," 1971; *Foundry Foreman*, 1980.

Analysis
Overall, Lloyd Zimpel's short fiction has a wide thematic range, but his
most compelling stories concern men at work. In stories thus focused the
author clearly seeks to define man's condition in terms of work. What work
means, or does not mean, is set forth with casually instructive detail about
specific jobs and how they are done. In his best stories, Zimpel lines out his
characters almost wholly by the way they do their jobs, not by the more
conventional fictional means of describing physical appearances. For all his
obviously sympathetic connection with them, Zimpel seems only a distant
cousin of the proletarian writers of the 1930's, whose frequent ponderousness
he sidesteps through a style informed with irony and humor, as well as a
measured authorial stance that permits closeness to, or distance from, a character as the story's dramatic needs demand. Often this creates a tension never
quite resolved in the story, leaving an unsettling sense of real-life ambiguity
that compares with all too many of the reader's own work-day experiences.

Major publications other than short fiction
NOVEL: *Meeting the Bear; Journal of the Black Wars*, 1971.
NONFICTION: *Business and the Hardcore Unemployed*, 1970 (with Daniel
Panger).

Diana M. Rathbone

HARRIET ZINNES

Born: Massachusetts

Principal short fiction
"Entropisms," 1966-1973; "Pure Will," 1977.

Analysis
All fiction deals with the outside world, and that world returns to the observing eye and heart in strange ways. Harriet Zinnes' fiction sometimes seems to make mysterious transformations: characters seemingly see what is not there, or find objects so elusive that illusion is more apparent than appearance. At other times, stories may leap about in time or be told from different points of view, yet they never replace the outer world with anything strange. A divorce can occur with repercussions to a child; a husband may not understand his wife's strange way of obtaining her freedom. A California artist may or may not have constructed a vulture. A man's encounter with a snake in Virginia may lead to another encounter with a young girl who has experienced more than snake venom. A mentally ill wife in a hospital entangles more than her knitting. Two young lovers face the insecurity of the modern world by affirming love even as they worry about commitment. Since Zinnes is a poet, her style, although changing as the fictional material changes, essentially catches that material in a language that is sensuous, passionate, and musical—in the sense that there is a music in our humanity that is sound and sense, at once exciting and calming. Frequently, perhaps again because she is a poet, Zinnes writes stories that are short and tense ("Pure Will"); yet still in their terseness they reach into the heart of contemporary woman's conflict between self and lover as she wills to extend her own consciousness and freedom.

Major publications other than short fiction
POETRY: *Waiting and Other Poems*, 1964; *An Eye for an I*, 1966; *I Wanted to See Something Flying*, 1976; *Entropisms*, 1978.
NONFICTION: *Ezra Pound and the Visual Arts*, 1980.

AUTHOR AND TITLE INDEX

"A & P" (Updike), 98-99.
Abbas, K. A., 649; *The Black Sun and Other Stories*, 649; "Sparrows," 649.
"Abbé Aubain, The" (Mérimée), 198.
"ABC to the Virgin, An" (Chaucer), 1101.
Abel, Robert H., 2487.
Abish, Walter, 2488.
"Abominable" (Brown), 564.
"Abominable History of the Man with the Copper Fingers, The" (Sayers), 758.
"About the Marionette Theater" (Kleist), 1759-1760.
"Abrazo de Vergara, El" see "Embrace at Vergara."
Achebe, Chinua, 819-823; "Girls at War," 822-823; "Uncle Ben's Choice," 821-822; "Vengeful Creditor," 820-821.
Ackerson, Duane, 2489.
Acres and Pains (Perelman), 2081.
"Act of Self-Defense, An" (Ford), 1386.
Acts of the Kings (William of Malmesbury), 440-441.
Adams, Henry; *The Education of Henry Adams*, 219.
Addison, Joseph, 155-156, **824-829**, 2264-2269; "The de Coverley papers," 828; *The Spectator*, 151, 155-156, 827-828, 2264-2269; *The Tatler*, 151, 155-156, 827, 2264-2269; "The Vision of Mizrah," 826-827.
"Admiral and the Nuns, The" (Tuohy), 2346-2347.
"Adolescence" (Wescott), 2423.
"Adoration of the Magi, The" (Yeats), 2473.
Adorjan, Carol Madden, 2490.
"Adulterous Woman, The" (Camus, A.), 1047-1048.
Advance of the American Short Story, The (O'Brien, Edward), 84.
"Adventure of the Camberwell Beauty, The" (Derleth), 1258.

"Adventure of the Egyptian Tomb, The" (Christie), 1146-1147.
"Adventure of the Empty House, The" (Doyle), 1304.
"Adventure of the Remarkable Worm, The" (Derleth), 1257-1258.
"Adventure of the Rudberg Numbers, The" (Derleth), 1256-1257.
"Adventure of the Speckled Band, The" (Doyle), 1299.
Adventurer (Hawkesworth), 1605, 1606, 1607, 1608.
Adventurer, The (Johnson, S.), 1708.
Adventures of Huckleberry Finn, The (Twain), 615.
Adventures of Pinnochio, The (Collodi), 684-685.
"Adventures of Shamrock Jolnes, The" (Henry), 1630.
Aeneid (Vergil), 135, 2386-2389.
Aerial Ways (Pasternak), 2061.
"Aeroplanes at Brescia, The" (Davenport), 1247.
Aesop, 377-379.
Aethiopica (Heliodorus), 489.
"After Holbein" (Wharton), 2431-2432.
"After the Ball" (Tolstoy), 2336-2337.
"After the Race" (Joyce), 1720.
Agnon, Shmuel Yosef, 422, **830-835**; "Fable of the Goat," 831-833; "The Kerchief," 833-834; "A Whole Loaf," 834-835.
"ahogado más hermos del mundo, El" see "Handsomest Drowned Man, The."
Aichinger, Ilse, 2491.
Aickman, Robert, 2492.
Aiken, Conrad, 258-259, **836-841**; "A Conversation," 840-841; "Silent Snow, Secret Snow," 787-788, 837-838; "Strange Moonlight," 838-839; "Thistledown," 840; "Your Obituary, Well Written," 839-840.
Aikin, John and Anna Barbauld; *Miscellaneous Pieces in Prose*, 470.
Alarcón, Pedro Antonio de, 842-848;

I

932; "Autobiography," 929; "Life-Story," 928-929; "The Literature of Exhaustion," 70; "Lost in the Funhouse," 928, 930-931; *Lost in the Funhouse*, 928; "Night-Sea Journey," 929-930; "Water Message," 928.

Barthelme, Donald, 560; "Some of Us Had Been Threatening Our Friend Colby," 725; "Robert Kennedy Saved from Drowning," 99-100.

Bartholomew Fair (Jonson), 1716.

Bartleby the Scrivener (Melville), 205, 207-208, 796-798, 1915-1918.

Bartlett, Paul Alexander, 2506.

"Basement Room, The" (Greene, G.), 272-273, 786, 1543-1544.

Basile, Giambattista; *The Pentamerone*, 682-683.

Bates, H. E., 270-271; "Breeze Anstey," 270; "The Child," 270; *The Modern Short Story*, 70; *My Uncle Silas*, 270-271; "The Palace," 270; "Purchases's Living Wonders," 270.

Battin, M. Pabst; "The Sisters," 710.

Battle of Maldon, 431-432.

"Bau, Der" see "Burrow, The."

Baumbach, Jonathan, 2507.

"Beach of Falesá, The" (Stevenson, R. L.), 2285.

"Beach Party, The" (Grau), 1531, 1532-1533.

Beach Red (Bowman), 130-131.

Beachcroft, T. O.; *The Modest Art*, 70-71.

Beal, M. F., 2508.

"Bear, The" (Faulkner), 11, 12, 13, 14, 1363-1365.

"Bear on a Plate" (Malgonkar), 650.

Beard, Thomas, 499; *The Theatre of Gods Judgements*, 499.

"Beast, The" (Brecht), 1005-1006.

"Beast in the Jungle, The" (James, H.), 232-233, 1683-1685.

Beattie, Ann, 552.

Beattie, James; *Dissertations Moral and Critical*, 470.

"Beau Monde of Mrs. Bridge, The" (Connell), 1178.

"Beautiful Stranger, The" (Jackson), 1670.

Beck, Warren, 934-936; "Art and Formula in the Short Story," 71; *The Blue Sash and Other Stories*, 935; "Conception and Technique," 71; "Detour in the Dark," 936; "Encounter on the Parnassian Slope," 935; "The Far Whistle," 936; "The First Fish," 936; *Into Thin Air*, 934; "The Jap," 935; *Pause Under the Sky*, 935.

Beckett, Samuel, 674, 937-941; "Dante and the Lobster," 674-675; "Ding-dong," 939; "The End," 938; "The Expelled," 939; *Fizzles*, 939-940; *More Pricks Than Kicks*, 938-939; *Stories and Texts for Nothing*, 939.

Beckford, William; *Vathek*, 471, 475.

Bede the Venerable; *Ecclesiastical History of the English People*, 428.

Beebe, Maurice; "A Survey of Short Story Textbooks," 71.

Beer, Thomas, 251.

Beerbohm, Max, 942-947; *A Christmas Garland Woven by Max Beerbohm*, 946-947; "Enoch Soames," 943-944; "The Mote in the Middle Distance, H*nry J*m*s," 946; "'Savonarola' Brown," 943, 944-945; *Seven Men*, 943.

"Before Parting" (Pasternak), 2062.

"Before the Law" (Kafka), 1732-1733.

"Beggars, The" (O'Flaherty), 2010-2011.

Beggarwoman of Locarno, The (Kleist), 1762.

Beginning on the Short Story, A (Williams, W. C.), 94.

"Beginnings of and for the True Short Story in England" (Harris, W.), 78.

"Behind the Automatic Door" (Robbe-Grillet), 2156.

Behn, Aphra, 502; *The Perjur'd Beauty*, 502; *The History of the Nun*, 502; *The Fair Jilt*, 502; *Oroonoko*, 502.

"Beim Bau der Chinesischen Mauer" see "Great Wall of China, The."

"Bekenntnis zur Trümmerliteratur" see "Defence of Rubble Literature."

Belfagor see *Story of Belphagor the Arch Demon, The*.

Bellamy, Joe David, 2509.

V

L